ALSO BY MARK SINGER

Mr. Personality

Funny Money

CITIZEN K

CITIZEN K

The Deeply Weird American
Journey of Brett Kimberlin

Mark Singer

ALFRED A. KNOPF   NEW YORK   1996

THIS IS A BORZOI BOOK
PUBLISHED BY ALFRED A. KNOPF, INC.

Library of Congress Cataloging-in-Publication Data
Singer, Mark.
Citizen K: the deeply weird American journey of
Brett Kimberlin / by Mark Singer.
p.   cm.
ISBN 0-679-42999-9
1. Kimberlin, Brett, 1954–   . 2. Criminals—United States—
Biography.   I. Title.
HV6248.K518S56   1996
364.1'77'0973—dc20   96-35413
CIP

Manufactured in the United States of America
First Edition

Note: All of the people in this book are real, though some have
been given fictitious names. They are: Jessica Barton, Yvonne
Barton, Jack Crosby, Louise Crosby, Justin Farrell, Darlene
Harvey, Larry Harvey, Susan Harvey, Henry Lake, Janet Marx,
Woody McDermott, Tiffany Perkins, Bobby Dale Pettibone, Jeff
Purdy, Jerry Richardson, Felipe Sanchez, Randy Stovall, and
Ricky Stovall.

For Caroline

I used to divert myself by wondering whether such consistency on my uncle's part made this element of his story more likely to be true, or more likely to be false.

—JULIAN BARNES

CITIZEN K

1

EVERY DAY for more than five thousand days, Brett Kimberlin thought of freedom as something he had coming to him—not eventually but right now. The problem was that the prosecutors in Indiana had asked for ninety-three years, and the judge had obliged with fifty. Kimberlin persevered and, at last, with not quite fifteen years behind him, he had reached the cusp of liberty. From Memphis, where he had spent four and a half years getting to know the interior of the federal correctional institution but missed out on Graceland and the ducks in the lobby of the Peabody Hotel, he was scheduled to travel by bus to the District of Columbia, where he still owed society three months in a halfway house. For several weeks, our daily phone conversations were punctuated by a countdown. The operator would announce a collect call, and I would accept and then hear Kimberlin's uninflected Midwestern voice: a laconic greeting segueing to an up-tempo "Thirty-six and a wake-up" or "Twenty-two and a wake-up" or "Nine and a wake-up"—a still youthful Rip Van Winkle anticipating his journey out of a bad dream. At night, as he slept, his brain processed images of menace and violence, quotidian treachery. He never regarded freedom as abstract or spectral, and he never dreamed of it. Freedom was a palpable entitlement, air he could taste, an opportunity to exploit.

Kimberlin's physical condition was superb; he didn't like cigarettes and had never drunk alcohol in his life. As a child, he had been found to have acute food allergies: wheat, milk and eggs, red meat. Given what the Bureau of Prisons dietitians had to offer, as well as the fact that most fights got started in the mess, this seemed a tolerable disability. Usually, he prepared meals in his cell, subsisting on oatmeal, rice, tuna fish, and fruit juices from the commissary, a monotony interrupted by contraband onions, peppers, and tomatoes. Though he entered prison a runt—five five, barely a hundred pounds—along the way he had become a successful competitive power lifter, and he was leaving as a buffed-out 130-pounder who could bench-press more than twice his weight. He had high cheekbones, a fine jawline, a pallid complexion, and hooded blue eyes which he tended to aim directly at yours. A few months shy of his fortieth birthday, he might have passed for ten years younger if not for his hair. Its natural color was light brown, but an invasion of gray had evidently begun, because it looked as if he had taken to rinsing with a dye.

Often, Kimberlin had noticed other convicts on the brink of release come unglued and chain-smoke, pop Valium, or rattle the bedsprings with insomnia. Recently, a self-help book entitled *Unlimited Power* had arrived in the mail, a gift from "one of my strongest supporters." The author, Anthony Robbins, seemed to be writing out of an eerie understanding of Kimberlin's own experiences, and Kimberlin had underlined many passages: "To me, ultimate power is the ability to produce the results you desire most and create value for others in the process. Power is the ability to change your life, to shape your perceptions, to make things work for you and not against you. Real power is . . . the ability to define human needs and to fulfill them . . . to direct your own personal kingdom—your own thought processes, your own behavior—so you produce the precise results you desire."

Never in his life, Kimberlin said, had he felt more empowered. "I'm not nervous, I haven't lost any sleep, I feel fine," he told me. "It's like when I've spent months training for a power-lifting meet: Let me on the platform! I feel like I've *created* this, my release, and I'm going to be living in that creation. Most people leave prison and all they do is react to stimuli. It's all too much for them to absorb. I'm not going to be doing that. I feel like I'm going out into what I've created, and I'm ready for it."

Kimberlin's case manager had suggested having his mother send a pair of Guess? jeans and a nice sweater, maybe a sport jacket. Kimberlin found this laughable and morally reprehensible. He harbored pure contempt for what he called "the convict mentality." He said he had never been tattooed, never joined a prison poker or pool game, never been sexually humiliated. Why get all decked out like a neon ex-con? He wanted to hit the sidewalk wearing Bureau of Prisons–issue army-surplus green fatigues. "I feel like a POW, and I want to walk out of here wearing POW clothes," he said. "That way, I'll be making a statement that I feel I have to make. They want me to pretend that everything's OK. And I want to say that everything is not OK until I shed this shit." He envisioned a cinematic moment, imbued with a beatific glow; later, at the bus station, with the videocam rolling, he could change into civvies.

"It may sound weird, but I feel like I'm kind of the conscience of the country right now," Kimberlin said. "I have this eagle's-eye view of the situation. Everybody else seems to have these very restricted, myopic views of what's going on. They don't have an overview. I feel kind of like John Lennon. Other people get caught up in details and specifics, and they don't see broad things. Clinton's that way. I feel as if I was carrying this weight and it doesn't feel heavy anymore. I've had all this experience and I feel that I've been incubating as the conscience of the country, and now I'm prepared to go out and express it. I think that's why I've been writing all this music lately."

In his previous life, Kimberlin had been, among other things, an accomplished drug smuggler. In his next life, he planned on being, among other things, a rock star. He had written the lyrics of about thirty songs, including one called "Butterfly." ("It took time for me to be reborn, I needed boundaries so my wings could form. . . . Butterfly in the wind, forget where you've been. You're finally free, to find your destiny. . . .") He had compiled a typewritten agenda that itemized his plans for the first ninety days: setting up an office in the basement of his mother's house, in suburban Maryland, visiting a couple of doctors, finding a friendly banker, getting a credit card, financing a car, buying clothes, and dropping in on several journalists, congressmen, and attorneys in and out of government, all of whom he assumed would be delighted to meet with him. Then he would line up a composer and some other collaborators and make this music thing happen. One way or another, he intended to become rich. "I want to have five million dollars before I move out of my mom's house," he said. "I figure that will take me a year or two at the most."

IT WAS seven-thirty on a silvery November morning, two and a half hours since Kimberlin's final prison wake-up. The temperature was in the mid-forties; the oaks and maples were turning. I sat in the back seat of a parked compact car, thirty yards from the prison gate. Dennis Freeland, the editor of the *Memphis Flyer,* a weekly alternative newspaper, was the driver, and Kimberlin's sister, Cynthia, and Roy Cajero, a photographer for the *Flyer,* were fellow passengers. The *Flyer* had published two cover stories and several shorter articles about Kimberlin during his time in Memphis. As we turned onto the service road and caught sight of the concertina wire and the corrugated-concrete outer walls, Cynthia started crying. Now we all waited silently. A steady trickle of employees, mostly black, arrived for the eight-o'clock shift. Just before the hour, the cab that would transport Kimberlin to the bus depot pulled up, and soon we could see him standing inside the prison portal's glass vestibule, counting money. Roy Cajero poked a long lens out the rear window of our car. When Kimberlin stepped outside, he deliberately faced us, smiling but not waving—a man comfortable posing.

We followed the taxi along the interstate, a twenty-minute dash downtown, during which Kimberlin occasionally glanced through the rear window, smiled, winked, and faintly waved. On the sidewalk outside the Greyhound terminal, he embraced his sister. Waiting inside was a friend who, though he lived in Memphis, Kimberlin had never met face-to-face. This was Clyde Stephenson, a pen pal who in recent months had written several rambling single-spaced letters, free-associational metaphysical and philosophical riffs that described his life as a figure-skating instructor, a Ph.D., a spiritual pilgrim, and a follower of Walter of Pontoise, the patron saint of incarcerated people. The correspondence began after Clyde saw an article about Kimberlin in *People.* The accompanying photographs, Clyde felt, revealed a striking resemblance to Saint Walter. In addition to the letters, Clyde sent the copy of *Unlimited Power* and several photographs of a statue of Saint Walter. In general, Kimberlin had no use for religion, but he was susceptible to the text of a rosary Clyde included with one letter: "Holy Walter of Pontoise, even as you suffered imprisonment and lived to triumph, I ask you to be my patron. . . ." The day after this letter arrived, he told me, "Clyde's very insightful about me, incredibly so." Clyde had brought a shopping bag that was loaded with fresh barbecued shrimp, a silver amulet that he said he had received from the Dalai Lama and had gotten blessed by Pope John Paul II, and some last-minute advice. "Tell Brett to watch it," he said to Cynthia. "He's going out of here totally fearless. A lot of people won't be able to deal with that."

Cynthia toted an insulated knapsack filled with food, a knapsack packed with clothing, a small duffel, and a carrying case for her video camera. Kimberlin's request to wear his prison uniform had been denied, a valedictory rebuff by the feds. Instead, he wore a black hooded sweatshirt with WOLF RIVER RECREATION CLUB in yellow lettering, blue jeans with rolled-up cuffs, and black-and-white running shoes. From a duffel, he removed the prison fatigues.

"Videotape this," he said to Cynthia. "Where's the fucking garbage? Oh, over here." He pushed the clothes through the opening of a receptacle. "This is garbage. It's trash. That's over. It's done. It's behind me."

Seasoned bus travelers refer to any trip on Greyhound Lines as "ridin' the dawg"—best forgotten but ineluctably memorable. The ambience of the terminal suggested that celebrity sightings in Memphis typically took place in some other setting. A skinny woman with dirty-blond hair and dark rings under her eyes walked over, carrying a four-foot-tall Barney the Dinosaur. Gesturing toward Kimberlin, she asked Clyde, "Who is he?"

"He's rich and famous," Clyde told her.

In that case, she wanted to be photographed with him. "Sure, I'll hold Barney," Kimberlin said. "Barney was born after I went in." He smiled at the cameras.

"This Barney has come all the way from Lakeland, Florida, today," the woman said.

After she moved away, Kimberlin said, "What the hell was that all about?"

Cynthia continued to follow his movements with her camera, Roy Cajero stayed busy taking photographs, Dennis Freeland and I were jotting things in notebooks. It occurred to me that together, unwittingly, we were turning what might otherwise have been a deeply private moment of transition into a minor media event. Then I caught myself and realized that each of us—from Cynthia, who idolized her brother, to Clyde, who was looking on with what appeared to be controlled rapture, to the serendipitous skinny lady with the stuffed purple dinosaur and all the mileage on her odometer—was a player in a performance directed and choreographed by the ostensible subject. Like Kimberlin himself, each of us had an investment in his being somebody.

· · ·

I FIRST MET Brett Kimberlin in the summer of 1992. Over two consecutive days, we spent fourteen hours in a glass-walled private cubicle off the main visitors' room of the Memphis Federal Correctional Institution. He did most of the talking. I took notes with a laptop computer, concentrating on what he was saying, curious to see whether the facts fell into a pattern and, if so, what that pattern implied. Kimberlin unspooled a tale that was both linear and marked by a byzantine complexity. I already knew that I was listening to someone who, as a teenager, had been convicted of perjury; that he had progressed from small-time marijuana dealer to big-time marijuana smuggler; that in the late seventies he was regarded as a suspect, though never charged, in a murder case that was never solved; and that in 1981, after a protracted prosecution in Indianapolis that included several bizarre elements, he was convicted of six apparently motiveless bombings in the town of Speedway, Indiana, the last of which left a man severely maimed. (In all, eight bombs detonated, but the government based its case on only six.) I knew that Kimberlin had defiantly maintained his innocence, and to our first meetings he brought a tall stack of legal filings and other documents that amounted, he said, to proof of his having been railroaded. He had a reputation as an exceptionally adroit jailhouse lawyer, and the papers he showed me included briefs he had written himself or collaborated upon with respected members of the bar.

Though I entered the room armored with a rational skepticism, as would any self-respecting journalist, it was impossible not to be impressed by Kimberlin's articulate intelligence and self-disciplined aura. He referred me to a sympathetic newspaper reporter who had known him for more than a decade, and whom I dutifully called to ask whether he believed Kimberlin's story. "Which one?" he replied. "Brett's an interesting character." When I remarked to an Indianapolis lawyer who'd briefly worked on Kimberlin's case that I was eager to try to understand this complicated saga, he chuckled and said, "You realize you're getting into the murkiest, most amorphous mass of story in the world. You're entering a black hole."

Two months after this first meeting, I published in *The New Yorker* a lengthy article about Kimberlin. Though it addressed in part his criminal convictions and his avowal of innocence in the bombing case, its main focus was a series of events that started during the presidential-election campaign of 1988, when George Bush chose Dan Quayle as his running mate. In the closing days of that campaign, Kimberlin began sharing with reporters his claim that in the early seventies, he had routinely supplied Quayle with small amounts of marijuana. The immediate consequences of his willingness to disseminate this allegation seemed not at all murky or amorphous.

At the time, Kimberlin was an inmate at a federal prison in El Reno, Oklahoma. Four days before the election, as fragments of the story began to surface and dozens of reporters called the warden's office seeking audiences with Kimberlin, he agreed to a prison official's proposal that, for the sake of efficiency, he appear that evening at a press conference. Before this event could take place, however, it was canceled on orders of the director of the Bureau of Prisons. Kimberlin, instead of being allowed to exercise his First Amendment rights, was placed in administrative detention, apart from the general prison population. He was released within twenty-four hours but was isolated again, the day before the election, when he had planned to participate in a press conference via telephone with a gathering of Washington reporters. This time, he remained incommunicado for almost a week. Then, after a press account of these incidents appeared in a legal publication several weeks later, he was placed in detention a third time.

When I caught up with Kimberlin, he was successfully pursuing a civil-rights suit against the director of the Bureau of Prisons and an official of the Justice Department. That he was still incarcerated made him, from a journalistic perspective, quite compelling. He had attended a parole hearing in the summer of 1988, shortly before Dan Quayle was nominated for the vice presidency. The subsequent denial of parole, compounded by denials of appeals of the parole decision, despite Kimberlin's having been in most respects a model inmate, lent credence to the notion that he had become—and I resorted to this phrase with sober hesitation—a "political prisoner."

From the outset, my motive was to write about Kimberlin not as a symbol but as a human being whose experiences would form, I hoped, a verifiable narrative. By 1992, he had acquired considerable skill at dealing with the press. There were times when he seemed impelled by a belief that there was no such thing as enough publicity; at other times, he would in a peremptory way decline interview requests from various quarters. When I first contemplated writing about him and spoke with him on the telephone, some weeks before our initial meeting, I tried to make it clear that my purpose was not to enhance his standing as a cause célèbre. I have no idea what, at that point—with his parole status unresolved, with his civil suit still being litigated, with Bush and Quayle campaigning for reelection—Kimberlin thought might be the real advantages or risks of being scrutinized by a reporter for *The New Yorker*.

I wanted to figure out and to convey to readers: Who was this guy? Where had he been and where was he heading? How was it that, simply by virtue of his being a convict, certain members of the press and the public could dismiss him as not credible? How was it that Dan Quayle, simply by virtue of his position in public life, could be deemed credible? What was the subtext of the silencing of Kimberlin in 1988? What inferences could be drawn from Quayle's statement that he had not only never met Kimberlin but also had never used illegal drugs, had never attended a party where drugs were used, and had no friends who had ever used illegal drugs?

Some months later, I signed a contract to write a book about Kimberlin's life. He agreed to cooperate, and in exchange he would receive a share of the book's royalties. This venture was predicated on the idea that there was an even richer and more elaborate story to tell than I had previously told. Looking back at that moment, I think we both assumed we had the same story in mind—an assumption that now strikes me as both conspiratorial and naïve.

BY TEN O'CLOCK, we were on the bus, rolling east. In western Tennessee, we cruised past beige autumn foliage as dull as the pewter sky, and ripe white cotton fields ready for harvest. For Kimberlin, every frame had a Technicolor brilliance. In the terminal, savoring a stick of chewing gum Clyde had given him, he said, "That's the first piece of gum I've had in a long time. That's contraband. They send you to the hole for that." Now Cynthia began to unpack provisions from her knapsack. He bit into a coconut-almondine bar, looked deeply satisfied, and said, "Real food." He drank from a chilled container of juice that Cynthia had squeezed from her backyard apples in Utah the previous morning. When she gave him an oatmeal cookie, he said, "I haven't had a cookie in fifteen years." Later, as he assembled a sandwich of avocado, tomato, ersatz cheese, and mayonnaise, he held up a piece of rye bread and said, "This is the first piece of bread I've had in fifteen years."

His conversation during much of the trip was a litany of what else he hadn't seen or done for a long, long while. A little Cessna flew over, about to land on a strip next to the interstate. Kimberlin, who had gotten his pilot's license at sixteen, craned his neck and crooned "Memories." Stopping over in Nashville, he asked Cynthia to lend him a telephone credit card. "I've got some people I want to call," he said. "Come teach me how to use the phones, Cynthia. I've never used a calling card. They didn't have them where I was." The price of gasoline hadn't changed much, but that of Life Savers had quadrupled. A visit to the men's room became a mild epiphany: "I can't tell you how wonderful it is to be able to go into a stall and close the door. If I have any psychic scars, it's been from the loss of privacy—having to shit and piss two feet away from someone else for fifteen years."

Back on the road, with dusk falling, Kimberlin put on Walkman earphones to listen to the evening newscast on National Public Radio. It struck him that, unaccustomed as he was to visual stimulation, the oncoming car headlights were beautiful. An hour later, however, while doing Transcendental Meditation, he was serenely lost in his thoughts when the bus went down a hill and the glare of headlights hit him in the eyes—like a guard's flashlight during nighttime count in the joint—and for a few moments, he panicked. Once he calmed down, he told himself there were likely to be lots of nights when he would awaken and not realize he was free.

Kimberlin met a girl on the bus, a pretty auburn-haired Mexican American seated in the row ahead of him. He began chatting with her in an aggressively amiable way, and when the seat next to her was free he took it. Staring out the window during a stop in Bristol, Tennessee, at eleven-thirty at night, I saw Brett and Cynthia stretching and doing half jumping jacks to stay warm. Then I saw him introducing his sister to his new friend. Monica was eighteen, on her way from Los Angeles to Philadelphia, chaperoned by an aunt and a grandmother. Later, nearing the Virginia border, he asked Cynthia to hand him a copy of *Powerlifting USA*, the November 1993 issue, in which he was listed as eighteenth on the all-time list of squatters in the 114-pound division. "I told this girl I'm one of the strongest men in the world, and she told me I'm full of shit," he explained. "I want to prove it." By Fort Chiswell, Virginia, at one-thirty in the morning, he was in a

McDonald's, paying for Monica's Egg McMuffin. Too tightly wired to sleep, Kimberlin was soon leaning his head on her shoulder and rhythmically stroking her hair. Monica seemed to be neither discouraging him nor reciprocating. Before dawn, she asked him about other girls. "Yeah, there are other girls," he said. "They're like flies. I mean, I like them, but they're not special. Not like you." And she replied, "Boy, you've got every line, don't you?"

Naturally, there were snappy lines and fascinating facts about himself that Kimberlin couldn't share. He couldn't tell her where he had just come from. He couldn't tell her that looking up at the stars wasn't just pleasant, it was the first time he'd seen them in fifteen years. He couldn't tell her there were people in Indianapolis who, if they stuck to their word, were going to start carrying guns now that he was free. Anyway, it sure was nice to smell a woman. And it was a challenge to learn how to talk with women again. He worried that he might be a little too blunt for some people on the street. Men in prison had a whole way of talking that might involve certain subtleties but didn't require certain courtesies. They said "motherfucker" a lot. They talked frankly about masturbation. He would have to adjust.

Kimberlin was seated next to me as we reached the outskirts of the District. His mother would be waiting in the bus terminal, along with a couple of friends. Knowing that Cynthia would be videotaping their reunion, I asked Kimberlin how he intended to explain this expectant entourage to Monica.

"You go out ahead of me and tell everyone not to mention prison," he said.

Dryly, I said I wasn't sure whether, journalistically, that would be proper.

"Come on, man," he said, laughing. "Don't blow some pussy for me."

Who was Brett Kimberlin? Where had he been and where was he heading? The literal answer—that he was a thirty-nine-year-old freshly minted ex-con ridin' the dawg toward a halfway house, where, within the hour, he would walk through the front door carrying a canvas satchel large enough for a few toiletries, a couple of books, and a change of underwear—meant nothing. I had already spent more than a year examining Kimberlin's life and reassessing my original perceptions of him. And if who he was and where he'd been had begun to seem ambiguous, where he was heading seemed impossible to predict. Verities that I had filed away as tangible and solid now struck me as hazy and transient. There were questions I could pursue endlessly, while their answers would grow yet more elusive. One of the few facts I felt confident of was that I was witnessing a middle passage of a long and strange American voyage.

2

O N 16 AUGUST 1988, George Bush arrived in New Orleans, the site of the Republican National Convention, to accept his party's nomination for the presidency, his reward for eight years of indiscriminate loyalty to Ronald Reagan. The lame-duck president, who had addressed the convention the night before, was scheduled to depart on Air Force One shortly after the ascendant vice president had flown in on Air Force Two. They met on the tarmac at Belle Chase Naval Air Station. Bush whispered to Reagan his choice for the vice-presidency—Dan Quayle, the junior senator from Indiana. Reagan weighed in with some last-minute elbow-in-the-ribs bonhomie, informing the assembled reporters that he had "just tried to make a deal with George—that I'd tell him where to find the best blackened redfish if he'd tell me who's going to be vice-president," and got out of town, lest he overshadow his successor.

The next person to whom Bush disclosed his decision was James A. Baker III, the campaign chairman. Though Quayle had pursued a deliberate strategy to position himself for the vice-presidency—what David Broder and Bob Woodward, in a January 1992 series of articles in the *Washington Post,* described as a "six-month attention-getting effort"—his selection reportedly "astonished" some of Baker's closest aides. "In 1988, when Bush surveyed Republican senators, not one of Quayle's colleagues listed him among the top three choices for the vice-presidency," Broder and Woodward reported.

Responsibility for screening possible candidates had been given to Robert Kimmitt, a lawyer and Baker protégé who, during Baker's tenure as secretary of the treasury, had served as the department's general counsel. Kimmitt had been busy for several weeks, and well before the opening of the convention he had vetted not only Quayle but also such other contenders as Jack Kemp, then a representative from upstate New York, and Senators Robert Dole of Kansas and

John Danforth of Missouri, and Dole's wife, Elizabeth, the former secretary of transportation. According to Broder and Woodward, Bush "let none of his top political aides read the background checks he ordered on Quayle and the other finalists." The screening process required Quayle and the others to complete a thirty-page form that amounted to a detailed financial disclosure, travel summary, and medical history. Kimmitt had modeled this questionnaire on a document routinely used by the Federal Bureau of Investigation for background checks on potential judicial and senior executive-branch nominees. For each vice-presidential prospect, Kimmitt also threw in some tailor-made skeleton-in-the-closet questions.

In midafternoon, Quayle received a message on his beeper to call Baker. "Hang on for the Veep," Baker told him, and then Bush invited Quayle to become the new veep. The formal announcement would take place within an hour or so at a rally on Spanish Plaza, along the Mississippi, with Bush arriving aboard a paddle-wheeler, the SS *Natchez.* In the opening chapter of Quayle's score-settling memoir, *Standing Firm,* he describes discussing with Baker the logistics of how he and his wife, Marilyn, would reach the rally location: "He just wanted me to show up, and to keep this a secret. Okay, I told him, we'd figure out how to get down there. He reminded me that this was my first assignment and I'd better not blow it. 'Remember,' he joked. 'This decision is revocable.' It was the last laugh I would have for a long, long time."

A charitable explanation for the ensuing unpleasantness is that the media, having failed to see Quayle coming, pounced with excessive zeal. However, it wasn't as if Quayle gave the jackals of the Fourth Estate nothing to work with. For starters, during the rally on Spanish Plaza he displayed what was either his own excessive zeal or an unsettling callowness. He cavorted about the platform like a high-school cheerleader, displaying an exuberance that made the hyperkinesis-prone Bush seem subdued by comparison. "Let's go get 'em!" Quayle shouted, grabbing Bush by the shoulders, hugging his arm, and in general rendering a believable impersonation of a loose cannon.

The next morning, the running mates held a joint press conference, during which the subject of Quayle's military service at the time of the Vietnam War arose. In a poorly ventilated room at the Marriott Hotel, reporters were kept waiting for about an hour before the candidates appeared. How was it, the overheated journalists asked Quayle, that he could pose as a hawk on defense matters when, evidently, he had availed himself of family influence to join the Indiana National Guard, thereby avoiding the draft and active duty in Vietnam? An unwillingness to bear a weapon into a highly dubious battle was not a punishable offense; hypocrisy, however, was. Quayle's reflection that "I did not know in 1969 that I would be in this room today, I'll confess" only exacerbated the problem.

Several of the campaign professionals enlisted by Baker quickly arrived at a bottom-line conviction they would never abandon: Quayle was a mistake, plain and simple. Instead of providing the two- or three-percentage-point boost that one hoped for in a running mate, he represented a potentially serious liability. That evening, the candidate was dispatched to four network anchor booths. Interrogated further about his National Guard service, he continued to provide clumsy replies. To Dan Rather, he acknowledged that telephone calls had been made on his behalf to his draft board in Huntington. Other questions addressed the novelty of having a baby boomer on a national political ticket, and certain implicit assumptions were aroused. When Peter Jennings asked whether he had ever smoked marijuana, Quayle replied, "I did not."

AT APPROXIMATELY the same hour that Bush and Quayle were holding their first press conference, the head of operations for the Drug Enforcement Administration, David Westrate, paid a visit to John Lawn, his director, in Washington. In his background investigations, Robert Kimmitt had consulted the FBI but not the DEA. As a matter of routine, the DEA shares information with the FBI only when asked. Therefore, Kimmitt had no knowledge of the issue that concerned Westrate—namely, that the DEA had maintained a file on Quayle since the early 1980s.

In 1982, a joint task force consisting of people from the DEA, the FBI, the United States Capitol Police, and the Metropolitan Police of the District of Columbia began to investigate the proliferation of illegal drug use by government employees—a by-product of the congressional investigation that, a year earlier, had resulted in the censure of two House members for having sexual relations with pages. The syndicated columnist Jack Anderson had also reported drug allegations and named several names, among them Barry Goldwater, Jr. (Republican-California), Ronald V. Dellums (Democrat-California), and Charles Wilson (Democrat-Texas). As a result, the Justice Department organized a broader investigation, as did the House Committee on Standards of Official Conduct. These inquiries lasted eighteen months and led to fourteen hundred allegations against government employees. The raw information gathered by the task force was funneled to a central DEA database called NADDIS, an acronym for Narcotics and Dangerous Drugs Information System. Grand juries were impaneled in Washington and Los Angeles.

In July 1983, a meeting took place in the office of William French Smith, the attorney general—a meeting requested by Dean Burch, a lawyer and a former chairman of both the Federal Communications Commission and the Republican National Committee. Burch, who had been dispatched by Senator Barry Goldwater, Sr., of Arizona, delivered a straightforward message: If the so-called Capitol Hill drug investigation did not stop, the Reagan administration could anticipate that none of its defense appropriation requests would progress beyond the Senate Armed Services Committee, of which Goldwater was chairman. Four Justice Department employees witnessed this encounter. Smith's passivity left as lasting an impression as Burch's bluntness. Smith didn't flinch. Rather, he listened quietly and thanked Burch for coming. After half an hour, the meeting ended—anticlimactically, it seemed to those present.

Within a month, a message from the office of Attorney General Smith was received at the task force headquarters, and the Justice contact person was instructed to shut down the operation over the next few weeks. No explanation accompanied this directive. The remnants of the investigation survive to this day—massive files of interviews and allegations concerning wrongdoing by public officials, as well as bitterness among many who believe that a grand opportunity was squandered. The indictment of well-known political figures, these investigators felt, would have powerfully conveyed the clear message that illegal drug use should not and would not be tolerated.

Barry Goldwater, Jr., left Congress in January 1983, after unsuccessfully seeking the Republican senatorial nomination from California. He contemplated returning to the House of Representatives in the fall of 1984 but ultimately chose not to run. This decision was influenced by his knowledge that, despite having avoided indictment—

"Daddy saved my ass," he joked to friends—the Capitol Hill investigation could haunt him.

As the senior DEA representative on the task force, David Westrate had been well aware that Dan Quayle was under surveillance. In fact, though misidentified as "Don" Quayle, he was included in the organizational flow chart, along with fifteen senators and representatives, and dozens of Capitol Hill employees and relatives of government officials. The activities of three men named Todd, Marshall, and Finkel formed the core of the investigation. On the chart, two large groups of names were gathered under the headings "Alleged Drug Customers, Drug Users, Re-Distributors, Etc., Identified Through Investigation of Todd/Marshall/Finkel" and "Allegations of Illicit Drug Usage Received Independent of Todd/Marshall/Finkel Case." Quayle was listed in the latter category.

Now that Bush, in 1988, had exposed Quayle to public scrutiny, it seemed to Westrate that to disregard what he knew would amount to negligence. Lawn received the information calmly and ordered Westrate to retrieve a printout of Quayle's file from a DEA field office in southwest Washington. A couple of days elapsed before the hard copy of the file reached Lawn.

It being a proprietary matter, Lawn was not about to surrender the file itself. He did, however, make a summary report of its contents, which he then sent to the office of the attorney general. (Edwin Meese, who had replaced William French Smith, himself had only a few days remaining in office, and was about to be succeeded by Richard Thornburgh.) The summary traveled from Meese's office to the White House, where it was received by C. Boyden Gray, then a counselor to the vice president (and, after Bush's election, to the president). At that point, only three officials at DEA headquarters—Lawn, his deputy, and Westrate—were aware that Quayle's file had been requested. The hard copy was locked in a safe in Westrate's office and remained there for several weeks before being returned to the DEA field office. Because no congressmen were formally charged as a result of the Capitol Hill drug investigation, Westrate believed that, as a practical matter, the Bush-Quayle campaign did not have a great deal to worry about. For his part, Lawn felt he had done his duty. "If anything had come up in the campaign," an aide later said, "he'd covered his ass by reporting it to the proper authorities."

Throughout the 1988 campaign, Bush and Quayle said that the vice president would be in charge of the government's "war on drugs." This notion was later abandoned. In time, the widely held assumption within the DEA was that if James Baker had learned of Quayle's file at any point prior to his nomination, the junior senator from Indiana would've remained just that.

3

EXCEPT FOR reasons of professional curiosity, I couldn't care less whether, as a young man, Dan Quayle smoked marijuana or ingested cocaine. Nor, provided that he wasn't supporting legislation mandating prison sentences for casual users, does it disturb me that he might himself have indulged while serving in the House of Representatives or the Senate. When, during his vice-presidency, he declared, "What a waste it is to lose one's mind," my first reaction was not that he had mangled the motto of the United Negro College Fund but that he was sanctimoniously abandoning a modus vivendi he had enthusiastically embraced as a college fraternity boy.

By the time I began to explore Brett Kimberlin's alleged connection to Quayle, virtually no other members of the mainstream press seemed interested in the topic. Covering a political campaign is a depleting ordeal, offering barely enough time after the tally to catch one's breath before it becomes necessary to get back to work serially fawning over and vivisecting the newly elected. By muzzling Kimberlin in the final days of the 1988 campaign, the Bureau of Prisons obviated a public airing of his claim—which, had it been allowed to play out, would have concerned not drug abuse but an elected official's credibility. Kimberlin's credibility, in the short term, was easily impeached; he had the burden of a perjury conviction as well as a reputation in Indianapolis as a bomb-planting terrorist. So as far as the national media were concerned, once the election was decided, Kimberlin ceased to matter—before he had even begun to matter. Years would elapse before the lawsuit that grew out of his treatment by the Bureau of Prisons swelled to its full constitutional and political ripeness.

I managed to remain oblivious of the whole business until one day in early June 1992, when Lawrence "Ren" Weschler, a friend and colleague at *The New Yorker,* wandered into my office and said he had a story idea that might be right for me. It took Ren about ten minutes to explain why he thought writing about Kimberlin would be worthwhile. If Ren hadn't been about to begin reporting a complicated story set in Czechoslovakia, he would have pursued it himself. Any article about Kimberlin, to have real relevance, would have to be published before the November election. Only one contingency could seriously undermine the project: if Bush, who was lagging in the polls, were to yield to the growing pressure to abandon Quayle as his running mate.

Weschler himself had first heard about Kimberlin in detail from Garry Trudeau, the creator of the syndicated cartoon strip "Doonesbury." In August 1991, and again that November, Trudeau had produced strips about Kimberlin and the existence of Quayle's DEA file. The latter series, which was based on a collaboration with a Washington journalist named Cody Shearer, extended for three weeks and contained specific allegations that hadn't previously been aired. Several newspapers decided they were too inflammatory to be published. After the first series appeared, Kimberlin naturally felt that in Trudeau he had a potent ally. Shearer, who had been interested in Kimberlin since 1988, suggested that he get in touch with Trudeau, and Kimberlin began phoning regularly—always collect. They would chat about politics, Kimberlin would ask this or that favor, Trudeau would try to accommodate him, and along the way Kimberlin began to recite his autobiography.

Because I don't routinely read a newspaper that carries "Doonesbury," I had missed the strips and the controversy they provoked. As it happened, Trudeau and I attended college together in the late sixties and have been friendly acquaintances ever since. From time to time, we run into each other in New York. When I called Trudeau to say I indeed wanted to hear more, he invited me to lunch at his studio. The gist of what he had to say was this: The image of Kimberlin that had been floated by the Bush-Quayle campaign in 1988 and afterward—that he was a con with a tale, nothing more—was, in effect, a cartoon; the full story had drama as well as a prismatic complexity; Kimberlin was highly intelligent and, in his smuggling as well as his legitimate enterprises, had been hardworking and imaginative; in a manner that seemed persuasive, he denied being the Speedway Bomber; whether or not he truly was responsible for the bombings, he had not received a fair trial; his account of his dealings with Quayle, particularly in light of the existence of the DEA file, had the ring of truth; strong evidence suggested that political interference had tainted his parole case; no reporter for any national publication had ever bothered to take a sufficiently detailed look at Kimberlin's life to place his allegations about Quayle in a historical and logical context; with the 1992 election only a few months away, the truth had value.

I asked Trudeau to have Kimberlin call me, and four days later he did. We talked for more than half an hour, and I wrote down almost everything he said. He spoke about his girlfriend ("She loves me to death"), his family, his experiences in the marijuana trade ("I sold many tons of marijuana in my time"), Quayle ("Danny was just a small-time customer"). His manner was matter-of-fact, and there was no tentativeness to our exchanges. That Kimberlin seemed so straightforward, with no edge of defensiveness, I attributed to our shared regard for Trudeau.

As well as I could, I explained to Robert Gottlieb, the editor of *The New Yorker,* who Kimberlin was and why I wanted to write about him. Gottlieb told me to go ahead. Within a couple of weeks, it was announced that Gottlieb was being replaced by Tina Brown, who for the previous eight years had been the editor of *Vanity Fair* and whose mission at *The New Yorker,* clearly, would be to transform it. I had already spent eighteen years at the magazine. I weighed the possibility that she might not want to keep me on the staff. Her first issue would be published in late September. Meanwhile, Gottlieb reassured me that I should proceed.

I spent three days in Indianapolis in late July, talking to people who knew Kimberlin. In the library of the Indianapolis *Star* and *News*—newspapers that constituted the core of the publishing fortune created by Quayle's grandfather Eugene Pulliam—I photocopied hundreds of clippings, mostly related to the Speedway bombings. I went to Washington and met with Kimberlin's mother, Carolyn; with Cody Shearer, who at that point knew more about Kimberlin than any other journalist in the country; and with Howard Rosenblatt, the attorney who was representing him in his lawsuit against the Bureau of Prisons. I flew to Memphis and spent two days listening to Kimberlin. My notes from this fourteen-hour conversation totaled twelve thousand words, and I departed with a briefcase full of documents: Kimberlin's college transcripts, press clippings of his power-lifting triumphs, chunks of the appellate brief and exculpatory affidavits related to the bombings case, copies of articles about the unreliability of posthypnotic testimony (a key component in the prosecution of the bombings), an affidavit supporting his allegations about Quayle, petitions to the U.S. Parole Commission and the U.S. pardon attorney.

"If Clinton gets elected, I'm out; I know I'll get a pardon," Kimberlin told me at one point. "But you can't say that. It looks like I'm doing this for political reasons, like I've got an agenda." The ex cathedra tenor of this remark made me think that he knew exactly what he was talking about.

One afternoon in Memphis, I checked my phone messages in New York and found I had a call from Tina Brown. I called her back, she asked what I was up to, and when I explained, she said, "That sounds like a very hot story." A few days later, in New York, she told me to have the story ready—she wanted it to be the lead article—for her first issue. The deadline was five weeks away. I had arranged to take my sons on a weeklong vacation, so that meant I was down to four weeks.

I ended up more or less domiciled in my office at *The New Yorker.* I slept three or four hours a night. "I am building a brick wall," I told myself—each brick being a fact of Kimberlin's private and public history, the facts accumulating in layers that paralleled Quayle's public life and putative private history. Take away a fact here or there and the structure would collapse, but with each brick in its proper place, the completed wall would stand as evidence that the 1988 election had been corrupted and that ever since, Kimberlin had suffered political persecution.

Kimberlin was calling me several times a day, occasionally to hand me a brick, usually just to ask how things were going. I knew, of course, that there is such a thing as proper journalistic detachment, that for the wall to have integrity I had to stand back at a consistent arm's length. Particularly where Kimberlin's accounts of his dealings with Quayle were concerned, or in discussing the bombings, qualifiers were essential: "Kimberlin says," "Brett recalls," "It is Kimberlin's assumption that." I avoided the first-person pronoun, interjecting myself into the narrative only at the very end, when I described a scene in the Washington law office of Erwin Griswold, a former solicitor general of the United States, a former dean of the Harvard Law School, and the epitome of judicious rectitude. Griswold had once represented

Kimberlin in a criminal appeal and had developed a personal fondness for him. "A man can enter the penal system and then, for various reasons—reasons of an essentially political nature—the procedures established for parole and reduction of time can be bypassed," Griswold told me. "And in Kimberlin's case the result is that, in substance, he has become a political prisoner." That became the concluding quotation of the article.

As the editing and fact-checking and legal vetting progressed, I got into voluble and contentious discussions with a prosecutor in Indianapolis and with Quayle's press secretary. I also found myself on unfriendly terms with Don Hewitt, the executive producer of "60 Minutes." I was critical of the handling of the Kimberlin story by several news organizations and singled out Hewitt because he had gone out of his way, unjustly, to malign Trudeau and Shearer in print. When Hewitt, who has a water buffalo's appetite for combat, realized what was coming, he called Tina Brown and complained that *he* was about to be maligned in print. She calmed him down and earned my gratitude by not asking me to compromise what I had written.

She did make one request that, at first, I resisted. "I want to know what you really think of Kimberlin," she said. "We need a paragraph somewhere near the beginning that tells us that." I said it didn't matter what I thought, that the brick wall, as it were, should speak for itself. "No," she said. "I want a more close-up sense of what he's like as a person."

"If you want to be closer to him, you'll have to go to Memphis," I replied. "He's locked up. I've gotten as close as I can." But she persisted.

"All right," I said. "I can tell you that he gives off a powerful aura."

"Then write about that," she said.

So I wrote: "Kimberlin's voice seems to float within an eerie magnetic nimbus, and, whether he is seated across a table in a prison visitors' room or is disembodied at the end of a wiretapped telephone, he radiates the unmistakable aura of a haunted survivor—a man who is both protagonist and victim."

At the time, I thought of this little passage as smartly poetic filler, if a touch melodramatic. I now think of it as a projection of a mild delirium. My home telephone, I had become convinced, was wiretapped. Urgently, inordinately, I wanted the Democrats to win the election; otherwise, I envisioned an unfriendly audit of my federal tax return. Worse, I entertained a fantasy that I would be invited to the Clinton-Gore inauguration—laughable not only for its inane presumptuousness but because large crowds make me uncomfortable—and that I would bring my mother along, to give her a thrill. For several months, my marriage of almost twenty years had been in a final phase of disintegration; I felt both grief-stricken and liberated. Writing about Kimberlin had the virtue of providing a socially useful outlet for my obsessiveness.

The first issue of Tina Brown's *New Yorker*, launched with unbridled hoopla, hit the newsstand five weeks and a day before the election. My piece ran to 22,000 words. Three days after it was published, I sat in a recording studio and did a twenty-minute interview for a National Public Radio program called "Fresh Air." The taping took place before noon and was scheduled to be broadcast later that day. A couple of hours before airtime, the show's producer called to say, apologetically but firmly, that they were canning it because I "sounded too intense." What did he mean? "We just don't feel comfortable going ahead with this," he said. "You sound like you're a little too close to the subject."

The following week, I gave a live interview on the "Today" show. Kimberlin also appeared, by satellite hookup from the prison in Memphis. Bryant Gumbel asked the questions. When Gumbel, who was seated opposite me in the studio, crossed his legs, I deliberately chose not to cross mine. I had given television interviews often, but when I saw the tape of this one I was appalled. My knees were locked rigidly, and I gripped the arms of my chair like someone taking his first airplane trip. The import of my remarks was that evidence suggested that during the 1988 election, officials of the Bush-Quayle campaign—I singled out James A. Baker III—had engaged in behavior that was intolerable in a democratic republic. I sounded articulate enough, and what I said had a logic, but I never once smiled, and my sense of irony seemed to have evaporated.

I recall this entire period of my life as having an overvivid, hyperreal texture—an extended drugless altered state. A lawyer friend who read the *New Yorker* piece told me he found it interesting but that he had no sympathy for Kimberlin, "because he's obviously such a bad guy." Garrison Keillor told me he detected something generally "off" in the tone of what I'd written. "I thought the conclusion—the inferred conclusion—was hanging there before one got to it, that it was too anxious to reach a conclusion about Quayle and the government," he said. "I thought the purpose of the piece was to get Quayle." I read a Garry Wills column in which he agreed with my thesis that Kimberlin had suffered political persecution, but remonstrated that "it would be irresponsible for a journalist to print Kimberlin's charges without more verification than he has been able to supply," and that I seemed "readier to believe Kimberlin than are some of [Kimberlin's] own lawyers." Though I pride myself as one who welcomes scrupulous editing and constructive criticism, these appraisals merely stung. I wanted to have no idea what these people were talking about.

4

KIMBERLIN'S VERSION of his dealings with Quayle:
"Larry Harvey introduced me to Dan Quayle. He's dead now. Killed himself. He was the older brother of Susan Harvey, who was my girlfriend all through junior high and high school and after that, even. Sometimes I would buy pot from Larry in Bloomington, a pound at a time. I was there visiting Larry, I had some joints with me, and I was just passing them around. This was at a fraternity house, but I don't remember which one. Danny was there in the room. We were bullshitting around and listening to music. And within an hour, this guy who looked really square—my friend Larry was a hippie, and my hair was down to my shoulders—this blond frat-boy says, 'Hey, do you have any of this for sale?' I looked at him. I was stoned and he was stoned. I said, 'Yeah, but I live in Indianapolis.' And he says, 'That's no problem.' I get the feeling that this guy's a narc. He looks real square compared to everybody else there, and then he tells me he's gonna drive sixty miles to Indianapolis to buy a fucking ounce of dope. I mean, something's wrong. So I said, 'I'll talk to you later.' I asked Larry, and he said he didn't know the guy, he'll check him out. A while later, he tells me he's OK. So I went back and gave him my phone number. I had no idea he was living in Indianapolis at the time. He was going to night school there, at [a branch of] Indiana University Law School. A week or two later, I get this phone call and this guy says, 'This is D.Q.' I said, 'Who?' He says, 'Remember, the guy at the frat house. Why don't we get together?' So we met at a Burger Chef at Kessler Boulevard and Michigan Road, near my parents' house, and I sold him an ounce of pot. . . . He called me once a month for eighteen months. He was a nobody to me then. I didn't know anything about [the] Pulliam [family]. He was just another guy that I sold pot to. He would come down from the north side, and sometimes he would meet me on the northwest side, right

off the interstate, at a motel. Keep in mind, these things are not big memories for me. At the time I didn't have that many customers—maybe a dozen. This is 1971. I wasn't selling big-time. This is before I went into smuggling. He was just another upper-middle-class kid; I was an upper-middle-class kid. He was just like me. . . . He used to talk about how boring the National Guard was, how he used to get high while he was on duty. . . . The only time I ever smoked with Danny was the first time I met him, in October 1971. Then I had some bad experiences with drugs, and that December I quit taking drugs for good. . . . I stopped selling to him by the time I was eighteen."

On one occasion, Kimberlin said, Quayle brought along a girl-friend, and that unnerved him slightly, because when he sold marijuana he didn't like having people around whom he didn't know. He said he got angry with Quayle and told him not to do it again. Another time, he said, Quayle complained that the merchandise wasn't refined enough—too many stems and seeds—and that he wanted only buds. In the fall of 1972, Quayle married Marilyn Tucker, a fellow law student. Kimberlin, who did not claim ever to have met Marilyn, said that this development surprised him.

Kimberlin: "I just got the impression he was a real playboy. Then out of the blue he tells me he's engaged, he's getting married. And it was very quick that he got married. He got married in the fall of '72. A couple of months before that, he was telling me about his lady. He pulled out a picture, a little photograph. I said, 'Oh, she looks nice.' "

The entire foregoing account by Kimberlin was published in *The New Yorker*—except for Kimberlin's claim that he had quit taking drugs by the age of eighteen, which I alluded to in a different passage. When Kimberlin mentioned Quayle's showing him a photograph of his fiancée—and his reply, "Oh, she looks nice"—he added that Quayle then volunteered a scurrilous, vulgar remark about his intimate experiences with his future wife. I deleted this, picking up the monologue with: "And he got married to her ten weeks later. So I gave him a wedding present of some hashish—the only time I ever gave him hash—and a little bag of Acapulco gold. I saw him several times after he got married [to sell him marijuana], but it kind of dissipated, because after that I moved out of my family's house. I never laid eyes on him again."

I wish I could say that I blue-penciled Kimberlin's indelicacy because it was irrelevant and in irredeemably poor taste, but in fact my thinking was more convoluted. It was grounded, first, in a belief that Kimberlin was telling the truth. Larry Harvey, the one person who could corroborate or refute Kimberlin's basic story, was unavailable, and it bothered me that Kimberlin was invoking a dead person—that a skeleton lurked within the substructure of the brick wall I was building. (Other provocative Kimberlin stories also contained corpses.) I felt reassured, however, that this brick was held in place by several others. I had no blueprint for deconstructing the wall, no method of decoding Kimberlin's syntax and determining that certain details were true and others were invented. Ultimately, as much as anything, the rhythm and cadence and colloquial familiarity of Kimberlin's narrative led me to conclude that it sounded credible.

Back to the specific offending sentence: I did not unilaterally choose to delete it; I needed encouragement. Both Tina Brown and my editor, Pat Crow, advised me that it was not worth the trouble to include it. Technically and tactically, it threatened to become a distraction in a piece of journalism that, otherwise, meant serious business. Nevertheless, I maintained that it might be printable in light of a hortative and widely quoted speech Marilyn Quayle had delivered at the 1992 Republican National Convention. She said, in part, "But, remember, not everyone joined the counterculture, not everyone demonstrated, dropped out, took drugs, joined in the sexual revolution or dodged the draft. . . . When it comes to rebuilding our families, our communities, the fabric of our society, our goal must be to go back to the future." In 1988, enterprising journalists had clearly established that Dan Quayle used extraordinary means to get into the National Guard and avert any close encounters with the Vietcong. If Kimberlin was telling the truth across the board, then Marilyn Quayle's shrill piety was a fraudulent tour de force worthy of Jimmy Swaggart before his fall from grace. At the time, I did not seriously consider that the best reason not to broadcast this crude anecdote might be because the entire story was a lie.

5

A LETTER dated 2 January 1980 was sent to the Honorable Judge Woodrow Seals, of the U.S. District Court in Houston, Texas, by Carolyn Kimberlin, a concerned mother. The letter pertained to the second-oldest of her four children, her twenty-five-year-old son Brett, whom she characterized as the product of "a Christian home and a patriotic family." After describing Brett's energy and pluck as a businessman, she added:

> Brett's love, care and concern for his fellow man are the qualities which mean the most to me. It is part of Brett's nature to help those who are in need, and he takes the time to do good turns even for strangers who may never know who he is and without thought for monetary remuneration. On icy days, Brett used to go out in his truck looking for stranded people and helping by pulling their cars out of ditches. On cold, snowy mornings, he used to plow the snow from driveways and streets. Recently, a neighbor who lived at the end of a country road stopped me to chat and said that there were many times when he would awake to find Brett plowing his driveway which he never would have been able to get out of otherwise. When another neighbor was widowed, Brett shoveled and took wagons full of manure for her garden. When an elderly man became ill at planting season, it was Brett who voluntarily plowed his garden. Brett counseled others by encouraging them to eat natural food and meditate, and he urged others to not smoke and to not take drugs. He helped to reunite some young people with their parents. When a car plunged over a bridge and overturned in a canal, Brett jumped into the water and wrestled with the car until he was able to rescue the stranger inside. . . . Brett's love and care extended to animals. . . .

Judge Seals perhaps found it curious that a young man who would counsel others "to not smoke and to not take drugs" had several months earlier been caught in flagrante, along with several confederates, while attempting to smuggle into south Texas a planeload of Colombian reefer. In the judge's own courtroom, Brett had already pleaded guilty to one count of possession with intent to distribute. But it was also true that, having decided that he had copped a dumb plea, Kimberlin now wanted to withdraw it. In any event, to question Carolyn Kimberlin's sincerity would have been churlish and misguided. For years, she had been extolling her son's virtues to school guidance counselors and judges and court-appointed psychiatrists and probation officers, many of whom were skeptical. Her fierce loyalty, however, was unmistakably genuine. She never deviated from the basic portrait—of the sweet-voiced boy who sang in the Episcopal church choir, studied the French horn, joined the Cub Scouts, played on the Little League baseball teams coached by his father, ran track, took in stray pets, nurtured horses, and threw a paper route and shoveled sidewalks and mowed lawns because his parents had impressed upon him the value of enterprise and the work ethic; the loving, gentle-spirited pacifist practitioner of Transcendental Meditation; the imaginative young dynamo who never flagged in his devotion to his family.

Like Brett, Carolyn was physically small. She had a pearly complexion, dimples, a weak chin, and wavy brown hair. She was neither pretty nor plain. Her eyes, her most memorable feature, were a deep and luminous brown, at once lively and doleful. She spoke with a soft, slow, singsongy lilt, in a tone that shifted between deferential and guarded, a mixture of innocent curiosity and weary caution. When something struck her as funny, her laughter came in a sudden burst and quickly subsided. If she did not like a question, she could become curt or hostile. Contrary facts she could ignore. Unlike Brett, she did not seem possessed of a persistent need to explain or to justify. She had no trouble keeping her story straight. He was the child, she was the mother; that was that. When it came to maternal devotion, she made Donna Reed look negligent by comparison.

Carolyn's own mother, Mary, had not done nearly so well by her. In the late forties, when Carolyn was a teenager, her mother abruptly left. The career of Carolyn's father, William E. Jackson, had brought the family from suburban Washington, D.C., to Indianapolis, where they settled in a neighborhood that seemed utterly parochial, with no evident charm. Before long, Mary decided she had to get out and, fearing that she couldn't support her daughter, took off alone. The strains in the marriage had been caused, at least partially, by Bill Jackson's frequent extended absences. In the mythology that Brett eventually subscribed to, however, his grandfather was an unalloyed romantic and heroic figure.

Bill Jackson was an electronics engineer, a graduate of Brown University, an aviation pioneer who helped design a number of radar, navigational, and traffic-control systems that were crucial to the development of the civil-aviation system. He spent most of his career with the Civil Aeronautics Administration (and its successor, the Federal Aviation Agency) and published widely on the subject of air navigation. In Europe during the Second World War, as a consultant to the United States Air Force, he helped set up the ground receptors that guided Allied bombers. He described carrying cyanide tablets in case he got captured during the war. He told his grandson that before Lindbergh's historic flight to Paris, he had installed radio equipment in the *Spirit of St. Louis*. He spoke of having met Amelia Earhart and Truman and Eisenhower. From South America, he brought back spears that he said had belonged to headhunters.

When Brett was fourteen, Jackson began teaching him to fly single-engine airplanes. He helped pay for the lessons that led to Brett's pilot's license, which he earned in 1970, when he was sixteen. Jackson witnessed Brett's first solo. In the spring of 1972, Brett flew a Piper 140 from Indianapolis to Gaithersburg, Maryland. His mother, his sister, his brother Scott, and a girlfriend were on board, and his proud grandfather was waiting on the runway with a camera. A month later, Jackson died. There was comfort to be derived from the fact that he was not around when, two weeks after that, Brett was arrested for the first time.

After Carolyn's mother left, her father sent her to a boarding school on the Maryland shore, where she was happy. From there she went to Indiana University, in Bloomington. Second semester freshman year, she met Greg Kimberlin. He had grown up in Indianapolis and, like Carolyn, was the only child of divorced parents. His father, Otha, and his mother, Louise, had split up by the time he was five. A dental technician, Otha moved around after the divorce—California; Detroit; Fort Wayne, Indiana; Arizona; and finally Texas, where he retired. To support herself and her son, Louise was forced to return to the glove factory where she had worked before her marriage. While Greg was still in grade school, she married Horace Bicknell, who spent virtually his entire working life as a custodian in the Indianapolis public-school system.

Greg and Carolyn dated steadily for a year and a half, heading toward the inevitable. In 1951, the summer after Greg completed his bachelor's degree in psychology—also Carolyn's major—they married. That fall, he enrolled in graduate school in philosophy, intending to pursue a doctorate, but within two years the academic job market looked so unpromising he switched to law. "The department chairman told me even *he* would have a tough time getting hired elsewhere," he later recalled. "I had a child, I knew we planned to have more. Law school started to look awfully good." A son, Kevin, had been born in October 1952. By the time Greg finished his law degree, there were two more—Brett came along in June 1954, Scott in December 1955. Except for the first semester of his undergraduate freshman year, when he had help from his parents, Greg paid his own way through school. He worked as a janitor, posed as a live model for art school classes, painted houses, clerked in the university bookstore. Carolyn managed to complete her undergraduate degree in four years and began taking graduate courses in psychology, eventually earning a master's degree in educational psychology. She held occasional part-time jobs—research assistantships, and the like—but her primary occupation was child-rearing. Greg and Carolyn were grad-student poor, nothing more dire, and they knew that would change. Their personal optimism reflected the prevailing expectations of the post-war middle-class American mainstream: the trinity of faith in oneself, readiness for opportunity, and confidence that the tide was rising.

Greg joined the legal department of Public Service of Indiana, the largest utility in the state. They settled in Plainfield, home of the PSI head office, a company town of five thousand people. Though less than half an hour from downtown Indianapolis, on U.S. 40, it was a cliquish world unto itself, one that Greg did not find welcoming. He knew how to fit in—he spent the next thirty-five years with PSI—but the Babbittry of Plainfield quickly got to him. In 1960, the same year Brett entered first grade, the family moved to a four-bedroom house on the north side of Indianapolis. There were now four children; Cynthia, the baby, had been born in the fall of 1957. One rationale for the move was a desire to be in a neighborhood where the elementary and junior high schools fed into North Central High School, which at the time was considered one of the best in the country. In 1967, they built a five-bedroom ranch-style house on a one-acre plot in the same part of town.

Greg retired early from PSI, in 1992, four months after being disabled by a fall down the basement stairs at home. The injury left him comatose for several weeks, and there was concern that he might not regain his speech. When I met him, after his successful convalescence, I encountered a sober, gravel-voiced man in his mid sixties. Though he had light auburn hair, with no visible gray, he looked at least his age. He had a square, jowly face, a drooping nose, thin lips, blue-gray eyes, and dense upswept eyebrows that seemed perpetually raised, as if in surprise. Other aspects of his demeanor, however, suggested he had already seen everything. His diction had a detached, euphuistic formality, and his humor was deadpan, often sardonic. When I asked him whether he thought being short might have contributed to Brett's bravado, he said, "I think his diminution, his self-perceived deficiency in size, probably had some effect upon his thought processes and his behavior." Describing to me his reaction, more than twenty years earlier, when he realized that strangers were dropping by the house to buy marijuana from his sons, he said, "That would usually trigger a discourse, either to a group or individually. I was trying to get at the bottom of the need and outline some of the realities of use. Arrest, jail, fines, bad publicity. Whatever motive I could think of to discourage that."

Because of Greg's injury, I wasn't able to speak with him when I first wrote about Brett. Nor were Brett's brothers available; he and Kevin, I was told, were "no longer close," and Scott was dead. I was curious about Kevin—the older brother, who, though described to me as less driven, less ambitious, less animated by entrepreneurial instinct than Brett, had a degree from the Harvard Business School and a successful career as a venture capitalist in New York—but I was even more interested in Scott. His death, in 1980, seemed a watershed moment. Beyond the ordinary calamity of a lost brother and a lost child, it loomed as a defining event in Brett's intricate fate. So the Kimberlin family story, as I first heard it, was basically Brett's and Carolyn's version, with some gaps filled by Cynthia. Its salient components were a selflessly devoted mother, a loving son, some bad judgment, even worse luck, and unconscionable acts of perfidy and mendacity by others.

WHEN a subject aroused Brett's interest, he focused upon it with intensity. He became fascinated with unidentified flying objects, created an organization called UFO, Inc., and anointed himself president. He collected newspaper clippings and books with titles like *UFO's for the Millions, The Report on UFO's, Letters to the Air Force on UFO's, Why Are They Watching Us?, Behind the Flying Saucer Mystery, Flying Saucers: Serious Business, The Expanding Case for the UFO,* and *They Knew Too Much About Flying Saucers.*

Another bookshelf contained *Snakes and Snake Hunting, Cobras in His Garden, A Field Guide to Western Reptiles and Amphibians, Reptiles as Pets, Reptiles of the World.* The iconography of Brett's childhood included, in addition to the usual tree houses and underground forts, bedrooms filled with caged monsters. His father's mother lived in northeast Indianapolis, in an area known as Broad Ripple, and her backyard sloped down to Broad Ripple Creek. Greg would take the children there on snake and lizard hunts, literally leaving no stone unturned. Scott became the most avid collector, but everyone participated. There were long car trips out West, where they would hunt rattlers at night. Returning from a vacation in Miami, they brought along a southern Florida king snake. At one point, the Kimberlin children had fifty-seven snakes living in the house—garters, kings, water snakes, water moccasins, copperheads, blue and black racers, an anaconda, boa constrictors, and pythons—as well as geckos, chameleons, salamanders, frogs, horned toads, and iguanas. In the basement, they raised rats and mice to feed to the snakes, and mealworms for the lizards. Once, after Brett had been dealing with the rodents—"I had this mice smell all over my arm"—he was in his room handling a boa, which latched onto his arm and would not let go. Scott had to come and grab the snake by the back of the head to loosen his bite. Dozens of snake teeth were embedded in Brett's forearm.

UNTIL the children hit adolescence, Carolyn often took them to Sunday services at St. Paul's Episcopal Church. Brett was confirmed there, along with his brothers and sister, but he had no faith.

Brett: "I was the only one who wouldn't pray. Mom used to tell me to wear a suit and tie to church. I said, 'Mom, if there's a God, he doesn't care what I'm wearing.' I went to Sunday school and learned the Lord's Prayer and stuff, but I felt totally alienated from this fraud. From the age of six, I didn't buy into it at all. No brainwashing this boy. I have a very open mind. For instance, I wouldn't say I believe in psychic phenomena. But I believe in the *possibility* of psychic phenomena. Just as I don't close my mind to the possibility of some universal force. There are obviously things that we still don't know about, but all this organized religion I just don't buy at all. I don't like any kinds of groups. A lot of people got into meditation for religious reasons. The reason I liked transcendental meditation was because there was no religion at all involved. There were no other rules."

AFTER I published my original article, while Brett was still in prison, we began having long phone conversations, which I tape-recorded. A picture of his father began to emerge that was more Rabbit Angstrom than Ozzie Nelson. As Brett and his siblings entered adolescence, Greg became increasingly remote, a development that Brett attributes partly to alcoholism, partly to the effects of the Kimberlins' waning marriage. In 1973, Greg and Carolyn divorced. The breakup came as something of a relief—at home each evening, for years, Greg drank steadily and solipsistically; another woman had entered his life—but it left Brett with a residue of resentment toward his father and a protectiveness about his mother. Carolyn confided her feelings to Brett, and her pain became a lens through which he came to view certain fragments of his childhood.

Brett: "My mom always figured out what I was interested in—music or art or track—and she'd support me in those endeavors. My dad coached baseball, and maybe basketball, and he had the top teams for about ten years. He won all kinds of championships. My dad tried to push me into things I really didn't like—basketball, football. He was a big IU fan, and those were the big sports, but I hated those sports. I couldn't dribble a basketball.

"He wanted me to play the French horn, but I would have rather played the violin. And he never bought me a French horn. I had to use the fucking French horn at school. He didn't want me practicing at home, so he never bought me one. So at a certain point I started rebelling against anything he wanted me to do. Anything he wanted I wouldn't do, because I wasn't good at it. I wanted to do what I wanted to do."

This is not to say that Brett today blames his father for any of his troubles; to do so would be to portray himself as a failure, which notion is thoroughly at odds with his relentless self-confidence. This could also force him into a troubling speculation that if he hadn't been convicted of the Speedway bombings, his father would have culminated his professional life as the general counsel of Public Service of Indiana. What happened instead was that as Greg Kimberlin confronted the finite dimensions of his legal career, his son Brett was building a reputation as one of the most gifted jailhouse lawyers in the federal prison system.

6

BILLY WALKER looks like what, as a practical matter, he was for most of his working life—a cop. He has a square face, a strong jaw, a thick neck, tight curly hair, and piercing blue eyes that make you want to confess to something, anything, just to get it over with. Until he retired, in the summer of 1994, his official title was Assistant Principal of North Central High School, alma mater of Brett Kimberlin, class of '72. Early in his career he taught geometry and phys ed, but in 1967, in time to prepare for Kimberlin's arrival on the premises, he was excused from his pedagogical obligations and given a chance to exercise his talents as what he calls "an enforcer."

"I was in charge of the parking lot, building, grounds, security," Walker explained when I paid him a visit a while back. "I kept a lid on things."

North Central is one of those seemingly indestructible JFK-vintage factory-size institutions—wide corridors, vinyl-clad walls, terrazzo floors, display cases filled with photographs of conference-champion swimmers, tennis players, hurdlers, and wrestlers, and trophies they collected. The enrollment is more than one-third African American, compared with two or three percent when Kimberlin was a student. This change reflects a general white migration ("white flight" seems too strong a term) to the north, toward the town of Carmel, where Dan Quayle and his family settled in 1993. Reassuringly, North Central lacks the ornamentation and ambience—metal detectors and a subliminal threat of mayhem—that have become the hallmarks of so many big-city public high schools. The speech, music, and drama programs are still well subscribed; the Spanish, French, and Multi-Cultural Clubs are active; the Science Olympiad and the prom remain big draws. Almost eighty percent of the graduates go on to four-year colleges. Smoking a cigarette in the bathroom gets you a three- or five-day in-school suspension. Smoking pot gets you ten days in a treatment program. To get kicked out altogether, you have to violate a state law. As the culture shifted, Walker felt his job becoming increasingly burdensome, but when it came time to retire, he looked back with satisfaction and without regret.

"In thirty-one years here, I don't know of any kid that I disliked," Walker told me. "I could always find something in a kid that I liked." After toying with the possibility that he was dissembling, I decided he was being both sincere and deftly ironic. Kimberlin he remembered with an odd nostalgia.

"I loved him because you played mind games with him," Walker said. "He'd bait me to try to see what I knew about whatever he was involved in. He would always be guilty of the minor things, but you could never get information on the major things. Minor things? Cutting class. He loved the trump card. He loved the upper hand. This is not an ordinary individual. He's very bright, and he's going to work the world to suit him. He was a master at manipulating the system to his benefit. I would describe Brett as never staying in a poker game unless he knew he had the right cards, and then he would play them very well. He'd tell some kids he knew were snitches that he had stuff he knew the local cops had done. He'd say these things knowing it would get back to the cops. Then the cops would stop him driving his car—trying to catch him—and they'd never find anything. It made the cops look stupid. He'd work on me to try to find out who the snitches were. He might tell three kids that he had some drugs in his car to sell. Then he'd try to get me to give up the name of whoever had told me what he'd told them—just to prove who was a snitch. Which wasn't realistic of him. You know, in dealing with and solving problems, you gotta have a snitch somewhere. If you don't have some canaries, you're in deep trouble." In Walker's defense, the point needs to be made that he was swimming against a strong tide. North Central High School in the early seventies was saturated by illicit drugs. "Ten percent of the kids at North Central were dealers," a fellow student and fellow dealer of Kimberlin's told me. "The other ninety percent were buying. Who's left?"

Friday afternoons, Greg Kimberlin and a group of semipro male-bonders would hang out in a bar in Broad Ripple "to have a couple of beers and shoot the shit," Greg told me. "It was a gathering place for a small number of the faculty at North Central and me. Things tended to become honest and relaxed." In this setting, Kimberlin's father averred, he occasionally saw North Central faculty members smoking dope.

THE DREAD that has forever vexed restless adolescents stranded in the white-bread heartland—a fear that nothing will ever happen—exists in counterpoise with their parents' anxiety that something actually will. Until the late sixties, the grown-ups in Indianapolis, somewhat by accident, seemed to have matters under control. A half-million picnickers would turn out every Memorial Day weekend for the Indy 500, things got temporarily rowdy, and for the next fifty-one weeks the local atmosphere would be tolerably serene. Then came the counterculture, and with it evidence of how aggressively cannabis and hallucinogens could fill a vacuum created by chronic understimulation; the superego couldn't get a handle on the id. A lot of parents who hadn't planned for this and didn't know what to do elected to go blind; the cops didn't want trouble with the parents. Well-to-do kids, instead of looking for work in the mall, started selling nickel bags of pot. It was as if Brett Kimberlin, guided by some preternatural Darwinian instinct, arranged the timing of his own adolescence.

Kimberlin was fourteen when he smoked his first joint. He and his girlfriend, Susan Harvey, found some marijuana in her older sister's desk drawer. They took it over to Brett's house and turned on. Within a year, he was smoking every day. If rearranging brain cells signified the zeitgeist, it also signified an economic opportunity. Brett was an academic underachiever, with a grade average between B and C, but he was also a born laissez-faire capitalist. He and his best friend, Paul Heilbrunn, started dealing—first pot, then hashish, occasionally mescaline, but nothing more exotic, he always insisted to me. They bought marijuana by the quarter pound, then the half pound, then the kilogram. Among their suppliers were friends of Paul's older brother, Richard, as well as friends of Susan's brother Larry.

Brett: "My position at that time, and it always has been, was, Look, I don't want to be involved in cocaine or heroin, you know. I'm not a drug pusher; I'm selling pot. People enjoy pot. I mean, I would never sell it anymore, but I still have this same feeling that pot is basically a wonder drug as far as society is concerned. You smoke it, you kick back, you don't get violent, you have fun, usually; you might eat a little more, but you're usually nice, you're friendly, you get along with people, you know?

"Remember, it was the Vietnam War. School had a bad rap. All institutions had a bad rap. I had long hair. When I was in tenth grade, Billy Walker would chase my brother Kevin and me around the school trying to get us to cut our hair. The school administration was antidrugs and I was into drugs, so I had this antipathy toward school. I felt they were trying to stifle my individuality."

ONCE, Kimberlin and Susan attended a Cream concert—Eric Clapton, Ginger Baker, and Jack Bruce—and the music just blew them away. It was a snowy evening in March 1968. When his father came to pick them up, Kevin was in the car. There was a second show that night, and Brett told his older brother he absolutely had to hear this band. Kevin bought a ticket and, the next day, a guitar. Brett already owned an electric bass. The idea of rock 'n' roll stardom wasn't too banal for their fantasies. They signed up for lessons at a music store in Broad Ripple and, as soon as they were presentable, started playing at school parties and community centers. The band's name changed approximately as often as they got a gig, which was about once a month. This lasted a year or so, until Kevin objected to the fact that Brett used drugs.

If you can remember the sixties, the saying goes, you weren't there. Nevertheless, Brett can remember a three-day rock festival in Goose Lake, Michigan, where he was so stoned he became immobile. If there was a concert within a reasonable radius, he wanted to be in the audience: Traffic, Rod Stewart, Janis Joplin, Blind Faith, the Who. He road-tripped to Dayton, Louisville, Chicago. The time he went to Chicago to see Jethro Tull, he had not yet turned sixteen. Paul Heilbrunn and some of his friends were along for the trip.

Brett: "We got up there the night before the concert. And there were, like, six of us. So what one guy did, he said, 'Look, I'll go in and get a room for two at the Holiday Inn. After we get the room, then the rest of you guys come up in about thirty minutes. Sit out here in the car until then.' I had some pot with me, and Paul had some pot with him. I also had about, oh, a couple hundred dollars. So the four of us followed these guys up. It was late at night, like one or two in the morning. There was a cop and he was working security detail there. He gets on the elevator with us and follows us up. We get to the room and he's right behind us. I'm starting to get paranoid a little bit and Paul's getting paranoid. We knock on the door and our friend opens the door from the inside. We walk into the room and the cop walks in behind us. Well, Paul gets scared and pulls this bag of pot out of his pocket and tries to throw it behind this dresser, but it lands on top of the dresser. It's a little one-ounce bag or something. The cop calls in some backup. So here come four fucking Chicago cops. And I'm thinking: Holy fuck, I'm up here in Chicago. We're going to get arrested. We're going to go to jail, and my dad and mom don't even know I'm smoking pot or involved in drugs.

"So what happened was, the cop comes up there and he's searching about and all this. Everything was illegal. What the cop was doing was all illegal, but I didn't know it at the time. He's talking about taking us downtown and all this bullshit. I got my wits about me—all these poor kids are just only like fifteen and sixteen and seventeen years old, and they're all crying and shit like that—so I got my wits about me and said, 'Which one of you is in charge?' The one cop says, 'I am.' I said, 'Can I talk to you out in the hall?' So I went out in the hall with this guy. All the other cops and all the other kids were in the room. I told this cop, 'Listen, we're up here to see this concert. Our parents don't know we're involved in drugs. How about if I give you a couple hundred dollars to forget this whole thing?' The cop says, 'OK.' So I peel out a couple hundred bucks and give it to him. And the cop says, 'Now I want you kids to hit the fucking road.'

"Well, we didn't have enough money to get another motel room. So we had to sleep in the car. On the way down to the car, Paul says, 'What did you do?' I said, 'I fucking paid the guy; I bribed him to let us go.' Paul got all pissed off and said, 'What the fuck are you paying that goddamn cop for? Fuck them. And *na*-na-na *na*-na.' The cop overheard Paul saying this. The cop says, 'Hey, come here.' Paul says, 'What do you want?' And the cop beat the fuck out of him right there. Right there in the parking lot. So that was my first experience with the police. I saw police brutality and bribery right there when I was fifteen."

AROUND this time, Kimberlin had a bad experience with LSD. A friend, Janet Marx, gave him some Orange Sunshine that was, as the stage announcer said in the memorable line at Woodstock, "not specifically too good." He says he took only half a tab. Whatever was in it besides lysergic acid diethylamide—most likely strychnine—caused his dinner-table etiquette to deteriorate so badly that Carolyn ended up calling a psychiatrist friend, who prescribed a Thorazine antidote. She gave Brett a dose and he went to sleep. The experience shook him so deeply he swore off drugs. A couple of months later, however, he backslid.

Brett: "There was this guy at school. . . . He was all into these weird herbs and esoteric herbal remedies and all this stuff. He was a student, but he was a weirdo. I'd quit using all drugs, and so he said, 'Look, I've got these organic seeds that you can take that'll get you high but you won't have any adverse effects from it.' So me and Paul and Susan were sitting at Paul's house, and this weirdo kid was there with us. He says, 'Here, take a handful of these seeds.' They were little black seeds that were maybe a little bigger than a poppy seed. He says, 'It'll give you a nice mellow high and maybe some hallucinations.' So I took a handful at about eight o'clock. About ten o'clock I didn't feel anything, so he says, 'Here, take a few more.' So I took another little handful. Paul did too. Susan didn't take any. I was driving by then, and about eleven o'clock I drove Susan home and went to my home, got in bed. I was at my parents'. The phone rang at about midnight. It was Paul's mother and she said, 'Brett, what did Paul take?' And I said, 'Well, I don't know what it was, but I'll call our supplier and find out.' So I called him at home. He said that the Latin name is *Datura stramonium.* And he said it's also called devil's apple. Anyway, in lay terms it's called jimsonweed. I said, 'What the hell's the deal? Paul's going crazy.' I wrote this down on a piece of paper beside my phone and called his mother back, and I said it was *Datura stramonium.* And she said Paul was hallucinating and seeing things and talking to people that weren't there and banging against the walls and shit like that. When I hung up the phone, that was the last thing I remembered.

"My mother heard some noise in my room and she came to my room and I was hallucinating and seeing things and nitpicking—picking [things] out in the middle of the air but there's nothing there. . . . And then I started hallucinating. Massive hallucinations—people coming from Mars, people coming in the window, all this stuff. I don't remember except bits and pieces, you know. I was completely out of it. So my mother called and got—I don't know—she gave me something from when the LSD . . . some Thorazine. . . . She watched me for two days, and my brothers held me down, kept me from doing something dangerous. When I woke up, she was sitting beside the bed and she said, 'Brett, do you know what day it is?' I said, 'Yeah, it's Saturday. Why? What are you doing beside my bed?' She said, 'Brett, it's *Monday*.' I said, 'Monday? What are you talking about? It's Saturday morning.' She said, 'It's Monday morning.' So I was completely out of it for two days, two and a half days, something like that. That was it. I never fucking touched another drug after that. And what it was, it was a profound experience for me. Number one, because I got so frightened during that experience, and I'm saying *during* the experience, not after. . . . I got so frightened that I was never afraid of anything anymore. So I became not afraid. You could kind of see it in my actions, because I started flying. Who goes out and starts flying when they're sixteen years old? Who gets a fucking plane when they're nineteen and flies all over the country, and flies at night, and flies in thunderstorms? And who flies all over the Bahamas in their own little single-engine plane and flies twins? And you know, I just had no fear."

JANET MARX wasn't through doing favors for Kimberlin. In the spring of 1970, he says, she introduced him to a hashish connection—a young man whose name Kimberlin doesn't remember, and his girlfriend. His instructions were to come to New Jersey with $1,800. He did as told but never laid eyes on the hashish.

Brett: "I went there and they just ripped me off. It was a little scam. It was the couple or the couple and another guy. They took me to this place and said the hash was inside, and whoever was selling it didn't want to meet me. The guy went in with the money and never came back out. I realized it was a rip-off, so I just got back on the plane and went home. They acted like they got ripped off too; it was a scam. I told Janet, and she got really pissed and called the couple up. . . . The girl felt bad and she eventually introduced me to Leo Casas, my first Mexican marijuana connection. First, the guy told Janet he was going to pay me back by selling me some marijuana. He was going to cut some of this wild Indiana marijuana left over from the Second World War—this ditchweed. But Janet knew that was just more of a scam, so she told me about it. I met with the guy and he had the pot. He showed it to me and tried to bullshit me. I said, 'I can't sell this stuff. It's too green.' Then Janet told me this guy was going to the Rio Grande Valley. I figured it was more bullshit. He was gone for about a month. When he came back to Indiana, Leo followed with this load of pot in the trunk of his car. They came and showed it to me. It was beautiful, Acapulco gold. I hadn't sold anything this big before—a hundred-and-twenty-five-pound load. Leo was kind of skittish, and he wanted to be in the vicinity when I unloaded it. It was gone in five days. I think they sold it to me for a hundred and twenty dollars a pound, and I sold it from a hundred and sixty to a hundred and eighty-five a pound. So I made thousands of dollars. I made five grand right there on top, plus they gave me the $1,800 back that they'd ripped off from me.

"I met Leo, but I was never left alone with him because this guy from New Jersey didn't want me to jump the connection. But I felt like this motherfucker had ripped me off already. So I took a matchbook and wrote my name and number on the inside and gave it to Leo. I wanted him to call me and leave this asshole out. Leo could see that I was the one selling the pot. I palmed this matchbook and handed it to Leo when this guy's back was turned. And a week and a half later, Leo called me. . . . 'You want some more?'

"Anyway, this started every fucking week. Sometimes two times a week, sometimes three times a week—at least a hundred pounds. Then it went up to two hundred. Within a month, I had regular customers and I could unload it within twenty-four hours. It was gone and it was just money. I'd sell them thirty or fifty pounds. I remember a few times I actually stored it in my bedroom. My mother would die if she knew this. To get it into my bedroom I had to throw it on the garage roof and pull it in through my bedroom window. There were a few times when I did that. I was buying it for a hundred and twenty, maybe a hundred and sixty-five a pound and selling it for fifty bucks a pound more. That was the normal markup. This was commercial Mexican pot. Sometimes, if the pot was really good, I could get more. I could sell as much pot as I could get my hands on."

By Kimberlin's account, his initial encounter with Leo Casas—and the events that immediately ensued—occurred in the spring or early summer of 1970. This was more than a year before, as he later maintained, he began receiving regular phone calls from Dan Quayle and meeting him at the Burger Chef and in motel parking lots on the north side of Indianapolis and selling him marijuana by the ounce.

7

A COUPLE of weeks shy of his eighteenth birthday, in May 1972, Kimberlin was indicted and charged with having sold 2.3 grams of cocaine to someone who turned out to be a government informer. "It's a terrible error" was Carolyn Kimberlin's reaction, as reported in the *Indianapolis Star.* "Somebody made a great mistake." Brett, of course, shared this sentiment. The prosecutor who directed the grand jury that returned the indictment believed, because of what he'd been told by witnesses and federal drug agents, that Kimberlin was a substantial trafficker in cocaine, LSD, marijuana, and hashish. After Kimberlin's arraignment, the prosecutor and the agents were greatly surprised to learn that, legally, he was still a juvenile. In time, the government and Kimberlin found themselves in accord on the premise that the cocaine bust fit a pattern: The authorities saw a pattern of criminal behavior, while Kimberlin detected error and malice on the part of people supposedly enforcing the law. From either perspective, the episode could be regarded as a first domino—although the domino metaphor, inasmuch as it implies a linear progression, seems inexact. More fitting, perhaps, would be to think of it as a spring-activated lever in the Rube Goldberg contraption that delivered Kimberlin to his complicated destiny.

Two decades later, Kimberlin told me that a casual acquaintance named Kelly Merritt, who turned out to be the government informer, had called and said he wanted to buy cocaine. "I told him I didn't sell cocaine," Kimberlin said. "He kept bugging me. Finally, I heard from another friend, who said he had some coke, so I delivered it to Kelly Merritt." Kimberlin insisted that he did this for no profit and that when Merritt hounded him for more cocaine he refused. Nevertheless, for this, his one and only coke transaction *ever*—"a fluke"—he got indicted.

"When they busted me, I was floored," Kimberlin said. "I didn't even remember it. For six months, I denied it because I didn't remember it, because I never sold coke. They kept telling me—and they wouldn't tell me who—they had this confidential informant, supposedly. . . . What happened was somebody came to the house with a warrant and said to me, 'You've got to appear in court.' I said, 'What for?' They said, 'For selling cocaine.' I said, 'I've never sold cocaine. This is crazy.' So my dad, he believed me and he got one of his friends who was a lawyer there in town to represent me for nothing. We went to court and they said, 'You sold three grams'—they kept saying three grams—'of cocaine eight or ten months ago.' So I kept trying to figure out what they were talking about. . . . I mean, they finally, just after eight months or nine months or whatever it was, they finally arrested me. . . . It was really bizarre that they pursued that damn thing. And they got so mad at me because they thought I was some kind of big dealer and all that, and I wasn't at that time."

At the time Kimberlin offered this denial, I lacked this piquant information: that his brother Scott had told a friend, Joe Majko, about Kelly Merritt's snitching; that Majko and another acquaintance had subsequently agreed to inflict some pain upon Merritt, which led to Majko's arrest for threatening a government witness; that the arrest had taken place at the Kimberlin residence, where, with Carolyn Kimberlin's knowledge, Majko was hiding in the attic; and that, though the charges against her were eventually dropped, Carolyn herself became the subject of an arrest warrant for concealing a felon.

IN JULY 1972, a hearing was convened in the courtroom of Judge William E. Steckler to determine whether Kimberlin, who had meanwhile turned eighteen, should be prosecuted as a juvenile or an adult. The government was represented by an assistant United States attorney named Scott Miller, Kimberlin by James Clark, an Indianapolis attorney. A psychologist, Gerald Alpern, and a psychiatrist, Toner Overley, appeared as defense witnesses. (Alpern, Kimberlin explained to me, was someone his mother knew professionally and with whom she had become "really good friends." Overley was "like my dad's best friend at school," he said. "They'd grown up together.") After conducting two evaluative testing sessions, Alpern concluded that Kimberlin had "above-average intelligence, bordering on superior intelligence," that he "suffers no psychiatric disability in any of the classic psychiatric categories of disability," that "he does not suffer from any character disorders." According to the Minnesota Multiphasic Personality Inventory, he was neither psychotic nor neurotic. Alpern discerned in Kimberlin a tendency toward "a degree of impulsivity that is more than most eighteen year olds [possess]," but he was "not pathological." He also felt that Kimberlin did not have "strong political beliefs that I can determine in any way which would make him revolt-prone in terms of the political ideology. He is really too self centered." A few months earlier, Kimberlin had become a partner in a retail health food store in Indianapolis. Alpern's evaluation led him to conclude that, whatever Brett's drug-dealing activities during high school, for pragmatic as much as for moral reasons this illicit activity was now behind him. To continue it would risk subverting his business ambitions and "long-term life goals."

In a written report to the court, Alpern elaborated: "His current anti-drug stance in terms of his own usage is based on a commitment to his own physical health . . . [and] his practical judgment that such activities are both insufficiently profitable and primarily endanger [sic] of restricting his freedom, i.e., getting caught." In another passage, Alpern described Kimberlin as "not antisocial but rather dyssocial . . . he has no needs to act out against society but rather prefers to live within a society he himself has chosen."

Dr. Overley, who corroborated Alpern's finding that Kimberlin was "dyssocial," further testified that his marijuana dealing signified a desire "to be a big shot." He added, "He also, I fear, was a little too active in his own P.R. work, because, as I understand it, almost anyone you talked to had the impression that Brett knew where to get drugs. I think his motivation was to be somewhat important or worthwhile to his then peer group."

Drs. Alpern and Overley, earnest men of science, were no doubt sincere in their generally sanguine assessments. Their assumption that Kimberlin was no longer dealing drugs, however, was mistaken. The source of the information that led them to this false assumption was, of course, Kimberlin himself.

UNDER questioning by his own attorney, Kimberlin testified that he had never been a big-time dealer, and that he had participated in a North Central drug-education program counseling students to stay away from "hard" drugs such as heroin, which he'd never seen in his life. Assistant U.S. Attorney Miller then interrogated Kimberlin about his transactions with various suspected dealers, most of them his contemporaries in central Indiana. He was further asked about his travels to south Texas, where drug agents had seen him in the company of Leo Casas, his connection in the Rio Grande Valley. The authorities also suspected that Casas was involved with heroin and cocaine. At one point, Kimberlin was asked about his experiences with two young men from the Bloomington area, David Pacific and John Buckley:

Q. Are you acquainted with one David Pacific?

A. Let's see, if I remember right he was associated with, him and John Buckley had a laboratory making LSD and psilocybin, it's an organic psychedelic. Like last year, two years ago, something like that, then they got arrested. I haven't seen them since, but I don't even remember if I saw David Pacific, but I just heard his name.

Q. Did you ever borrow any scales from David Pacific for the purpose of cutting and weighing hashish?

A. I don't think so, I mean, not to my knowledge, I should say.

Q. Did you ever sell any LSD to David Pacific or Jenkins, John Jenkins?*

A. No, I wouldn't be selling it to Pacific or John Buckley because they are the ones that had the laboratory, they are the ones that made it all. If I was to do anything I would get it from them, that's my answer.

This testimony would eventually come back to haunt Kimberlin. In the short term, however, he didn't do badly. The original indictment was dismissed, and instead of being charged with a drug offense he was found guilty of juvenile delinquency and placed on probation for three years. This was reported in a story in the *Indianapolis Star* headlined ATTORNEY'S SON GETS 3-YEAR PROBATION IN DRUG TRAFFICKING. The article quoted Judge Steckler as saying: "I have concluded that the court should place you on probation. And, I do that with the anticipation that you will be difficult to handle."

The *Star* went on to say: "Kimberlin first drew the notice of Federal drug agents who heard of his reputation of being a 'multi-kilo'

---

* The prosecutor's reference to John Jenkins was a slip of the tongue; Jenkins was another dealer, whereas John Buckley was known to be Pacific's associate.

dealer in drugs. An informant told agents the youth was selling marijuana as a freshman at North Central High School." Finally, the article referred to a narcotics agent who worked on the case as having "testified at an early hearing that Kimberlin was known to have contacts with large-scale dealers in cocaine and heroin in Texas. He flew a private plane on some trips, the agents said."

KIMBERLIN was back in court in October 1972, this time to testify before a grand jury that was, again, under the guidance of Assistant U.S. Attorney Miller. And Kimberlin again was asked about Pacific and Buckley.

When I originally wrote in *The New Yorker* about Kimberlin's grand jury appearance, I recapitulated what he had told me: that he testified to marijuana and hashish dealings with Buckley but not Pacific, and that when asked whether he had bought or sold LSD or methamphetamines he said no. Not long thereafter, he said, Pacific and Buckley were arrested for manufacturing various hallucinogens, including LSD. He assumed that the authorities told Pacific and Buckley that he had given damning testimony about them and that, to return the favor, they claimed he had sold them hefty quantities of LSD. Another grand jury was convened, and this one indicted Kimberlin for perjury. At trial, his lawyer repeated the assertion that it made no sense for his client to be selling LSD to people who were in the business of manufacturing LSD. To no avail; Kimberlin was found guilty of perjury and given a thirty-day sentence.

In 1992, Kimberlin also told me that Cody Shearer had spoken with Pacific and Buckley, who acknowledged inventing the story that he was a supplier of LSD. To even the score, in other words, *they* had committed perjury. Hoping they would confirm Kimberlin's account, I tried to get in touch with them. When I failed, I let it slide, because this was a relatively tangential subplot. The manner in which Kimberlin had mentioned Shearer's contacts with Pacific and Buckley was so offhanded that, though I recorded it in my notes, I neglected to discuss it with Shearer. Expediency and circumstance led me to accept Kimberlin's version of this chain of events. To avoid libeling Pacific and Buckley, I omitted their names from *The New Yorker* article, and a year and a half elapsed before I finally tracked them down.

8

GOING to jail the first time taught Kimberlin some useful lessons, if not precisely what the judge who sentenced him had in mind. His perjury trial and conviction took place on a single day, in November 1973, but Kimberlin didn't actually enter custody until the following February. In the interim, he considered and then decided against filing an appeal. The official sentence was one year, with eleven months suspended and tacked onto the probation from his juvenile delinquency conviction. With credit for good behavior, Kimberlin ended up serving only twenty-one days. He did his time in Wayne County, an hour east of Indianapolis, which was a relatively unthreatening place for a potentially vulnerable youth— and where one thing he learned was that "good behavior" was legally a fuzzy concept. During this temporary inconvenience he had visits from family members and drug partners, as well as limited use of the telephone, and thus managed to buy and sell five thousand pounds of marijuana. This virgin incarceration confirmed his belief in his remarkable resourcefulness. Here was proof that even when his mobility was restricted he could remain profitably engaged with the outside world.

Another bit of wisdom Kimberlin picked up—not immediately, but as a direct result of this experience—was that not everything your lawyer tells you is true. Though Kimberlin contended that the jury could not have found him guilty if John Buckley and David Pacific had testified truthfully, his ultimate complaint had less to do with the trial itself than with the procedural technicalities of his sentencing. Kimberlin claimed that his attorney, Forrest Bowman, had assured him he would automatically be sentenced as a youth offender, under the terms of the Federal Youth Corrections Act. Accordingly, upon the completion of his probation, this felony conviction would automatically be expunged from his record, rendering an appeal superfluous. Several years elapsed before Kimberlin realized that he had in fact been sentenced as an adult. By then, his choice not to appeal had resulted in such unwelcome consequences that Kimberlin still refers to it as "one of the worst decisions in my life." As he headed off for the slammer, however, there was no way to see this coming. Nor was he temperamentally inclined to anticipate pessimistic scenarios. He was a young man in a hurry, an entrepreneur with a desire to broaden his profit-making opportunities.

Already Kimberlin had expanded his horizons. In the fall of 1971, while a high school senior, he invested in a health food store, in the Broad Ripple neighborhood, which had been in business only a few months. Some of the Good Earth's original partners, one of whom was the older brother of Brett's best friend, Paul Heilbrunn, had diversified in the same way Brett envisioned for himself; when they weren't pushing tofu and bulgur wheat retail, they were pushing marijuana wholesale. Their decision to bail out of the Good Earth was prompted by an overriding desire to go to India, where they planned to put on saffron robes and smoke hashish with the shamans at Goa Beach, getting simultaneously closer to Nirvana and farther from Indiana. Kimberlin paid $5,000 for his interest in the Good Earth—in money he told me he'd saved from his days delivering newspapers and cutting grass and shoveling driveways. But it seems more likely that he had earned the money toting bales with Leo Casas down Mexico way.

Within a couple of years of buying into the business, Kimberlin owned the building it occupied, a two-story wood-sided converted house that looked as if it belonged exactly where it was, in a neighborhood of head shops and tie-dye boutiques. Later, the Good Earth acquired an Earth Shoes franchise, which flourished in a room upstairs. Kimberlin also became a quarter-owner of the Earth Garden Café, which didn't do so well. He always maintained that he never mixed his legitimate and illicit enterprises. His annual net from the Good Earth, he said, ran between $30,000 and $50,000. Evidently, this was a fraction of his drug profits.

Regardless of how or where the cash flowed, the Good Earth provided a convenient cover. If Kimberlin needed plastic-lined burlap bags for packing Mexican marijuana across the border, he could order through the same vendor who might sell him similar bags for bulk whole grains. If asked why he made so many plane trips in

Texas, he could answer that the Rio Grande Valley was a source of excellent organic produce. A hardworking New Ager could plausibly tool around in a Jaguar or a Mercedes. Kimberlin once won a businessman-of-the-year award from the Broad Ripple Merchants Association. In his most vivid memory of that occasion, his electronic pager went off during the proceedings and he had to excuse himself abruptly to go unload thousands of pounds of marijuana—contraband bound for Michigan, Ohio, and south-central Indiana. "As I was leaving the award banquet," he said, "I thought to myself: Boy, if these people only knew what a wonderful businessman I *really* am!"

Though Kimberlin was discreet, his contemporaries, at least, had few illusions about the provenance of his prosperity. At North Central High, it was rumored that by the time he graduated he'd made a million dollars—a big, magical number, but who knew for certain? A similar assumption surfaced on his twentieth birthday, when he threw a masquerade party for himself at his new, large house, rented from the city and remotely situated in Eagle Creek Park, on the northwest side of Indianapolis. Kimberlin came as Uncle Sam. As party favors, he distributed T-shirts whose slogan traded on another of his fantasies: BORN TO BE PRESIDENT. The crowd was not large, but his major clients, as it were, all showed up to pay homage. Uncharacteristically, Kimberlin let them gather in the same place at the same time. "Brett was a master at keeping his people separated," I was told by Woody McDermott, a steady jobber who ended up delivering a hundred pounds of Kimberlin's Mexican weed every Friday to a black neighborhood near downtown Indianapolis. "These were his connections. It was kind of understood that we weren't to make any buddies at this party." Whatever excess and revelry took place Kimberlin was in a position to view with a certain detachment, having by now permanently sworn off drugs.

McDermott remembered his first meeting with Kimberlin, in the fall of 1972. Larry Harvey introduced them: "Harvey is telling me, 'This kid is cool, man. He looks like a fucking kid, but he's cool.' Larry Harvey was an incredible guy, who turned into an incredible dirt bag. But before he went bad, he could see things. He said to me, 'Woody, the fucking kid thinks he's gonna be Howard Hughes.' "

It didn't take McDermott long to figure out what Larry Harvey meant. "Brett recognized certain qualities in other people that he didn't have, and he also learned how to manipulate those qualities. If he could get you to operate under the pretense of camaraderie, then he would use that. He preferred to play upon your greed and your insecurity about your meal ticket. He talked about going straight, but he had no interest in that. He had an interest in being a robber baron. Selling pot was love and peace to the rest of us, but to Brett it was figuring out the angles. To him, it was money and power from the git-go. Everybody dealt with Brett very carefully, because when he was on the street he was a force. Everybody had this one face they showed Brett. You certainly had to respect him. He had a pilot's license about the same time most kids were learning to drive. While everybody else was doing dope, chasing girls, doing lines, and conducting business with a handshake, Brett was calculating."

Kimberlin owned a green Dodge pickup that had been converted into a camper, complete with kitchen, bathroom, and curtains. "Every time I'd go anywhere I'd buy these travel stickers, and I stuck 'em all over that truck," Kimberlin told me. "That thing had supposedly been everywhere." It also had air shocks to accommodate the loads Kimberlin concealed within its hidden compartments.

McDermott: "Brett's attitude was: Never have anybody do anything for you that you can do yourself. B.K. was centered, he was collected. He wasn't wild. He wasn't like the rest of us, who were our own best customers. The rest of us are waking up at noon because we've gotten wasted the night before, but Brett's up at eight o'clock to go to a welding class. When he learned welding it wasn't to build a piece of sculpture. It was to weld a false wall inside a truck. He learned how to drive an eighteen-wheeler. Doing that made him feel big. And that was one thing B.K. wasn't—big."

The Mexican connection that Kimberlin established in 1970, though rewarding, had within six months become insufficient to satisfy the demand from his customers. Once or twice a week, one of Leo Casas's drivers would arrive in Indianapolis, having traveled from the Tex-Mex border with two or three hundred pounds in the trunk. "I kept pushing Leo to send more and more and more," Kimberlin told me. (For less than a year, he said, starting in 1970, he had a second Mexican connection—"not more than three or four thousand pounds, total"—which operated out of Nogales, Arizona.) Casas's drivers tended to speak marginal English and often brought along their wives and children as camouflage, the pot packed in suitcases.

No one got busted, no one ever lost a load. Kimberlin assumes Casas paid his drivers about a thousand dollars per circuit. In late 1971, a wholesale produce shipper and pot smuggler in McAllen, Texas, named Lorenzo Reyes paid one of Casas's mules what Kimberlin assumes was a much larger amount to deliver Kimberlin himself—that is, to reveal the name of whoever up north was buying so much marijuana. When Reyes phoned Kimberlin, their first conversation was necessarily oblique. Maybe they could work together, the caller suggested. Kimberlin pondered the possibility that he was being set up but agreed to a meeting. A week later, Reyes arrived in Indianapolis with two Plymouth Furys, whose capacious trunks, Kimberlin fondly recalls, were "filled with fucking pot, beautiful pot, marvelous pot—eight hundred pounds in all, at least. And I said, '*This* is what I want.' " Reyes, who was known to his familiars as either "Papa" or "Frank" but never as Lorenzo, was asking thirty dollars a pound less than Kimberlin had been paying. He was also able to keep the supply flowing with a clockwork, assembly-line-like regularity—deliveries every two or three days, a ton of merchandise a week, transported in cars with air shocks on the rear axles, chauffeured by drivers who never broke the speed limit. "Papa and I hooked up and we were best friends," Kimberlin said. "From then on we made lots of fucking money. We sold many, many, many tons of pot."

GREG KIMBERLIN once told me, with apparent candor and sincerity, that he and Carolyn supported Brett's adolescent flying lessons because this avocation afforded "an opportunity to keep him from having to compete with his brothers, and it provided a diversion from drugs." This was of course a wishful notion, of a piece with the expert psychiatric opinion that drugs were inconsistent with Brett's ambitions as a health food merchant. Flying amplified his mystique, encouraged his willingness to take physical risks, and, as a practical matter, was a worthwhile tool in the smuggling trade. The only plane he ever owned was a single-engine Piper 235. For one six-month stretch, he leased a twin-engine Piper Navajo. The latter had a cargo capacity of two thousand pounds, but Kimberlin said the most exotic agricultural product he ever hauled was organic mangoes. He flew all over the country and in the Caribbean, occasionally doing smuggling reconnaissance, sometimes carrying cash, but never moving drugs.

There would always be a market for the Mexican pot that was Kimberlin's mainstay, but when his customers' customers found out about Jamaican ganja, and then traded up another notch and discovered high-end Colombian—the stuff capable of placing the brain in deep freeze for a few lost hours—Kimberlin knew he had to expand his inventory. Compared to Mexican, which brought from $100 to $150 a pound, Jamaican went for up to $225 and Colombian as much as $325. Though profit margins varied from one shipment to the next, Kimberlin said his average net was about thirty dollars a pound. He found that he could boost the price of Mexican—if not exactly its potency—by shipping it in pineapple wrappers and passing it off as Hawaiian. When he worried that a load might be too dry, he would stick it in a sauna, add a quart of sweet rum to the humidifier, and steam it back to an appealing texture and spicy fragrance. Once, when McDermott complained that Kimberlin was in effect selling water at a dear price, he defended himself by saying, "Woody, I'm *conditioning* it."

Kimberlin cultivated several Colombian and Jamaican connections, working with middlemen in Miami, Atlanta, New Orleans, New York, and Kentucky. Sometimes he merely fronted money, but at other times he provided operational guidance. To this day, he speaks proudly of a plan he devised—in the summer of 1973, when he was already on probation but had not yet gone to trial for perjury—for refueling Indiana-bound flights from Colombia and Jamaica. The planes were light twin-engines, capable of carrying fifteen hundred or two thousand pounds, and Kimberlin outfitted the pilots with corporate-style uniforms, which he thought added a credible touch of class. Flying his little Piper in the Bahamas, he had observed that a plane landing in, say, Freeport would be examined by a customs inspector and, if all was well, the pilot would receive a stamped and dated form called a transair. With a properly executed transair in hand, a pilot could land anywhere in the Bahamian chain without submitting to additional inspections. In Indianapolis, Kimberlin had a hundred or so counterfeit transairs made, as well as counterfeit rubber stamps from various Bahamian ports.

Kimberlin: "From then on, a plane could come in from Colombia and land at Georgetown, in the southern chain. He'd be running low on fuel, but he could pull out his transair that says Freeport, Bahamas, and say he just came from there. He wasn't searched, and they'd gas him up because it's a pretty long haul from Freeport to Georgetown. It was a beautiful way of going through. I was in jail with hundreds of smugglers, and nobody I met ever used this scheme. If you got enough fuel, you could haul ass all the way to Indiana. We landed at the airports in Brownsburg or Columbus or Bloomington. I owned property in Jackson County, ninety miles south of Indianapolis, and there was a huge field in the valley that I was going to make into an airstrip. I never got around to it. But sometimes they'd just come in and buzz that valley and throw the pot out. I've met smugglers who thought that some of my methods were too ballsy. I looked at it as just the opposite. If you do something right out in the open, as long as you don't trip up and make a mistake, then nobody's going to suspect it. These other assholes, they want to come in at night and land on some paid-off strip in the Bahamas, and I personally thought that was a greater risk than landing in Freeport in daylight and getting gas and hauling ass."

AT DIFFERENT times and in differing degrees, Kimberlin said, his younger brother, Scott, was his accomplice. Brett also had a long-term partnership with someone whom I will call Justin Farrell. Several of Brett's other drug-dealing associates retain vivid memories of encounters with both partners. Scott had an agreeable nature, a sweet unguardedness, but many people found him flaky and, on occasion, irritatingly erratic. From adolescence, he was in Brett's thrall. "If Brett said shit," McDermott told me, "Scott's pants hit the ground." The nature of Brett's relationship with Farrell was considerably more complex; by now, several years have passed since he and Brett exchanged a cordial word, and Farrell refused my requests for an interview. During Brett's final semester in high school, he lived alternately with his parents and with Farrell and a girlfriend, who had rented a house in a suburb called Zionsville. He then spent three or four months in a small town called Greenfield, and moved to the house in Eagle Creek Park in the spring of 1972. That same year, Farrell moved to New York to pursue a career as a rock musician. A year or so later, however, discouraged, he returned to Indiana. According to Brett, when Farrell left for New York he took with him a substantial amount of money—"I don't know, maybe a quarter of a million bucks." At some point, Kimberlin said, his mother and younger siblings became dependent upon him. Moreover, in 1975, Cynthia and Carolyn moved in with him at Eagle Creek. Scott was then enrolled at Indiana University, in Bloomington. In Greg Kimberlin's absence, Brett began to think of himself as the family breadwinner, and he justified his smuggling as a necessary consequence of this obligation. In our earliest conversations, he stated explicitly: "I was the only one bringing in any money."

I ONCE asked Kimberlin if his drug-dealing had ever drawn him into physically perilous situations, and he replied that there had been several. In Bloomington, when he was sixteen years old, a junkie pulled a .38-caliber pistol on him while trying to steal thirty pounds of marijuana. They were in Kimberlin's parked car, the junkie in the passenger seat, when a confederate suddenly appeared and assaulted Brett; he managed to wrestle the gun away, but the two culprits escaped with the pot. I thought that sounded scary enough, but then he described a far scarier episode. In the fall of 1971, he said, he was living with Justin Farrell in Zionsville, and a deal involving a Mexican source—out of Nogales, Arizona, where the supplier was a serious businessman named Manny—went seriously wrong.

Kimberlin: "Manny was introduced to me by this one fucking asshole named Bobby Dale Pettibone. Well, I paid Pettibone, I don't know, five or ten thousand dollars for the connection. But then Pettibone heard that I was doing a lot of business with this guy. Pettibone lived north of Dayton—I don't remember the little town; I could find it on a map. So anyway, it was on a Halloween night and I'm asleep by myself in the house. This house was so weird. It was out in the middle of the woods. They used to call it the haunted house, because it was just like something you'd see in a fucking movie—all these pillars in front, like a mansion that had become all dilapidated and old, with the wind blowing through it. This place had these balconies off the bedrooms upstairs. So about one o'clock in the morning there's this pounding on the door, and I hear these people screaming, 'Open up! Open up! DEA!' and all this bullshit. So I go out on the balcony and I'm getting ready to—it was cold as hell that night, and rainy— and I get ready to jump off the balcony and haul ass. Anyway, there were like three guys altogether and one of the guys was out front and he saw me getting ready to jump off the balcony. So they grabbed me and tied me up and broke into this—I had this drawer that had a lock on it, you know, and I had, I think, like thirty-two thousand dollars they stole. They left me there tied up. We all moved away from there very shortly thereafter because they condemned the house and everything.

"About a year or two later, this guy calls me up. He lived in Dayton and his name was Jeff Purdy. Purdy was the one that introduced me to Pettibone in the first place. Purdy called me up at my store and he says, 'Hey, Brett, Pettibone says he wants more money.' It was a strong-arm tactic, you know. And I said, 'Let me tell you something. Tell Pettibone that he came and he robbed me for that money. I went down and I pressed charges against him. And there's a felony charge pending against him right now in the state of Indiana. If he comes to the state of Indiana, the guy's going to get arrested. He's going to get charged for kidnapping, robbery, assault'—and I ran down this fucking list of things. I said, 'Tell him to quit fucking with me.' That was the last I heard of that motherfucker."

Kimberlin described another unpleasant situation, in New Jersey in 1972. Two years earlier, also in New Jersey, he'd said, he had gotten ripped off while trying to buy $1,800 worth of hashish. This time the product again was hashish, but the stakes were higher and the circumstances more complex.

Kimberlin: "There were two brothers, Randy and Ricky Stovall, and I sold a lot of pot to them. I don't even know how I met these guys. They called and said this guy had some hash and we could buy it for $40,000. I went there. It was three cars. One car had the money and they were taking it to the exchange place. We get there and they asked for the briefcase and I gave it to them and I was supposed to get a briefcase with the hash. And before I got the hash they drove away, they absconded. And the Stovalls were furious. I was their main source of pot and it made them look terrible. So they took me back to the motel and said they would handle this. They knew the guy who had set this up, the middleman. I just figured it was a rip-off. I was making so much money I didn't care that much. I would've just raised the price on the pot I sold these guys and made the money back in six months. I lost hundreds of thousands of dollars over the years because of different things that happened. So anyway, I wasn't that worried. Forty thousand—I made that in a couple of hours some days. So I just went to the motel and a couple of days later the Stovalls call and say everything's cool and they bring me the forty grand and tell me the story. The middle guy was involved. They found him and basically kidnapped him and put him in a basement and tied him naked to a chair in the corner and kept threatening him. He kept denying that he was involved. The Stovalls had a conversation that they wanted him to overhear and said, 'Look, if he doesn't tell us tomorrow, let's just kill him.' So the next day, the guy ended up calling his girlfriend and telling her to get forty grand from his safe-deposit box. And he gave it to them and admitted he was involved in the setup. After that I never went to New Jersey again. I sold these guys pot, but I never went back. I never liked New Jersey after that."

As Kimberlin narrated these vignettes, during our taped telephone conversations in the spring of 1993, I was more intent upon getting him to talk than upon listening carefully. I certainly wasn't inclined to find these stories literally incredible, because at the time I had yet to encounter anyone who was in a position to set forth a version of reality that diverged sharply from Kimberlin's.

9

KIMBERLIN said he followed self-imposed rules that, for many years, enabled him to survive unscathed in his high-risk occupation. He never did business using his home telephone. He didn't use the same pay phone repeatedly. He wrote down few of the phone numbers of his business associates, relying instead upon his "incredible memory." If he did write a number down, he would invert certain digits. He never transported dope in his own car. He never told a woman what he was actually up to. When he checked into a hotel or bought a plane ticket, he paid cash and used an alias. He rotated through dozens of aliases. (When he went to Washington, he was "Mr. Smith.") He carried false identification—Social Security card, passport, driver's license. When the federal authorities finally caught up with him, they attributed to him aliases he'd never even heard of, among them half a dozen Hispanic surnames.

The federal and state governments, in Kimberlin's view, were a collection of occasionally laughable but mainly irritating bureaucrats, who were far less entitled to his money than he was. He had not yet turned nineteen when he first sought professional tax advice. "When I first started dealing dope, I went to see a lawyer in New York, who told me how to beat the tax people," he said. "I had to pay this guy $2,500 or $3,000 for a couple of hours of consultation. Plus I had to fly out there. But it was worth it." Other than driving an expensive car and owning a small airplane, he avoided ostentation and, along the way, the scrutiny of the tax authorities. Each year, he figured out how much he'd spent, extrapolated the income that would be required to support such a life, added ten percent, and filed a short-form tax return, taking the standard deduction. The tax code did not specifically require him to list his occupation, so he left that space blank. The only money he ever put in the bank, he said, was the money he used to pay taxes. He wrote only two checks a year—one to the Internal Revenue Service and the other to the Indiana Department of Revenue.

Kimberlin had a friend, an orthodontist and a devoted right-wing-conspiracy theorist, who gave him books to read that were part anti-Communist proto-survivalism, part Armageddon prophecy. Kimberlin said the books contained "a lot of John Birch crap" which he "never bought into," but he was definitely susceptible to the underlying libertarian dogma. The experience of reading Ayn Rand, specifically *Atlas Shrugged,* "changed my life." He admired the way Rand's characters rigidly "stuck to their principles" and jealously guarded their independence.

In 1974, not long after serving his time for perjury, Kimberlin went to Bermuda for a financial planning seminar that was attended by "all these multi-multimillionaires going around making all this fucking money." His curiosity was aroused when "everybody kept saying that they had one thing in common: Transcendental Meditation." Back in Indianapolis, he and his older brother, Kevin, found their way to a TM center in Broad Ripple. They signed up, paid the money, and received their mantras. "The first time I meditated, I couldn't stop smiling for weeks," he said later. In time, his mother, his father, and his sister became meditators as well.

For about a year and a half, between 1974 and 1976, Kimberlin said, a number of factors moved him to drop out of the drug trade: he wanted to complete his probation without any complications; Colombian and Jamaican marijuana had made Mexican marijuana seem relatively burdensome to market; he'd already made plenty of money and was losing his appetite for the risk; he welcomed the challenge of his legitimate business activities. Some of Kimberlin's customers had the impression he hadn't actually retired but was a shadow in his brother Scott's ongoing ventures. Scott had customers as nearby as Bloomington and as far away as Alaska, and he was plugged into Brett's marketing network. On the supply end, he dealt with some of Brett's Colombian and Jamaican suppliers, in Florida. For a while, he dealt with Papa Reyes down in McAllen, but this didn't last. Nor were the Heilbrunns or Woody McDermott or several other of Brett's familiars willing to deal with Scott.

"With Scott, you never knew what he was going to say or do," a dealer named Tim Young told me. "He was never serious about business. I never thought of Scott as intelligent. You'd meet him in a parking lot to give him money and he'd be trying to *look* like something shady was going on. He was just a kid. He was not mature for his age. I'd have liked him if I wasn't doing business with him. He liked to party and he was a fun guy to be around. But if there was business, it was not him talking. I felt like he was fronting for Brett. You could just tell. And he was always messing up figures. If you owed him ten thousand, it was always him saying you owed ten thousand seven hundred. Just dumb shit. He was a pain in the ass to do business with."

Brett was relieved when he found out that Reyes no longer wanted to deal with Scott. "My Mexican partners were real sophisticated people," Brett said. "I'm a very sophisticated and serious business person, and my brother was just kind of the opposite. My brother was very young and wild. I just didn't think it was the right thing. I thought it would cause people to get busted." Kimberlin had already had some close calls himself. His Mexican connection in Nogales had dried up after his supplier, Manny, got stopped by the police in the Indianapolis airport and was found to be carrying almost $40,000 inside his boots. According to Kimberlin, he was detained by the police and the money was eventually returned.

Money—how to cope with excessive amounts—always presented a challenge. Early on, Kimberlin kept cash in a bank safe-deposit box, but he stopped doing that after he learned that the feds, in untoward circumstances, could seize the contents. Even after he emptied the box he continued to rent it—a perverse fantasy. "I'd keep the keys right in my bedroom with the name of the bank and the box number on a tag. In case I got raided, they'd go to the bank and there would be nothing there." The safest method for concealing cash was to stuff it inside a polyvinyl chloride pipe—the type used for plumbing and electrical conduits—which would be sealed with silicone and buried. The tricky part was to remember exactly where the pipe was interred, because a metal detector couldn't find it. Kimberlin learned about PVC pipe the hard way, after water once seeped into an underground safe.

Kimberlin: "We had a real bad spring and it flooded. About six months later, I went to get this money out of the safe, and this fucking money was all wet. And it was moldy. I had to bring it into the house and peel these bills apart. I had thousand-dollar bills in that safe and five-hundred-dollar and hundred-dollar bills. This was like hundreds of thousands of dollars. And I had to peel these goddamn things apart and I had them all over my fucking bedroom, lying out. Some of them, the mold had gotten so bad it smelled like hell. I had to go to the bank."

On many other occasions, he went to the bank for a less literal version of money-laundering. If he had a hundred thousand in twenties, he'd divide it into three- or five-thousand-dollar bundles and, within a couple of hours, hit a dozen or more banks: "You won't believe how much money I took to the bank and changed into hundreds—millions and millions. You don't know how well I got known in these fucking banks. I used to know exactly how much a hundred thousand weighed in twenties, fifties, and hundreds, down to the gram."

Some of the money that he didn't stick in the ground he invested in silver. In his house, he had a "secret room," a six-by-eight enclosure, access to which was hidden behind a row of shelves in his bedroom. "I bought about $250,000 in silver," Kimberlin told me. "I bought gold too—about ten or twenty thousand. I had these $1,000 bags of solid-silver U.S. currency stashed in my house, in my secret room. I also bought antique rugs—Afghani, Iranian, kilims. The price of silver fell and I sold a bunch. I bought tons of food—grains, rice, nuts, dried fruits. Don't compare me to David Koresh, but I had enough food to last for ten years. Every kind of food you could imagine. I had an enormous walk-in cooler. It was as big as a one-car garage. I had five-gallon jugs of bottled water. And I had figs and dates and prunes and raisins and ground wheat and all kinds of seeds for sprouting and big blocks of cheese. You name it, I had it. I bought six thousand or eight thousand gallons of diesel and gasoline and stored it underground. This was during the Arab oil embargo. My attitude was, 'Hey, they're not slowing me down.' I didn't want to wait in any lines."

When the happy drudgery of counting cash started wearing blisters on his fingers, Kimberlin invested in an electronic money counter the size of a portable typewriter. To avoid suspicion that he was buying "drug-related paraphernalia," he bought the money counter through the Good Earth. He did the same thing when he bought portable platform scales that were capable of handling half-ton loads. He liked both the scales and the money counter so much he started ordering them in large quantities and selling them to other dealers.

He recalls paying $1,800 apiece for the money counters and turning them around for almost $4,000. The money counters, when they got busy, crooned a delicious tune, a whirring lullaby, a song that to Kimberlin's sensitive ear was utterly seductive, sweet music, a tantalizing melody he could hum all day long, as soothing as a mantra.

10

THE NOTION that, after a hiatus of eighteen months or so, Kimberlin resumed marijuana trafficking to support his family has about it an air of quaint, homey virtue—an implicit, if selective, endorsement of some of the cherished values Dan Quayle would later champion on the stump. Coincidentally, 1976, the year Kimberlin plunged back into the business—on a more ambitious scale than ever—also marked the beginning of Quayle's career in politics. A cornerstone legend of Indiana Republican favorite-sonism is the story of how Quayle, at age twenty-nine, was invited by Orvas Beer, the GOP county chairman in Fort Wayne, and Ernie Williams, the editor of the *Fort Wayne News-Sentinel,* to run for the congressional seat then held by Ed Roush, an eight-term Democrat and by local standards a decent fellow but a hopeless liberal. Quayle told Beer and Williams he first had to ask his dad if it was OK. Despite Gerald Ford's loss that year to Jimmy Carter, Quayle went on to beat Roush by ten percentage points. An oddment for the Colorful Footnote Department is nestled in the 16 March 1977 edition of the *News-Sentinel,* under the headline QUAYLE IN SUPPORT OF TAKING A LOOK AT LEGALIZED POT. Two months after his arrival in Washington, in an interview with a reporter named Mark Helmke, Quayle suggested that the resources devoted to prosecuting marijuana users could be more fruitfully employed "prosecuting the rapists and burglars who are a menace to society."

In 1992, Kimberlin told me that once he stopped selling marijuana to "Danny" in 1973, he never thought about him until he saw his photograph in a newspaper article about Quayle's first campaign for Congress. He referred me to his sister, Cynthia, who in 1976 was nineteen years old. Cynthia said, "Brett showed me the newspaper and said, 'Look at that guy. He's running for Congress. I used to sell pot to him. Can you believe it?' I just made a joke, and we laughed. I didn't really think about it again until Quayle was running for vice president, and then it was like 'Hmm.' " When I questioned Cynthia about this a second time, in 1994, her recollection seemed less specific: "All I remember is this was an important guy who was running for some political office and Brett had sold him dope. It's a vague memory. I don't remember him running for the Senate. When Brett brought it up in 1988, that was the first time I'd thought of it, and then I could remember him showing me that picture and telling me that this was an important political figure. And I remember having bragged to one of my boyfriends at the time that my brother had sold dope to government officials, but I didn't even know what I was talking about."

The volume of merchandise that Kimberlin began to move in 1976 suggests a cupidity that exceeded a basic imperative to stock the family larder. Customers who retained their earliest impressions of him—a barely pubescent pipsqueak in a top hat who would travel to Bloomington with thirty pounds of Mexican dope and, when necessary, interrupt business proceedings to call his mom and ask permission to stay out past the dinner hour—might continue to regard him with a certain degree of bemusement. He had indeed been a prodigy, a peewee Dr. Feelgood spreading relatively innocuous cheer and enriching himself in the process. That image would serve the earliest versions of the Kimberlin mythology, until it became clear that business had gotten more serious, at which point the Kimberlin emanations metamorphosed from oddly diverting to flat-out weird, and a new and decidedly more ominous mythology began to emerge.

DURING his retirement, Kimberlin said, his brother Scott would apprise him of big deals and big problems, and in 1976 one of the former became one of the latter. Along with a partner, Scott had bought an airplane with a range of 2,500 miles, sufficient to transport Colombian marijuana nonstop to the States. Scott had invested $150,000 in the plane and had fronted $100,000 for a load of pot and borrowed an additional $50,000 from Brett, all of which went down the tubes when the pilot hired by his partner turned out to be a DEA agent. Dimming Scott's prospects even further was the fact that government interdiction of illegal Colombian and Jamaican exports was becoming more effective. The good news was that Brett had not forgotten Papa Reyes's phone number.

Kimberlin: "Scott was pressuring me. He said, 'I can't make money like you did. Every time it's going good it fucks up.' I said, 'I gave you every one of my connections. Why do I have to do this anymore? I'm *done* with this. Please, don't make me do this.' It went on like this for a couple of months until finally I said OK. I flew in a private plane down to Harlingen, rented a car, found Papa. I hadn't talked to him in years. Papa was somebody I could always depend on."

Within a week, Kimberlin was up and running again, with what proved to be an ideal connection: a steady flow of inventory, a comfortable profit margin, and logistics that required him to get his hands only a little dirty. Papa had two other partners—a Mexican American in Cuernavaca, who dealt with the growers, and a Mexican national who moved the pot to the border at McAllen. This maneuver incorporated an impressive subterfuge—a secondhand propane tanker that had belonged to Pemex, the government-owned oil-and-gas concern. In the cargo tank was a nominal volume of propane, enough to make it smell authentic. On the tank's underside was a small hatch that led to a compartment that could conceal up to seven tons of baled marijuana. The partner on the border, whose name was Francisco Gonzalez, had a corruptible friend who worked as a customs officer; the tanker always arrived at the checkpoint at a propitious hour. In McAllen, Papa would supervise the transfer from the Pemex truck to a box truck and then to a forty-foot refrigerator trailer. Eventually, five or six or seven tons of marijuana would be transported to Indianapolis hidden among, say, thirty thousand pounds of oranges or grapefruits. "We never had one fucking problem, never got busted, nothing," Kimberlin said. "It was a beautiful, beautiful setup."

The original partners in the Good Earth, as it happened, decided not to relocate permanently in India. By the time Kimberlin had built up a business that involved multiton cargoes, Richard Heilbrunn had repatriated to Indianapolis. Along with his brother, Paul—Kimberlin's pal from his junior-high, nickel-bag days—Richard had opened a health food distributorship that also carried a line of contraband. Heilbrunn and Associates, as it was called, eventually blossomed into a $50- to $100-million-a-year marijuana enterprise, which, when finally broken in the late eighties, would result in seventy indictments and prison terms for the Heilbrunns and their colleagues ranging from two to twenty-four years. Before this disappointment, however, Heilbrunn and Associates occupied a warehouse in an industrial complex northwest of Indianapolis, near the interstate that leads to Chicago. In this same complex, Kimberlin and his crews would often rendezvous with Papa's refrigerator trucks. From there, the marijuana would be conveyed to various stash houses in the outlying countryside. Kimberlin would canvass the real-estate classifieds for downscale rentals, recruit a female companion to pose as his wife, arrive driving a car with misleading license tags, offer a pair of aliases and six months' rent in advance, bring in electric timers for the light switches and a token load of Salvation Army furniture, and remember to stop by occasionally to pick up the junk mail. He never stored marijuana at the Good Earth, he said, and only rarely at Eagle Creek. When he designed a country hideaway in Jackson County, ninety minutes south of Indianapolis, he included underground storage vaults, one of which had a capacity that exactly matched that of the Pemex tanker. Typically, however, the pot never spent long on the shelf. Within three days of arriving in Indianapolis, the shipment would be out of Kimberlin's hands—well on its way to becoming smoke from the pipe of a grad student in Ann Arbor or a Harley-Davidson rat in Dayton or a lathe operator in Flint.

During what was to be the remainder of his career, Kimberlin said, he dealt with very few customers. On a regular basis, there were about half a dozen, among them his brother Scott. Brett gave Scott a break on the price—if everyone else was paying $180 a pound, Scott could come in for $150—but he didn't want him as a partner. For that matter, once a load reached Brett's possession, he didn't want *any* partners. He wanted to have the market levers in his grip, and he wanted no surprises.

"Brett wouldn't come to me with a deal unless he had control," I was told by one of his main customers, Jerry Richardson, now a successful legitimate businessman in northern California. Until Kimberlin resurfaced, Jerry had been dealing directly with Papa. "If you brought Brett a load, he'd say, 'If you'll allow me to control it, if I'm the only customer in the area, then I'll do business.' He wanted to control the action. He wanted no competition on up the line. He wanted to be the only person at the stage of master distributor. He wouldn't want to have Papa selling me the same thing he was selling him in the same geographical area. Remember, he went for the throat when it came to pricing. He liked a monopoly."

THE REWARDS were straightforward. Kimberlin was making more money than ever and spending it as if there was plenty more where that came from. In 1975, he had bought the Jackson County property, three hundred fifty acres surrounded by national forest. After selling fifty acres to his reactionary orthodontist friend, he hired an architect, who drew plans for a five-bedroom, four-thousand-square-foot house. It had both active and passive solar design features, as well as security accoutrements that might have seemed the product of a paranoid imagination but, in context, mainly seemed *echt* Kimberlin—a concrete tunnel, for example, three feet in diameter, that extended from the basement to a camouflaged exit in the woods a hundred yards away. Kimberlin conceived it as a potential escape route in case intruders broke in while he was at home. Or, if he returned home and suspected criminal trespass, he could sneak up on them by approaching the house through the tunnel. On the ground floor was a huge fireplace that separated the kitchen and the living room. A trapdoor in a closet upstairs provided access to a vertical passageway that ran parallel to the smokestack and contained a built-in ladder that terminated in the basement, near the entrance to the subterranean tunnel. At midpoint in the vertical passageway was a vent through which it was possible to peer into the living room without being seen, and a gun rack was built into the wall at that spot. Kimberlin could capture unwanted guests in his rifle sights and "take offensive action without them knowing where the bullets were coming from."

As he had at Eagle Creek, he installed storage tanks for gasoline and diesel fuel. He built a dam, forty feet tall by a hundred fifty across, that created a five-acre lake. Though the pace of construction in Jackson County was leisurely, he was in no particular rush. The Good Earth was humming along, as was the Earth Shoes franchise. To capitalize upon the tax incentives created by the energy crisis, he started a company that installed polyurethane insulation. The company, Kimberlin said, had contracts with both the federal government and the Indianapolis public school system, and "the phone was ringing off the hook." It stayed in business for only a year and a half but would've lasted longer if a partner had not "absconded with tens of thousands of dollars." When Kimberlin's investment in Earth Garden Café, the health food restaurant, became a drain, he attributed that difficulty, as well, to the foibles of an unreliable partner.

Kimberlin got around in his Mercedes or a four-wheel-drive pickup. He also owned a mature Dodge pickup with a camper fitted over the cargo area. At Eagle Creek, he always kept a junker handy, a sedan that ran fine and that he never had to worry about keeping clean. And for dope deals he went through dozens of throwaways—cars bought under assumed names for not much cash and, after a month of useful labor, easily abandoned. He had a small tractor with a front-end loader and a backhoe, which, if necessary, could be hauled to Jackson County aboard his flatbed trailer. His six-horse trailer was occasionally loaded with pot but mainly was used for its intended purpose. There was a five-stall stable at Eagle Creek, and not long after moving there he started keeping horses. Caring for them was a time-consuming chore, of course, and it came as a relief when his mother introduced him to an acquaintance who, in exchange for boarding her own horse, was willing to feed and groom Brett's small herd.

Her name was Sandra Barton, and she and Carolyn Kimberlin had met while working in a research lab at IU-PUI, the campus that Indiana University and Purdue University shared in downtown Indianapolis. Sandi Barton was eleven years older than Brett and about that many years younger than Carolyn. She had dark-blond hair and blue eyes, and like Brett she was short and slightly built and looked much younger than her age. Eventually, under oath, she would describe Brett Kimberlin as her "best friend in the world"—her distillation, for consumption in a public courtroom, of a relationship that to some observers seemed obscure and ambiguous. With one of Sandi Barton's two daughters Kimberlin would establish a bond that would seem even more obscure and ambiguous—incongruous at best and, in the eyes of some law enforcement officers, disturbingly inappropriate.

In time, the connections between these people would be reduced to blood and ashes. Many years down the line, Kimberlin would respond to questions about Sandi Barton by saying he had no idea whether or not she was still alive. Her daughters would become impossibly elusive, so intimidated by the prospect of uttering to a reporter their feelings about Kimberlin's role in their lives that they would seem to prefer shriveling and disappearing into the wind. For me, Kimberlin's connection to the Barton family would become an opaque knot of intrigue and dread, a little black hole unto itself. And the moment their paths crossed would come to represent one more eerily inevitable increment, the magnetic gears of Kimberlin's fate meshing silently, ratcheting forward another notch.

11

I N THE spring of 1978, during what Kimberlin said was a pleasure
trip to New York with his girlfriend Susan Harvey, he made a pil-
grimage to the home of a man named Marinus Dykshoorn. A
question was nagging at him, and though he felt he already knew the
answer—whose implications were abysmally unsettling—he hoped
Dykshoorn might confirm his intuition. Dykshoorn's own intuition
amounted to his bread and butter, since he made his living as a psychic. One of his distinctive techniques was to survey a crime scene
while holding a loop of piano wire: this procedure, he maintained,
enabled him to absorb the vibrations of whatever had taken place,
as if the wire were an antenna that received signals from the past.
Dykshoorn was born in the Netherlands—an inordinate number of
modern psychics have been of Dutch origin—but had been in the
United States for many years. Displayed on the walls of his apartment in the Bronx, Kimberlin recalled, were dozens of commenda-
tions and citations from police departments that had enlisted his
help with investigations.

Kimberlin didn't need to refer to the wall decorations to be persuaded that Dykshoorn possessed a strange gift. He had recently read
Dykshoorn's autobiography, *My Passport Says Clairvoyant*. Books
on clairvoyance and similar subjects had appealed to Kimberlin since
adolescence, when he read "all kinds of stuff about psychics." Several
professors at Duke University were engaged in academic research
about psychic phenomena, he said, and he corresponded with some
of them. In his travels he had visited psychics in various cities, though
when I asked for specifics he couldn't remember any names. As a
child, he had been captivated by magic—"I was a big fan of Hou-
dini"—and he traced his interest in psychic phenomena to that.

Carolyn Kimberlin encouraged these pursuits. She and Brett
shared a fascination with Edgar Cayce, the "Sleeping Prophet," who

laid the groundwork for the New Age hoodoo of trance channeling. Brett thought of himself as open-minded but not overcredulous. Palm reading, for instance, he found unconvincing. Certain aspects of astrology, however, made sense. Generally, he had no use for divinations of the future, because he simply didn't believe in "fate"—not a word in his vocabulary, he decreed. Every individual had the potential to create his own destiny. Nevertheless, a genuine psychic, as if plumbing some universal force, could perhaps tap into a person's prior history.

A few months earlier, someone had stolen $152,000 of Kimberlin's money. It had been concealed in a hidden compartment inside an antique dresser in his bedroom at Eagle Creek. One autumn afternoon, Kimberlin left the house on health food business for four hours, and when he returned he saw that a burglary had occurred. The house had an elaborate security apparatus, but the thief had broken and entered through a window that happened not to be wired into the system. Kimberlin's prime suspect was his partner Justin Farrell. The weekend before the robbery, Farrell had seen Kimberlin in his bedroom, counting the proceeds of a large marijuana transaction. A few weeks earlier, Kimberlin told me, he'd given Farrell $25,000— a gift Farrell considered insufficient. Farrell, he added, was aware of the hidden compartments in the dresser, and he knew the fine points of the security system.

"I called Justin on the phone the day of the robbery," Kimberlin said. "At first, I acted like nothing happened. I asked him what he'd done that day, and he said he'd been to school. Then I confronted him, and he denied everything. Later, I called Scott and asked him to go by Justin's house and spy on him. He called me back and told me he saw Justin standing in front of a mirror, looking at himself. I went down there the next day and told Justin I wanted him to take a polygraph. At first, he said OK, but then he refused. He had this terrible scrape on his left arm. When I asked him how he did that, he said he'd tripped while jogging. I think he did that when he went through the window or when he was running through the woods from my house. Justin's the worst liar on earth—and there was nothing I could do about it."

If Kimberlin expected Dykshoorn to exercise his psychic powers and arrive at a positive identification of the culprit, he also expected him to summon the truth without the benefit of accurate raw data.

He laid out the case against Farrell, but then, on the assumption that six figures in cash would arouse suspicion that he was a drug dealer, he described the loss as a few thousand dollars. Either this was too trifling an amount to seem worthwhile or the nature of the problem failed to engage Dykshoorn's curiosity, or else Dykshoorn's superior intuition told him Kimberlin was indeed a dealer, who was lying about the sums involved. For whatever reason, he declined to get involved. If Kimberlin would cover his expenses, however, he was willing to come to Indianapolis to deliver a public lecture and to perform private psychic readings.

Kimberlin already had experience arranging lectures by psychic healers and nutritionists and the like. The Good Earth would function as a cosponsor of these sporadic events, and Kimberlin would in effect collect a promoter's fee. For Dykshoorn's visit, though, he far surpassed his previous efforts as an advance man. He rented a hall in a Ramada Inn and booked Dykshoorn for three interviews on television and more than fifteen on radio. Hundreds of people attended the lecture. Despite having given complimentary tickets to many friends and acquaintances, Kimberlin said, he cleared a profit of about a thousand dollars. Dykshoorn did even better. So impressive was his public performance that he attracted scores of volunteers for private psychic readings, at thirty bucks a pop. These sessions took place over several days, in Dykshoorn's hotel suite. One afternoon, Kimberlin dropped by and brought along the younger of Sandi Barton's daughters. Jessica, who was fourteen, wanted Dykshoorn to answer a straightforward question: Her maternal grandfather was sick with cancer. Was it going to kill him? As grim as this possibility was, if Dykshoorn could reveal the future she wanted a glimpse.

WHEN Jessica was born—on April Fool's Day, 1964—her father had already walked out of her life. A sister, Yvonne, had been born two years earlier. Sandi's marriage was a shotgun affair that had taken place before her twentieth birthday, and its collapse forced her to return home to her parents, Fred and Julia Scyphers. There she stayed for eight years, in a three-bedroom ranch-style house in Speedway, a predominantly blue-collar community on the west side of Indianapolis. Fred Scyphers assumed a necessary and influential role in his granddaughters' upbringing, but his wife loomed even larger. Julia

Scyphers was a physically imposing, opinionated, and emotionally overbearing figure. The escape from her mother that marriage might have provided Sandi turned out, bitterly, to be only a brief respite. Her only sibling was a sister, Louise, who was three years younger. Louise's marriage took her to Texas, where she began to raise a family. So eager was Sandi to lead an independent existence that when she finally moved the girls to a two-bedroom apartment a couple of miles away from her parents' house, she didn't have the money to furnish it. It was around this time that Kimberlin entered their lives.

When I asked Kimberlin to describe the Barton girls, he said both were pretty but that there wasn't much of a family resemblance. Though each had blue eyes, Yvonne was a brunette and Jessica was a honey blonde. He compared Yvonne to Lynda Carter, the actress who appeared on the "Wonder Woman" television series, while Jessica was "more like Cheryl Tiegs." Of greater significance was the history of Kimberlin's relationship with each of them, and here the contrast was far more striking.

From the beginning of his friendship with Sandi, Kimberlin said, her younger daughter developed an attachment to him. Sandi would come to Eagle Creek to tend his horses and ride her own; Jessica would tag along, and "she used to hang on me, she didn't want to let me go." Jessica was ten years old and Kimberlin was twenty. Before long, Sandi accepted his offer to pick Jessica up after school one day a week and take her "somewhere fun—horseback riding or swimming or to the zoo or whatever." Though he never gave Sandi or the girls money outright, he extended himself in kind, buying birthday gifts, school supplies, clothing. The summer after they moved into the apartment, the Bartons went on a vacation with Sandi's parents and asked Kimberlin to feed their pet rabbit. While they were away, he bought and arranged for the delivery of a couch that opened into a bed, a matching chair, beds for the girls' room, lamps, and end tables. He brought over a table saw, he said, built an eight-foot-wide bookcase and storage unit in the living room, painted the entire place, and put up a WELCOME HOME sign. "When they came back from their vacation, they thought they were in the wrong apartment," he said. From then on, he had a key to the place.

Kimberlin described his relationship with Sandi as platonic. She became acquainted with his girlfriend, Susan Harvey, and Susan wasn't jealous, "because there wasn't anything to be jealous of." His closeness with Sandi was such that, across the years, she became privy to intimate entanglements that indeed made Susan jealous. In turn, he recalls meeting Sandi's boyfriends, including one who was bewildered and perturbed that Brett would occasionally sleep on the couch in the living room. When I asked why he spent nights there, he said, "I don't know. Like, maybe I'd bring Jessica home and I'd be too tired to drive home"—too tired to drive himself to Eagle Creek, all of six miles away.

Sandi worked part-time at the Good Earth. Brett bought her an Arabian horse, and she named it Arad Taibeh, which in Arabic meant "good earth." Many weekends, she and Jessica stayed at Eagle Creek. His ties, he said, extended to Sandi's parents. When her sister and brother-in-law and their children visited one Christmas, Kimberlin showed up at the Scyphers house dressed as Santa Claus—even though, at 105 pounds, he could more easily have passed for one of the elves. When a tree blew down in the Scypherses' backyard, he helped Fred cut it up and haul it away. He says he tilled their garden and—drawing from his repertoire of youthful good deeds—plowed their driveway. Later, when damning rumors surfaced that he and Mrs. Scyphers had feuded, he dismissed them as outright fabrications or exaggerations of minor disagreements, and in either case specifically designed to assassinate his character.

BRETT attributed Yvonne's failure to share Sandi's and Jessica's affection for him to her personality: she was "distant, bitchy, and cold," and "unappreciative" of her mother, with whom she "never got along." Yvonne was perhaps old enough to have retained some memory of her father before his abandoning act. Conceivably she ascribed their subsequent hardships to a failure on her mother's part, or supposed that if Sandi had done things differently, the father would have stuck around. Or maybe Yvonne resented her mother's decision to move into an apartment and away from her grandmother, who doted on her and to whom she was especially close. In any event, she resisted Kimberlin. Once, inscribing a wallet-sized junior high school photograph, her gesture of graciousness was no match for her youthful candor: "Brett: A guy that I do respect . . . even though there is a barrier. I don't know if it will ever be broken and I can't say I want it to be, but just so we think differently don't mean I can't say, yer okay!

Yvonne." In a deposition she gave in a 1982 civil suit, she testified that Kimberlin "tried to buy my friendship more or less on various occasions . . . he bought me all kinds of presents . . . a bicycle, a stereo, clothes . . . on Christmas, birthdays and stuff like that."

His attachment to Jessica was quite a different matter. Their weekly after-school outings, Kimberlin said, were "very special days" for her. She and her mother and Kimberlin and his sister traveled together to Transcendental Meditation retreats around the Midwest. He took the mother and daughter camping in national parks in Kentucky and Indiana. Sometimes he hitched a horse trailer to his pickup, and the camping trips would include long trail rides. If Jessica brought along a girlfriend her own age, Kimberlin would sleep in a separate tent. For three consecutive summers, 1974 through 1976, they took vacations of a week or longer in Disney World, Mexico, and Hawaii. Sandi couldn't get time off from work, so on these summer trips it was just the two of them—Brett and Jessica.

Eyebrows levitated. A drug-dealing colleague had memories of conversations with Kimberlin that struck him as odd: "We'd see a girl who was pubescent or prepubescent, and Brett would get this smile and say, 'Hey, what do you think? Isn't she great?' It made me very uncomfortable." Another recalled Kimberlin introducing Jessica as "my girlfriend," and if irony was intended, it was too subtle to register. To a coworker at IU-PUI, Sandi confided that Kimberlin was "grooming Jessica to be his wife." To another, Sandi explained that though Kimberlin's relationship with Jessica was chaste, he intended "to wait for her and would marry her."

Kimberlin recorded some of his experiences with Jessica on film. When I asked him to show me photographs of the Bartons, he could find only the one school picture of Yvonne and none of Sandi, but he had a trove of snapshots of Jessica: nuzzling a black-and-white mutt named Snoopy, admiring a porpoise at an aquarium in Ohio, standing on the beach in Florida, on horseback in southern Indiana, on horseback along the beach in Hawaii, posing at the entrance to a cave in Hawaii. Several others were taken poolside at Eagle Creek: Jessica treading water, Jessica diving, Jessica in a yellow-and-white bathing suit, resting an elbow on the red-brick apron at the pool's edge, her hair wet and slicked back, revealing every feature of her face: her high, smooth cheekbones, her perfectly straight teeth, her ingenue's smile—a nymphet worthy of the heart-piercing torment of Humbert Humbert.

I had also requested photographs of the Kimberlin family, and the packet he sent me included, in addition to dinner-table and birthday-party scenes and posed groups in the living room, some shots that I hadn't expected and didn't know what to make of. There was one of Kimberlin, poolside at Eagle Creek, nose-to-nose with a dog in the foreground, while a woman with long, dark hair stood in the distant background. He lay prone on a lounge chair, nude, seemingly unaware of the camera. He wasn't certain who had taken this picture—"maybe my sister or one of her friends." In another, he was on his belly in a bathtub, with his knees bent, but this time he was facing the camera and smiling, and he was extending his heavily bandaged right hand. He'd cut the hand, he said, on broken glass. A contemporaneous shot—some of his fingers bandaged, lacerations on the others visible—showed him seated on a toilet, smiling goofily, with his pants below his knees. The photographer? I asked. "Probably Sandi," he said.

How, I asked, did he define platonic friendship?

"Hey, we don't have any hang-ups about nudity, if that's what you're getting at," he said. "When you make a big deal out of these things it affects kids, but when you don't make a big deal there's no consequence. That's just the way things were. Very informal. Shit. Sometimes I'd go out there and weed the garden in the nude for two hours. Sometimes when I'd go to my property down South, I'd swim nude. Sandi would sometimes swim nude. My sister and her friends would swim nude. My mother still sees me naked. Hell, my sister, growing up in our house, probably saw more dicks than most women do in a lifetime. It was no big deal. Nudity was no big deal to me."

What about Jessica, I wondered. How might she have been affected?

"When Jessica was young she had kidney surgery and she had this big scar on, I think, her right side and she was very self-conscious," he said. "She never wore a two-piece bathing suit. She was very shy. I don't remember ever seeing her swim nude."

Then what about Yvonne? Did he think Yvonne would have said something to her grandparents about his casual attitude toward nudity?

"No."

JESSICA had a capacity for rebelliousness that Kimberlin interpreted as typically adolescent—petulance, more or less—and he said he knew better than to let it get to him. During the spring of 1978, for instance, marijuana dealings in Texas crowded his schedule and made it hard for him to honor a couple of dates with her.

"She knew I was into doing something illegal, though she didn't know exactly what it was," he told me. "She said, 'Brett, I hate it when you go to Texas.' I said 'Why?' She said, 'Because I'm afraid you'll never come back.' But I had to go. So she started getting back at me for going away on her special days. Like when I came home, I told her, 'I'll pick you up on Thursday,' and she'd say, 'No, I have other plans.' This was her way of getting back at me.

"One day in June, I called her at the apartment and said I'd come pick her up. I told her I was coming and I had a friend with me. She said 'Who?' It was Bill Bowman"—a drug-dealing associate. "When I got there she wasn't there and she left a note that she was at her grandmother's. I called over there and said I was coming to pick her up and the grandmother said, 'Well, Jessica's with me today. You'll have to see her later.' It was like Jessica was doing this little head game, you know. I wouldn't call it a rebellion against authority. It was more 'Hey, you're fucking with me because of your dope. I can fuck with you too.' "

JULIA SCYPHERS could be a nuisance, Kimberlin acknowledged, but he emphasized that in no sense did she and he have a running dispute.

"People call it a falling-out, but I don't know that's what it was," he said. "I think it was more jealousy on her part. The grandmother was a control freak. She was always trying to control Jessica and Sandi's lives, even after they'd moved out of her house. Maybe the grandmother thought I was instigating Sandi's independence. She would call and say she wanted Jessica over at the house at a certain time on a certain day, but Jessica would've already made plans with friends. Then the grandmother would lay this head trip on her. I never had a falling-out with her. I never had a blowout with the grandmother or an argument or a disagreement. She never threatened me."

THE AFTERNOON of 23 June 1978, Julia Scyphers appeared at the office of Judith L. Johnson, an employee of Born's Management Company, a real estate management firm whose portfolio included the

Port O' Call apartment complex, where Sandra Barton was the lessee of unit 68-A. According to a statement that Johnson later gave to the Speedway Police Department, Mrs. Scyphers paid fifteen dollars to have the front-door lock on 68-A rekeyed. Johnson wrote that Mrs. Scyphers wanted the lock changed because "her grandchildren had been approached by a man prior to her visit to our office. She was concerned for the safety of her grandchildren."

Subsequently, Judith Johnson has recalled, either Kimberlin or Sandi intercepted a Port O' Call maintenance man and prevented him from changing the cylinder on the lock.

The morning of June 26, Judith Johnson continued in her statement to the police, she had another surprise visitor.

> Brett C. Kimberlin came to our office. He came into my office and closed the door, talked very low, was nervous, introduced himself as living with Sandra Barton, 68 POC #A, and stated he had lived there for a good many years. He told me that his girlfriend's mother was harassing them, that she hated him and their situation (living there with her daughter and grandchildren) . . . he said that Mrs. Barton's mother was insane and that *he* wanted them to get away from her but that Mrs. Barton was afraid of her mother and would not stand up to her.

Listening to Kimberlin, Johnson realized she'd made a mistake when she accepted money from Julia Scyphers to change the lock. Nor did she care to hear much more of what he had to say. But Kimberlin persisted.

> He wanted me to evict them so it would be a good reason for them to have to move away and therefore Mrs. Scyphers would believe them and think they had to move and were not just getting away from her. I told him I couldn't evict Mrs. Barton for something like that. He then told me the apartment was destroyed due to Mrs. Barton having 4–6 animals, that the odor was very bad and that he sometimes had to step out on the patio in warm weather. He said the carpet was ruined. I advised I would have it inspected. If it was true and was this dirty we would ask her to move. He agreed. We also discussed the date and arrived at 8/1/78.

On a three-by-five index card, the detective from the Speedway Police Department who interviewed Judith Johnson—the interview took place 3 August 1978—recorded the following quotation from her, separate from her signed statement: "Brett Kimberlin had vengeance on his face when he talked about Mrs. Scyphers. He radiated hatred."

WHEN, during Marinus Dykshoorn's visit to Indianapolis, Jessica Barton approached to ask about her grandfather's prognosis, Dykshoorn went out of his way to accommodate her. Knowing that she was a friend of Kimberlin's, he gave her fifteen minutes of his time, gratis. While Jessica sat with the psychic in one corner of the hotel suite, Kimberlin chatted with his wife. A memory of this occasion lingered with Kimberlin—of Jessica bringing along a photograph of her grandfather or some other object that could yield a clue to his destiny. When it was time to leave, Jessica seemed distressed. If Dykshoorn indeed had the capacity to foretell the future, then the outlook for her grandfather was bleak. "Oh, I'm sorry. Things don't look very good at all," Dykshoorn told her, or "He's not going to live very long," or words to that effect.

"Afterward, she was visibly shaken," Kimberlin said. "But it came true. Exactly as he said."

Well, actually no. Not exactly.

THE *Chicago Reader,* in its 25 February 1983 issue, published a lengthy article about Kimberlin that examined the vicissitudes of his career as a drug smuggler as well as his encounters with the law. Following leads from Kimberlin, the author, Deanna Silberman, spent time in Indianapolis interviewing Kimberlin's attorneys, family members, and Sandi Barton. She also spoke with government agents who had investigated Kimberlin and with reporters for the Indianapolis newspapers. In later years, Kimberlin supplied copies to journalists or potential allies, hoping to interest them in his case.

Silberman recounted Kimberlin's delineation of his involvement with the Barton and Scyphers families. Referring to Jessica and events in 1978, she wrote: "Their relationship had been so strong for the previous five years, Kimberlin says, that he felt he had 'raised' this child. But early that summer she started to break away from him, to rebel against his control. Sandra Barton was later to testify that when she asked Brett, in May or June of 1978, to stay away from her daughter, he became very upset and said it wasn't worth going on anymore."

ACCORDING to Kimberlin: He never had a conversation about Julia Scyphers in the offices of Born's Management Company—on 26 June 1978 or any other date—and the meeting Judith Johnson described to the Speedway Police Department never occurred; any suggestion of impropriety between himself and Jessica Barton was a delusion that flowed from Julia Scyphers's neurotic need to control the lives of her daughter and granddaughters. "Nobody ever explained to the grandmother anything about the relationships," he told me. "The grandmother never had any idea what was going on. Sandi had these boyfriends but she would spend time with me. My conjecture is maybe the grandmother thought Sandi was whoring around. The grandmother couldn't figure it out. But so what? I never had any conflict with the grandmother—never, ever." All insinuations of exploitative or unsavory behavior on his part were figments of the imaginations of unscrupulous people whose object was to impugn and persecute him.

What was not a figment of anyone's imagination, however, was what happened to Julia Scyphers on 29 July 1978. Shortly before three o'clock that afternoon, she was mortally wounded with a gunshot to the head, in a fashion that bore the earmarks of a contract murder. Within twenty-four hours, Kimberlin said, he called Marinus Dykshoorn and asked him to help determine the identity of the killer.

12

KIMBERLIN did not shoot Julia Scyphers, nor did anyone ever insist that he had. Only two people—the victim and her husband—got a close look at the killer. The description Fred Scyphers gave to the police was of a white male, thirty years old, six feet tall and weighing about 180 pounds, with collar-length dark hair and a neatly trimmed mustache. Two weeks before the murder, the Scypherses had had a garage sale at their home, at 1651 Cunningham Drive. A man who claimed to be interested in some unsold objects of china, crystal, and silver called and made an appointment to come by. He drove up in a white late-model Oldsmobile—Fred and Julia watched from the living room window as he parked in their driveway—and got out, carrying an attaché case. Fred made a disparaging observation about the length of his hair. Three years earlier, Fred had retired after putting in thirty-five years as a plant engineer at a nearby General Motors factory. Julia was active as a library volunteer, Girl Scout leader, and member of the Speedway Christian Church. They met the visitor at the door and walked with him to the garage. Fred moved a leaf mulcher that was blocking the table where the sale items were on display, then checked the oil in Julia's car. He was inside the house, washing his hands, when he heard "a loud pop." The white Olds was pulling rapidly out of the driveway. In the garage, Fred found his wife lying in an expanding pool of blood. Yvonne Barton, who'd been sunbathing in the backyard, came running and then sought help from a neighbor who was a doctor. An ambulance arrived quickly and delivered Julia to a hospital a couple of miles away, but within the hour she was pronounced dead. The calm manner of the killer—as well as the apparent lack of motive, since nothing was stolen—suggested the work of a professional. Neighbors who saw him drive off reported that he stopped within a block of the Scyphers house and placed his attaché case in the trunk of the car, which had out-of-state plates. In the fifty-six-year history of Speedway, only two previous homicides had been recorded.

Kimberlin said he spent time that Saturday in Martinsville, thirty miles to the southwest, and was driving back toward Indianapolis when he received a voice message on his beeper—his sister, Cynthia, telling him to call home right away. He said that in Mooresville, a blink-and-you-miss-it hamlet along Highway 67, he pulled into a drugstore parking lot and used a pay phone to call Cynthia, who told him Yvonne had just delivered the news that her grandmother was dead. "I asked if it was a car accident," Kimberlin told me. "Cynthia said she didn't know and she [Yvonne] wanted to find her mother. So then I called Yvonne from there. I asked what I could do and she said I could get ahold of Sandi."

Only Kimberlin knew why Sandi and Jessica were out of town, and at the time of the murder, he said, he knew their rough coordinates but not their exact whereabouts. They were in south Texas, doing him a big favor. That spring, Kimberlin had bought five tons of Mexican marijuana, much of which turned out to have an uncharacteristically extended shelf life. Its arrival in Indiana coincided with the growing public awareness of a cooperative effort by the American and Mexican governments to spray cannabis plants with a synthetic herbicide called paraquat; when smoked in sufficient quantities, this tainted marijuana could cause the scarring of lung tissue. By the spring of 1978, the spraying campaign had penetrated between two and twenty percent of the Mexican crop—depending upon who was compiling the statistics. Smoking Mexican weed thus became a kind of Russian roulette, though certainly less risky than the real thing. But regardless of its actual public-health consequences, the paraquat program seriously curbed the demand for Kimberlin's inventory.

"Normally, that pot would have gone anywhere from one fifty to one eighty a pound," Kimberlin said. "And at the end I was trying to sell it for seventy-five or eighty dollars a pound, and I couldn't get rid of it. If someone had offered to buy a thousand pounds for fifty grand, I would've taken it. When that happens, a lot of people would turn to customers they don't normally deal with. I could have sold that Mexican if I wanted to put myself out, but I wasn't about to do that. That whole fucking deal was a nightmare."

The damage was mitigated when his partners, Papa Reyes and Francisco Gonzalez, agreed to find another buyer if Kimberlin could ship half a ton of pot back to them. Kimberlin wasn't prepared to drive it himself, of course. Instead, Sandi agreed to hitch a U-Haul trailer to the back of her station wagon and transport it to Beeville, Texas, for a thousand dollars—"a free vacation for her and Jessica," as Brett put it. Ostensibly, the trailer contained furniture. When I asked if Sandi knew its actual contents, Kimberlin said, "Well, I never told her. She never asked. She was delivering it to a bunch of Mexicans. What she surmised I don't know. She knew I was involved with pot. Not that I told her. Not that we ever talked about it. But she wasn't born yesterday."

After speaking to Yvonne Barton, Kimberlin said, he called Sandi's sister, Louise Crosby, who lived in Austin. Sandi's itinerary led her from Beeville to Austin, where she planned to spend a few days with her sister's family. "Louise told me that after hearing the news about her mother, she'd called the police and they'd put out an all-points bulletin for Sandi's car," Kimberlin said. "This put me in a panic. I thought: Oh, my God. I didn't know if she was down there yet. I thought the state police were going to pull her over with a trailer carrying a thousand pounds of pot." Next, he said, he spoke with Gonzalez and learned that the trailer had already been dropped off. This news, obviously, inspired a sensation of deep relief. In retrospect, however, it seems plausible that had Sandi been discovered in possession of a U-Haul full of marijuana—and had Kimberlin, as a consequence, been busted on a drug conspiracy charge—his life would ultimately have taken fewer frightful and time-consuming detours.

THAT evening, in Indianapolis, Kimberlin received a phone call from Sandi, who reported that before heading to Austin, she and Jessica were planning to spend a couple of days on Padre Island, off the coast of Corpus Christi. "She was at a motel," Kimberlin said. "She sounded real happy. She was all excited about going to Austin. She loves Louise's kids. I said, 'Sandi, I've got something to tell you.' My mom was standing right there and she said, 'I think I should tell her.' So my mom actually gave her the news."

SANDI and Jessica's efforts to get back home were thwarted by a tropical storm out of the Gulf of Mexico, which halted commercial air traffic. Kimberlin said he booked a charter jet to fly them, but it was also grounded by the weather. Finally, three days after the murder, they were able to catch a flight. (Kimberlin arranged for someone to return Sandi's car to Indianapolis.) Meanwhile, the Speedway police were feeding the press their unfolding theories of the crime. The *Indianapolis Star* ran a banner headline that said: HIRED GUNMAN KILLED WOMAN? The story posed a series of hypothetical questions— "innocent victim . . . in a tragic mix-up? . . . crazed 'thrill' killer? . . . why . . . an active church member and grandmother?"—and then concluded that "Police know of nothing in the background of any family member that would explain the slaying."

Meanwhile, Kimberlin had initiated his own investigation, in the form of a plea to his psychic adviser. "I called Dykshoorn and said I needed his help. I told him a friend of mine's mother got murdered and the killer got away. He asked what happened and I told him what I knew and he said, 'I can't get involved. I don't get involved in murders involving drugs.' And I said, 'Nobody said anything about drugs. This was a robbery.' And he said, 'This case involves drugs.' I taped the conversation. I argued with him. I implored him to come."

Kimberlin said Dykshoorn's insistence that the killing was drug-related left him feeling "kind of pissed off," and as a result, "I never spoke to Dykshoorn again." In other words, Kimberlin was rejecting a scenario Dykshoorn evidently had envisioned through the medium of his superior intuition—the very attribute that had drawn Kimberlin to him in the first place. The plotline Kimberlin preferred began with some sort of robbery and ended abruptly in a random act of anonymous violence. A drug-related script didn't fit any reality that he wished to reckon with.

BY THE time Sandi reached Indianapolis, the police were eager to talk with her, and so was Kimberlin. When he arrived at the Scyphers residence that evening, however, she ran outside and warned him that he wasn't welcome. Her father was brandishing a gun and claiming that Brett was somehow responsible for the murder. "Sandi was being interrogated about her trip, and she was all freaked," he told me. "And her sister starts asking her all these fucking questions. And she was telling it like I'd told her—that the trailer was loaded with furniture. But the circumstances were terrible. It looked like she was being very evasive. It's like being caught with your pants down when you're not try-ing to fuck somebody, you're just trying to look at a scar on their ass."

Naturally, Kimberlin said, he was thoroughly taken aback by this development, and there was nothing he could do to mollify Fred Scyphers or Louise Crosby. But he did have the tape recording of his conversation with Dykshoorn to play for Sandi: "If there was ever any doubt in her mind that I was even remotely, tangentially involved in the murder—she never said so, but it might have been in the back of her mind—listening to that tape eliminated any doubts."

The police were more skeptical, and the next day they summoned Kimberlin to headquarters for questioning. He arrived in the com-pany of an attorney. Press accounts, which did not mention Kimber-lin by name, stated that he was advised of his rights, offered no response to several "pertinent" questions, and declined to take a "psychological stress evaluation test," or polygraph. The *Star* said that Julia Scyphers "reportedly had a series of bitter disputes with a wealthy Marion County businessman" that "stemmed from the busi-nessman's refusal to stop associating with certain members of Mrs. Scyphers' family," and that "the victim had informed friends she was considering filing a peace bond to put a legal stop to his visits."

Kimberlin's refusal to submit to a polygraph, he said, was his at-torney's idea. As far as the murder was concerned, he had nothing to hide. Any questions about Sandi's trip to Texas, however, would re-quire an evasive response that would flunk him. "At first I was will-ing to take a polygraph," he told me. "I said, 'Sure, but you have to have everybody else in the family take a polygraph too.' But then my attorney wouldn't let me."

A NEWSPAPERMAN in Indianapolis has referred to the Speedway Po-lice Department of this era as "Barney Fife and Company." Early on, public pronouncements by Robert Copeland, the chief of police, sug-gested that a solution was imminent: "MAJOR BREAK" IN MURDER SEEN and KILLER SUSPECTS NARROWED TO 3. Before long, though, it became apparent that the murder investigation was testing the author-ities beyond their capacities. The department had only three detectives, one of whom was assigned as a juvenile officer. Crime in Speedway was a tiny industry: half a dozen robberies a year and only fifty or sixty burglaries.

Within a week and a half, the police were nakedly frustrated. "We're almost sure we know what happened," Copeland complained. "But just go try to prove it. We were very optimistic last week, but the investigation is taking a lot longer than we expected. We're running into a lot of roadblocks." On the advice of an attorney, Sandi formally refused to submit to a polygraph, and she failed to attend her mother's funeral. The police wanted to know exactly where in Texas she had been and what she was doing at the time of the murder, but according to the *Star*, she "refused to answer several questions posed by investigators." Fred Scyphers and the two witnesses who'd seen the killer put the attaché case in his trunk were placed under hypnosis by a Marion County sheriff's deputy, in the hope that they might recall more precise details. A *Star* headline said: POLICE BAFFLED BY MURDER VICTIM'S DAUGHTER. In the *Indianapolis News* was a short item: SCYPHERS CASE NEAR STANDSTILL.

Kimberlin said that after being questioned, he tried to resume his routines. The police "had been fucking with me," but he thought of them as "like Keystone Cops, a bunch of bungling fools." He was working on building an addition to the Good Earth. He stayed busy, as always, with his smuggling scams. Sandi's boyfriend at the time, a medical student, moved out-of-state. She had rented a new apartment, in the western suburb of Brownsburg. Jessica and Yvonne had moved in with their grandfather, and "Sandi didn't really have anybody to be with," so Kimberlin said he spent a lot of time with her.

Four weeks following the murder, after a ten-day hiatus in newspaper coverage, the *News* revealed a fragmentary detail of Sandi's trip to Texas: she allegedly had initialed rental papers when the trailer was picked up in Indiana and dropped off in Texas. The story also noted that federal narcotics agents had previously investigated Kimberlin, identified not by name but as "a primary suspect." Mainly, the newspaper report reiterated the theory from which the police had not budged: Julia Scyphers was the target of a "revenge murder"; the investigation "centered around a relationship between a female relative of the victim and a young Indianapolis businessman"; Julia Scyphers "had argued with the businessman on several occasions."

Six days later, the bombs started going off.

13

THE FIRST night—Friday, 1 September 1978—four explosions occurred, at irregular intervals: shortly before ten o'clock, in a trash container in front of a stereo equipment store in a shopping center; fifteen minutes later, in a Dumpster in a motel parking lot; half an hour after that, in a residential area; finally, more than three hours later, under a crab apple tree near the entrance to a school. The shopping center was called the Speedway Shopping Center, the motel the Speedway Motel, and the school Speedway High School, so there was no choice but to call the perpetrator the Speedway Bomber. It had an evocative ring—name-brand recognizability. All the bombs detonated within a half-mile radius and could be heard five miles away. The third excavated some shrubbery in the 1600 block of Whitcomb Avenue, which ran parallel to Cunningham Drive. As the crow flew, it went off less than a hundred yards from the Scyphers residence.

Bomb squads from the Indianapolis Police Department and the 64th Ordnance at Fort Benjamin Harrison, officers from the Indiana State Police and the Marion County Sheriff's Department, and agents from the federal Bureau of Alcohol, Tobacco and Firearms (ATF) reported for duty. They found bits of wiring and springs that seemed to have come from alarm clocks, and pieces of metal from six-volt batteries. That no one was injured seemed more a matter of luck than of design. A fifth blast and then a sixth—in a cornfield and outside the Speedway Lanes bowling alley—took place the following two nights. The ATF people gathered fragments and sent them to the lab for analysis. While awaiting the results, the supervisor of the local ATF office publicly theorized that each bomb consisted of a soft-drink can packed with smokeless gunpowder, triggered by a simple timing device.

The bomber decided to take a day off—which did nothing to lessen the tension—and then upped the ante by planting one beneath a Speedway Police Department patrol car parked at an apartment house near Cunningham Drive. "Now we know we've got a real nut," Chief Copeland told the press. Local businesses began receiving phoned-in bomb threats that turned out to be hoaxes. Clearly, the real bomber preferred a strategy of complete surprise. The town was terrorized out of its collective wits. A woman who was living in Speedway told me, "The whole place was paranoid. If you saw a paper bag in the road, you'd veer into oncoming traffic to avoid running over the bag."

"There's no rhyme or reason to this thing. Police headquarters could be next," Chief Copeland said, reflecting such a lame grasp of the fundamentals of spin control that quite possibly there were citizens who hoped that would indeed be the next target.

As it happened, however, the next explosion destroyed Carl DeLong's right leg.

AND WITH that the bombings stopped. No more predictably than they had begun, they stopped, never to resume, as if the bomber had experienced a revelation: Well, I didn't mean to blow off some guy's leg, particularly some guy I've never met, so maybe I need a new hobby.

Carl DeLong and his wife, Sandra, had attended a football game at Speedway High, where their son, Steve, played on the freshman team. The game had ended, the players were in the locker room, and the DeLongs and other spectators were idling in the parking lot when Carl noticed a small brown-and-yellow gym bag lying on the pavement. His wife, who also received relatively minor shrapnel injuries to her legs, later recalled that as he approached the bag he made an offhand allusion to the bombings. There were conflicting reports as to whether he kicked the bag or merely nudged it with his foot.

The ATF analysis indicated that the fifth, sixth, and seventh bombs differed from their predecessors in that each appeared to have contained large quantities of .445-caliber lead balls, the marble-sized variety used in muzzle-loading weapons. The composition of the eighth bomb, ironically, was relatively benign. Had it also been packed with lead shrapnel, it almost certainly would have produced Speedway's fourth homicide in fifty-six years. Only by that warped standard could DeLong count himself lucky. One of his eardrums was shattered, and two of his fingers had to be reattached. The force of the blast lifted him into the air. "I remember looking down on the tops of cars and wondering why they were there," he later testified. "I stood up to take a step and fell down, hitting my head. I tried to get up again but fell." DeLong, by coincidence, worked at the same General Motors plant where Fred Scyphers had spent his career. He was a Vietnam veteran and was sufficiently familiar with traumatic limb injuries to instruct innocent bystanders on how to tie tourniquets around both of his legs. "I looked down at my right leg, and my kneecap was blown up on my thigh," he recalled. "My left leg was just shredded away to the bone. I yelled, 'Oh, God, get those kids out of here,' and tried to crawl away from there." Then he passed out.

A sifting of the debris turned up a piece of plastic embossed with the name of a manufacturer in Connecticut: the back casing of a sixty-minute Mark Time timer switch. Within a week, investigators had determined the Indianapolis distributor, pored over the store's receipts, identified three recent sales involving a total of fourteen timers, and interviewed employees of Graham Electronics. The timer switches were designed to turn off a flow of electric current, and one clerk described having explained to the buyer how to reconfigure a timer to do just the opposite—to open a circuit. When used in a time bomb, this would allow current to heat a blasting cap, causing the explosive material to detonate. The sales clerks were subjected to hypnosis, in sessions conducted by the same Marion County sheriff's deputy who had hypnotized the Scyphers murder witnesses. The posthypnotic interviews yielded details that enabled an artist to come up with a composite portrait of the buyer. When members of the Speedway Police Department saw the sketch, they recognized an image with which they had become familiar—the face of the same person they believed had arranged the killing of Julia Scyphers.

KIMBERLIN was placed under surveillance. Surreptitious photographs, taken as he entered and left the Good Earth, were then shown to the Graham Electronics employees, in the hope of identifying him as the buyer. Photo spreads were also presented to employees at retail stores where the lantern batteries and lead balls that went into the bombs were stocked. Physical evidence from the explosions went to ATF laboratories in Cincinnati and Washington; their thorough analysis would require several months. Minus eyewitnesses, building a case based on circumstantial evidence is necessarily incremental and time-consuming.

In the short run, what amounted to a culture clash developed among the law enforcement people who, in the wake of the first bombings, had been camped out in the Speedway police headquarters. Six of the eight bombs had exploded at sites that were engaged in interstate commerce—a sine qua non for federal jurisdiction. The U.S. Attorney, Virginia Dill McCarty, assigned the case to an assistant prosecutor named Bernard L. "Buddy" Pylitt. Despite Pylitt's exhortations against unauthorized discussions with the press, Chief Copeland blabbed promiscuously. ATF agents discovered that after engaging in conversations with Copeland—conversations they'd assumed were confidential—they could read their own words, anonymously cited, in the next day's newspaper.

Three weeks into the investigation, heralded by the front-page headline BOMBING SUSPECT IS LINKED TO MURDER, the *Indianapolis News* reported that a suspect was under surveillance, that he was a Broad Ripple businessman previously arrested on drug charges, and that the bombings were connected to the murder of Julia Scyphers, "who was fatally wounded at her home, which is near the scene of the third of the eight bombings." A front-page story in the next day's *Star* revealed Chief Copeland in remarkable form:

> Copeland expressed doubt about the bombing-murder connection . . . and hinted that federal authorities might be hindering his investigation by discussing it with the press. "Mrs. McCarty better do some explaining to someone because she's put everyone in a trick bag," Copeland said. "They better get their stories straight because they're jeopardizing our murder investigation." Copeland pointed out . . . that the idea of a connection between the two bizarre sets of crimes was pursued by both reporters and police during the bombing investigation. "We ran down all the tips and dropped it because we were chasing our tail," Copeland said. "If the ATF people have gotten on to him (a murder suspect), it would have been in the last day or two." Copeland acknowledged, however, that he did not know all the details of the federal end of the investigation. . . .

In at least one respect, Copeland's instinct was accurate: he didn't know what the feds were up to. His ignorance was not likely to diminish anytime soon, either, because that very day the U.S. Attorney ordered all federal personnel to relocate to an office in downtown Indianapolis. The feds, for their part, were busier than ever trying to figure out what Kimberlin was up to. During "the last day or two," their puzzlement had deepened. Kimberlin had been arrested at a printing shop on the west side of Indianapolis. He was apprehended by an FBI special agent who had no idea that the Speedway police and the ATF and the U.S. Attorney were interested in his peregrinations. For several hours after the arrest, he gave the FBI a phony name. Thus did one arm of the United States government—notwithstanding its mandate to monitor Kimberlin—fail to realize that another arm had taken him into custody.

NOR DID Kimberlin deign to clarify matters for his captors. Halloween was still a few weeks away, but Brett was already in costume. He had on navy-blue trousers, a medium-blue short-sleeved shirt with a sew-on cloth *Department of Defense Police* shoulder patch, and a gray wide-brimmed felt hat. The overall effect—especially the Smokey the Bear flourish of the hat—bordered on slapstick. The eventual charges against Kimberlin were impersonating a Department of Defense officer, illegal possession of military insignia, and illegal possession of a facsimile of the Great Seal of the President of the United States. The latter two offenses were so obscure that Kimberlin said his later search of case law turned up no other criminal prosecutions under the relevant statutes—a statistic that seems to fit the novel circumstance under which he managed to get himself busted.

Kimberlin and his partners in Texas had come up with a baroque ploy for bringing planeloads of marijuana into the States. Beeville was the home of a naval air base, and about thirty miles away was a rarely used and lightly manned naval auxiliary airstrip. In a maneuver Kimberlin said the smugglers had employed half a dozen times without a hitch, a World War II cargo plane that began its flight in Colombia would land at the auxiliary airstrip late at night, and its crew would be met by a group of confederates disguised as military officers. To gain access to the airstrip, the ground crew would arrive in trucks just as the flight was coming in, flash phony identification at the sleepy pair of genuine military sentries on duty, and announce they were there on top-secret Defense Department business. Then the convoy would meet the plane and unload the pot. The plane would refuel and head back to South America, while the trucks would head north to Indiana.

From the printing shop, Kimberlin had ordered counterfeit Department of Defense license plates and counterfeit military driver's licenses. This became necessary, he says, after similar equipment was lost during a prior escapade in Texas. From uniform and army-surplus stores in Dayton he bought his own getup, including the sew-on patch, as well as similar outfits for other crew members. At a shopping mall in Indianapolis he bought a supply of embossed plastic name tags. Kimberlin said the printing shop owner, John Dottenwhy, knew him and had done work for him in the past, though Dottenwhy later denied even having met him. In any event, the printer subcontracted the phony driver's licenses and a reproduction of the presidential seal. "I just wanted a copy of a very light presidential seal in the middle of a plain sheet of paper," Kimberlin told me. "In case I ever needed it. It wasn't being used for anything specific. I'd found it in the *World Book Encyclopedia*. I was in a library and saw the thing and I kind of liked it." The subcontractor shared with Dottenwhy his concern that Kimberlin might be engaged in illegal activities, which prompted him to call the FBI.

Late on the afternoon of 20 September, Kimberlin went to the printing shop to pick up his order. A well-built man—the FBI agent—was loitering unobtrusively near the counter. Dottenwhy politely apologized to Kimberlin for not having the job finished, but the scene became less polite as Kimberlin headed for the exit. The FBI man tackled him and bent one of his arms behind his back. With his free hand, Kimberlin wadded up and threw the prototype for the military IDs into a trash container. While being wrestled to the floor, he slipped the image of the seal into his mouth and began chewing and swallowing it, then got his car keys from his pocket and slid them beneath the photocopying machine.

The FBI agent had a backup, a special investigator from the U.S. Army, waiting in a car outside the printing shop. For the next few hours, Kimberlin said, he sat in their car and tried to charm them into letting him go. "I was pretty freaked out," he said. "But I played it cool. I figured I had this uniform on and I figured maybe I could work it out." The feds asked why he was wearing the uniform and, in general, what sort of scam he was running. "I'm not allowed to discuss it," he replied. This was not well received.

Kimberlin then tried a different tack. A government document later obtained under the Freedom of Information Act describes how Kimberlin had attempted to "talk the agents out of formally charging him with any violations in exchange for information which he had concerning . . . drugs [and] an Ohio millionaire businessman, and a Congressman of the United States." Kimberlin was referring to Dan Quayle, then running for a second term in the House of Representatives. The Ohio businessman was years later arrested on state drug charges, convicted, and sent to prison. These were promising and distinct bargaining chips, since Quayle and the businessman had nothing to do with each other. Because he wasn't sure whether the FBI would be willing to cut a deal, Kimberlin says he did not mention either Quayle or the businessman by name. And in fact, his captors weren't buying what he said he had to offer.

BEFORE taking Kimberlin downtown, the agents asked what he wanted to do with the ratty-looking white 1970 Chevrolet Impala, with blue vinyl roof, that he'd driven to the printing shop. Kimberlin tried denying that the car was his, but the backup outside had seen him drive up in it. For a number of reasons, Kimberlin said, he wanted to dissociate himself from the car, which had been bought in Dayton, Ohio, a week earlier for a few hundred dollars. "That was a throwaway car that we were going to use in a drug deal," he told me. "I wasn't even the person who bought the car; I was just using it. I knew my brother [Scott] had been driving the car for a couple of days and it contained some materials to use in a smuggling operation, like flares for lighting a runway. I had a Department of Defense police jacket and a rubber stamp that said *Top Secret* and some ID tags in the car, and I didn't want them to see that stuff." The keys that he slid under the photocopying machine opened the driver's door and operated the ignition, he later claimed, emphasizing that he never possessed the key that opened the trunk.

On balance, it had not been a good day for Kimberlin, and there was more unhappiness to come. At FBI headquarters, he was promptly deprived of his alias when another agent recognized him.

He called Forrest Bowman, his attorney for the perjury trial and, more recently, during the Scyphers murder investigation. Kimberlin was booked into a holding cell at the Marion County Jail, where the population was nearly all black. He immediately consulted the largest of his fellow inmates, he said, and for fifty dollars bought a night's worth of protection against predators. He also called an attorney whose expertise, said Kimberlin, was fixing parking tickets. The attorney came to see him late that night, and during their conversation Brett described the location of the Impala and explained that inside was a jacket with $3,500 in a pocket. If the attorney would have the car removed from the printing shop parking lot and towed to a safe location, he would pay him $500. Kimberlin says the attorney assured him that he'd take care of it.

The next morning, Kimberlin appeared before a U.S. magistrate for a bail hearing. Forrest Bowman argued that given the nature of the charges, all misdemeanors, the bond should be minimal. Despite the presence of a number of federal agents, who Kimberlin said "were going bananas," bond was set at a mere thousand dollars. Taxpayer money was hard at work that day in Indiana. Before the bail hearing began, the magistrate granted the FBI a warrant to search the Impala. Meanwhile, ninety miles south, a group of ATF agents and Marion County sheriff's deputies, acting without warrants, were searching Kimberlin's place in Jackson County. They went, at least in part, because the bombing investigation had produced information that Kimberlin had detonated explosives on the property. If the agents had limited themselves to surveying the grounds, seeking superficial evidence of an explosion, no search warrant would have been necessary. Self-restraint and legal niceties eluded them, however, so they opened an underground storage tank and discovered half a ton of marijuana, part of the Mexican load Kimberlin had been stuck with since the paraquat scare. DEA agents were summoned, and confiscated it. Perhaps to express annoyance that they turned up no bomb components—but mainly to torment Kimberlin and make it appear that he'd been ripped off by other dope dealers—someone in the posse attached a note to the front door of the house. With no apologies for lapses of punctuation or gentility, the note said: "Smoke this, however, please leave a little paper to wipe your fucking ass, Brett you prick!"

At eight o'clock that evening, Kimberlin was released from jail. Sandi Barton picked him up, they ate dinner at the Earth Garden, and then she drove him home to Eagle Creek. The next morning, he said, he went to the "safe location" where the Impala was to have been towed—a car dealership. He was unpleasantly surprised when told that the car had never been delivered, and after a round of phone conversations, he learned why: the FBI had impounded the vehicle. Early that afternoon, Kimberlin went downtown to meet with Forrest Bowman. Along the way, he said, he passed a newspaper vending machine and saw the *Indianapolis News*'s proclamation BOMBING SUSPECT IS LINKED TO MURDER.

"I saw this headline about the bombing investigation and I bought a newspaper and started reading it," he told me. "I think: Oh, this might be interesting. And then I read the first couple of paragraphs—about a Broad Ripple businessman—and I realize they're talking about me and I'm just floored. I didn't even read the rest of the article. I just ran to Bowman's office. He didn't know anything about it yet."

In his haste and alarm, Kimberlin added, he initially didn't focus carefully on the newspaper story's details—for instance, in the fourth paragraph: "It also has been learned that Federal officials have confiscated timing devices from a car reportedly owned by the suspect."

For a vehicle intended to be thrown away, meticulous attention was being lavished on this Chevrolet. Several FBI agents, as well as a peer from the ATF, Bernard (Ben) Niehaus, were present when the search got under way in the printing shop parking lot. The original warrant was limited to evidence related to the misdemeanor possession charges. The agents would later testify that after forcing open the trunk—and this would become central to the prosecution of the bombings case—they discovered objects that had nothing to do with the misdemeanors. Niehaus phoned a fellow ATF agent, Patrick Donovan, and described particulars that provided for yet another search warrant. The most provocative item Niehaus saw that morning was a black leather suitcase imprinted in gold with the initials BCK—the monogram of Brett Coleman Kimberlin. Inside, the government would one day explain to a jury, were four Mark Time timers. Each had been altered so that it was identical to the devices that triggered the bombs in Speedway.

14

A CERTAIN theory of the bombings crystallized at the moment when Kimberlin emerged as the prime suspect, and it went like this: The bombings were calculated to distract the Speedway police and derail their investigation of the Scyphers murder. The violence was appalling, and the unanswered questions about Kimberlin's involvement with the Barton family were quite unsettling; but the sequence of events, in its own grisly way, had a linear clarity and logic. The arrest at the printing shop, on the other hand, seemed to come out of left field. The unrevealed purpose of Kimberlin's masquerade—the smugglers ploy—was, in the larger context, rather tame. In the minds of the investigators who were trying to divine what was going on in the mind of the suspect, however, the episode introduced an unintelligibly queer element into the case. Given the evidence that had emerged thus far, they felt justified in assuming that any inexplicable behavior on Kimberlin's part was animated by motives as malevolent as the murder and the bombings.

The search of the Impala yielded, in addition to the timers, a six-volt battery, an ohm meter (for measuring electrical current), two twenty-five-pound bags of double-aught lead shot, three boxes of .445-caliber lead balls, four types of ammunition (approximately eighty rounds in all), and four gallons of Coleman lantern fuel. The government's agents had no basis for believing that the car belonged to anyone other than Kimberlin, nor were they disposed to regard its contents as innocuous.

Kimberlin would later explain—in his courtroom testimony and, adding refinements, in our conversations—that he'd driven the car from Ohio to Indianapolis but it hadn't been in his possession in the days immediately preceding his arrest. The lead shot, battery, lantern fuel, and ammunition, he said, must have belonged to Scott Kimberlin and his best friend, Scott Bixler. He would hypothesize that the lead shot might have been intended to weigh down portable lights on a landing strip during a nighttime smuggling run, and this could also account for the battery and the lantern fuel. The ammunition? Well, Bixler had always been preoccupied with guns. And the four altered timers inside Kimberlin's suitcase? These, along with the lead balls, which were inconveniently identical to the type used in three of the bombs, suggested a knottier mystery. Eventually, of course, Kimberlin would propose a tidy explanation for them as well.

AROUND DUSK, two days after the Impala was seized, Kimberlin and Sandi Barton were feeding horses at Eagle Creek when he noticed a car parked in the brush near the corral and surmised that its occupants were official visitors. While his mother called the sheriff and complained that poachers were trespassing on the property, Kimberlin said, he looked through his room "to see if I could find anything that might look bad, but I couldn't." Then Sandi drove him to a motel, which meant he was absent when a full search party showed up bearing a warrant seeking "firearms, ammunition, instrumentalities and other evidence associated with the fabrication of an explosive device." The following day, Kimberlin went to Jackson County and discovered that he was missing half a ton of marijuana and that whoever took it had left a truly unfriendly message on his front door. "There were only a few people who knew about that pot and I couldn't imagine any of them doing it," he told me. "I figured it was probably the feds."

Despite all this heat—"Things were coming at me like missiles from every direction"—Kimberlin said he sought refuge in his knowledge that he hadn't really done anything wrong, the printing shop raps being peccadilloes. Though he knew he was being watched—transparently atypical customers would check him out at the Good Earth and then, awkwardly, buy a single trifle—he did his best not to let the strain show. Above all, he said, he had "this weird feeling—it was obviously naïve—that I would never be arrested for the bombings because I didn't do them."

Citizens who read the newspapers were developing a contrary impression. The *Indianapolis News* reported that the suspect had been "identified by Speedway Police and Federal authorities as 'extremely dangerous' and a person 'who has all the money and connections he needs to have anyone killed at any time or any place.' " Four weeks after the first bombs went off, articles about the case began mentioning Kimberlin by name. The Eagle Creek search produced only a small amount of ammunition and no deadly weapons, but stories clearly leaked by the authorities speculated that Kimberlin might be connected to a wider range of crimes: cocaine dealing, drug-related shootings in Indiana and Florida, "an international drug-trafficking ring, operating from South America to Alaska." The seizure of the half ton of marijuana merited a front-page banner headline. A related article about the Jackson County property described "a secret tunnel leading to an underground bunker."

Superficially, Kimberlin got a break when, a week after his arrest at the printing shop, Forrest Bowman filed a probable cause motion with the U.S. magistrate for the searches of the car and the Eagle Creek house. The government responded abruptly and unexpectedly by dismissing the insignia and presidential-seal possession charges, and the motion thereby became moot. When Bowman persisted, the U.S. attorney opposed him on the ground that opening the probable-cause affidavits "would result in possible jeopardy to and harassment of government witnesses." The dropped charges, however, could be reinstated at the U.S. attorney's discretion, which meant that Kimberlin hadn't really got a break after all. The government strategy was to bide time, cultivate witnesses, and build an all-inclusive case: high-volume drug running, the Scyphers murder, the bombings.

When I first met Kimberlin, he spoke as if he possessed instant recall of the bombing case's complex minutiae. A couple of years later, however, as I was closely rereading all the pertinent newspaper clippings, I asked how he had reacted when the misdemeanor charges were dropped, and his response was anomalous: he said he couldn't remember any significant tactical maneuvering during or in the wake of the hearing before the U.S. magistrate. Rather, according to his recollection, "Forrest said, 'Nobody's ever been prosecuted for an army patch,' and I figured they looked at the statute and figured that out." Then Kimberlin told me that what had lodged in his memory most vividly was another morsel of Bowman's counsel: "Forrest told me, 'Brett, just go to work every day and go home every night and just follow your normal routines.' And that was it. I walked out [of the courtroom]. I was obviously confused. Here there'd been all this stuff in the papers and now they were dismissing the charges. I talked to Forrest about theories and he said, 'Brett, they obviously don't have a case against you. Moreover, they think you're not the bomber but are affiliated with him and you will lead them to the person who did it.' "

Following normal routines without deviation while being dogged was a practical impossibility for Kimberlin, since the routine he maintained was smuggling. His willingness to do so indicated an entrepreneurial zeal that superseded good judgment. Over the next few months, he said, he did "some really successful loads." He was using planes—DC-3s mainly—that could accommodate between one and two tons. His connection in Colombia, an expatriate American on friendly terms with several air cargo companies, wanted to fly bigger planes and bigger loads. Stepping up to a DC-4, for instance, could increase the cargo potential to five or six tons. Kimberlin was ready. If that went well, the connection knew where he could get his hands on a C-130, a converted military transport plane that could handle more than twelve tons. Kimberlin felt ready for that too.

Between October and December, he made three trips to Texas, each time for a week or ten days. He would stay with Papa Reyes in McAllen, or across the border, in Reynosa, on a ranch owned by one of Papa's friends. He called his family frequently, always from pay phones, but spent no more than a day or two at a time in Indianapolis. His mother agreed that he was prudent to make himself scarce. Carolyn was "so pissed off at all this crazy stuff people were saying, she thought it was highly inappropriate for me to be hanging around home." He rarely flew into or out of Indianapolis but instead used the airport in Dayton. He always bought plane tickets with cash, always under an assumed name. He kept in touch with Sandi by phone but felt that "with the estrangement she was having with her family, I thought the less time I spent with her, the more time she could concentrate on her family."

Sandi's family, though they tried, failed to persuade her that Kimberlin was capable of inflicting harm. Patrick Donovan of the ATF met with her two and a half months after the bombings, and interviewed her for five hours. She had seen Kimberlin within the past week; they had discussed grand jury subpoenas; she was convinced he wasn't the bomber. The night of the first four explosions, they had eaten dinner at the Earth Garden and then gone to Eagle Creek, where they fed the horses, watched television, meditated, and went to sleep early. During the bombings, Brett never expressed concern about becoming a suspect. To now read the things that were being reported in the newspapers seemed literally "incredible" to him, and Sandi concurred. Donovan deemed her replies "responsive but not truthful."

15

IN MID-NOVEMBER of 1978, Kimberlin was in Washington, D.C., where he had a mail drop and, he says, a girlfriend. But the mail drop was his priority. The goal of this visit was a passport, and to apply for one successfully he needed a local address. Under the circumstances, a passport issued in his real name would've been useless. He had cultivated the alias on his application—Christopher Columbus Shipley—with his usual resourcefulness. Kimberlin had gone to a library, consulted death notices published in a southern Indiana newspaper during the 1950s, and lifted the name of the genuine Christopher Columbus Shipley, a boy who was born around roughly the same time as he was, but who had died as an infant. On half a dozen other occasions, Kimberlin used this ruse to obtain birth certificates. As Shipley, he acquired a fraudulent Social Security card and driver's license and, eventually, the passport. His motive was uncomplicated: on short notice, he wanted to be able to launch himself on a foreign excursion of indefinite duration. "I thought it was an appropriate response to all the ludicrous things people were saying I'd done," he told me.

A MAN who introduced himself as Chris Shipley was arrested by members of the Kingsville, Texas, Police Department and deputies from the Kleberg County Sheriff's Department in the early morning hours of 16 February 1979. He was driving a four-door 1979 Chevy Silverado pickup truck with Indiana plates, a vehicle owned by Kimberlin but otherwise unregistered. Not much time elapsed before the Texas lawmen confirmed that Shipley was in fact Kimberlin, and they already had a clear idea of his line of work. In Kimberlin's estimation, his delivery into their grasp was the result of remarkable good luck on the law's part and remarkable bad luck on his. As usual, the government had a contrary perception.

The arrest at the printing shop five months earlier did not convince Kimberlin that the Department of Defense stratagem was no longer viable. He said his cohorts in Texas employed it on two or three subsequent occasions, each time without a hitch. However, the whole thing had to be shelved when one of Kimberlin's partners, Francisco Gonzalez, fell out with someone in Beeville who was aware of the scheme. Kimberlin said Gonzalez also got into a disagreement with the Internal Revenue Service, which caused him to want to lie low in general. As a consequence, though Kimberlin normally avoided getting his hands dirty at the point of entry, he agreed to manage the ground crew receiving a DC-4 full of Colombian marijuana. The plane was due to arrive at a makeshift airstrip, a neatly mowed pasture twenty miles west of the town of Alice, at eleven o'clock the night of February 15. If everything proceeded according to plan, by eleven-thirty the cargo—five and a half tons, in forty-five-pound bales packed inside chicken-feed sacks and wrapped in burlap, all of it destined for Indiana and Kimberlin's distribution network— would be unloaded into two box trucks and driven to a stash house, and the refueled plane would be en route back to Riohacha, Colombia. But nothing proceeded according to plan.

In Alice, almost two weeks earlier, Scott Bixler, accompanied by Kimberlin, had rented a single-engine Cessna that they used to determine the navigational coordinates the DC-4 pilots would rely upon. They rented the plane again a few days later and flew to McAllen, along with William Bowman (no relation to the attorney Forrest Bowman), a steady customer from Dayton who had come to work on the ground crew. Kimberlin said that he and his crew had also readied a backup airstrip and that at the last minute he elected to switch to that contingency. But when he called his connection in Colombia to propose a change of plans, it was too late—the pilots were already on their way. During their eight-hour flight, a cold front arrived in south Texas, producing mist and an impenetrable fog. The ceiling fell below four hundred feet. Not only were the pilots unable to find the landing strip but the weather made even the Texas Gulf coastline indiscernible. Kimberlin and the others waiting at the landing strip never even heard the plane's engines.

When air traffic controllers at a naval air base in Kingsville picked up the DC-4 on radar, the pilots explained that they were low on fuel and were directed to a civilian airport in Cotulla. The DC-4 was the only craft on Kingsville's screen that had not filed a flight plan—a fact sufficient in itself to generate suspicion. The plane was also flying without lights. As it happened, the U.S. Customs Service had already alerted the controllers, after the smugglers had been seen taking on a load of aviation fuel in their tanker truck. Despite the poor visibility, a Customs Service plane was in the air above the landing strip. A second CS plane took off from Alice to meet the DC-4 in Cotulla. Meanwhile, evidence that things had gone awry was accumulating in several counties; along with the steady drizzle, it was raining marijuana. Rather than touch down in Cotulla with eleven thousand pounds of contraband, the pilots had decided to unload in midair. A lot of bales wound up in Lake Corpus Christi. Plenty of others were found by ranchers, who joked the next day about feeding the stuff to their livestock. One bale landed at the main intersection of Alice. Another crashed through a barn roof and killed a goat. Eventually, the detritus of this fiasco was recovered along a swath one hundred twenty-five miles long. POT BOMBS FALL ON AREA FARMS was the front-page headline in the *Corpus Christi Caller-Times*.

When Kimberlin describes the accoutrements he had lined up for this operation, he sounds wistful, as if imagining a happy outcome that barely eluded him. From a high-tech surveillance firm in New Jersey he had treated himself to "night scopes, parabolic microphones, high-frequency radios—about ten thousand dollars' worth of this shit." Wearing night scope goggles, he could identify a porcupine waddling through the mesquite a hundred yards away. In addition to these toys, a police search of the airstrip and the crew's vehicles produced strobe lights, walkie-talkies, a twenty-thousand-watt searchlight, bulletproof vests, handcuffs, two Taser electric-shock-inducing stun guns, several military uniforms and berets bearing *United States Special Forces* and *Special Officer* and *Department of Defense* and American flag patches, U.S. Postal Service uniforms, a 20-gauge shotgun, a .22-caliber revolver, a .22-caliber automatic pistol with a silencer, a .38-caliber revolver, a box of silicone-sealed .38-special shells loaded with cyanide, a gas mask, and eight pairs of panty hose. One piece of equipment the mission lacked was a high-frequency radio aboard the plane. Both the pilots and Kimberlin had VHF radios that would have enabled them to communicate within about a fifty-mile range. When the plane strayed far off course, however, communication was thwarted. Kimberlin had no way of knowing that the flight had been diverted to Cotulla.

It was almost one-thirty in the morning when Kimberlin finally decided to leave the landing strip. If he'd cleared out half an hour earlier, he claimed, he never would have been caught and his life would have turned out differently. Kimberlin knew that he and Bixler and the landing strip were under surveillance from the moment they rented the Cessna for their reconnaissance. He knew that Customs agents followed him to McAllen. He knew they rented rooms in the same motel where he and his crew stayed in Alice. But he refused to conclude that the venture was doomed. Eventually, the government put together a case file whose narrative terminated, inexorably and triumphantly, with Kimberlin squarely nailed. No matter. In Kimberlin's cosmology, he was always several IQ points and steps ahead of the law. If the plane had landed on time and unloaded and departed without mechanical complications, all would have been right with the world.

A miniconvoy—the box trucks and the tanker—tried to exit unobtrusively down an unpaved road. They had traveled less than two miles when they were greeted by Customs agents and Duval County sheriff's deputies. Kimberlin and two passengers—Bixler and Bowman—were about a mile behind the convoy. Kimberlin saw flashing lights and announced he was making a detour. Bixler announced he was bailing out on the spot. He disappeared into the darkness, not to surface again for five months.

Kimberlin and Bowman quit the road and set off bumpity-bump across the range, headlights doused, destroying fences in the process. An unmarked car carrying two Customs agents picked up their trail at the point where Kimberlin came through a fence onto a numbered highway and began heading toward Kingsville, fifty miles east. The agents said they pursued Kimberlin at a hundred miles an hour but couldn't gain ground; Kimberlin said no such chase took place. The agents said they could hear the tread separating on one of their tires and feared a blowout. They radioed ahead for help. In Kingsville, Kimberlin briefly lost them in a residential neighborhood. The ride ended a mile south of town, when patrol cars from Kleberg County and the Kingsville P.D. blocked the road. "Real Texas pigs" was Kimberlin's phrase for the men who took him into custody. "They pulled Bowman and me out of the truck," he told me. "They slammed us up against the truck. I said, 'Why are you stopping us?' I said, 'You have no right to do this.' "

AFTER an abbreviated night in a rural county jail, Kimberlin and
Bowman and a crew member named Louis Sill, a part-time trapper
who had been hired to scout the landing-strip location and then stuck
around to unload the plane, were driven to Corpus Christi by a pair
of DEA agents. The trip took about an hour, and along the way, Kimberlin said, he asked the agents, "What are we under arrest for?"

"Conspiracy with intent to possess and distribute marijuana,"
one agent replied.

"What marijuana?" asked Kimberlin.

"We got your airplane," said the other agent.

"What airplane?"

"Your pot was scattered all over south Texas."

"What pot?"

In this manner Kimberlin learned what had taken place the previous night in the sky above while he waited anxiously in the mud
below. After being delivered to the Nueces County Jail, Kimberlin,
Bowman, and Sill were taken down the block to the federal building
for arraignment before a U.S. magistrate. Bail for Bowman and Sill
was set at fifty thousand dollars; for Kimberlin, the amount was a
quarter of a million in cash or surety bond. Though he'd brought
plenty of walking-around money to Texas, when he checked his wad
he saw that he was short by $240,000. The delight of the Indianapo-
lis authorities at the news of Kimberlin's capture was tempered by
concern that he might make bail before a grand jury in Indianapolis
could indict him for the bombings. U.S. ATTORNEYS SEEK TO KEEP KIM-
BERLIN IN JAIL, ran a headline in the *Indianapolis News* five days after
his arrest. The reason was simple: the U.S. attorneys feared he would
flee. Kimberlin himself told me their apprehensiveness was justified.
If he had made bail, jumping was "a distinct possibility."

KIMBERLIN'S second day in Corpus Christi, he received a visit from
Ben Niehaus, the ATF agent who had witnessed the search of the
Chevy Impala in Indianapolis. According to the report he filed, their
conversation lasted five hours. By the time Niehaus returned the following day, eager for more, Kimberlin's court-appointed lawyer had
intervened, and the prisoner was no longer available. Niehaus's re-

port began by stating that he had properly informed Kimberlin of his constitutional rights, then continued:

When advised that the topic of conversation was to be the Speedway bombings, he said he was happy to talk about them. He said he wasn't involved and was willing to do what he could to cooperate with the government to prove his innocence. He stated he would be willing to take a polygraph examination concerning the bombings. When asked if he had not been offered a polygraph on other occasions and had agreed to submit to the test until the actual time of the examination and then refused, he said that was true, and that he had done so on his attorney's advice. When asked if that would happen this time, he said "probably, but I don't know." He also said he would like to testify before the grand jury concerning the bombings.

Kimberlin also said he was being framed for the bombings and the ATF should be looking for three FBI agents who had a vendetta against him, and had been conducting the vendetta for years. He said the vendetta was a result of the fact that his father, an attorney for Public Service of Indiana, had won the largest cash settlement in history from the United States government, and that the only way the government could get back at Mr. Kimberlin was through Brett. When asked the names of the three FBI agents, Kimberlin refused to name them and said he refused because he is not a snitch and did not want to get anyone in trouble even if they were framing him.

Kimberlin also said he had read in the newspaper that the bombs were set off as pranks by racing fans and wondered if this had been explored.

Kimberlin also said he did not know where he had been each night during the bombings except that he had been doing the floors at his health food store part of the time.

Relative to Sandra Barton, Kimberlin told me to "get off her goddamn back." He said she is "straight as an arrow" and would not do anything wrong. He also referred to Julia Scyphers, Barton's mother and the victim of a murder, as a "goddamned bitch." He further stated that if we wanted to find out who murdered Mrs. Scyphers, we should consider Sandra Barton's brother-in-law in Austin, Texas, who Kimberlin said was a CIA agent.

As to his arrest in Texas on federal drug charges, Kimberlin stated that he had just happened to be out in the desert in the middle of the night and was wrongly arrested. He said the situation would be cleared up. When asked why he presented false identification at the time of the arrest, he said that he had not given false identification to the agents, they had found it in his wallet.

Several days after being arraigned, Kimberlin attended a bail-reduction hearing, by which time he was represented by Gerald Goldstein, a high-dollar drug-defense specialist from San Antonio. His fellow defendants, all of whom had comparatively modest bond requirements, were already free on bail. The morning of the hearing, Kimberlin said, he was placed in a holding tank in the federal courthouse. From the wire-mesh cell, he could see a teletype machine spitting out paper with his name on it; the machine chugged away, it seemed, for at least half an hour. Kimberlin couldn't make out the content of the printout. The thought occurred that it might be a copy of his criminal record, but his wasn't *that* extensive. When he was taken before the magistrate, an assistant U.S. attorney was holding the document. "It was about thirty feet long, it was dragging on the floor," Kimberlin said. The government attorney, Robert Berg, explained to the magistrate that the dispatch, freshly arrived from Indianapolis, was the text of a thirty-four-count federal indictment: six of the eight bombings; possession of unregistered firearms; unlawful possession of explosives; unlawful transport of ammunition; unauthorized possession of military insignia and the presidential seal; impersonating a federal officer; and the injury to Carl DeLong. The Texas magistrate declined to reduce Kimberlin's bail. Meanwhile, in Indiana, the barrier to freedom had been raised by several multiples. The judge there had set a separate bail of $800,000.

THE DAY of the indictment, 28 February 1979, was, for Indianapolis, uncommonly eventful. Though an account of the grand jury's action occupied a prominent position in that evening's *Indianapolis*

News, the lead story was actually the Scyphers murder—back on the front page after several months. Mug shots of Kimberlin and his companions in Texas had been forwarded to the Marion County prosecutor's office, where investigators "acting on a hunch" had compiled a photo lineup that was shown to Fred Scyphers. The result was immediate: Scyphers identified William Bowman as the man who seven months earlier had come to his front door and put a bullet into his wife's skull.

OHIO MAN IN COURT, DENIES SCYPHERS GUILT, blared a *Star* headline the next day, above an account of Bowman's appearance in Municipal Court during a probable-cause hearing. "Huh? I've never heard of these people before," Bowman said when the judge read the murder charge. Bowman had an alibi. The day of the killing, he said, he was visiting his parents in Florida. Prosecutors then leaked to the press records of a call to Bowman's house the day of the murder, from a pay telephone Kimberlin was known to frequent. Bowman's alibi changed: he had indeed been home and was able to produce half a dozen witnesses who had seen or spoken with him between 9:00 a.m. and 4:00 p.m. Bowman's wife's rabbit had been sick that day, some of the witnesses recalled. A dated veterinarian's bill was introduced as proof. Scyphers did not waver. He had gotten three good looks at the suspect: "I could tell by his face and his eyes. The expression in his eyes. That's the same man."

"I never saw you before in my life," Bowman replied from the defense table.

Bowman's attorney declared that his client stood ready to submit to a polygraph, and the prosecutor declared that he stood ready to submit the case to a grand jury. After posting a fifty-thousand-dollar bond, Bowman went home to Ohio.

In time, the prosecutor was forced to acknowledge that Bowman had indeed twice passed a polygraph, though by then the issue had been eclipsed by another circumstance. For a murder trial to proceed, eyewitness testimony was essential, but Fred Scyphers was no longer available. Nine days after confronting Bowman in the courtroom, he collapsed and died of a stroke.

"OH, I'M SORRY. Things don't look very good at all," Kimberlin said Marinus Dykshoorn had told Jessica Barton nearly a year before, when she'd asked the psychic about her grandfather's prognosis. Now both her grandparents were dead, relations with her mother were greatly strained, and Kimberlin, once a major presence in her life, was locked up in Texas. Not since Julia Scyphers's murder had he been allowed to see or speak with Jessica. From his jail cell, he composed a handwritten letter which he addressed "To the Family" and sent care of the Scyphers residence in Speedway:

> My sincerest condolences to your family. I just heard the tragic news about Fred. I'm truly sorry that his life ended with such sorrow. He is surely much happier in the absolute with his lovemate of so many years. I have always held a special place in my heart for Fred. I remember when he came over to pick the kids up and he'd have to wait and I would always go out and talk to him, usually about cars, and every time I was always awed by his handshake—so strong and sincere—and his wonderful smile and his warm heart. No matter what his problems were, he radiated love eternal. . . . Jessica loved him above all else and always when she talked of him she smiled a warm smile. Sandi's heart was broken when he rejected her. She would cry, sometimes for hours, and ask why or what she should do or could do to make him understand her undying devotion to her mother and father. Fred was a very good man, one who had my deepest respect. He wanted so much to get the slayer of his other half that he made a mistaken identity. I'm sorry for you and for Bill [Bowman], for he did not do it. But I'm glad for Fred, for he died with peace and peace is what he wanted so dearly. . . . He deserves the best, for he truly earned it. He is a lucky man to have passed on into eternity and his soul will live on forever as will the love he brought to you.

The letter reached its destination. Sandi Barton's sister, Louise Crosby, opened it and showed it to her nieces, and then they did the only thing that made sense to them: they turned it over to the federal government. This was how Kimberlin confirmed, years later, that the letter had indeed been received: a photocopy arrived in a packet of documents he'd requested under the Freedom of Information Act. I once asked him whether he had expected to receive an acknowledgment of gratitude for his expression of sympathy.

"I didn't expect a reply," he said. "I knew the family hated me. I just wrote it because it was the way I felt. It was my true feelings. I felt bad for Jessica too. They hated me because of what they were told by the government. They didn't hate me because of anything I did to anybody. I've always been very consistent with the family. I've been consistently myself. That's just the way I felt when I heard Fred died. I wanted to express my feelings. I would like to have heard back, but it didn't hurt my feelings not to. To hurt my feelings after what I'd been through would have been pretty hard. I'm pretty immune to that stuff. I'm a forgiving individual. To this day, if anybody in that family wanted to be on speaking terms, wanted to be nice, I'd forgive them."

16

URING his two-month stint at the Nueces County Jail, Kimberlin received a letter from his brother Scott. The envelope bore an Atlanta postmark and a phony return address—Scott never lived in Atlanta—and the message inside was signed "Scizoid," a nickname Scott embraced without bothering to learn its proper spelling. The purpose of the letter, evidently, was to elevate Brett's spirits: "Things seem a bit more positive these days," Scott wrote. "Your case there [Texas] is being widdled [*sic*] at by your attorney. Motions filed and some evidence surely to be dropped. The Government has fucked up already so you may get off on technicality. Will not go in detail but it looks good. Circumstantial evidence even less on rediculous [*sic*] charges in Indy. Many will be dismissed. Perhaps all!"

Scott's own situation hardly merited optimism. The marijuana that got dumped over south Texas included more than a ton that had been reserved for him—merchandise he had been counting on to help dig him out of a financial hole. Business administration was never Scott's strength, and his account with Brett was seriously in arrears. The previous summer, just before the paraquat scare, Brett had fronted him a few thousand pounds of Mexican pot. Though he worked hard enough to find buyers for about a ton, at the moment of Brett's arrest Scott still owed more than $100,000. The loss of the airplane and its cargo immediately set Brett back a quarter of a million dollars, not including legal bills that began with a $25,000 retainer and would eventually run well into six figures. Since childhood, Brett had provided Scott with practical guidance and emotional ballast, but now there was not much he could do for his younger brother, financially or psychologically. Brett's inaccessibility, and the circumstances that had rendered him inaccessible, seemed to deprive Scott of his stability.

Many years later, when Carolyn talked with me about Scott, her description was as rosy and syrupy as her accounts of Brett's boyhood: "Scott was the first one of the children to graduate from college. He was the third-born but the first one to graduate. Scott was so sensitive. He just tried to do the right thing. He was a tremendous athlete. Natural athlete. Long-distance swimmer, great baseball player."

Carolyn's pride in Scott's completion of his college degree offered a poignant illustration of how well he concealed from his parents large segments of his actual life. One truth was that he had been only nominally a university student. Except for courses in psychology, his undergraduate major, he subcontracted to fellow students the distractions of attending classes, writing papers, and taking exams. His primary occupation was incompatible with serious scholarship: he was supplying marijuana to a significant portion of the population of Bloomington, and he also served regular customers in California, Kentucky, Florida, Ohio, Michigan, and Alaska. "He was in Bloomington for the living, for the enjoyment, not for the schoolwork," a friend of his told me. "Scottie was very motivated, he did a lot of things, but most of them were scamming."

Like Carolyn, Scott's friends held warm, heartfelt memories of him. When in peak form, "he was a jammer, he was full of energy, ambition, outgoing, he was definitely different from most people you ran into on the street." Everyone else in the family, including Carolyn, practiced Transcendental Meditation, which, in theory, required abstinence from drugs. Scott never bought into it. He faced life overmedicated and without a mantra. He restricted himself mainly to dealing pot and Quaaludes, but as a consumer he was less discriminating: downs, hallucinogens, cocaine. Brett's technique was to operate in the shadows, and he knew how to deflect other people's curiosity about his illicit activities. Scott was less calculating, and his idiosyncrasies and dubious habits were more overt. He dressed down—T-shirts and blue jeans, nothing fancy—but when he was rolling in dough he enjoyed inviting pals to a pinkie-in-the-air French restaurant in a bank building in downtown Indianapolis, where they ordered hundred-dollar bottles of wine with their dinners. Afterward, he would cruise home in a '65 Chevy or one of the other pitiful junkers he felt comfortable driving—a car that, a day or two earlier, might have had fifty grand in the trunk.

"Working continually in your behalf," he wrote in the letter from Atlanta. "Have acquired some funds and hope to get more." Some fellow dealers from Bloomington had a place in Gainesville, Florida, and by the time of Brett's arrest Scott was spending most of his time in an apartment he'd rented there. In June, Cynthia Kimberlin and her friend Lori Levinson went to see Brett in Corpus Christi, and he dispatched them to Brownsville and McAllen to collect debts. Later that summer, Scott paid for a cash-scavenging junket the women made to Bermuda, where he had a shrimp boat to sell as well as drug partners who owed him more than $20,000. Some of the money they came up with—$14,000 in all—went to a pair of Miami lawyers who, Brett had been assured by another prisoner, could arrange to have him freed on bail. With the combined Texas and Indiana bails exceeding a cool million, what the Kimberlin family needed was several '65 Chevy trunkloads of liquid assets.

Scott Bixler, the only Texas conspirator to escape the dragnet, made his way down to Gainesville, where Scott Kimberlin helped him find a place to stay. While Cynthia and Lori were in Corpus Christi, Carolyn Kimberlin joined them. One day, in her motel room, Carolyn was talking on the phone with Scott, who was reassuring her that everything in Texas would work out all right; since he had Bixler under control, the charges against Brett were certain to be dismissed. Then Cynthia and Lori rushed in and said they'd just seen Bixler in the motel coffee shop, sharing a table with ATF agents Pat Donovan and Ben Niehaus.

A TRIAL on the Texas charges was set for mid-July, five months after Kimberlin's arrest, then pushed back to early August. As the trial date approached, Kimberlin said, he received a list of potential jurors, and he happened to show it to a fellow inmate named Felipe Sanchez, a veteran pot dealer from the Rio Grande Valley. Referring to one name on the list, Sanchez told him, "Brett, I can't believe it. This is my cousin." Kimberlin then asked, "Can you get to your cousin—you know, with money?" Through an intermediary, he said, Sanchez arranged for Kimberlin to pay a $5,000 bribe. Justice, however, was neither as swift nor as cheap as Kimberlin would have liked. The sensational elements of the case—the chase, the bales of marijuana falling from the clouds—had generated extensive media attention, and seventy-four of eighty-one members of the juror pool said they'd heard or read about it. Without bothering to entertain any other pre-trial motions, the judge ordered a change of venue to Houston.

Kimberlin was transferred to the Harris County Detention Center, on the outskirts of Houston, and there he was given a job as a file clerk in the classification department. The sheer volume of paperwork, its tedious redundancy, and its overriding purpose, he said, exposed him to what he regarded as systematic patterns of injustice and inspired what he thought of as "my revenge." Whenever the lieutenant in charge and the other clerks turned their backs, Kimberlin started shredding documents—"tens of thousands of fucking documents." After a busy shredding session, "I'd have this huge bag of documents and I'd have to sneak them down the hallway when nobody was looking and put them in the trash barrels at the end. You could see me hauling this huge bag like Santa Claus down the hallway—almost too big to carry."

In late August, Kimberlin appeared before federal District Judge Woodrow Seals, petitioning yet again for a bond reduction. Superficially, Kimberlin seemed caught between the competing interests of prosecutors in two jurisdictions. Government attorneys in both Texas and Indiana were eager to crucify him, but the Indiana sanctions were potentially far more severe. As long as he was being held in Texas, the U.S. Attorney in Indianapolis had no urgent reason to formally arrest and arraign him. Kimberlin said he wanted to go on trial *first* in Indiana, adding that he assumed acquittal was inevitable. Even if he was subsequently found guilty in Texas, he further assumed, the judge would impose a light sentence, perhaps limited to the time he'd already been incarcerated. Carolyn and Greg attended the bond hearing, and their presence aroused Judge Seals's sympathy. "Unfortunately, in this courthouse the people who suffer usually are the parents, the wives, and the close relatives," the judge said. "I think they are the type of parents that would probably exhaust all of their resources down to selling their home to make a bond."

Rather than holding Kimberlin in lieu of the original surety bond, which required a nonrefundable deposit of $25,000, Judge Seals reduced both the amount and the terms, enabling Greg and Carolyn to spring their son with $5,000, which moreover was refundable if he didn't flee. Still, from the perspective of the court, this was a low-risk proposition. No sooner had Kimberlin posted the bond than he was arrested on a warrant arising from the bombing indictments. He would now head north for arraignment and could go free while awaiting trial only if he could meet the requirements of an $800,000 bond, or any lower amount that the court in Indiana might decree. Five days later, he was placed on an airplane bound for Indianapolis. Brett would've enjoyed manning the controls himself, but the U.S. marshals who were his escorts had harnessed him with a restraining device—a sophisticated cuffs-and-shackles called a "black box"— that instead took control over his immediate destiny.

KIMBERLIN'S expectation that he would proceed expeditiously to trial in Indiana was unfulfilled. This resulted, he contends, from his having been sandbagged by both prosecutors. Pretrial transcripts suggest conflicting interpretations of what the courts and the government attorneys intended. During the Texas bond hearing, for example, Judge Seals speculated that a conviction in Indiana would "wash out this offense one way or another"—since even if Kimberlin was also found guilty of the drug charges, any sentence would presumably run concurrently with the bombings sentence. Nevertheless, the judge set a trial date for October 15, which was six weeks away. The Indiana case had an early-November trial date. When October 15 rolled around, Kimberlin was still in Indianapolis, residing in the Marion County Jail. His lawyers, Richard Kammen and Michael Pritzker, had filed a number of motions, including one for a continuance. "We were seeking a continuance until after the first of the year," Kammen recalled. "We had to do a lot of investigation—check out the documentary evidence, locate various witnesses." Other pending motions included requests to change the venue to Chicago, to examine potential jurors on an individual basis, and to suppress certain evidence (including that gathered from the Chevy Impala and from Kimberlin's Mercedes-Benz). Kimberlin told me that it was actually the government that wanted to delay the Indiana trial. Despite the investigative work that had led up to the grand jury indictments several months earlier, he said, "The government knew they had no case, they were still trying to manufacture evidence and find witnesses who would perjure themselves."

On October 22, Kimberlin's lawyers filed an application for a bond reduction and the government filed its response. The matter was still unresolved when, on October 31, Judge Seals signed a writ ordering Kimberlin back to Texas. The trial there, having been briefly postponed, was due to begin within two weeks. The morning after the Texas writ arrived in Indiana, a bond-reduction hearing took place in the courtroom of Judge James Noland. Its outcome, according to Kimberlin, amounted to "a wink and a nod" on the part of the judge.

"The Texas court . . . had jurisdiction of the defendant prior to the time that this court ever attached any jurisdiction to him," Judge Noland noted; in other words, if Texas wanted him back, well, they had first dibs and they could have him. Bond was reduced from $800,000 to $450,000, but Kimberlin was given no time to come up with the money. All Saints' Day turned out to be his last day in Indianapolis for a long while. The next morning, he was flown back to Texas.

WHEN Kimberlin returned to the Harris County Detention Center, he wound up alone in a basement cell he called "the dungeon." This second episode of solitary confinement, he said, made the first seem like a long weekend at a health spa. Kimberlin's "attitude" might have been the problem. Or there may have been a misunderstanding; the U.S. marshal's office would later maintain that Kimberlin was placed in isolation because his father had expressed concern for his safety. Or, actually, there might have been, explicit or implicit, a calculated disregard for his sense of comfort and well-being. For whatever reason, as Kimberlin wrote in a letter to Judge Seals a few weeks later, his sojourn in solitary reduced him to a demoralized frame of mind that severely undermined his judgment. He went on to describe the conditions:

> It was not a protection cell, it was totally isolated, the room was approximately 6′ × 7′ and kept dark except for a few hours per day if I was lucky. The only human contact was when they shoved food through the door or gave me a towel. I was not allowed "any" phone calls nor the privileges given other inmates. The cell was infested with rats and cockroaches. Since I had nothing to do, I kept track of how many times I would see one of these "critters." During one 24-hour

period, I counted 147 roaches and 17 rodents, not including the times I brushed them off me at night. Also, I was awakened twice each night by the deputies who would ask me simple questions like "What is your name?" or "How are you feeling?" or "What is your number?" and then tell me to go back to sleep. I got very irate after several nights of this harassment and told them not to wake me up any more and put a big note on my door reminding them. It did no good and, when I questioned them about why, they told me that the "higher echelon ordered it."

When Kimberlin recounted this experience for me in 1992, he included these embellishments: the cell had shrunk to five by six; it was bitterly cold; the toilet was broken and he had to insert his arm into the bowl to drain it; the place smelled like a sewer, and the stench forced him to tie a towel over his nose in order to sleep; there was neither hot water nor soap; the food was inedible; when he asked a guard why he was thus confined, he was told that he had killed a policeman; though not suicidal himself, he noticed hanging from a wall a noose that had been used by a previous occupant.

Eleven days passed before the date of his trial arrived. The preceding evening, he met briefly with his attorney, Gerald Goldstein. Their conversation culminated in Kimberlin's electing to plead guilty to one count of conspiracy to possess with intent to distribute approximately two tons of marijuana. The other charges would be dropped, and he wouldn't have to testify against his fellow conspirators. Later, Kimberlin would complain that Goldstein, who has served as president of the National Association of Criminal Defense Lawyers and is an adjunct professor of law at the University of Texas, provided ineffective counsel, that their plea discussion lasted only half an hour, and that he was insufficiently apprised of the consequences of his decision. Goldstein said that their meeting on the eve of the guilty plea was indeed brief, but added that this wasn't their first exploration of the general topic. "We had certainly talked about this considerably before—his guilt and whether they could prove it," Goldstein recalled. "The conversations at the time of the plea were much more pragmatic."

Four of Kimberlin's codefendants, some of whom had been out on bail and none of whom had been locked in "the dungeon," also pleaded guilty the same day. Judge Seals had a duty to ascertain whether Kimberlin grasped the implications of his plea. He reviewed the potential penalty—five years and a fifteen-thousand-dollar fine and a minimum two-year parole term—and then put both Kimberlin and Goldstein through a litany of pro-forma questions. Among Kimberlin's replies were several that later would prove inconvenient.

Judge Seals: Have you ever been under the care of a psychiatrist or received treatment for mental disease?

Kimberlin: No, sir.

Judge Seals: You have an attorney here. I know him quite well, Mr. Gerald Goldstein. Are you satisfied with him?

Kimberlin: Yes, very much so.

Judge Seals: Have you had sufficient time to consult with your attorney about the law and facts of this case and your plea of guilty?

Kimberlin: Yes, sir.

Judge Seals: Have you had sufficient time to investigate the law and facts, Mr. Goldstein?

Goldstein: Yes, I have, Your Honor.

Judge Seals: Does your client understand the nature of the charges pending against him?

Goldstein: I believe he does, Your Honor. He has been able to assist me in his own defense. I believe he understands the nature and the consequences of these proceedings.

Judge Seals: Does he have sufficient present ability to consult with you with a reasonable degree of rational understanding?

Goldstein: I believe he does, yes, Your Honor.

Judge Seals: Does he have a rational as well as a factual understanding of the proceedings against him?

Goldstein: I believe he does, Your Honor.

Judge Seals: In your opinion, is he now mentally competent?

Goldstein: Yes, Your Honor.

Judge Seals: Are you pleading guilty because you are guilty, Mr. Kimberlin, or for some other reason?

Kimberlin: Yes, sir, I am guilty.

WITHIN two weeks, Kimberlin had changed his mind. This was the import of the letter to Judge Seals in which he catalogued the indignities of dungeon life. In the concluding passage, he wrote: "I have talked with Gerry Goldstein as well as other Houston attorneys about withdrawing my plea. I am certain that it was made under duress in an abnormal state of mind without enough legal counseling, and that I was misled or misunderstood some very important aspects of the plea. Therefore, I beg this honorable court to allow me to withdraw my guilty plea or in the alternative to dispose of this case with 'time served' so that I can receive a reasonable bond on the other case."

In accepting Kimberlin's guilty plea, Judge Seals had set a sentencing date less than two months away. Kimberlin would later aver that his guilty plea included an explicit quid pro quo that no sentence would be imposed until a verdict had been reached in the bombing case. Such an arrangement would have meant that his guilt in Texas could not be used to impeach him in Indiana, and he would thus be far more inclined to take the stand in his own defense. Analyzing this protracted to-and-fro with hindsight, Kimberlin would view it through this lens: The prosecutors in Indiana were engaged in an unscrupulous manipulation, the object of which was to make certain that he not go free on bail before standing trial for the bombings. And the government was further determined that the Indiana case not get under way until his malefactions in Texas had become a permanent blot on his record.

ON 5 JANUARY 1980, Kimberlin filed a formal motion to withdraw his guilty plea. The trial of the two pilots who had flown the DC-4 from Colombia to Texas had recently ended in a mistrial after the jury failed to reach a verdict. This development encouraged Kimberlin's belief that he had cut a dumb deal. He further reasoned that the motion to withdraw made him immediately available to begin his trial in Indianapolis, though of course the government had different ideas. Judge Seals took the motion under advisement. Kimberlin's next stratagem was to fire Gerald Goldstein and replace him with Jerry Patchen, another well-established Houston criminal-defense attorney. When Patchen proposed that Kimberlin be examined by a Houston psychiatrist who would assess his mental state at the time of the guilty plea, the government's attorney, Robert Berg, countered with a motion to consign Kimberlin to the U.S. Medical Facility for Federal Prisoners, in Springfield, Missouri, for a ninety-day psychiatric evaluation. The judge signed an order to that effect, and Kimberlin arrived in Springfield in mid-February.

Kimberlin: "Indiana put pressure on Berg to send me to Springfield. The real reason they sent me to Springfield, instead of having me examined in Houston, was because they had this informant—a professional informant—and they would put him in prison to try to get people to confess to crimes. This guy's name was George Balboa. George Balboa was put right next to me, in the crib in Springfield. The government sent me there because I told them that, you know, I was forced to plead guilty in the dungeon, with all the rats and torture and everything. So this was a way to retaliate against me, but also to put the snitch in with me. So they put this Balboa in with me and he starts befriending me and going to lunch with me and never leaving me alone. And he started interrogating me about my crimes in Indianapolis, my charges. He did all kinds of things that I thought were weird, but I'd never been in federal prison before, so I didn't really know at the time. I just started figuring that there was something wrong with this guy, that he was an incredible con man or he was an agent. Then somebody came into the prison and said, 'That guy's a fucking snitch, and he works for the U.S. Attorney's office in New York.' So anyway, Balboa kept getting all these visits. Well, I found out later that the visits were from the ATF agents in my case— Donovan and Niehaus. And they would feed him all these questions to ask me."

KIMBERLIN'S assertion that the court had the discretion to order a psychiatric evaluation in Houston was technically correct, but the inferences that flowed from the decision to send him to Springfield seem not to be supported by facts. "I don't have any recollection of anyone putting pressure on me to send him to Springfield," Robert Berg told me. "If they had, by nature I would have resisted. Mainly, the economics of the situation influenced me. To do this in Houston would have meant paying for a twenty-four-hour-a-day guard. On top of that, the court would have to pay for a psychiatrist. These guys at

Springfield were already on the government payroll. And as a prosecutor, I would want him examined by doctors who had exposure and experience dealing with people who had been charged with crimes."

And Balboa, though indeed a snitch, was not the puppet that Kimberlin imagined him to be. As a result of litigation initiated years later by Kimberlin, evidence emerged that Balboa, rather than acting for the government, was a freelance speculator. Having determined that Kimberlin was a man in need, Balboa contacted an investigator he knew in the office of the U.S. Attorney for the Southern District of New York; this man, in turn, got in touch with the U.S. Attorney for the Southern District of Indiana. Donovan and Niehaus were dispatched to Springfield, met once with Balboa, and concluded that he had nothing of value to tell them. No one from the U.S. Attorney's office in Indianapolis ever spoke with Balboa, nor did the government ever compensate him with regard to Kimberlin. Nevertheless, this endeavor did prove rewarding for Balboa. Before determining that he wasn't a trustworthy ally, Kimberlin had become sufficiently convinced that Balboa had "friends in high places" and could fix the outcome of the Texas case that he agreed to pay him $2,500.

LESS than the full ninety-day observation period was required for the medical staff in Springfield to render an opinion. A report signed by the hospital's chief of forensic psychiatry concluded that Kimberlin "was not suffering from mental disease or defect and was mentally competent to stand trial in that he had a rational as well as factual understanding and could communicate with his attorney." In early May, in Judge Seals's courtroom—a week and a half after being returned to Houston—Kimberlin formally withdrew his motion to withdraw his guilty plea. In other words, he reverted to the bargain that had been struck when he emerged from solitary confinement. During this hearing, Jerry Patchen elicited from Dr. R. H. Eisaman, a staff psychiatrist from Springfield, the following testimony:

> Patchen: Based on your observations and the tests that you conducted on Mr. Kimberlin, did you form an opinion as to whether or not he was a violent-type individual?
> Dr. Eisaman: This was not specifically addressed by the court at that time. However, I think I can safely say he is not a violent-type individual.

Patchen: Could you tell Judge Seals whether or not you consider Mr. Kimberlin, then, a threat to society?

Dr. Eisaman: No, I do not consider him a threat to society.

The authorities in Indiana were unmoved. At the request of Patchen, Judge Seals agreed to defer sentencing for ninety days, which theoretically might have allowed the bombing trial to take place in the interim—but only if the U.S. Attorney in Indianapolis formally issued a writ of habeas corpus. Not surprisingly, no writ was forthcoming. Anticipating this recalcitrance, Kimberlin said, he decided to take matters into his own hands. He had rejoined the general population at the Harris County Detention Center and was available for a work assignment, but his old job in the classification department was filled. Instead, he went to work in the front office as an intake-outtake clerk. He would type paperwork related to incoming prisoners, and when a prisoner was about to be released, he would type that paperwork as well. When he had been at the job only a short while, the thought occurred: "Fuck it, I can release *myself*." Kimberlin decided that Memorial Day weekend, when staffing levels were low, offered the ideal opportunity. He typed a release form, forged a U.S. marshal's signature, and stashed it away. The document designated his release for 12:01 a.m. on a Saturday; no staff member, he reasoned, would be inclined to call a marshal at home at midnight to inquire if the release form was legitimate. For extra measure, he removed all the marshals' home phone numbers from the Rolodex in the front office. "I figure what they're going to do is let me out the front door, I call a cab, and I'm history," he said. "I had money out there on the street. I could leave the country. I had a fake passport, fake driver's license, and all that shit."

The Wednesday before he intended to pull this off, he said, a prisoner named Henry Lake was brought from one of the regular units to an individual holding cell in the front office, complaining of stomach pain. When Kimberlin went to Lake's cell to see if he needed anything, the pain had become more acute. He said he spoke to the lieutenant on duty and explained that Lake required assistance, and the lieutenant replied, "Ah, fuck him." Later that night, Lake died. According to Kimberlin, the lieutenant and "three or four of his goons" had entered Lake's cell and spent ten or fifteen minutes beating him. Afterward, when Kimberlin "went back down there to check on him to see how he was doing," Lake lay motionless on the floor. Kimberlin said he informed the lieutenant of Lake's condition and an ambulance was summoned. Before Lake was placed on a stretcher, "he was in a fetal position and they had to pry him apart." Though Lake's death was attributed to appendicitis, Kimberlin thought otherwise. "I was so outraged at this thing," he said. "You know, the injustice of it." The next day, Kimberlin encountered an FBI agent who was accompanying a prisoner to a court hearing. Kimberlin said he confided to the agent his belief that Lake's civil rights had been terminally violated, and the agent told him, "We'll look into it."

Kimberlin: "Well, the next thing I know, Friday morning, I'm on a bus getting transferred to the fucking Harris County Jail, downtown. This was the day before I'm getting ready to escape. I mean, it's terrible luck, you know? What happened was the fucking FBI told the goddamn lieutenant that I snitched him out, and so to punish me and to get me away they put me down there in the fucking city jail."

Kimberlin did not have to stay for long in this new domicile. On June 11 he returned to Judge Seals's courtroom for sentencing. He had abandoned his effort to go to trial first in Indianapolis, he said, because "I was worn down by eighteen months of torture, basically." He was also relying upon Judge Seals's reputation for leniency, to which several friends and family members also appealed with epistles on Brett's behalf. Among them was Carolyn's memorable testimonial that depicted a selfless humanitarian who spent so much time plowing snowy driveways throughout the neighborhood and pulling stranded motorists out of ditches that it was a miracle he had any time left over for smuggling pot. Bob Landman, who had become Kimberlin's partner in the Good Earth, wrote to acquaint the court with the defendant's "belief in a sober, industrious, and healthy way of life." Kimberlin's old girlfriend Susan Harvey, who was by then a law student, wrote that the time he'd already spent behind bars had provided ample deterrence and punishment, and that "allowing him to rejoin society as soon as possible would be the most beneficial to him."

Carolyn appeared in person the day of the sentencing and testified that Brett was "the backbone of the family." She continued, "We love Brett very much. He is a successful businessman, a hard worker and he has sometimes worked fourteen to sixteen hours a day in his businesses. I would like to have my son back home. I'm very proud of him. He has a lot of potential, intelligence and creativity. But most important of all, he is a caring, loving human being who shows great concern for his fellow man."

Judge Seals heard all these entreaties, as well as a peroration by Kimberlin's attorney, and, without pausing to offer editorial comment, revealed that he was in a less indulgent mood than usual. He gave the defendant four years and sent him home to Indiana, knowing that the prosecutors there were eager to give him plenty more.

17

THE UNITED STATES government invested three years and enormous expense in prosecuting Kimberlin for the Speedway bombings and ancillary offenses. This excruciatingly protracted, bitterly fought process generated three separate jury trials—one of them the longest in the history of the Southern District of Indiana—as well as copious publicity, a dramatic appeal, and civil litigation that continues to this day. Contrition and mea culpa, on the other hand, have been in scarce supply. The abiding subtext has been a pair of opposing mythologies: the Evil Kimberlin versus the Evil Government. Across the years, Kimberlin has grasped every opportunity to burnish the latter concept, a task that proves laborious for both him and his audience. What most taxes the stamina of a tolerant listener is Kimberlin's unrelenting insistence that evidence of guilt is not an issue worth pursuing, and that what merits scrutiny and redress is the purposeful effort to deny him justice.

On 26 September 1980, slightly more than two years after the most unsettling week in Speedway's history, opening arguments were delivered in a trial that consolidated relatively minor charges (impersonating a federal officer, and the insignia and seal possessions) with the far more serious bombing and explosives offenses and the grave matter of Carl DeLong. The Honorable James E. Noland was the presiding judge, Buddy Pylitt and Kennard Foster appeared on behalf of the government, and Kimberlin was represented by Michael Pritzker and Richard Kammen.

Pritzker—who came from Chicago and didn't mind explaining that he happened not to belong to the megabucks branch of the Chicago Pritzkers—had formed a law firm, along with Gerald Goldstein and several other lawyers, that was active in drug defense cases. One of the partners operated out of Denver, a couple of others were in Washington, another was in Atlanta, and Goldstein covered Texas.

With ample geographic diversity, they hoped to attract clients from a broad national market. Pritzker had a background in general criminal defense work, as did Kammen, who had been in practice in Indianapolis for several years. After the Texas case, with Kimberlin feeling less than well served by Goldstein, it perhaps isn't surprising that he should have become critical of Pritzker and Kammen's performance. This would manifest itself as personal antipathy—a sentiment that, particularly on the part of Pritzker, was reciprocated. "I'm sure that in a social setting he could be very charming," he said of Kimberlin many years later. "I just couldn't take him." Still, a thirty-four-count indictment was on the table, and Kimberlin was footing the bill.

Pylitt explained in his opening statement that, lacking eyewitness testimony, the government would prove a circumstantial case. "There will be no witness who saw him put together a bomb and there will be no witness who saw Mr. Kimberlin place a bomb," he said. "Nevertheless, the evidence will show that Mr. Kimberlin did make those bombs and did place those bombs." Pylitt likened the case to a jigsaw puzzle consisting of "many small pieces that may seem insignificant, but when put together there will be an overall picture." The government needed a week to present its version, during which it called thirty-nine witnesses. The jigsaw puzzle that Pylitt promised to construct included these elements:

(1) Enough fragments were recovered for chemists and other experts to testify that at least six of the bombs consisted of an altered Mark Time timer that, when triggered, allowed current to flow from a six-volt Ray-O-Vac battery to an electrical blasting cap that was inserted in an explosive material called Tovex 200, the trade name of a dynamite substitute manufactured by du Pont. Each bomb contained between one and three sticks of Tovex. Three of the bombs also contained .445-caliber lead balls.

(2) Two cases, each containing fifty sticks of Tovex and fifty electrical blasting caps, had been sold in 1975 to Stephen Miller, an architect and contractor who was building Kimberlin's house in Jackson County. (Kimberlin's 1973 felony conviction for perjury barred him from directly buying or possessing explosives.) Initially, the Tovex was used to excavate the underground storage containers that Kimberlin, in his survivalist speculations, had incorporated into the project. About seventy sticks of Tovex remained, and workers tes-

tified that the unused explosives had been left in the cargo area of Kimberlin's pickup truck. Vacuum sweepings and swabbings of both Kimberlin's 1976 Mercedes-Benz and the 1970 Chevy Impala he drove to the printing shop were submitted to a laboratory, and both cars tested positive for Tovex residues.

(3) Six witnesses agreed to be interviewed by law enforcement agents while under hypnosis; none was hypnotized during Kimberlin's trial. Four of these witnesses worked for Graham Electronics Supply, whose three retail stores in Indianapolis were the only local vendors of Mark Time timers. Store records showed that, starting ten days before the first bombing and continuing through the day of the next-to-last bombing, Graham Electronics sold fourteen Mark Time timers. (Eight were used in the bombings, four turned up in Kimberlin's luggage in the trunk of the Chevy Impala. The trial testimony did not account for the whereabouts of the two other timers.) On one occasion, the customer gave his last name as Martin. Ten days later, with a different salesman, he identified himself as Thomas. A few days after that, at a different store, he said his name was Johnson. One Graham salesman recalled showing "Martin" how to modify a timer so that when it completed a cycle it would open rather than close a circuit.

The three boxes of .445-caliber lead balls that were found in the trunk of the Chevy Impala bore labels from the Broad Ripple Sports Shop, which, like the Graham Electronics outlet where most of the timers were sold, was only a few blocks from Kimberlin's health food store. Tracy Carr, a clerk at the sports shop, had submitted to hypnosis and given a statement. In court, he testified that he had sold a dozen boxes of lead balls to someone resembling Kimberlin. Asked if he could identify him, he said, "I sure can," and pointed to the defendant.

The sixth hypnotized witness was an automobile mechanic named Andy Jones, who testified that while working on Kimberlin's Mercedes the day of the seventh bombing, he had seen in the trunk two boxes of .445-caliber lead balls, a six-volt Ray-O-Vac battery, a du Pont pamphlet describing the safe handling of explosives, and a one-gallon can of Coleman fuel. Under hypnosis, Jones had offered a subjective appraisal of Kimberlin. He described him as having "the personality of a foreskin," then elaborated: "Dressed like a turkey. He's got bib overalls on, and . . . looks like a fruit from

I.U. [Indiana University] and he's . . . kinda looks like a jerk. He's got Earth Shoes on and bib overalls. He's a little guy. His arms are about the size of my wrists. He looks down a lot. He doesn't want to look you in the eye and talk to you. . . . The guy's a wimp. He's got a twenty-thousand-dollar car, treats it like a garbage can."

(4) Two authorized searches had turned the humble Chevy Impala into the government's Golconda. John Yara, a special agent for the FBI, identified a number of items that were found during the first search. These included Kimberlin's wallet, Selective Service card, library card, pilot's license, and driver's license; Marinus Dykshoorn's business card; Kimberlin's membership card in the Florida Association of Private Investigators; a bag of five stamped metal badges that said *Security Officer;* a pair of rubber stamps reading *Top Secret* and *Department of Defense United States;* a radio scanner tuned to the frequencies reserved for the police and fire departments of Speedway, the police department of Brownsburg (a western suburb, where Sandi Barton lived), and the Marion County Sheriff's Department; a light-blue uniform shirt with a shoulder insignia reading *Department of Defense Police* and a pair of dark-blue uniform trousers; and assorted police gadgetry, including a blackjack, handcuffs, and a Mace-like chemical spray.

Kimberlin, wearing a uniform with Department of Defense insignia and using the alias Drew Jacobs, had gone to the printing shop to order and later to pick up Defense Department driver's licenses and license plates and a replica of the Presidential seal. He used the same alias when he wore the uniform in two other stores, where he bought embossed plastic name tags and emergency flares. A woman named Andrea Mazzone, a waitress in Dayton, Ohio, and an occasional girl-friend of Kimberlin's, described how she had picked up a uniform that he'd ordered from a Dayton store in the name of Jeff Duvall and, in her apartment, tried on. Her sister, Dorene, was also present in the apartment, and she recalled seeing military insignia sewn on the sleeve of the shirt. A photograph of Kimberlin in full regalia, taken at the time of his arrest, was introduced into evidence.

(5) The ATF agents Bernard Niehaus and Patrick Donovan testified further about the Chevy Impala. Two days after Kimberlin's arrest, Niehaus said, the keys to the car, which Kimberlin had tossed beneath a photocopying machine at the printing shop, were found by a customer and turned over to the FBI by the shop's owner. Niehaus

received two keys on a paper clip, he told the jury, and one of them opened the driver's side door and started the ignition.*

Donovan described objects that were found in the trunk during the second search: Kimberlin's suitcase, the four timers, the lead balls, a six-volt battery, two twenty-five-pound bags of small-gauge lead shot, an ohmmeter, four one-gallon containers of Coleman fuel, and two boxes of Remington .223-caliber shells. The shells—the type used in a Colt AR-15 rifle, the semiautomatic version of the military M-16—bore price tags from a store in Dayton. Also found were a box each of 30.06 rifle and twelve-gauge shotgun shells. The ammunition had no apparent connection to the bombings, and the government made no effort to indicate any causal link. Rather, it was established that the car had also been bought in Dayton and that Kimberlin had driven it in that city and in Indianapolis—circumstantial evidence of unlawful transport of ammunition. The Tovex residues in the Chevy Impala and the Mercedes were introduced to prove unlawful possession of explosives and to tie Kimberlin to the bombs themselves. Also found inside Kimberlin's suitcase were a copy of *Hustler* and a book titled *Strange Powers of Unusual People*. These had no real evidentiary value, but the government investigators seemed pleased by them nonetheless.

(6) Carl and Sandra DeLong, who were wounded by the eighth bomb, described their injuries. This was the occasion of Carl's chilling account of being thrown into the air by the blast, landing and then trying to walk, falling to the pavement and banging his head, and seeing that his left leg was "just shredded away to the bone." The damage to his right leg was even more severe, and he recounted its amputation, the rebuilding of his left leg, the reattachment of two fingers and an ear, and the repair of a shattered eardrum. He was still removing bomb fragments from his body, he said. He handed Pylitt a bottle of same.

KIMBERLIN presented an alibi defense. In anticipation, the government had called Jan Confer, the wife of one of his partners in the Earth Garden Café, who testified that Kimberlin often ate at the restaurant and that he had been there every day during the bombings.

---

* See Appendix, pages 370–1.

This testimony suited Kimberlin fine. His alibi witnesses were mustered to depict someone going about his routines in a casual, unhurried manner, whose behavior was inconsistent with the furtive actions of a clandestine bomber. A woman named Lorraine Fint, who identified herself as a longtime friend of Kimberlin's, testified that on September 2, the eve of the fifth bombing, Kimberlin had taken her teenage daughter, Lisa, and her teenage niece, Helen Conwell, shopping for school clothes and to dinner in Indianapolis. The Fint family lived in Martinsville, midway between Indianapolis and Bloomington. Kimberlin brought the girls home about 11:00 p.m. and remained there forty-five minutes or an hour, Mrs. Fint said. The bomb exploded at 12:15 a.m., September 3. The driving time from Martinsville to Speedway was at least half an hour.

Lisa Fint and Helen Conwell gave corroborating testimony. Kimberlin had picked them up in Martinsville around three o'clock on a Saturday, they said. Their first stop was the Good Earth, where he bought Helen a pair of Earth Shoes. They went to an equipment rental store and Kimberlin, who planned to refinish part of the floor at the Good Earth over the Labor Day weekend, picked up a floor-sanding machine. At a mall called Castleton Square, he bought a blouse for Lisa and jeans for both girls. Their next stop was the Glendale Shopping Center, where he bought them custom-made T-shirts.

There was a Graham Electronics store in the Glendale Shopping Center, and three Mark Time timers were sold on September 2—exactly when the alibi witnesses placed Kimberlin there. The store manager, who handled the transaction, testified that the customer had a light beard, wore a yellow T-shirt with a nondescript design, and was accompanied by two girls. Under direct examination, Lisa Fint said Kimberlin had been wearing a plain T-shirt. Before a grand jury, she had testified that he had a scruffy facial growth—a beard that "was just like in the beginning." At the trial, both girls testified that the T-shirt emporium was the only store in the shopping center that they entered with Kimberlin. After leaving the Glendale Shopping Center, they said, he dropped the floor sander off at the Good Earth, took them to dinner at a seafood restaurant, and then drove them home to Martinsville.

Lorraine Fint testified that she had met Kimberlin at a party in 1972, when he would have been eighteen and she twenty-five. At the time, she said, she was separated from her husband, Rodney, and she and Kimberlin dated "on and off." Kimberlin told me, however, that this aspect of her testimony was fiction; they never had any romantic involvement. The truth, he said, was that he knew Lorraine because Rodney was one of his steadiest marijuana customers.

SANDI BARTON provided Kimberlin's most elaborate alibi, a running account of his activities that seemed impossible to reconcile with the government's portrait of him as the lone bomb plotter and planter. On September 1, for example, according to her testimony, she met him at his house early in the evening, went to dinner with him at the Good Earth, returned to the house around nine o'clock, fed the horses, and briefly chatted with Carolyn (who had invited a male friend over for dinner) before retiring for the night. Sandi and Brett did Transcendental Meditation for twenty minutes. After he fell asleep, around ten or ten-thirty, she stayed awake reading for forty-five minutes or an hour. He slept in his bedroom and she spent the night on a mattress in the hallway outside. By daybreak, four bombs had detonated. The next morning he drove her to work, and along the way they stopped at a drugstore, where he picked up a newspaper that reported a series of bombings in Speedway. She was concerned, she testified, because "my parents lived there and my children were staying there." (Actually, given her mother's murder, only one of her parents still lived there.)

Sandi's testimony concerning the day of the fifth bombing dovetailed with that of the Fints. After taking the girls home to Martinsville, Kimberlin had come by her apartment in Brownsburg and asked her to spend the night at his place in Eagle Creek. She couldn't pin down the exact time—only that it was very late, after midnight—when he knocked on her door. While she got her things together, he meditated. When they arrived at Brett's house, Carolyn was still awake and in the kitchen. By now, it must have been 1:00 a.m., so they went to sleep.

In the morning, he got up early because he had to get started on the floor-refinishing at the Good Earth. In the late afternoon, he called and asked her to meet him again that evening at his house. Sandi arrived around 8:00 p.m. and had spent about fifteen minutes visiting with Carolyn when Brett came in. He was filthy with sawdust and floor stain. After he had showered, she gave him a back rub, and "he was asleep in two minutes." Again, she stayed the night. Shortly before 10:00 p.m., the sixth bomb went off, at the Speedway Lanes bowling alley.

They spent much of the next day, Labor Day, together. Sandi couldn't account for Kimberlin's activities after 3:00 p.m., but it didn't matter—the bomber was observing the national holiday. She helped Brett deliver his Mercedes to a repair shop the following day, then went to work, and at the end of the day she drove him back to the repair shop to pick up the car. During this interval, Andy Jones testified, he'd seen incriminating evidence—the lead balls, the du Pont explosives pamphlet, the battery—in Kimberlin's car. Also that day, the customer who called himself Johnson bought five timers from Graham Electronics. The seventh bomb exploded that night. The next evening, Carl DeLong lost his leg.

Sandi characterized Brett as "one of my very best friends." The duty to determine precisely what that implied was not included in the judge's charge to the jury. Most likely, they were as puzzled by the anomalous nature of this relationship—what amounted to a chaste intimacy—as anyone who had pondered the topic. In her testimony, Sandi mentioned that late in the summer of 1978 she had felt lonely because a serious boyfriend had moved out-of-state. She also alluded to Kimberlin's dalliance with Andrea Mazzone and spoke of his attachment to her younger daughter.

The intense but almost ineffable entanglements in Sandi and Brett's lives could be rendered for the jury only in elliptical terms. During cross-examination, Pylitt managed to extract the information that Kimberlin and Sandi's younger daughter had traveled alone together to Disney World, Mexico, and Hawaii. For Pylitt to delve extensively into *that* particular anomaly, however, would have risked a mistrial. In the courtroom, the Scyphers murder was off-limits, and the theory that early on had galvanized the government's investigation—that the bombings grew out of the murder—could not be delineated. At the conclusion of the trial, newspaper interviews with jurors indicated that their deliberations were free of musings about the murder. Several jurors simply hadn't realized that Sandra Barton was Julia Scyphers's daughter. The *Indianapolis News* quoted one: "I didn't know about it until I got home and my wife told me. Had we known, there might have been some more questions about her testimony." Thus the apparent lack of motive for the bombings increased the prosecution's burden of proof.

EVEN without Kimberlin's alibi witnesses, the government's case appeared less than airtight. Connecting Kimberlin to the Chevy Impala was crucial, and despite the proliferation of his personal effects in the car, the defense could argue that a link was missing. The car had been sold in Dayton by a dealer named Donald Wiltheiss to someone calling himself Ray F. Eaton. Presuming that this was one of Kimberlin's aliases, the government subpoenaed Wiltheiss to testify. When asked to point out Eaton in the courtroom, Wiltheiss selected an attorney who had wandered in and was seated in the spectator section. Later, the defense presented a handwriting expert who compared the purchaser's signatures on the car's sales documents with samples of Kimberlin's penmanship and concluded that "Ray F. Eaton" was someone other than the defendant. (This analysis was accurate; Eaton was the pseudonym of a drug colleague whose true identity never surfaced in court.) For Kimberlin to be convicted, Ray F. Eaton and the bomber did not have to be one and the same. On the other hand, "reasonable doubt" was all Kimberlin's lawyers needed to evoke. Deprived of the latitude to put the defendant himself on the witness stand—and thus to open a Pandora's box of complications—Pritzker and Kammen recognized that their best hope was to attack the government's credibility.

Only one of the six hypnotized witnesses, the mechanic Andy Jones, had encountered an unveiled Brett Kimberlin. A great deal rode on how the others described the buyer of the bomb components. Statements given by these witnesses in the wake of hypnosis were introduced into evidence. Tracy Carr, who sold the .445-caliber lead balls, alone seemed on the mark. He described the buyer as five feet five or six inches tall, with "sparse hair on his cheeks, as if he was starting to grow a beard." The four Graham Electronics employees described a white male dressed in a T-shirt and blue jeans, slender, in his early or mid twenties, with an incipient beard—characteristics that fit Kimberlin—but neither the height nor the weight dimensions really matched. Two witnesses said he was five eight, one said five nine, another said between five six and five eight. Two estimated his weight at 145 pounds, a third put it between 140 and 150, and a fourth at 135. His hair was variously "brown," "dark," and "dark brown." One witness mentioned dark eyes. The defense rebutted that Kimberlin's eyes were not dark but blue. His hair, though brown, was not especially dark. Most notably, Kimberlin stood five five and weighed only 110 pounds. In court, Kimberlin wore a white suit instead of a T-shirt and blue jeans; he was boyishly clean-shaven. From the witness stand, two of the Graham Electronics employees identified him as the man who bought the timers but admitted they weren't certain, another clerk was unable to identify him, and the fourth wasn't asked to do so.

At the time of the trial, hypnosis was frequently employed in Indiana as a criminal investigative tool. Elsewhere, the suitability of posthypnotic testimony had become the object of a burgeoning debate in medical-legal circles. Scientific evidence had accumulated that for posthypnotic testimony to be taken seriously, the hypnotist must work independently of either side in a case; information given to the hypnotist before the hypnosis must be recorded; the witness must present the hypnotist with the facts as he remembers them before hypnosis; contact between the hypnotist and the witness must be videotaped; and only the hypnotist and the witness can be present when there is contact between the two. In Kimberlin's case, however, the hypnotists were neither independent qualified psychiatrists nor psychologists but state and local police officers involved in the bombings investigation, who had received their training at weekend seminars. ATF agents were also present in the room. In five of the six instances of hypnosis, none of the information given to the hypnotists before the sessions was recorded, nor were any of the sessions recorded on videotape.

Kimberlin's lawyers presented two psychologists to discredit the practice of hypnosis altogether. These experts bracketed the proceeding: one taking the stand at the outset of the trial in an unsuccessful effort to block the testimony of the six hypnotized witnesses, the other appearing at the conclusion of the defense case to negate the damage they had inflicted. In the interim, Judge Noland had decided to allow the testimony, his only concession to the defense being to warn the jury not to give any unusual weight to their statements. The first psychologist, Dr. Milton V. Kline, testified for more than four hours, during which he cited American Medical Association policy opposing teaching hypnosis techniques to non–health-care professionals. He went on to catalogue the shortcomings of hypnosis: its ability to enhance blocked memory and inability to enhance normal memory; the likelihood that a person under hypnosis will distort his recollection with pseudo-memories or confabulations; the tendency of the hypnosis subject to be influenced by overt or covert suggestions to please the hypnotist; the danger that hypnotism can imprint faulty memories which the subject adopts as actual memories and which cannot be fairly challenged by normal cross-examination. Having examined the transcripts of these particular sessions, Dr. Kline asserted that one witness—the man who sold five timers to the five-foot-nine, 145-pound "Thomas"—was probably not in a hypnotic state. Dr. Eugene Levitt, the second expert, reiterated Dr. Kline's basic arguments.

Paradoxically—or, perhaps, typically—the lawyers on both sides wanted it both ways. The government vouched for the reliability of posthypnotic testimony but desired a generous margin of error. And the defense, though arguing that posthypnotic testimony was unreliable, sought to exploit the fact that several witnesses had summoned from their memories a suspect who did not necessarily resemble Kimberlin.

"PUT YOURSELVES back in September 1978, when Speedway was a quiet town and Carl DeLong had two legs and two ears," Buddy Pylitt, presenting his summation, implored the jury. "Go back and put all the items back in Brett Kimberlin's car, and you will have to convict." Two weeks earlier, in his opening statement, Pylitt had promised: "The evidence will show that Mr. Kimberlin did make those bombs and did place those bombs." But Pylitt and his fellow prosecutor, Kennard Foster, though they had laid open an incriminating chain of events and physical evidence, were never able to provide a graphic image of Kimberlin making or placing a bomb. Michael Pritzker hammered at this point in his closing remarks: "What they hoped would be proved hasn't been proved. They would have you guess or speculate. The government wants us to bring all of the threads of this case together. We can't. We just don't know, and you can't infer and you can't guess." Richard Kammen played the same note one last time: "You've got to be sure in your heart, soul, and mind. You can't be guessing. If you're guessing and speculating, then there is doubt."

The jury, sequestered throughout the trial, began its deliberations around dinnertime and put in four hours before retiring. They worked through the next day without reaching a verdict on the major counts. The proverbial "hopelessly deadlocked" had not been uttered, but at eleven o'clock the following morning Judge Noland declared a mistrial. The jury's labors had not been fruitless: Kimberlin was acquitted of the single count of possession of ammunition by a convicted felon, and convicted of the nine counts related to unauthorized possession of military insignia and the presidential seal. Still, twenty-four charges remained unresolved. Immediately, the government announced that the case would be retried.

In 1992, Kimberlin told me that the jury had been on the brink of acquittal on the bombing charges. The vote had been 9–3 or 8–4, momentum running in his direction, when Judge Noland, fearful that the government was about to lose, intervened prematurely with his ruling. The source of this information, he said, was a juror who had spoken with one of his attorneys. When I first heard this, in 1992, I believed him. Only a year or so later did I come across an *Indianapolis News* clipping, published two days after the mistrial, that caught me short. The lead paragraph stated: "Nearly all the jurors in the Brett Kimberlin Speedway bombings trial felt Kimberlin had a hand in the bombings, but a number of them believed the government failed to prove its case beyond a reasonable doubt, according to comments by individual jury members to the *News*."

David Rohn, who wrote the story, had covered the case from the beginning. On many occasions, Kimberlin told me that he felt the Indianapolis media were in general gratuitously and occasionally viciously hostile to him, but he often cited Rohn's coverage as a balanced and reasonable exception. Rohn recalls that he obtained a list of jurors, in exchange for which he agreed to protect their anonymity, and that he interviewed about half the panel. "Several of the alternate jurors, who heard the entire case but did not participate in the ultimate deliberations, voiced the strongest feelings of believing that the government had proven its case," Rohn reported. The jury members, he added, "were fairly evenly divided on whether to convict or acquit. A slight majority reportedly favored convicting . . . on at least some of the bombings charges."

Kammen's memory of the trial was less vivid than Kimberlin's— he had taxed his brain with a few other cases since then—but he didn't recall an acquittal near at hand. However, he did support Kimberlin's contention that the tide seemed to be running in his direction. "Usually, a defense attorney grabs the chance for a mistrial," he told me. "In this case, though, I think we objected. We really wanted Noland to let them deliberate." At the opposite end of the spectrum was the federal investigator who told me: "I remember hearing from people not associated with the defense team that it was 10–2 for conviction. The problem with the bombings case was that when the jurors compared the circumstantial evidence with the direct evidence from the military insignia charges, the bombings case seemed less impressive."

THE *Indianapolis Star* story that reported the government's intention to retry the case included this cryptic sentence: "Kimberlin's attorneys countered that any effort to retry Kimberlin would run into 'some problems,' but they refused to comment further." Meanwhile, Pritzker and Kammen had some problems of their own with Kimberlin, and their representation of him was about to terminate. All along, they had resisted his advice on strategy and tactics. When I asked Kammen what was distinctive about Kimberlin as a client, he replied, "His self-destructiveness. Brett's judgment almost always seemed to us to be bad and counterproductive. Brett was unusual because he was so bright and intuitive, and yet his judgments seemed to be so wrong." Pritzker told me that on the eve of closing arguments, he dispatched Kammen to visit Kimberlin in jail to ask what points he wanted covered in the summation. Kimberlin didn't realize this gambit was guided by inverse logic. "I wanted to make sure I didn't use a single thing Brett wanted us to say," Pritzker said. "He has the worst taste of anybody I've ever met."

Pritzker's valedictory chore in Kimberlin's behalf was an appearance at his sentencing for the military-insignia and Presidential-seal possession counts. This hearing took place 3 November 1980. The previous day, a small item in the *Star* noted that Kimberlin was among a dozen prisoners at the Marion County Jail whose attempts to vote in an imminent general election were being thwarted by an Indiana law that disenfranchised criminals during their imprisonment. Kimberlin was thus deprived of the chance to cast his ballot either for or against Dan Quayle, who was then on the eve of election to his first term in the U.S. Senate.

In Judge Noland's courtroom, Kimberlin learned that his disenfranchisement would last much longer than he'd anticipated. The misdemeanors he'd been convicted of carried, technically, a combined maximum sentence of fourteen and a half years. However, Kimberlin said Pritzker and Kammen had led him to believe the sanctions would be less severe. Later, on appeal, he would argue that he had been unfairly accused of multiple offenses; instead of being indicted for four counts of possession of military insignia and four counts of impersonating a federal officer, he should've been charged with only one violation of each statute because his transgressions were "continuous" rather than discrete.

But mostly Kimberlin thought the whole thing was a bad joke grounded in bad luck. High on the list of unlucky particulars was having the case turn up on the docket of Judge Noland, who, during the sentencing hearing, seemed affronted by the jury's failure to return a guilty verdict for the bombings. Kimberlin described Judge Noland as "a lunatic; he was literally shaking with rage" when he pronounced the punishment.

"This case unraveled a series of bizarre events in which there was serious damage to both person and property," the judge concluded. "The bulk of the charges which were tried against the defendant resulted in a hung jury. At this time we do not know for certain what will happen as to the balance of the counts remaining. The trail of this case and the evidence demonstrated certain things with a very compelling force. What this court saw and heard made a lasting impression on this judge. We have here a defendant who has masqueraded as a reputable citizen, when, in fact, he has been operating on the fringes of drug traffic for several years. His business activities appear to be a front while he callously preyed on his fellow citizens. His conduct reveals the complete disregard for the welfare of his fellow citizens, and his associates have been composed of a criminal element. Indeed the defendant appears to have a double personality. . . . There is every reason to believe this defendant will resume his attempts to spread human misery with his drug trafficking when he is released from custody. In an attempt to limit the evil effects of this defendant's activities, the court will impose the maximum sentence provided for." He then gave Kimberlin twelve years, which in fact was actually two and a half below the maximum.

Judge Noland had not been moved by Pritzker's trumpeting, in the court-mandated presentence report, that Kimberlin had "great rehabilitative potential"; and like Judge Seals in Texas, he was able to resist Carolyn's by now boilerplate paean to a loving, caring son. Greg Kimberlin had spoken, noting that Brett had told him: "Dad, I never realized how precious freedom was until I had been in this situation as long as I have been in it. I will never knowingly do anything to jeopardize my freedom again."

I would like to know what Judge Noland thought as he listened to Greg's and Carolyn's pleas for leniency, but he died in 1992, before I had a chance to inquire. And though I had opportunities to ask Greg and Carolyn what *they'd* been thinking at that moment, I refrained for fear that their replies would've seemed unbearably sad. They had dragged themselves into the courtroom, I imagined, in a state of numb desperation. Brett's immediate plight was not even the source of their deepest pain. Sixteen days before the sentencing, Greg Kimberlin, returning home on a Friday evening, was greeted in his driveway by police officers bearing the news a parent dreads more than any other. The Indianapolis Police Department had received a call from a homicide detective in Ohio about a body found on the outskirts of Dayton. A formal identification was required, but the murder victim was unmistakably Scott Kimberlin. The sole mercy was that death had apparently been instantaneous, a gunshot through the heart.

18

THE BULLET that killed Scott Kimberlin was a .223-caliber round from his own gun, an AR-15 semiautomatic rifle with a collapsible stock. Within the context of a tale flush with spiraling intrigues and echoing ironies, the circumstances of the murder had a hollow dullness, and its principals lacked the grandeur required for tragedy. The shooter was a seventeen-year-old punk named George Shingleton, and the motive was a banal combination of robbery, petty jealousy, and drug-and-alcohol-fueled impulsiveness. The site was a motorcycle club in southwest Dayton, in a wooded area whose low-grade magnetism stemmed from adolescent rumor that Bigfoot-type pawprints had been spotted there.

Scott had gone to Dayton on drug business. He was driving a red Chevrolet van, and on the street he met a group that included Shingleton, another seventeen-year-old boy, a sixteen-year-old girl, and her fourteen-year-old brother. At Shingleton's trial, they testified that Scott had tried to conscript them to deal drugs. For three days, he treated them to a binge featuring beer, whiskey, marijuana, cocaine, and methaqualone. They divided their time between driving around and hanging out at Scott's motel. Late in the afternoon of the murder, he gave the three boys the keys to his van and dispatched them to buy beer. When they returned, they discovered Scott and the girl in flagrante. Either Scott was oblivious or he didn't care that Shingleton was also attracted to her; in any case, he told them to come back in half an hour. Rummaging in the rear of the van, Shingleton discovered the AR-15 and an ammunition clip.

Around midnight, they all wound up in the Bigfoot forest. At one point, Shingleton returned to the van, ostensibly to root out some more beer. He loaded the gun, toted it back to the woods, and fired once, point-blank. The chief assistant coroner testified that Scott's heart was "obliterated." His pockets were turned out. He'd been carrying a couple of hundred dollars in his wallet, and Shingleton split the money with his companions. They also stole a briefcase that, according to Brett, contained a long list of people who owed Scott money. Shingleton would have taken the van too, but as he ran down an embankment, he lost the keys in the dark. The next afternoon, the motorcycle club's grounds attendant discovered the body. A chilly rain had fallen meanwhile. Scott lay faceup, with his hands over his head and mud in his palms.

BRETT was in the Marion County Jail when Scott was killed, and his parents paid him a late-night visit to break the news. Because the facts behind the murder had not yet emerged, Brett told me, his initial assumption was that "the feds were the reason Scott was dead." The trauma and misery of the moment, he said, did not prevent him from thinking clearly and acting decisively: "I called these guys who I knew Scott would've seen in Dayton. At first I thought maybe one of them did it, though the guy I called I knew very well and I knew this wasn't his kind of thing. Anyway, they told me Scott had been staying in a motel near the interstate. I found the motel and called from jail and asked whether he'd been staying there and they said yes. He and these teenage kids had all gone to his motel room together. The girl called her mother from the motel room. I asked the people at the motel to give me a list of the phone numbers he'd called from his room and they did. There were a couple of calls I recognized and then this number I didn't recognize, which turned out to be this girl's number. I gave that to the police and they went over to talk to this girl and she broke down and spilled her guts. It was my quick detective work that solved this crime."

THE MURDER weapon, abandoned inside the van, was traced to Dayton Sports Headquarters. More than two years earlier, the gun had been sold to a man who identified himself as Allen M. McGaughey. Store records indicated that McGaughey also bought two boxes of Remington .223-caliber shells and two twenty-five-pound bags of double-aught lead shot. The same day, the same individual made at least one other noteworthy purchase—a white 1970 Chevrolet Impala with a blue vinyl roof.

The two boxes of Remington shells discovered in the trunk of the Impala at the time of Brett's arrest bore price stickers from Dayton Sports Headquarters. Two twenty-five-pound bags of double-aught lead shot were also found in the trunk. To obtain the rifle and the ammunition, the purchaser was required by Ohio law to disclose his real name—which was indeed Allen M. McGaughey. He had a straight job working in the street-maintenance department of the city of Dayton, but according to Brett, he moonlighted as a bar bouncer and, infrequently, as a gofer for Scott. Because the regulations governing automobile title transfers were relatively loose, McGaughey, in buying the Chevy Impala, was able to get away with posing as the fictitious Ray F. Eaton.

Five weeks after the murder, ATF agent Patrick Donovan went to Dayton to see McGaughey, who did not extend a cordial welcome. Though McGaughey could not credibly deny having bought the rifle, he did deny remembering to whom he had subsequently given or sold it, a memory lapse that Donovan found unconvincing. McGaughey was a cousin of Rodney Fint, and he acknowledged to Donovan that he was acquainted with Brett Kimberlin and with Bill Bowman, who had been arrested with Kimberlin in Texas and then, for a time, charged with the Scyphers murder. Donovan possessed a finely tuned familiarity with the details of the bombings investigation, and the contemporaneous purchase of the Scott Kimberlin murder weapon and the Chevy Impala was a coincidence he was in a position to take note of. Nevertheless, he said he didn't draw a connection between the two seemingly unrelated transactions and therefore didn't ask McGaughey any questions about the car. For his part, McGaughey neglected to volunteer that he was its buyer.

McGaughey was never charged with any crimes as a result of having procured the AR-15 or the Impala. Brett told me he had no idea why Scott needed a semiautomatic rifle or why, instead of buying the car himself, he enlisted McGaughey. Kimberlin found it galling that the government wasn't dissuaded by the evidence that McGaughey was Ray F. Eaton. From their perspective, of course, who controlled the Impala just before its seizure was of far greater interest than who nominally owned it. Kimberlin naturally regarded the government's persistence as incriminating proof that its goal was not uncovering the truth so much as seeing him convicted.

"HE WAS gentle as a hummingbird," I was told by a smuggler who knew Scott well. The man added, however, that toward the end of his life Scott frequently was in the grip of delusional fantasies. Before driving to Dayton to meet his murderer, he visited the smuggler and asked him to hold his AR-15. The man didn't want any guns around his place and told Scott to bury it. To many, looking back, it seemed as if Scott had a premonition that fought a losing battle with his death wish, with paranoia supplying both sides of the struggle. So clearly was he headed toward an emotional meltdown that his death, however sordid, came as more a shock than a surprise. Family members, friends, and acquaintances had witnessed a lot of behavior that suggested psychosis. A classic instance was his refusal to go to the dentist because he feared transmitters would be implanted in his teeth. He also observed Russians and CIA agents hiding in trees.

The theme that Carolyn, years later, preferred to emphasize—Scott's deep bond with Brett, his devotion to the cause of his brother's freedom—masked a turmoil that often rendered him barely functional. Drug abuse and the vicissitudes of drug dealing generated a stress that seemed to swallow him whole. A lawyer in Bloomington recalled for me Scott's desperate effort to raise Brett's bail money, as well as the glaring evidence that he was strung out on cocaine. He invested in a drug deal that was supposed to deliver a shrimp boat of Colombian marijuana to a port on the Gulf coast; when the boat arrived, it carried not marijuana but Quaaludes, and marketing the stuff was a nightmare. Getting any of his money back required Scott to front the Quaaludes to several smaller dealers. The money was still due when he died, and all the dealers collected windfalls.

Brett said that from the time of his arrest in Texas until Scott's murder, he saw his brother rarely. Scott came to visit once or twice in Corpus Christi, and their final face-to-face encounter took place at the federal penitentiary in Terre Haute in September 1980, shortly before Brett's trial in Indianapolis. "The only thing I remember about the whole visit was I asked him if he was feeling better," Kimberlin told me. "And he looked at me as if to say, 'What? Do you mean I've been feeling bad?' It was as if he was denying that he'd ever had any delusions or anything like that."

A diagnosis of schizophrenia seemed plausible. No formal determination or treatment ever took place, however, because when Greg and Carolyn intervened to have him involuntarily hospitalized, he literally jumped over a balcony railing, climbed a fence, and fled. Just how mad Scott Kimberlin was, and what that madness implied, would subsequently become a factor in Brett's defense. During the trial in Judge Noland's courtroom, Brett says, Scott went to see McGaughey and persuaded him to inscribe, several times, the front page of that day's edition of the *Dayton Daily News* with the message "I am Ray F. Eaton"—graphological proof that Brett was not the buyer of the Chevy Impala. The newspaper survived as an anecdotal artifact, but Pritzker and Kammen decided against formally introducing it as evidence. By then, the dealer who sold the car had already failed to identify Brett in the courtroom—a solid point for the defense. To admit the newspaper into evidence was potentially confusing and, moreover, would've required Scott to testify. Pritzker and Kammen knew better than to risk exposing him to cross-examination; there was no telling what questions he might be asked or how he might respond.

Scott never actually attended the trial, and a week after it ended he was dead. A friend of the family told me, "When I heard he had died, my reaction was, 'Thank God, he's out of pain now.' " His body was barely in the ground when the facts took on an entirely new spin. Did Scott's willingness to do whatever he could to win Brett's freedom include, subconsciously, a readiness to die? Might Scott's emancipation from his demons in fact become Brett's independence? In death, was Scott now free to volunteer for the role that, during the trial just ended, no one had suggested? If Brett Kimberlin wasn't the Speedway Bomber, who was?

19

I N THE spring of 1980, a man named Richard C. Curry, Jr., went on trial in federal court in Indianapolis for drug conspiracy. According to the attorneys on both sides—the defense conceding much to the prosecution—Curry was an important operative in an enterprise that moved prodigious volumes of marijuana, cocaine, and methaqualone from Colombia to the United States. An indictment returned a few months earlier had described an organization whose principals were mostly Indiana residents and whose distribution network extended to Kentucky, Michigan, Tennessee, Texas, Georgia, the Carolinas, and Florida. Twenty-three conspirators were named, and their alliance was called "The Company." Since Curry was skillful as both a pilot and a flight instructor, the government considered him indispensable to the venture's enduring success.

"The Company" monicker, smacking so redolently of multitentacled malfeasance and derring-do, suited headline writers as well as government attorneys. The quaint reality exposed by the Curry trial, however, was that the world of drug smuggling in Indiana was in many respects cozy and circumscribed. Another indicted pilot, for instance, was George R. Green, of Remington, Indiana. Though there was no apparent pattern of business dealings between The Company and Kimberlin, Curry and Green had been at the controls of the plane seized in the Texas fiasco; it was they who flew the DC-4 from Riohacha, Colombia, were parties to the heaving of the 11,000 pounds of marijuana into the foggy darkness, and were greeted at the Cotulla airport by sheriff's deputies and customs agents. Their resulting trial produced a hung jury, which outcome emboldened Kimberlin's decision to withdraw his original guilty plea in the same case.

Curry's courtroom experience in Indiana impressed Kimberlin even more. Most of Curry's codefendants, including Green, made plea bargains and were available to testify against him. Imaginatively, Curry's attorney, Nile Stanton, concocted a coercion defense. Yes, Stanton acknowledged, over a two-year period the defendant had indeed transported planeload after planeload of illegal cargo, but he had done so only because of intimidation and threats of violence from his associates. Stanton's maneuver put the government in the awkward position of claiming that The Company was a confederation of pacifists—this despite colorful testimony about internecine strife, kidnappings, the shooting down of a plane piloted by Curry, and intrigues involving various corrupt Colombian government officials. On his initial flights, Curry testified, The Company's organizers sent along as chaperons "armed motorcycle hippies." When asked why he hadn't availed himself of his many opportunities to escape these oppressors, he replied that to have done so would have jeopardized his life. A resident of south Florida, Curry claimed no desire to try swimming in Biscayne Bay wearing concrete shoes. Nile Stanton milked this stratagem unabashedly. Curry might be human and fallible, he told the jury during his summation, but he lacked malevolence. He was no Boy Scout, but—and here Stanton offered a comparison that a jury of central Indiana citizens could readily grasp—"he's not violent, he's not a bomber, he's not a Brett Kimberlin."

Of course, this invidiousness was displeasing to Brett. However, months later, as he pondered his own situation and the remarkable result of Stanton's labors—an acquittal for Curry, a verdict that so disturbed the judge he chastised the jurors en masse—Kimberlin managed to swallow his irritation. He was fed up with Pritzker and Kammen; the mistrial and prospect of a retrial made him impatient. For the next go-round he wanted an attorney who would do his bidding and oppose the vindictive prosecutors with an inventiveness and vehemence worthy of the cause. So he did what seemed sensible. He hired Nile Stanton.

JUDGE NOLAND had withdrawn from the proceedings, evidently for reasons of his own well-being—mainly, that propinquity to Kimberlin tended to infect him with apoplexy. For the defendant this should've been a salutary development, except that the case was next assigned to the Honorable William E. Steckler, who almost a decade earlier had given Kimberlin three years probation on the juvenile delinquency rap arising from his cocaine-dealing arrest. During that sentencing hearing, Steckler had told Kimberlin, "I do that with the anticipation that you will be difficult to handle," and there was no reason to assume the judge's prescience had given him any satisfaction in the intervening years.

More important to Kimberlin than the jurist on the bench was the one at his defense table. In Nile Stanton, he had an advocate of proven skills, whose rhetoric and temperament meshed with his own ideals. Best of all, Stanton was willing to allow him to participate, in effect, as a cocounsel. "As a client, Brett was fully cooperative," Stanton said years later. "If we had disputes, we would talk about them. If he could convince me that I was wrong about a point of strategy, we would talk about it and I would listen. And vice versa. He was a very beautiful client to have, very bright, very knowledgeable. I trusted him and he trusted me. He understood what was going on, and he would internalize it very quickly."

By Indianapolis standards, Stanton was the closest thing around to a William Kunstler, a homegrown contrarian who combined a reflexive contempt for the established order (i.e., government lawyers) with equal measures of theatricality and assiduous trial preparation. He had grown up an hour north of Indianapolis in Fairmount, Indiana, a small town whose principal distinction was as the birthplace of James Dean. After graduating from college in 1966, he taught high school history while working toward a master's degree in history. His mother was an earnest Quaker, and he avoided Vietnam by registering as a conscientious objector.

While teaching in an accredited high school program at the Indiana State Reformatory, a maximum-security institution in Pendleton, Stanton became "very sympathetic to the rights of prisoners." Simultaneously, he enrolled in the Indiana University Law School branch in Indianapolis, where Dan Quayle and his wife-to-be, Marilyn Tucker, were fellow students. (Stanton made law review; the Quayles did not.) Even before completing his degree, he became executive director of the Indianapolis Lawyers Commission, a do-good arm of the Indiana Bar Association, and in that capacity he focused his attention on prison reform. His mission, he later said, was to introduce the powers-that-be in state government and the legal establishment to "the realities of prison life." Once, referring to a client he'd first encountered in those years, he told me: "He's a beautiful man. He's a fantastic prisoner. He's a great prisoner. Real witty, bright. He's a convict's convict. I love him like a brother."

By the time Stanton assumed the defense of Kimberlin, his reputation had been bolstered not only by the Curry trial but also by several other high-profile triumphs. In 1977, he had used an insanity defense to win an acquittal for Anthony Kiritsis, a businessman who had kidnapped a mortgage company executive, publicly marched him through downtown Indianapolis with a shotgun wired to his neck, and then held him hostage for sixty-three hours while an army of lawmen waited outside the apartment where they were holed up. A columnist for the *Indianapolis Star,* Dan Carpenter, reviewing Stanton's career, once wrote: "Ah, Tony Kiritsis. When Stanton won him an insanity acquittal . . . his office became Lourdes to defendants needing miracles. And while he didn't always work miracles, he worked juries like nobody else in town."

Two years after that trial, Stanton successfully petitioned for a retrial for Larry Hicks, a death-row inmate convicted of a double murder in Gary, Indiana, and, when Stanton met him, only two weeks shy of an execution date. Stanton's standing offer was to represent gratis anyone who could pass a polygraph. There were caveats: the polygraph would be conducted by an expert chosen by Stanton, and the prospective client had to pay for the procedure. In Hicks's case, Stanton actually waived the latter requirement. Twice, Hicks passed polygraphs administered by John O. Danberry, who for more than two decades was the chief polygraph examiner for the Indiana State Police. Convinced of Hicks's innocence, Stanton mobilized private investigators to gather evidence of negligent police work as well as prosecutorial misconduct.

On retrial, Hicks was acquitted and set free. The jury arrived at its not-guilty verdict without referring to the polygraph findings, because the prosecution was able to suppress them; in Indiana's state courts, such evidence is inadmissible unless both sides agree to allow it. In the federal Seventh Circuit, of which Indiana is a part, prevailing opinion holds against polygraphs.

The examinations conducted by John Danberry in the Hicks case were confirmed by Leonard Harrelson, of Chicago's Keeler Institute. I once heard an Indianapolis attorney describe Harrelson as being "at that time perhaps the leading polygraph examiner in the country"; another referred to the Keeler Institute as "the Harvard of polygraph training." Legal experts who are skeptical of the practice would argue, of course, that these are empty encomiums.

Nevertheless, polygraph examiners continue to find work, often for the privileged enlightenment of defense attorneys. Indeed, before the first Speedway bombings trial, Pritzker and Kammen decided to subject Kimberlin to a polygraph. Pritzker told me, "I did it as an investigative tool to determine to what extent I could open Brett to questioning"—to calibrate the risk of allowing Kimberlin to testify and face cross-examination. The examiner whose services the lawyers happened to engage was Leonard Harrelson. Usually, when a polygraph suggests that a defendant is innocent, his attorney will share the result with prosecutors and propose they corroborate by bringing in an examiner of their choosing. This, Kammen told me, had been his habit; but he also said that when Harrelson had completed his examination of Kimberlin, "we didn't want to breathe a word about Harrelson to anybody." The results of Kimberlin's polygraphs never became part of any public record.

That Harrelson had in fact been retained, however, did become public. On 18 May 1981, the *Indianapolis News* featured a front-page interview with Kimberlin, the first he'd granted since his indictment. The reporter, David Rohn, elicited several pure Kimberlin nuggets: he was a libertarian entrepreneur; the government's prosecution of him for the bombings was mistaken and misguided; vindication was inevitable. In one passage, Rohn wrote: "Kimberlin revealed that at the outset of the bombing trial he was given a lie detector test by his attorneys to convince them he was innocent. He said he passed that lie detector test." Once the government's attorneys read this, they checked the visitors' register at the Marion County Jail, deduced the identity of the examiner, and prepared a subpoena for Harrelson.

THE ROHN interview was published at a time when Judge Steckler was entertaining various pretrial motions, skirmishes in which Stanton and his cocounsel, Kevin McShane, were experiencing mixed results. Attacking the validity of the second search of the Chevy Impala—the linchpin of the government's case—Stanton filed a motion to suppress the critical evidence gathered from the trunk of the car. This motion was denied. A motion to quash statements made by the hypnotized witnesses was denied. Stanton next presented an involved argument seeking dismissal of the two charges of receipt of explosive devices by a convicted felon. In this instance, Kimberlin was forced to confront the fallout from his adolescent criminal behavior. Six years earlier, he had done his first jail time: thirty days for perjury, a felony. Had he received that sentence as a "youth offender," as defined by the Federal Youth Corrections Act, the conviction eventually could've been erased from his record, eliminating with it the subsequent rationale for the explosives possession charges. Stanton argued that the judge in the perjury case had committed a "judicial error" in sentencing Kimberlin as an adult. Judge Steckler denied the petition to expunge the original conviction, but as a consolation he granted Stanton's motion to sever the explosives possession indictments from the bombings indictments. This meant that there would now be two trials: one limited to the explosives case, and a separate trial to resolve the twenty-two counts related directly to the bombings.

THAT in the summer of 1975 Kimberlin had participated in the purchase, from a du Pont dealer in Belmont, Indiana, of a hundred sticks of Tovex 200—the same explosive material that went into the bombs—had been demonstrated at the first trial. Several witnesses who had testified then, including the architect and members of the construction crew involved in the excavation work at Kimberlin's Jackson County property, also testified at the second trial. The Tovex was bought and the blasting completed within a single day. Two cardboard cartons containing unused Tovex were left in the cargo space of Kimberlin's pickup truck. None of the crew members recalled anyone other than Kimberlin taking possession of the leftover Tovex at the end of the day. After establishing this proximity, the government's burden of proof was to show that, once the blasting was finished, Kimberlin *controlled* the explosives.

Kimberlin's architect, Stephen Miller, testified that he took to his own home, in Nashville, Indiana, four sticks of Tovex and four blasting caps, which he had planned to use to do excavation for a greenhouse. Two months after the Speedway bombings, Miller was visited by Patrick Donovan and Bernard Niehaus. He had never built the greenhouse. Miller signed a statement that said, in part: "Of the remainder, I kept four sticks of Tovex and four blasting caps. Brett Kimberlin kept the rest. I subsequently turned my Tovex and caps over to S.A. Patrick Donovan, of ATF, and we took it to the same du Pont dealer and turned it over to them."

The government called Ronald Confer, who had been a partner in the Earth Garden Café. (His wife, Jan, had been a minor prosecution witness during the first trial.) During the summer of 1975, Confer testified, he helped Kimberlin unload from his pickup truck some old barn siding that had come from Jackson County and was intended for the Earth Garden's interior decoration. While unloading the wood, he also saw two cardboard boxes, which Kimberlin said contained explosives. Kimberlin reassured him that the cargo wasn't dangerous because no detonation was possible without fuses or blasting caps, and those were inside the truck cab, on the driver's seat.

Confer's testimony was neither the beginning nor the end of the perjury that would be deployed against him, Kimberlin explained to me. After the first trial, he said, Carolyn tried to collect from Confer $10,000 that Brett was owed from the sale of his interest in the restaurant. Instead of paying, he said, Confer retaliated with an incriminating falsehood. Stanton challenged Confer with his own grand jury testimony, in which he had said of Kimberlin, "I have never seen him with any [explosives] and I don't know him to possess any explosives." Confer explained the inconsistency by saying that his memory had been jogged during or shortly after Kimberlin's first trial, when he received a phone call from an assistant to Pritzker and Kammen. The caller asked whether he remembered accompanying Kimberlin years earlier to an antiques shop where he had bought some wooden crates—army surplus items whose markings suggested they originally had been used to store dynamite. The crates were mentioned in a government affidavit supporting a warrant to search Kimberlin's home in Eagle Creek. To verify that these were innocuous, Kimberlin told his lawyers to consult Confer. In remembering the crates, Confer testified, he also recalled the cardboard boxes in the back of Kimberlin's truck. This information he shared with the ATF.

To impeach Confer, Stanton asked about his knowledge of Kimberlin's marijuana smuggling—the first time an Indiana jury caught a glimpse of this dimension of Kimberlin's life. Confer's denial of any such knowledge, Kimberlin claimed, compounded his perjury. Confer, he said, was a professional printer who had assisted some of his illicit schemes. When Kimberlin decided to pass off a load of unexceptional Mexican weed as high-potency Hawaiian, for example, Confer printed wrapping material that looked as if it had been designed to ship pineapples.

AFTER the defense rested, the *News* headline said: CASE GOES TO JURY WITHOUT TESTIMONY OF BRETT KIMBERLIN. Actually, he had spoken under oath, in Judge Steckler's chambers. Leonard Harrelson, responding to the prosecution's subpoena, had met with government attorneys and investigators in Indianapolis and was then called as a witness, with the jury excused. Stanton urged that the public and the media also should be prevented from hearing testimony from Harrelson, as well as any lawyers' debates about whether he should even be allowed to testify. Steckler convened the ensuing arguments behind closed doors.

Both sides now found themselves in tricky postures. Stanton objected to Harrelson's testimony on the ground that Kimberlin's examination fell within the attorney-client relationship and its contents were privileged. And of course, the results themselves were inadmissible as evidence. Implicit in Stanton's argument was his desire to steer as clear of the polygraph findings as possible. This seemed a curious stance if, one, Stanton was being candid when he told the court of polygraphs in general, "I think if a professional gives them, I think they are very scientific, they're highly reliable, I do believe in them"; and, two, Kimberlin was being truthful when he claimed to have "passed" the test.

On the other hand, the government's argument was the certitude that Brett *hadn't* passed. Still, Kennard Foster explained that he didn't want to ask Harrelson about the content of the polygraph, but wished only to inquire about statements Kimberlin had made *before* the examination began. During that preliminary conversation, Foster told Steckler, "Mr. Kimberlin told Mr. Harrelson that he, during the period 1975 to '78, when he was working on his property in rural Indiana, had possession of explosives." Moreover, Foster asserted, Kimberlin's disclosure to the *News* reporter constituted a waiver of privilege. Unable to restrain himself, Foster added (not quite parenthetically) that "Mr. Harrelson ran Mr. Kimberlin on polygraph and found—and based upon the questions asked and the answers given by Mr. Kimberlin relative to all the counts—that his answers were deceptive."

Judge Steckler ruled for the defense, though disturbed that Kimberlin's interview "might have some bearing on potential jurors." Kimberlin's disclosure per se, however, did not signify an unambiguous waiver of the attorney-client privilege. To allow Harrelson to testify, the judge concluded, would be "a hazardous step."

WHETHER Kimberlin would testify in open court had yet to be resolved when the *News* misconstrued the discussions in Steckler's chambers. If the defendant did take the stand, David Rohn wrote, "the government is expected to call rebuttal witnesses, including Leonard Harrelson." The article's erroneous premise was that, quid pro quo, Harrelson would then be allowed to testify freely. Foster and Pylitt, meanwhile, relished the prospect of cross-examining Kimberlin. Without success, Stanton asked that his client be permitted to offer limited testimony—his goal being to prevent the government from impeaching Kimberlin by dragging in his prior criminal convictions, matters ostensibly unrelated to the explosives possession charges. Judge Steckler replied, in effect, "Put him on the stand, let him testify and be cross-examined, and then I'll let you know what is and what isn't admissible." Ultimately, Stanton decided it wasn't worth the risk.

Instead, the jurors ended up hearing from Greg and Kevin Kimberlin, whose collective testimony, reduced to its essence, was this: Scott Kimberlin, not Brett, controlled the unused Tovex. They weren't sure what he'd done with it (maybe he'd blown up some tree stumps on the Jackson County property) or where he'd stored it (possibly at his residence near Bloomington). Neither was Greg sure of the name of the town near Bloomington where Scott lived; as a father, he also found it "embarrassing" not to be able to tell the court exactly how old Scott was in the fall of 1975, when he revealed that Brett had placed him in charge of the explosives. Greg couldn't recall specific rooms in his house where specific conversations about the Tovex had taken place. He could, however, definitely recall being concerned about safety, because Scott was "at that point in his life [the] most unresponsible of my children." Still, he and Kevin had never seen Brett in possession of explosives, nor had Brett ever mentioned them.

Most of what Stanton had hoped Greg and Kevin would tell the jurors never reached their ears. The hearsay doctrine kept getting in the way; whatever Scott might've said about possessing Tovex was inadmissible, since a dead man can't be cross-examined. Even Stanton conceded "it rather amazes me" that, before the first trial, no one in the family had advised the U.S. attorney that Brett was not the proper object in the government's case.

THE VERDICT came after ten and a half hours of deliberations. Its indignity—guilty as charged, good for five more years once Judge Steckler delivered the sentence—was exacerbated by its having arrived on Kimberlin's twenty-seventh birthday. At the sentencing hearing, Stanton argued that Kimberlin was not a violent criminal. "It is just a technical violation of the law," he pleaded. "He is a loving and caring human being." A juror told the *Indianapolis Star* that his panel had discounted Ron Confer's trial testimony because it conflicted with his grand jury testimony. On the other hand, they hadn't believed Greg or Kevin Kimberlin, either.

20

B ETWEEN the second and third trials, Buddy Pylitt left the U.S. Attorney's office and was replaced by John C. "Jack" Thar, a methodical professional. Kennard Foster stayed on as lead prosecutor and never wavered from the tone he had set during the first trial. For Foster, a brawny, choleric ex–FBI agent, going to trial meant waging war, and when the last shot was fired he and Nile Stanton would not be saluting each other as noble adversaries. Indeed, they appeared to nurture a heartfelt reciprocal loathing. Had Judge Steckler ordered them to settle their disagreements with boxing gloves, neither would have retreated. For the benefit of the jury, Foster mastered his enunciation of *Brett Cole-man Kim-ber-lin*—lingering over every syllable with such distaste that the name itself sounded like a crime.

The third trial lasted longer than the first two combined: nine weeks, one hundred seventeen witnesses. Much of the testimony—the posthypnotic accounts of the purchase of bomb components, the defense counterattack on the reliability of hypnosis, the trail of the Tovex, the catalogue of evidence from the Chevy Impala, Carl De-Long's account of his injuries, Kimberlin's alibi witnesses—felt redundant to the point of déjà vu all over again. However, there were also novelties, moments of pure surprise, wonders rich with entertainment value.

"The evidence . . . will indicate that no one saw Brett Kimberlin make a bomb, possess a bomb, set off a bomb at the scene of the bombings. The reason they didn't is he didn't do it," Stanton told the jurors during his opening statement. Hearing this no doubt thrilled Foster and Thar, who knew that their final witness would be a thirty-seven-year-old machinist named Lynn Coleman, who would recount how, around nine-thirty the evening of 1 September 1978, in a shopping center parking lot at 6000 Crawfordsville Road, he saw

Kimberlin place in a trash receptacle the first of the eight Speedway bombs.

Coleman and his wife were looking for a sofa at a used-furniture store, he testified. They were parked near the store when a light-colored Mercedes pulled alongside, advanced a few car lengths, made a U-turn, and stopped about a hundred feet behind them. Watching through a rearview mirror, Coleman "saw a man get out, fairly well-dressed, reach for a large sack, take it over to the trash container and put it in the trash container, got back in his car and left." A few minutes later, Coleman and his wife headed toward home. While waiting at a stoplight, they "heard a loud explosion." Foster asked Coleman to "look around the courtroom here today and see if you see an individual that is or resembles" the person he observed in the parking lot.

"Yes, I do. He is right there," Coleman said, pointing at Kimberlin.

According to the *Star*, while Coleman answered Foster's questions, Stanton "sat openmouthed, nervously tapping his left foot"— a spectator astonished and perturbed by the choreography he was witnessing. And Kimberlin, "who has at times displayed jovial laughter to the jury during the eighteen days of testimony, paled, his boyish grin replaced with a stern scowl."

Coleman had neither appeared before the grand jury nor signed any written statement setting forth his allegations. Nor had any investigators kept contemporaneous notes of interviews with him. If such statements or written notes existed, the government was required to share them with the defense during the pretrial discovery process. Unveiling an eyewitness without forewarning was, from Kimberlin's indignant perspective, symptomatic of the government's chronic underhandedness. What rock had Coleman been hiding beneath during the first trial? Judge Steckler evidently regarded his sudden emergence as, at worst, a piece of technically legal legerdemain, or he would have barred his testimony. Obliging Kimberlin with the moral outrage he felt entitled to, Stanton routinely impugned the government attorneys' integrity. He filed objection after objection, motion after motion to suppress evidence. On almost a dozen occasions, he requested a mistrial. At other moments, seemingly swept up by the tide of the testimony and the court's rulings, he projected the image of someone in less than full possession of his equilibrium.

FOR KIMBERLIN to testify on his own behalf, preemptive damage control was required. Presumably, the hazards of cross-examination could be mitigated if the defense acknowledged Kimberlin's criminal convictions before the government luxuriated in reciting them to the jury. Acknowledging *everything,* however, was not what Stanton had in mind; the trick was to persuade Judge Steckler to limit the disclosures to the troubles in Texas. This amounted to a Brett's-a-pot-smuggler-but-he's-no-bomber strategy—a variation of the tack Stanton had used in successfully defending Richard C. Curry, Jr. He did not look forward to telling the jurors, for instance, "He's a perjurer but he's not a bomber," or, worse, "He's been convicted of illegal possession of explosives but he's not the bomber." So, in his opening statement, when Stanton referred to Kimberlin's arrest and guilty plea in Texas, he said, in essence: "The uniforms, the military patches, the lead balls and lead shot that were found in the Chevy Impala—it was all connected to a marijuana importing venture. None of it had anything to do with the Speedway bombings."

Ultimately, Judge Steckler issued a ruling that provided Kimberlin only limited protection from his past. The explosives-possession and juvenile cocaine-possession convictions were proscribed, but everything else was at the government's disposal for impeachment purposes. "If you read the trial transcripts, you'll see that ninety percent of the trial had nothing to do with the bombings," Kimberlin later complained. "It was all about army patches, marijuana, weapons possession." (Weapons had been confiscated in the Texas bust.) Foster and Thar were out to "bad-man" his client, Stanton argued—by which he meant that, with their demonological view of Kimberlin, they had decided, irrespective of the relevant facts or the exigencies of due process, that he simply deserved locking up.

In return, Stanton hatched the defense theory of the alternative bad man. He used the opening statement to affirm Kimberlin's innocence and to float an intrepid hypothesis: "The government, in attempting to make its case against Brett Kimberlin, has ignored evidence which we submit the defendant is likely to present to you, and that is of activities engaged in by another person at approximately the same time in purchasing other things in this city and activities engaged in by another party who, we'll submit to you, is the Speedway Bomber."

During Kimberlin's adolescence, several boys who had become alienated from their parents turned up as fixtures in the Kimberlin household. Carolyn indulged these waifs in a maternal way, baked cakes on their birthdays, and managed simultaneously to lend an ear and avert her eyes. "Basically, it's my mom's fault that we took in all these losers," Kimberlin told me. In 1972, when he gave the grand jury testimony that led to his indictment for perjury, he offered a poignant description of the most frequent drop-in, Joe Majko: "He has been my little brother's best friend for three years. His dad's a convict, his mother's an insane-o. . . . He would always come to our house because he knew we would accept him and we didn't hold anything against him. The only way he could live when he wasn't at our house was to steal." His name had come up in the grand jury inquiry because months earlier, following Brett's cocaine bust, Majko had been charged with threatening the government's chief witness. This was the occasion when the police, pursuing an arrest warrant, tracked Majko down to the Kimberlins' home and found him hiding in the attic.

Another Dickensian charmer who thought of himself as Scott Kimberlin's best friend was Scott Bixler. Unlike Majko, Bixler came from an affluent family; his father was a dentist, his mother a magazine editor, and his stepfather owned a thriving car dealership. In common with Majko and the Kimberlins, he was not a likely candidate for the Boy Scouts or Youth for Christ. Good-looking, with light-brown hair and blue-green eyes, he stood five ten and weighed about 180 pounds. He was muscular and kinetic, hard-wired for bravado; physical confrontations didn't frighten him. Bixler frequently got into fights and usually came out ahead. He knew a lot about guns and liked to load his own shells. For years, "Scottie K. and Scottie B." were, according to Carolyn, "inseparable." Bixler had been riding shotgun in Brett's truck just before his arrest in Texas but had fled into the night and escaped the dragnet, eventually making his way to Gainesville, Florida, where Scottie K. gave him refuge. Months later, Bixler surfaced in Texas, having meanwhile made arrangements with the DEA to testify against Brett and the other smugglers. Bixler told federal agents that he and Scott Kimberlin were as close as brothers, but this did not extend to Brett; the substance of their relationship was business.

When Stanton promised the jury, with a flourish worthy of Erle Stanley Gardner, that the evidence would exonerate Brett Kimberlin and point toward the real Speedway Bomber, the culprit he had in mind was Bixler. At the time, Stanton seemed sincere in this belief, which is to say he had not devised a theory—adding the burden of establishing another man's guilt to the daunting task of exculpating his client—just so Brett could repay Scott for having turned snitch. To identify Bixler by name during the opening statement offered no tactical advantage. Nor was Stanton ready to reveal that the witness who would help verify this solution to the Speedway bombings was Joe Majko.

One wonders how scrupulously Stanton weighed the implications of this strategy. Brett had assured Stanton of his innocence. He also told him that the two Scotts had used the Chevy Impala in the days preceding its seizure. Stanton knew that Carolyn would testify that Scott Kimberlin had behaved erratically in 1980, and he knew that Greg and Kevin, as they had during the explosives-possession trial, would vouch for Scott's general flakiness and unreliability. Within the constraints of the hearsay rules, Greg and Kevin would testify that Scott took possession of the Tovex in 1975.

How did Stanton think the jurors would fit these pieces together? The Impala was filled with Brett's belongings, including bomb components and residues of Tovex, and no tangible evidence tied any of this to Bixler. Was the Speedway Bomber a hybrid? Were there many Speedway Bombers? How did Bixler figure in? What was Scott Kimberlin's role? What if Scottie B. and Scottie K. had been doing Brett's dirty work? What gerrymandering of the facts could isolate Bixler as the lone bomber? How eager was Carolyn, mother of lost boys, to have her dead flesh-and-blood fingered for the crimes? Was this the defense the Kimberlin family was paying for?

If Bixler took the stand, Stanton would have no way of knowing how he might answer in cross-examination. What if the trial's outcome was reduced to Bixler's credibility versus Brett's? Bixler, mind you, had never been convicted of a serious crime, and if Majko's word—with eight felony convictions behind it—was stacked against his, whom would the jury believe? Among the potential complications Stanton never accounted for was that Bixler would produce an alibi even more persuasive than Brett's—an alibi that would also acquit, of all people, Scott Kimberlin.

CALLED as a defense witness in the fifth week of the trial, Majko gave the following testimony:

At the Indiana State Reformatory, in Pendleton, he was serving an eight-year sentence for burglary and possession of narcotics. He had four previous convictions along those same lines. In October or November of 1978, he helped Scott Kimberlin move furniture and other belongings from an A-frame house a few miles south of Bloomington to a miniwarehouse in the nearby town of Spencer. Among the belongings was a cardboard carton labeled EXPLOSIVES. He hadn't actually seen the carton's contents, but Scott Kimberlin referred to them as "plastic explosives."

During a trip to Aspen, Colorado, three months after the bombings, while changing a tire on a pickup truck, he witnessed an argument during which Bixler said to Scott Kimberlin, "I didn't mean to mess up that man's leg."

Asked by Stanton to characterize the two Scotts, Majko answered, "A little bit on the wild side. Real erratic." Would he apply that same description to himself? "Yes. Yes, I would. I guess I have to."

Early in 1979, by then at Pendleton, he received two visits from a member of the Speedway Police Department. The second time, an ATF agent came along. The lawmen asked Majko a few questions, but he wasn't very cooperative. He did, however, describe for them the incident in Aspen, including the quotation from Bixler.

Stanton showed Majko a photograph of the Chevy Impala and asked whether he'd ever seen Bixler driving it. Around the middle of September 1978, Majko said, outside a tavern on the north side of Indianapolis, he saw Bixler remove some money from the glove compartment of a similar-looking vehicle. "I can't say positive it was the same car," he testified, "but it was a car of that model."

During cross-examination, Foster dragged Majko through a detailed discussion of his crimes—breaking and entering drugstores was his specialty—as well as his accomplishments as a pharmacological epicure.

Arthur "Buddy" Ellwanger and James Richardson, the Speedway detective and the ATF agent, were also subpoenaed by the defense. It is easy to imagine that had Stanton not called them, the government would have—as rebuttal witnesses. Ellwanger testified that Bixler's name had not come up in either of his conversations with Majko at Pendleton, though Scott Kimberlin was mentioned. He said the subject of a trip to Colorado never arose. Then Richardson was asked by Stanton, "Did you discuss with Mr. Majko a man by the name of Robert Scott Bixler?" and Richardson replied, "No,

I did not." On cross-examination, Foster asked, "You say that you didn't discuss Robert Scott Bixler with Mr. Majko. Who did you discuss with Mr. Majko?" and Richardson replied, "Mr. Brett Kimberlin."

AFTER cooperating in Texas, Bixler had been placed in a federal witness protection program. Stanton asked the court to order the government to produce Bixler. Acknowledging that the government knew his whereabouts, Foster stated that he was no longer enrolled in the witness protection program but continued to "fear for his life." At the conclusion of Majko's testimony, Bixler, at Stanton's request, was escorted into the courtroom. He was not sworn as a witness but, rather, was required to pose before the jury for a few minutes. Stanton's object was to demonstrate that, at five eight and 150 pounds, with brown hair and hazel eyes, Bixler bore a close enough resemblance to Kimberlin that the hypnosis witnesses and Lynn Coleman could have confused them.

Bixler returned two weeks later, this time called by the government. Foster asked the questions, and Bixler gave the following testimony:

During the summer of 1978, he bought seven Colt AR-15 semi-automatic rifles from the Broad Ripple Sports Shop, with funds provided by Brett Kimberlin. "I kept one for myself and I turned the remaining six over to Brett," he said. He later resold the one that he kept to the same dealer. That same day, he bought Kimberlin a box of .223-caliber shells that fit an AR-15. On an earlier occasion, he'd bought Kimberlin shells for a twelve-gauge shotgun. (Both types of ammunition were found inside the trunk of the Chevy Impala, as were 30.06 rifle shells.)

On 1 September 1978, when the bombings began, Bixler recalled being in either Bloomington or Indianapolis. He did not then or at any other time possess any explosive device. The next day, he and Scott Kimberlin flew in Bixler's Cessna 206 from Bloomington to Louisville, Kentucky, where they attended a wedding. On September 3, they flew from Kentucky toward Fort Lauderdale, Florida. En route, they spent a night in Dublin, Georgia, where they received service for a minor mechanical problem. The next night, weather conditions forced them down in Ocala, Florida. They arrived in Fort

Lauderdale on September 5 and stayed "approximately two weeks," after which Bixler returned to Indianapolis.

Back in Indianapolis, did he borrow any vehicles from the defendant?

"No, no."

When shown photographs of the Chevy Impala, he said he had never seen it.

How had he spent the remainder of the fall?

"Business, marijuana trafficking."

During cross-examination, Stanton asked Bixler the exact date he'd returned from Florida to Indianapolis. (He had left his Cessna in Fort Lauderdale and flown home commercial, buying his ticket with cash and an alias.) Bixler said he couldn't remember a specific date—"approximately September twentieth, thereabouts." Could it have been a couple of days earlier? "Yes, it could very well be."

Nine other witnesses—among them the bride and the groom, an airport service facility owner, a motel clerk—substantiated Bixler's alibi. The import of this corroborating testimony, of course, was to place both Bixler and Scott Kimberlin far from Indiana when the last four bombs exploded, including the one that messed up both of Carl DeLong's legs.

To imagine a parody of a stage magician in a flop sweat, groping inside his top hat, desperate for anything to materialize—a dove, a rabbit, a bouquet of flowers, a successful mistrial motion—is to empathize with Stanton at that juncture. The truly bad news, however, was that Bixler was not even the government's most jarring rebuttal witness.

FRANCISCO MANUEL GONZALEZ—otherwise known as Frankie Gonzalez, Kimberlin's longtime smuggling partner in McAllen, Texas—was called. In response to questions from Foster about his travels in Texas with Kimberlin, Gonzalez testified:

Sometime in the fall of 1978, he and Kimberlin had gone to Austin—a three-and-a-half-hour drive from Beeville, where they were setting up a drug deal—"to see some girls." They stayed in a downtown hotel. At one point, Kimberlin left the room, saying "he'd be right back to get the girls." Upon his return—the length of his absence wasn't specified—Kimberlin said, "Let's take a drive." Gonzalez was behind the wheel, and Kimberlin gave directions. They took Interstate 35 north about "five or six minutes," left the highway, and drove into a residential area. Kimberlin told Gonzalez to let him out, then said, "Come back for me in about fifteen minutes." Later, when Gonzalez picked Kimberlin up, he asked what was going on, and Kimberlin said, "Forget it. Let's just drive back." They then returned to Beeville.

Gonzalez was testifying under a grant of immunity. To ease his conscience, it seemed, he concluded his testimony with kind words for the defendant: "As long as I have known Mr. Kimberlin, Brett Kimberlin, he has always been my friend. We had never had any misunderstanding or any kind of—how do I say?—unusual respect. Okay? And I have not in any way seen Mr. Kimberlin or heard him act in a violent way or commit violent action toward anybody."

Even with allowances for odd syntax, what any of this signified was quite mysterious. When Stanton objected on the ground of relevancy, Judge Steckler allowed Gonzalez to continue but agreed to strike the testimony if the government failed to connect it to the charges against Kimberlin. With the next witness, the other shoe swiftly dropped. Louise Crosby, Sandi Barton's sister, gave the following testimony:

She resided in Pflugerville, Texas, a middle-class bedroom community north of Austin, where she lived in a brick ranch-style house, in a subdivision "two to three minutes" off Interstate 35. Her street dead-ended at the boundary of a cow pasture. On the afternoon of 10 March 1979, she was clearing her backyard of debris that had gathered over the winter. On the side of her house was a cedar with branches "low enough that they touched the ground." Using a hoe, she began to rake papers from beneath the tree and saw a black plastic garbage bag. At first she thought it was stuck in the mud, but then she realized it was heavy. She finally dragged it out and tried to open it, but it was very tightly wrapped, so she set it aside. Next, on the other side of the tree, her hoe hooked into the handles of a red-and-white vinyl gym bag. She pulled it out and saw inside a "blue and white square box, and it had a cord, a plug at the end of the cord." Then she noticed another such electrical device. Further inspection revealed "white capsule-shaped bags, and on one I could see was written 'Explosives—Danger.'" Now she was frightened. She went to the phone and called Ben Niehaus, in Indianapolis, and he arranged for an Austin-based ATF agent to come to the Crosby house and take control of the materials.

Subsequent witnesses, including the ATF agent, elaborated. The blue-and-white boxes inside the gym bag turned out to be a pair of Mark Time timers, and the white capsule-shaped bags were sticks of Tovex 200—fourteen sticks in all. The bag also contained three blasting caps. Each stick of Tovex was factory-wrapped with a white plastic sheath upon which had been stamped a code that specified the date, time, and location of manufacture. These so-called date-shift codes on each stick, however, had been effaced with scissors or a knife. Inside the heavy, tightly wrapped black garbage bag, the ATF agent found a Colt AR-15 semiautomatic rifle. The provenance of the rifle was impossible to trace because its serial number had been filed off. Enough of the date-shift codes on the Tovex wrappers were still legible—bits of letters and numerals—for a laboratory analysis to conclude that the Tovex came from the same batch that had been used at the Jackson County blasting site and in the Speedway bombings.

Frankie Gonzalez returned, for cross-examination. Stanton asked, regarding his account of a trip on the interstate, "Has the government shown you any pictures of anything to ask you if you can describe an area or any particular home or where you went?"

"I was asked about a name of a town," Gonzalez replied, "but I couldn't remember that."

Asked whether Kimberlin, when he got out of the car, had been carrying a gym bag or a black plastic bag or digging tools, Gonzalez replied, "The only thing that he had was a very small bag where he kept all his vegetarian things . . . a very small bag."

LOUISE CROSBY'S testimony was the occasion for one more loaded revelation. After she described rooting around under her cedar tree, Foster asked her to identify a handwritten document, and she did so. It was a letter she had received from her niece Yvonne Barton—Sandi's older daughter. Following Stanton's cross-examination of Gonzalez, Yvonne briefly took the stand. Her testimony was a single-thrust assault upon the foundation of Kimberlin's alibi. The evening of 1 September 1978, she said, around seven-thirty, her mother arrived, alone, at the Burger King on the west side of Indianapolis where Yvonne worked as a waitress. Sandi waited until Yvonne finished her shift, then drove her to Fred Scyphers's house, reaching there about eight-thirty. This was an event far enough out of the ordinary—Yvonne was then living with her grandfather, not with her mother—that she noted it in a letter to her aunt, with whom she maintained a steady correspondence. "It was really weird tonight at work," the letter said. "I was running for drive-thru, and we had a rush. I had just gotten a fish sandwich and taken it to the window and somebody goes 'Yvonne.' So I looked out, and Mom was sitting there. It totally flipped me out."

Sandi could not have been simultaneously with her daughter in a Burger King on the west side of town and having dinner with Brett at the Earth Garden Café, on the east side of town. If the letter was in fact written on September 1—to discount any suggestion that she was mistaken about the date, the government introduced into evidence another letter she'd written to Louise Crosby, this one dated September 2—Yvonne had effectively nullified the defense's entire version of Kimberlin's whereabouts and activities the night of the first four bombings.

21

THE FORMALITY of a criminal trial permits a defendant to face his accusers with his vanity intact. What typically ensues—particularly when the crime is nasty—is a process of being stripped bare, reduced to a naked aggregation of scars and blemishes. People in love engage in similar rituals, and if later they become alienated, the truth emerges that each has engraved in memory a meticulous taxonomy of the other's tiniest flaws. There was a sense in which Kimberlin and the prosecutors came to resemble the parties to a sadomasochistic entanglement, each driven by a compulsive belief in, even an appetite for, the other's capacity for perversity. In the years that followed the bombing investigation and trials, Kimberlin's absorption with his experience seemed inexhaustible. Retold and retold, his chronicle retained a vigorous, evergreen freshness. No mere litany of injustice and violation, it seemed to have become his most treasured possession.

He spent three days on the witness stand. The first day, according to the *Indianapolis Star,* he wore a three-piece blue suit and "calmly recited his alibi for the first week in September, 1978." Hour by hour, Kimberlin's version jibed with the testimony of other defense witnesses in a manner the *Star* called "nearly letter perfect."

"The first time I learned of the bombings, was when I bought a paper at a drugstore and read the headline that said THREE BLASTS ROCK SPEEDWAY," he testified. He set forth his biography: health food promoter, aviator, vegetarian, practitioner of Transcendental Meditation, all-around pacifist. He portrayed himself as a beacon of New Age wholesomeness; his construction project in Jackson County was conceived as a "self-sufficient home to retreat from the headaches of the city." His alibi shimmered with grace notes. When the seventh bomb detonated, he said, he was at home in Eagle Creek with his mother and sister. He heard about it during a television broadcast and thought immediately of his grandmother, who lived in Speedway. "My concern was about my grandmother, because she is about seventy-five years old and has a bad heart," he testified.

Kimberlin's testimony fell in the middle of the trial, before Scott Bixler, Frankie Gonzalez, Louise Crosby, and Yvonne Barton turned up as rebuttal witnesses. So to explain how he happened to be driving a vehicle that brimmed with evidence, he adhered to Plan A: Bixler and Scott Kimberlin had used the car in the days preceding his arrest. Brett conceded ownership of the military uniforms and insignia, the police badges and apparatus. Only one Scott or both, however, could explain how the unambiguously incriminating stuff found its way into the trunk, because Brett—how many times did he have to say it?—*never had a key to the trunk.* Recapitulating his defense from the second trial, he recounted how Scott Kimberlin had taken possession of the Tovex after the initial blasting. "At that time, we still had to take out some trees and work at the bottom of a valley," he testified. "We had to use the explosives to take out tree stumps."

And so forth. The eyewitness, Lynn Coleman, could not possibly have been describing Brett when he told of a bomber who was neatly dressed in a sport coat and tie and drove a clean Mercedes. Kimberlin invariably dressed in blue jeans and T-shirts, never in a sport coat and tie; his Mercedes had body damage and he rarely washed it. Nor had the hypnosis witnesses ever done business with Brett; two Graham Electronics clerks gave statements that they had sold timers to a customer who wore a wristwatch, but Brett hadn't worn jewelry or watches since junior high school. The lead shot that the hypnotized Mercedes mechanic, Andy Jones, recalled seeing in the trunk of Kimberlin's car was actually a box of lead pellets, for a nonlethal pistol that he used to round up horses.

Implicit in his testimony was that evidence had been tampered with to frame him. His suitcase and a paper bag containing security officer badges and embossed plastic name tags, he claimed, were on the backseat of the Impala when he parked at the printing shop. Somehow—there was no delicate way to level this charge—these objects wound up inside the trunk. And somehow—the same somehow, of course—the timers, which bore no fingerprints and which he'd never laid eyes on until they were displayed by the government at trial, wound up inside the suitcase. Stanton warned him against explicitly stating in open court that this evidence had been planted. Instead, Stanton insinuated this during his closing argument. "Sometimes the government goes awry," he said. "Sometimes the government assumes guilt and then finds something [that] makes them think the man is guilty and then just gets real wrong-headed about something. I suggest to you that that is what has happened in this case."

The verdict enabled Kimberlin to shed his inhibitions about calling his accusers cheaters and liars and enemies of the Bill of Rights. In time, he could anatomize the government's duplicity with the dexterity of a vascular surgeon. At the first trial, Assistant U.S. Attorney Pylitt likened the chain of evidence to a giant jigsaw puzzle. That new pieces emerged during the second and third trials—Ron Confer's tale of having seen cartons of explosives in Kimberlin's truck; Lynn Coleman's eyewitness testimony; Frankie Gonzalez's Texas travelogue and the dramatic unearthing in Louise Crosby's backyard; Yvonne Barton's letter to Louise Crosby; Bixler's assertion that he bought weapons and ammunition for Brett—Kimberlin cited as proof that the prosecution's evidence and testimony had been confected. Any piece of the puzzle that didn't quite fit—or, more tellingly, one that fit too neatly—further confirmed that he had been made the victim of corrupt collusion. If the government insisted on depicting Kimberlin as a homegrown Hannibal Lecter (vegetarian style), he could come up with a countermythology of his own and expound it with the passion of moral certainty. If he never possessed a key to the trunk of the Chevy, and if the trunk was pried open with a crowbar in the presence of FBI and the ATF agents—revealing a suitcase bearing his initials and, inside, four Mark Time timers—the only conceivable interpretation was that the government, not Brett Kimberlin, deserved to be on trial.

I ONCE asked Kimberlin to itemize the investigative irregularities and breaches of due process perpetrated by the government, and he replied with three and a half single-spaced pages. When I studied this document and tried to distinguish between conjecture and provable fact, the exercise struck me as folly. The allegations were familiar—I had heard most of them in our earliest conversations—and I had long since learned that to cavil over minor details, let alone contradict Kimberlin's version of reality, meant coping with a bristling eruption of offended pride. Ultimately, the minor details mattered enormously, because they were what had made Kimberlin's narratives compelling and credible at first blush. He was a master at leveraging a tree here and a tree there into an entire fog-shrouded forest. What most dampened my appetite for a point-by-point dissection, however, was a perception of the Speedway bombing case that I had developed, a feeling of epistemological futility that I summed up with a tautology: I don't know what I don't know. Again and again, Kimberlin's explanations* contained elements that seemed to extend the margins of the plausible into the sphere of the apparitional. All my attempts to nail down an empirical "truth" were doomed: Scott Kimberlin was dead; Bixler had disappeared; the Bartons weren't talking; the prosecutors Foster and Thar, having taken umbrage at what I had written about Kimberlin in *The New Yorker,* also refused to talk. Not only was I deprived of certain information; I didn't even have a firm fix on what information I was deprived of.

ONE PART of the puzzle—the Tovex, timers, blasting caps, and rifle found beneath Louise Crosby's cedar tree—bewildered me more than any other. How did they get there? Their serendipitous discovery—was that really how it happened? The government postulated that Kimberlin put them there when he and Frankie Gonzalez went to Austin in the late summer or early fall of 1978—but never broached the thundering *Why?* The prosecution case was a kaleidoscope of curious details that, severed from their subtext, could never be pulled into crystalline focus. In the minds of the investigators and prosecutors, the motive for this errand flowed logically from that subtext: Kimberlin's disturbing attachment to Jessica Barton, which led to the murder of Julia Scyphers, which led to the bombings. That these causal linkages were unmentionable in open court meant that when Louise Crosby came to the witness stand and spoke of finding what she had found, the jurors grasped that, yes, she was the sister of the defense's main alibi witness and, yes, the two women represented opposing sympathies—but not that the corpse of their mother lay between them.

What did the government suppose the jury would make of this evidence? When Stanton denounced Foster and Thar for trying to paint Kimberlin as a bad man, he was not hallucinating, but he was

* See Appendix, pages 367–381.

ignoring the fodder that Kimberlin himself had provided for their assault on his character. Repeatedly, Stanton objected that the prosecution's digressions—references to Kimberlin's drug-dealing or military-insignia convictions, or unflattering appraisals of his personality—were irrelevant to the charges in the indictment. More often than not, however, Judge Steckler overruled, having accepted the government's line that the defense had opened the door to the evidence or testimony in question.

To counter Kimberlin's claim that he was temperamentally incapable of violence ("not prone to assaultive behavior"), for instance, the government cited the array of weapons that had been seized during the drug bust in Texas. Among them was a .22-caliber semiautomatic pistol equipped with a silencer. The testimony of Bixler placed this gun in Kimberlin's hands, along with the half-dozen AR-15s he said he had bought for the defendant. To show that Kimberlin was not necessarily an unalloyed altruist who catered to the needs of children and grandmothers, the government confronted Sandi Barton with her grand jury testimony that, on at least two occasions, Brett had slapped Jessica. Another time, Sandi had told the grand jury, when Jessica refused to speak to Brett he seized her beloved dog, Snoopy. To undermine Kimberlin's credibility in general, Foster maneuvered him into invoking the Fifth Amendment. On September 7, the day after the last bombing, Kimberlin testified, he had flown to Texas from Dayton. Foster asked whom he had met with there, and Kimberlin declined to answer. Further questioning along these lines evoked the same nonresponse. Kimberlin's rationale—he had gone to Texas on drug business, and it was dishonorable to give up the names of Frankie Gonzalez and his other associates—never reached the ears of the jurors. What they received was the defendant's evasiveness. If Kimberlin had known that Gonzalez was waiting in the wings as a rebuttal witness, would he have answered Foster's questions differently? Foster had him in a box.

Still: why hide bomb components and an untraceable rifle in the Crosbys' yard? In theory, the apparent lack of motive for the bombings might have worked to Kimberlin's advantage—by permitting the worm of reasonable doubt to burrow into the minds of a few jurors— but the psychology of terrorism doesn't really work that way. If someone had anonymously claimed responsibility for the bombings as political acts, the crimes would have been no less egregious yet would've *seemed* less random and therefore less frightening. As it was, the mysterious provenance of the cache under the cedar tree, instead of absolving Kimberlin, tended to amplify one's revulsion at the transgressions he was accused of. Louise Crosby's testimony echoed the government's favorite theme: Only a bad man would plant bombs and expose innocents to mortal harm, never mind the intent. And only a truly depraved soul—unpredictable, sinister beyond reason— would secrete evidence thousands of miles away, in a location and manner that compounded the original terror.

Three days after the verdict, the *Indianapolis Star* published a story that described Kimberlin's encounter with Ben Niehaus in Corpus Christi following his arrest in February 1979. This conversation, according to an investigative report filed by Niehaus, lasted five hours—or, according to Kimberlin, about five minutes. Niehaus noted that Kimberlin "stated that if we wanted to find out who murdered Mrs. Scyphers, we should consider Sandra Barton's brother-in-law [Jack Crosby] in Austin, Texas, who Kimberlin said was a CIA agent." The *Star* reporter, Joe Gelarden, paraphrased Niehaus's written report: "According to sources, Kimberlin knew the [Crosbys] were helping police in the Julia Scyphers murder probe. He once tried to get Niehaus to investigate the [Crosbys], who took in Sandi Barton's daughters after their grandmother was murdered. Informants reported Kimberlin left the bag at the [Crosby] residence to frame them for the Speedway bombings."

The treatment Kimberlin received from the Indianapolis media often provoked his outrage, and he was most offended by the *Star*. Gelarden, he explained, was a government stooge who would print anything the prosecution fed him. Complaining about this lack of integrity, he referred to "an article written by Gelarden saying that I had told [Niehaus] that the Scyphers murder weapon was buried in the Crosbys' backyard."

This was a startling remark. I had read and indexed all the Indianapolis newspaper clippings about the murder and the bombings, but I'd never come across any reference to the murder weapon being buried anywhere. A rereading of Gelarden's clippings confirmed this for me. I had, however, recently *heard* from a government source that Kimberlin had indeed made the remark to Niehaus about the murder weapon. My bewilderment deepened: If I had never mentioned a buried murder weapon to Kimberlin, and if no such detail had ever been reported in the newspaper, what had prompted his denial? When a person claims to know where a murder weapon is buried, even if he's trying to finger someone else, what does that imply? Each step I took in the direction of the truth, it seemed, added to my inventory of slippery questions.

The government, Kimberlin told me, in cahoots with Louise Crosby, had rigged the evidence under the cedar tree—just the sort of theatrical flourish Niehaus relished. "I think Niehaus was involved with the Louise Crosby thing up to his fucking ears," he said. "I think when he went down to Texas to see me he planted it. I think she was lying about how she found it. He's in Texas and less than a month later she finds this stuff? Come *on*. . . . It was too coincidental. I think it was some harebrained scheme of Niehaus's, similar to the one where they raided my property in Jackson County."

But how, I asked, could Niehaus have planted Tovex from the same batch that Kimberlin bought in 1975?

The date-shift codes were effaced because it *wasn't* from the same batch, Kimberlin said.

What about the testimony from the ATF chemist who said that enough of the date-shift code lettering remained on the plastic casings of the Tovex to confirm that it *was* from the same batch?

"That testimony was bullshit. It's absolutely ridiculous to determine that that was from the same date of manufacture. When this agent came in and said this, Nile and I were laughing."

The proof that *he*—Kimberlin—hadn't planted it, he explained, was that the testimony of Gonzalez and Crosby caught Stanton completely off guard. "If I'd been involved with this thing, Nile would have known about it," he said. "Neither Nile nor I knew what was going on when Gonzalez was called to testify. I thought he was going to talk about marijuana."

So what about Gonzalez's testimony? I asked. Did you drive with him to suburban Austin and get out of the car for fifteen minutes? What were you doing there? Gonzalez testified that you went to Austin to see some girls, but then you left town without seeing any girls. Why did you go there?

"Listen, Frankie's testimony was basically a lie," Kimberlin said. "We never went to any fucking hotel. I never left his side. We didn't go to Austin to meet any girls; we went to buy pot. We went over to this guy's house to buy some pot. It was Mexican foot-long buds. And it was in egg cases. The only time I ever bought pot that way. They packed it that way so that the buds didn't get smashed. I remember that we paid a hundred sixty-five dollars a pound. I think I sold it for two twenty-five. Frankie and I never left each other's side. We went to this guy's house and that was it. The only thing I had with me was food. The feds granted Frankie immunity from everything he ever did in his life. They had him on taxes, conspiracy. We know that they took him to the grand jury twice and he took the Fifth. If somebody granted me full immunity from everything I'd ever done, I would get up on the stand and say what he said. He tried to give the government enough to make them happy. Niehaus flew down to Texas during the third trial and brought Gonzalez back. Niehaus is the one who put the words in his mouth, no doubt about it. If it had really happened, they would have taken him on that interstate, told him, 'Show us where you went, what you did.' It was very weak testimony. We did go on the interstate, we did go to a suburb. This guy with the pot lived in a suburb. I don't know directions in Texas. I didn't know Austin. I wouldn't have known where Pflugerville was or where the Crosbys lived if my life depended on it. Nobody ever told me where they lived. I never was there."

When I asked Stanton what he thought of the evidence beneath the cedar tree, he said, "If Brett put it there, either he was involved in the bombings and picked a real dumb place to put it, or somebody else asked him to do it and he picked a real dumb place to put it. And if he was trying to implicate the Crosbys, somebody would have had to tip off the feds."

Yes, I thought. Leading Niehaus to the Crosbys' backyard by telling him there's a murder weapon buried there—isn't that a form of tipping off the feds?

Finally, I tried out these serpentine theories on Patrick Donovan, Niehaus's partner, and realized that he had already given them plenty of thought. "If we planted the timers in the Chevy Impala, why didn't we plant all six of them?" Donovan said. "What were we trying to do—save two to frame the Crosbys? If we had extra explosives and timers, why not plant those in Brett's house in Indianapolis, at Eagle Creek? Why plant those in Texas and bury them? Why go to all that trouble? Why move your conspiracy all the way to Austin when you can just plant the stuff in his bedroom or at the Good Earth? If the government had a conspiracy, why not line up an expert witness to say that the serial number on the AR-15 that was beneath the tree was legible and that it was one of the guns Bixler had bought for Kimberlin? Or if the government's that sophisticated, why not get an AR-15 and stamp one of those serial numbers on there? The reason this evidence wasn't used at Kimberlin's first trial was because an immunity agreement hadn't yet been worked out with Frankie Gonzalez. This stuff was discovered within a month of Kimberlin's arrest down there. If we planted it, that means we've already lined up Frankie and we know he'll testify—or else we're just sure we're going to be able to find someone to perjure himself and give testimony consistent with the theory that Brett planted it there. If the purpose of planting that stuff was to frame Brett, why not figure out a way to use it at the first trial? If it's all a conspiracy, why did we fall short in the first trial?"

THE JURY began its deliberations late on a Tuesday and by early Thursday afternoon sent word that it had reached a verdict. Before the panel filed into the courtroom, Kimberlin used a pencil and a yellow legal pad to record his feelings: "Today is a sad day in the pages of American history. Today I wonder to what sub-species of animal I belong. Today I see that I will pay for the errors of others."

The pessimism—if not the narcissism—was warranted. "Guilty" on all twenty-two counts, the foreman announced. The eyewitness testimony of Lynn Coleman had been pivotal, jurors later told reporters, as had Yvonne Barton's letter to Louise Crosby. Not that other aspects of Kimberlin's alibi hadn't given the jurors pause. The *Indianapolis News* reported that one juror "said there was considerable speculation that Kimberlin had an accomplice in connection with the bombings and added, 'Maybe he did, but we don't know who it was and we figured that he would have been along to see that the bombs were planted.' "

Carolyn, though tearful, said, "Don't feel sorry for me. Feel sorry for our country. It is a sad day for everyone in the country when an innocent young man is convicted." Stanton echoed this sentiment: "The last time Brett was convicted, he told the people to feel sorry for the country, and not for him. Today, I add myself to those comments. I don't consider we lost the case. The American people did."

Kimberlin didn't go to the trouble of sounding statesmanlike. As the U.S. marshals escorted him away, he told reporters, "I expected the verdict because the government is corrupt."

WITHIN forty-eight hours of the verdict, Kimberlin got in touch with
an alternate juror named Debra Jane Irey and persuaded her to meet
with Stanton. Debbie Irey was twenty-one years old, worked as an office clerk, lived with her mother, and had spent her whole life in Indianapolis. She was not listed in the telephone directory, and her
mother had a different surname. To track her down, Kimberlin called
an Irey who turned out to be her brother, identified himself as an old
friend, and explained that he had misplaced her number.

That Kimberlin assumed she was sympathetic didn't really surprise her. During the trial, some of the jurors said they had noticed
him looking at her—she was pleasantly pretty, pale-complexioned,
with blond-streaked light-brown hair, brown eyes, and high, broad
cheekbones—and she often found herself studying his reactions to the
proceedings. It bothered her that he'd used a deception to contact her,
but she put that in perspective. If she had been a regular juror, she
would not have voted to convict. She possessed rigid personal standards—she had never smoked a cigarette, never drunk alcohol, never
used illegal drugs—but these predilections had no bearing upon her
sense that the prosecution had used unfair tactics. She was engaged to
be married, but eventually she broke off the engagement because her
fiancé could not abide her compassion for Kimberlin. Her fiancé, she
would conclude, was a hypocrite; somehow it was all right that he
smoked marijuana with his friends, but it wasn't all right that Kimberlin smuggled the stuff. Dragging Kimberlin's drug running into the
bombing case was a prosecution trick to cloud the facts. The bad-
man mythology offended her, and so did the use of hypnosis. The government, she believed, was capable of manufacturing evidence. She
was suspicious of the five-month lag between Kimberlin's arrest at the
printing shop and his indictment. Lynn Coleman, she thought, was
not credible.

Irey went to see Kimberlin at the Marion County Jail, accompanied by one of Stanton's associates, and Kimberlin made certain the
press became aware of the visit. An interview that she gave to David
Rohn, of the *News,* carried the headline ALTERNATE JUROR IS PRO KIM-
BERLIN. In conversations with both Kimberlin and Stanton, she cited
what she said were examples of juror misconduct: Some jurors discussed the case during recesses, in defiance of Judge Steckler's warn-
ings not to do so; some jurors referred to events that occurred when

they were excused from the courtroom, which could only mean that they had been following news accounts; one juror frequently napped during the presentation of evidence; another once declared, "They ought to hang him now, so that we can go home"; a juror who had worked as a legal secretary told the others that Stanton represented only guilty individuals and got them off "scot-free."

Irey's allegations were incorporated in a motion Stanton filed requesting a new trial, but this was rejected by Judge Steckler. When, next, she repeated her claims in a letter and an affidavit that she sent to Judge Thomas Fairchild, of the U.S. Court of Appeals for the Seventh Circuit, she received a perfunctory, noncommittal response. In time, her suggestions that the jury's deliberations had been tainted would become part of Kimberlin's comprehensive appeal to the Seventh Circuit. Also, in time, her relationship with him would acquire an entirely different content and significance.

"DEAR SARAH" was the salutation, and 18 November 1981 the date, on a letter Kimberlin addressed to Sarah Evans Barker, the U.S. Attorney for the Southern District of Indiana.

It has been a long month since that fateful day in October, a month filled with trial and tribulation for myself and all of those who love America like I do. I am writing you today, in the hopes that I am not premature, to express myself with pencil on paper. . . . Needless to say I was disgusted and disappointed with the verdict, but admittedly, not surprised. I say that because of the case that was presented by "your boys." . . . The case that was presented was an indictment against the Constitution, it greatly saddened me. As I told Nile many times throughout the trial, "I can deal with the truth, it's just all the lies that I can't defend against." . . . I did not do the bombings. . . .

Sarah, I promise you that I will not end my fight for liberty and justice until I am vindicated. I promise you protracted litigation on all fronts. I promise you appeals on all levels. I promise you that someday I will win and I will be liberated. . . . I promise you that I will fight for my Constitution, drafted by my Founding Fathers. . . . Sarah, when you think of me you can smile—for I am fighting for all Americans including yourself. . . . I am happy with myself. I am smiling. I hope and pray with all sincerity that you are, too. I will close with the words of another American hero, words that I affirm everyday, "I have not yet begun to fight." Truly, Brett.

At his sentencing hearing, six weeks later, Kimberlin held forth in this same spirit. When Judge Steckler invited him to share any thoughts he might have as to why the court should not impose a sentence, he showed no reticence: "Well, first of all, I think probably the—the only mitigating reason is that I'm innocent, and I have taken this trial—I have been to three trials on this same indictment—because I am innocent."

After this halting beginning, Kimberlin briskly accelerated: "If I am sentenced to one day or one hundred years, to me it's a travesty and a tragedy and an injustice, and for that reason I would ask that I don't have an executed sentence. And furthermore, I have decided and am prepared to take this on appellant levels and do everything possible to vindicate myself, whether through the district court, appellate court, Supreme Court. If I have to go to the United Nations I plan on doing that, and I plan on going to the World Court. I plan on filing lawsuits against every person that I know that lied against me and any agencies that were involved with corruption and use of perjured testimony. And I plan to ask the United States Attorney for the Southern District of Indiana and the Justice Department in Washington to conduct a full grand jury investigation of any use of perjured testimony and government misconduct in this case. I plan on asking for full support from the media and from all people in Indianapolis, and some friends and relatives and supporters have started a freedom committee. And I have thousands of signatures to present to the judge at this time to show that I have support and there are people that know that I am innocent, as well as myself.

"I plan to file very soon with this court a motion for a new trial based on the government's use of perjured testimony, and I have the proof. I plan to present it, and I hope that the court will see that the government did use perjured testimony and grant me a new trial at that time."

Judge Steckler wasn't interested in seeing Kimberlin's signed petitions, he said, nor, for that matter, had he relied upon a sentencing memorandum prepared by the government. The memorandum reflected the prosecutors' wish that, as Kennard Foster noted when his turn to speak arrived, "that man not walk the streets to terrorize any other citizens." Foster emphasized that the law allowed for the imposition of sentences totaling two hundred thirty years, but the government felt that ninety-three years would suffice. Steckler, however, had independently made up his mind.

"You haven't learned some of the very simple, basic lessons of social living, living in society where people have the right to go unmolested, unharmed, uninjured from the use of drugs because someone wants to make a profit in trafficking in drugs," the judge told Kimberlin. "You should know this. I think it's time for you, rather than to be spending all your time on preparing documents, to go into the basic knowledge of mankind. Go back to some of the early scholars. Read what they have proven throughout the course of history. Go back to the cradle of knowledge. Read what the great Greek philosophers spoke for our benefit, which we still can rely upon today. They haven't been proven to be wrong. And so I am disappointed; I am disappointed that I took it upon myself to exercise the courage to put you on probation the first time you were ever in trouble. I am sorry that you let us down. So I feel today it is my duty to protect society from your conduct. . . . I am convinced after hearing the evidence that you are not only guilty of the offenses with which you were charged but that you have not done one single thing to cooperate with the government to clarify what may have happened or what did happen which you could help clarify.

"The evidence shows your implication so deeply that any reasonable person could ask the question, 'If he is so implicated, why doesn't he do something to aid the government in establishing the real bomber?' If you are not the real bomber, why don't you do that? Why haven't you done it? You haven't done it, and your failure to do it does not assist you under the circumstances. . . . Do you have anything you wish to state before I pronounce the judgment?"

"Nothing except I am innocent," Kimberlin replied. "I am innocent and I don't think you should hold it against me that I didn't cooperate with the government. That, to me, is not a crime, and it is not punishable by law."

Whereupon Judge Steckler—whose eleventh-hour expectation of contrition or remorse seems, by turns, quaint and ludicrous—gave him fifty years.

22

EXCEPT for the part about the United Nations and the World
Court, Kimberlin wasn't bluffing when he told Judge Steckler
his plans. By the time of his sentencing, he had already been in
custody almost three years. Twelve more years elapsed before his release on parole, and he spent virtually every intervening day petitioning for an audience—before Bureau of Prisons administrative panels,
with parole commissioners, in state and federal courts, in trial-level
and appellate courts (including the U.S. Supreme Court), and, of
course, in the media.

He had not yet been convicted of the bombings when he wrote to
Sarah Evans Barker, the U.S. Attorney, requesting a grand jury investigation of the Jackson County search. His next dispatch to her was
the "Dear Sarah . . . 'I have not yet begun to fight' " manifesto, and
a month later he wrote again, this time demanding the appointment
of a special prosecutor "to investigate the illegalities with the construction and presentation of my case . . . the use of planted evidence,
perjured testimony, destroyed evidence, prosecutorial misconduct
and vindictiveness . . . and violations of my civil rights by government agents and attorneys." The coup de grâce of this epistle was diverting: "I hope you don't think for one minute that I am doing this
out of frustration or revenge. I can honestly tell you that had I been
acquitted, I would have done the same thing." To assume that his demeanor was ironic or less than sincere was to misread and underesti-
mate him. The same day he put that letter in the mail, he filed a $24
million damage suit against Ronald Confer, claiming his testimony
contained "malicious falsehoods" that were intended to "cause
harm." When nine months passed without Barker's appointing a special prosecutor, he sued her as well, along with two dozen law enforcement officials (including William French Smith, the attorney
general of the United States) and several witnesses (including Lynn

Coleman and, for good measure, Confer again). There could be no mistaking his fundamental jurisprudential strategy: Sue the bastards; then sue them some more; then some more.

"The same laws that put you in will get you out," Greg Kimberlin advised his son, adding that when you're locked up, there are worse places to kill time than the law library. Even without his father's prodding, Brett would have found his way there. What any given convict did to wind up in prison mattered far less than whatever *they*—the ubiquitous and odious *they*, the government's morally rancid agents and prosecutors—had done to make the charges stick. Brett did not take long to realize that in the joint, nobody had more juice than a jailhouse lawyer. Here was a craft whose rewards included power and protection and access to worthwhile information. The ultimate carrot, of course, was freedom. Jailhouse law suited all of Kimberlin's aptitudes: It appealed to his peripatetic imagination and disciplined habits, offered rich opportunities for creative sophistry, and gratified his bottomless capacity for self-justification.

FOR THREE months, Kimberlin resided at the federal prison in Terre Haute, Indiana, in a unit reserved for convicts awaiting long-term assignments to other institutions. This was a relatively sheltered form of incarceration. He had long since accommodated himself to the protocols of prison life, however, and he harbored no illusions. On earlier rotations through Terre Haute, between trials in Indianapolis, he had been housed in the open population. He had seen one convict having sex with his own preadolescent daughter in the visitors' room. He had seen other convicts having sex with each other. He had resisted a sexual predator by tossing powdered chlorine cleanser in his face. The predator was African American, Kimberlin told me, and as he fended him off he shouted, "You fucking nigger! You motherfucking nigger! Get the fuck away from me! I'll kill you, you motherfucker!" Kimberlin enjoyed telling this story. When I asked whether he hadn't feared reprisal, he said, "No, I wasn't afraid of reprisal because, let me tell you, anytime you show strength in prison, nobody will fuck with you. When you show weakness, you get fucked with."

Terre Haute lived up to its reputation as one of the grimmest institutions in the federal prison system, but when Kimberlin learned that his next home would be in Oxford, Wisconsin, he was not eager to depart. Going to Oxford meant being too far away from his family and his attorneys; he preferred to be designated to the Metropolitan Correction Center in downtown Chicago. Without having seen MCC Chicago, he knew that compared to Terre Haute and Oxford, "it was like a Holiday Inn," with carpeted floors, wooden cell doors instead of metal bars, private shower stalls.

At Oxford, he was assigned as a quality-control clerk at a prison factory that manufactured cables for military aircraft and tanks. His task was to inspect the finished goods. Each day, he said, he did his work quickly and then tried to immerse himself in a book, but the prison guard who was his overseer objected to his reading on the job. When he persisted, the guard threatened to give him a "shot"—to write an incident report that could lead to disciplinary action. So he stopped bringing a book to work, he said, and instead devoted his spare time to sabotage. "I'd run the cables through quality control," he said. "I'd check them. I'd sign off on them. And then I'd cut some of the damn wires."

NILE STANTON had no evident flair for post-conviction legal practice. While preparing for the third trial, he represented Kimberlin before the Seventh Circuit, where he argued, fruitlessly, for a new trial on the military-insignia charges and related counts. Because Kimberlin intended to challenge each of his convictions, he was in the market for a full-time appellate specialist. Stanton referred him to a Chicago attorney named John Gubbins, who until recently had served as the senior staff attorney for the Seventh Circuit. What Stanton did not realize was that Gubbins had serious limitations as a manager and organizer of his time. For Kimberlin, this became a source of both exasperation and motivation, proof that "no lawyer was going to be as dedicated as I was to my own case."

Kimberlin had been at Oxford less than three months—not quite long enough to cripple the United States armed forces with his wirecutters—when his request for a transfer to MCC Chicago was granted. Now his career as a jailhouse lawyer began in earnest. Within a week of his move, he received coaching from another convict and was able to file Freedom of Information Act disclosure suits against the FBI, the U.S. Customs Service, the DEA, and the U.S. Navy. He was fishing for any information that might prove useful for his appeals. On his work detail, he was a clerk; he allocated jobs to the sixty or so other convicts in his unit. These duties demanded a couple of hours in the morning, and he was free to spend his afternoons in the law library.

In the fall of 1983, a staff member at MCC Chicago asked Kimberlin to prepare a list of cases in which he was either a plaintiff or an appellant, and there were more than twenty. "I began working on motions for reductions of sentences and motions to vacate convictions," he said. "Then I branched into tort claims against the Bureau of Prisons and other civil litigation. I filed a shitload of civil suits. I started suing everybody—all the people who lied about me. I sued the agents who performed the illegal search and seizure of my home and property." Eventually, Kimberlin filed more than a hundred lawsuits and motions in the federal courts on his own behalf, and nearly that many for other convicts. In a barbed denial of one of his many motions for a reduction of sentence, a panel of Seventh Circuit judges remarked: "Kimberlin is no stranger to the appellate proceedings." He sued an Indiana probation officer who he alleged had arranged for false and defamatory information to find its way into his prison file. When he felt he had been unfairly denied a parole hearing on his drug conviction, he sued a warden. Claiming he had been unjustly deprived of "good time" credit, he sued the U.S. attorney general. When he thought he had found a loophole in a federal sentencing-reform law, he sued the Parole Commission, claiming that he and thousands of other convicts should immediately be put on the street.

HE ALSO learned what it felt like to be on the receiving end of a lawsuit. On the eve of the first bombings trial, in September 1980, Kimberlin was sued in Marion County Superior Court by Carl and Sandra DeLong, who wanted $5 million for their pain and suffering. Because any finding of liability hinged upon legal proof that Kimberlin had caused the explosion that caused the DeLongs' injuries, the lawsuit was held in abeyance until after his conviction at the third trial. Along with their son, Steve, the DeLongs attended Kimberlin's sentencing hearing, and a few days later a front-page feature story appeared in the *Star*, with the headline SPEEDWAY BOMB VICTIM NOT INTERESTED IN REVENGE. The article, which was written by Joe Gelarden, Kimberlin's favorite media antagonist, described the family as it joined the crowd filing out of the courtroom: "Carl D. DeLong, 43, husband, father, soldier, victim, the man whose right leg was ripped from his body by the finale of Kimberlin's Tovex charade, felt the familiar pain as the plastic and steel prosthesis locked in place." DeLong told Gelarden, "I think justice has been done . . . so far. But it is hard to sort out in your mind. I guess it'll take two or three days to get it straight. I want justice. Not revenge, justice."

Steve DeLong made known his pure contempt for Kimberlin: " 'I hate his guts. He is just a little rat,' snapped the handsome, broad-shouldered former football middle linebacker"—whose game Carl had just finished watching the evening his leg was blown off.

A mysterious encounter—a sensory experience comparable to a divine visitation—had saved DeLong's life, he told Gelarden. As he lay on the pavement, bleeding, he yelled, "I want to die!" A neighbor who was applying a tourniquet shouted, "You aren't gonna die!" And then, DeLong said, he heard another, unearthly voice:

"All of a sudden, it wasn't him (the neighbor) talking at all. I heard a voice that said 'Do you believe in me?' I said 'What . . . who are you?' And there wasn't anybody around. He [the voice] said, 'Stay awake, fight, and believe in me.' " In the emergency room, though he had been sedated, DeLong tried to obey the voice's instructions until it spoke again: "The voice said, 'You showed me you believed in me. Now go to sleep.' And I was out." Once more, weeks later, in De-Long's hospital room, the voice returned, and he asked it, "What do you want from me?" The voice replied, "Nothing. Go out and be seen. Show what you can do." A photograph of the DeLongs—Carl smiling assuredly and Sandra appearing equally sanguine—illustrated this article. The caption said: "Bombing victim Carl DeLong, wife Sandra, restore lives."

IN FACT, family members would later testify, Carl DeLong had been less and less able to put his life back together. Whatever promises he had made to the mysterious voice became harder to keep. His daughter, Deanne, would recall that she had seen him remove his artificial limb and beat it on the ground in frustration. He still worked at his job as a quality inspector at the General Motors plant, but his physical and mental health had deteriorated. The difficulty of ambulating with a prosthesis caused chronic back pain, and there was a serious possibility that his remaining leg would have to be amputated. He was drinking heavily, usually late at night at the American Legion post in Speedway. He refused offers of help. The only time he would discuss his problems with family members was when he was drunk; when he sobered up, he couldn't recall these conversations. Often, he seemed to be in the grip of frightening flashbacks, though it was unclear whether they emanated from his experiences in Vietnam or his experience in the parking lot of Speedway High. His irrational bursts of hostility alarmed the family. He would disappear for days at a time. Finally, it all became more than Sandra could tolerate, and she filed for divorce.

On the morning of 24 February 1983, a bit more than a year after the sentencing and three days after the divorce filing, Carl was awake early. He reviewed several letters that he had written: to his wife, his son, his daughter, his son-in-law, and his granddaughter, declarations that sounded one constant theme—sorrow and regret, but not anger. Then he went to his garage and, with the door closed, turned on the ignition of his automobile and gave himself permission to go to sleep one last time. The coroner's certificate listed the death as a suicide caused by carbon monoxide intoxication.

The DeLongs' lawsuit came to trial eight months later, in the courtroom of Judge Michael T. Dugan. Kimberlin was at MCC and was not permitted to attend the civil trial in Indiana. The latter was a bifurcated affair—facts first, damages second—and its resolution amounted to both a whimper and a bang. A single ruling from the bench dispensed with the fact-finding portion of the proceeding. In September 1982, the Indiana legislature had passed a law—inspired in part by the Speedway bombings—that made it possible to use a felony conviction as evidence in a civil complaint. Invoking this statute, the DeLongs' attorney, Paula Thrun Kight, said that Kimberlin's guilt was conclusive proof of his liability, and she filed a motion for summary judgment, which Judge Dugan accepted.

Monetary compensation was the only issue that the six-person jury had to reckon with. As they were poised to begin their work, Kight moved to amend the original complaint. Now the lawsuit sought damages not for Carl's injuries but for his wrongful death. Kimberlin was represented by David Hennessy, an associate of Nile Stanton's. Hennessy's request for a continuance was denied, and the plaintiff's motion was granted; Kimberlin later protested that the court never gave him a fair chance to contest the assumption that De-Long's suicide was a consequence of his maiming. The testimony was completed in less than a day, with DeLong's wife and children serving as the main witnesses. After brief deliberations, the jury awarded Sandra $360,000 for her own injuries and $1,250,000 on the wrongful-death claim. Kimberlin of course immediately mobilized an appeal. In a separate action, in federal court, he succeeded in having himself legally designated a pauper. The civil tort judgment—for what it was worth—meant that for the remainder of Kimberlin's imprisonment, Sandra DeLong was in a position to attach a lien against any identifiable income or assets.

THE INTANGIBLE perquisites of jailhouse law—foremost among them status—allowed Kimberlin to cultivate a comfortable aloofness. His diatribes against the "profoundly corrupt" nature of the American judicial and penal systems tended not to culminate in solidarity fests with his fellow convicts. He knew he had more to gain by promoting himself as an oppressed individual than as a member of an oppressed class. At our first meeting, in the visitors' room in Memphis, he told me, "When I come to a prison I find out who the smartest, most interesting guys are and I hang out with them. I mind my own business. I don't get involved with other people's business. You don't hang around with trash, with something that stinks, or you start smelling too."

Stanton's associate Kevin McShane said to me, before I'd even met Kimberlin face-to-face, "Brett's never allowed himself to be institutionalized. He's always kept his head on the outside." This observation, on its surface, seemed eloquently apt. Kimberlin was a virtuoso of the telephone. Another convict introduced him to a woman who worked as a switchboard operator for a Chicago manufacturing company that had a WATS line. For the price of a local call, Kimberlin would, with her assistance, stay on the phone for hours. "She was just like a personal operator for me," he recalled. "It was great. As soon as a call was done, it would click right back to her. I mean, she saved me tens and tens of thousands of dollars." In a separate scam, he claimed, he and two other convicts availed themselves of a corporate telephone credit card access code, ran up charges well into six figures, and never got caught. Kimberlin seemed to have memorized the contents of a large Rolodex. There was no one he was too timid to call, no favor he was loath to solicit. "Media mogul is my middle name," he liked to half joke. "During my first trial, my lawyers told me to stay away from the press. But later I realized that I had to deal with the press. I was pissed off because it was the press that was doing me in, so I needed to get them on my side. I just started working them. I beat 'em to death."

Did Kimberlin recognize that his great skill at manipulating others depended upon his being locked up? For a year and a half, I had almost daily conversations with him while he was still doing time in Memphis, and whenever the phone rang and I heard his voice, I sensed a special hollowness in the timbre of the connection—an added dimension of long distance. This distance corresponded to my understanding that no matter how well he succeeded in keeping his head on the outside, I could never project my head *inside*. Empathy with Kimberlin was impossible because, questions of guilt or innocence aside, he had witnessed events and experienced emotions that I could only imagine, only with dread. Given that he literally and metaphorically had my home phone number, this was an unequal arrangement I had decided I could live with. Consciously or intuitively, Kimberlin grasped that this was the essence of his relationship with the outside world, and he used it brilliantly as a lever. Again and again in our conversations, he characterized as "close" friendships his transactions with people who, having discovered themselves wedged into a corner by a combination of his presumptuousness and their own fear of closeness, had tacitly agreed to be manipulated in ways that felt safely antiseptic. The switchboard operator who facilitated his phone calls, for instance, was "one of my girlfriends"—though he never laid eyes on her. Other people who were clearly even more marginal, but who at some point had accepted his collect calls, he would refer to as "some of my strongest supporters." In time, I stopped debating whether his narcissism was a fundamental component of his personality or an adaptive trait acquired for prison survival. What mattered was that it was the engine powering him. And I came to see his talent for keeping "his head on the outside" as, in actuality, a propensity for keeping his public head deeply submerged within his own private head.

. . .

BY THE TIME Kimberlin arrived in Chicago, Debbie Irey had made the transition from sympathetic alternate juror to paramour. For more than a year, they sustained a long-distance romance. They talked on the phone every day, and she would visit once a month—until, finally, she moved to Chicago. This was an enormous leap; everyone she had ever known was back in Indiana. She found an office job in a North Shore suburb, and each evening after work she would head to the Loop, to MCC, where she would sit with Kimberlin for two hours in the main visitors' room. If one of the private attorney rooms was free, and if an accommodating guard was on duty, they would sneak what Kimberlin described as conjugal visits. She stayed in Chicago a year and had no other friendships the entire time. Kimberlin's head was more on the outside than hers.

The personal nature of their relationship was not disclosed in the letters that Kimberlin drafted and Irey signed and sent to various congressmen. The first of these mailings, which went to the members of the Senate and House judiciary committees, called for hearings on the use of hypnosis in criminal investigations. Describing her experience as an alternate juror, Irey mixed melodrama with a plea for enlightened public policy awareness: "Immediately after the verdict I committed myself to righting the miscarriage that occurred that day. I have developed a keen interest in hypnosis, and in my investigations the more I learned the more convinced I became that the use of hypnosis as a tool of the prosecution in a criminal case is extremely dangerous to the accused and a hoax perpetrated on [the] American Judicial System."

Kimberlin's routine encounters with indifference and rejection rarely deterred him. He pressed ahead, like a drone in a telemarketing boiler room, motivated by alternating currents of optimism, cynicism, and cunning. "I've never been depressed to the point of inaction—or never for more than twenty-four or forty-eight hours," he said. "Most people in prison just tend to react to what happens to them. I knew I always had to have a plan. I would think and analyze and methodically do what I had to do. I took the attitude that I couldn't let a week go by without trying something new to push this case. I'd try this, and if it didn't work I'd try that, and if that didn't work I'd try something else."

An ostensible casualty of posthypnotic testimony had far greater potential media appeal than an unadorned drug smuggler or bomber or victim of prosecutorial zeal, so that became Brett's leitmotiv. He built a pyramid. To various Chicago publications and television and radio stations he sent clippings from the Indianapolis newspapers about Debbie Irey's belief in his innocence. Early on, after James Warren, of the *Chicago Sun-Times*, did a story, he circulated the clipping, and as new articles about him appeared, he added those to his mailings. In this manner he accumulated ink in, among other places, the *Chicago Tribune*, the *Chicago Daily Law Bulletin*, *Chicago Lawyer*, *Chicago Reader*, *Chicago Magazine*, and *Judicature*, a national magazine read primarily by judges. He got airtime from a National Public Radio outlet and a CBS television affiliate in Chicago, and from a CBS affiliate in Pittsburgh. He hounded "Good Morning America," "Donahue," "60 Minutes," "The MacNeil-Lehrer Report," *Time*, *Newsweek*, *U.S. News & World Report*, *Playboy*, *Hustler*, *People*, *The Village Voice*, the *New York Times*, the *Washington Post*—confident that, sooner or later, he would wear them down.

His roster of press contacts grew to more than two hundred. The journalistic allure of the hypnosis angle lay in its combination of "Twilight Zone"-iness and accessibility. Kimberlin had absorbed virtually all the extant medical-legal literature on hypnosis, and he often corresponded with scientific experts who opposed its admissibility in criminal trials. He could lay out the case against posthypnotic testimony with fluency and specificity. Thus did many reporters and editors, responding to Kimberlin's articulateness, intelligence, legal scholarship, and upper-middle-class background, become seduced by the illusion that they were dealing with someone who was actually or potentially like themselves.

IN INDIANAPOLIS, where name recognition was not a problem, Kimberlin spiced his communiqués with an unintentionally ironic hometown-boy-made-good flavor. During his first summer in Chicago, his high school class held its tenth reunion, and he sent a three-minute tape-recorded pontification. According to the *News*, Kimberlin gravely reminded his classmates that "domestic and international events . . . keep the world in an upheaval, and these conditions create the greatest burden on youth, especially our generation. [But] our generation's impact against these systems is our only hope for the future." He said his "greatest tip of advice" was to "love and respect your freedom and liberty with a passion, for this is the greatest thing you or any American can possess today." In an op-ed column he wrote for an Indianapolis alternative weekly called *Taboo,* he railed against Ronald Reagan's judicial appointees and urged anyone doing jury duty to vote for acquittal: "When you vote, vote for liberty, freedom of choice and the pursuit of happiness. A 'not guilty' vote will, more likely than not, be a vote *for* justice and against an unjust law. Your 'not guilty' vote will be your way of nullifying the laws passed by a Congress you did not support. . . . It takes a strong conscience and a tremendous adherence to individual rights and values to vote 'not guilty.' Don't be afraid to do it. It is one of the best highs going. Well, that's it from the typewriter of Brett Kimberlin for today. Have a wonderful summer and when you have fun, have a little fun for me, too. Until I am able to join you, I remain, unjustly incarcerated."

23

I N FEBRUARY 1984, a 273-page appellant's brief in the matter of
U.S. v. *Kimberlin* was delivered to the clerk of the United States
Court of Appeals for the Seventh Circuit. Several cases titled *U.S.
v. Kimberlin*—all the convictions from the 1979 indictment in Indiana, as well as motions for new trials—had been consolidated into a
single appeal, which sagged under the burden of the disparate factual
and constitutional complexities the petitioner wished to address. This
hernia-inducing brief grossly overshot the fifty-page maximum length
permitted by the court, and it was rejected by the senior staff attorney of the Seventh Circuit without receiving even a cursory reading.

Listed as the petitioner's lead attorney-of-record was John Gubbins, the former senior staff attorney in the Seventh Circuit. If Gubbins's ex-colleagues intended the summary rejection as a personal
reproach, the disapprobation was misplaced, because Gubbins had
contributed virtually nothing to the research or drafting of the appeal. Listed as cocounsel was a Chicago solo practitioner named
Donald V. Morano. The reality was that Morano had assumed the
duties that the Kimberlin family had hired the dilatory Gubbins to
carry out. And Morano in turn had engaged the services of a young
lawyer who, though not a member of the bar and therefore not qualified to be officially listed as cocounsel, was one of the most diligent
and ambitious young advocates in the federal system. This, of course,
was Kimberlin himself.

More than two years elapsed between Kimberlin's final conviction and the filing of the appeal. Procedural arguments had dragged
on for many months, and there had been an added delay while the
court reporter prepared the transcript of the third trial, which ran to
almost 7,500 pages. Though Gubbins was not to blame for these obstacles, Kimberlin had concluded early on that the task at hand was
beyond his capacities. He asked for the name of "the best writer of

appeals in the city," and Gubbins referred him to Morano. "Don came to see me," Kimberlin recalled. "And after that he and I were two peas in a pod."

In fact, the sight of Kimberlin and Morano side by side would have evoked some other image altogether. Kimberlin was youthful, trim, and wiry; Morano was twenty years older, graying and rumpled, with a receding hairline, round face, doughy complexion, thin lips, strong nose, and a general look of soft middle-aged capitulation. Nor were there significant parallels in their backgrounds. Morano was a former Roman Catholic seminarian who, after abandoning plans to join the priesthood, had earned a Ph.D. in philosophy and had taught at Northwestern University, the University of Tennessee, Notre Dame, and Loyola of Chicago. He was an intellectual nomad, and his passions were eclectic. As an undergraduate, he entered Harvard with the class of 1956, and though he left after only a year, he contributed a personal narrative to the class's thirty-fifth-reunion report. In six hundred words, he included references to Swift, Blake, Spinoza, William James, Karl Jaspers, and the Synoptic Gospels, and described two books he hoped to write, *Justice Denied: Representing Inmates in the Federal Courts* and *On Divine Providence*. At forty, he enrolled in law school at UCLA; after receiving his degree, he spent only a year in private practice in Chicago before returning to academic life, teaching civil procedure, equity, and legal research and writing at John Marshall Law School. (There he had met Gubbins, who was an adjunct professor.)

One day in August 1983, Morano paid his first visit to Kimberlin at MCC. Kimberlin arrived for this meeting toting more than a dozen volumes of *The Federal Reporter*—the published opinions of the courts of appeals. Each book was opened to a different case that he felt was integral to his appeal. The meeting lasted five hours, during which Kimberlin recited the history of his tribulations at the hands of the government, outlined his strategy for vindication, and inspired in Morano a feeling that he came to refer to as "rejuvenation." On the spot, he agreed to take the case. "I said, 'Oh, yes, Brett, we're going to do this,' " he recalled. Later, Morano would regard the crossing of his path with Kimberlin's as a turning point—the moment in his life when he committed himself to working full time defending the rights of convicts, a calling no less ennobling than the priesthood might have been.

For the next several years, Kimberlin and Morano had an alliance that was more a partnership than a standard attorney-client relationship. One was a natural pedagogue, the other an avid student. "Don taught me how to write and how to research," Kimberlin said. "He was my mentor. He was ruthless with me. He corrected my spelling, sentence structure, and punctuation. He taught me about parallel construction." Morano was fascinated by Kimberlin's intensity and single-mindedness and what seemed "an encyclopedic knowledge of the cases." He was quick and prolific, Morano immediately saw, and his gift for mimicry lent his writing a professional gloss. When it came to analysis, "Brett would twist the ruling to make it fit what he wanted the result to be. But we worked on it."

In addition to representing him in the Seventh Circuit, Morano took up the appeal of his smuggling conviction in the Fifth, and they collaborated on the appeals of many other convicts, who, having retained Kimberlin inside the joint, in turn hired his preceptor to pursue their court filings. Morano lived on the North Side, less than a block from Lake Michigan, and conducted his legal practice out of his apartment. Almost daily, he rode a commuter train downtown to MCC to confer with Kimberlin or other clients. In his spare time, Kimberlin did typing for Morano. The MCC visitors' room began to function as Morano's satellite office. Kimberlin once was typing a final draft of a brief when he encountered the phrase "most unkindest cut of all" and deleted "most." Morano upbraided him for tampering with Shakespeare, but Kimberlin explained he was just trying to rectify an obvious grammatical error. Pound for pound, idiosyncrasy for idiosyncrasy, each had met his match. Morano lacked Kimberlin's instincts for pragmatism and opportunism; instead, he complemented those traits with what he referred to as "a crazy sense of loyalty." (After Kimberlin was granted "pauper" status, Morano's fee was paid by the court.)

The first appeal Morano ever argued in the Seventh Circuit had wound up before the U.S. Supreme Court, and he was confident that Kimberlin's case offered another opportunity to make law. Early on, he and Brett identified sixteen discrete rationales for reversing various convictions. Morano concentrated upon two issues: search and seizure (the manner in which the Chevy Impala had been explored) and "duplicity" (whether the indictment presented the sixteen counts of manufacture and possession of destructive devices in a manner that enabled jurors to distinguish among the specific alleged offenses). Kimberlin did most of the drafting of the arguments about hypnosis, prejudicial pretrial publicity, violation of the right to a speedy trial, improper cross-examination by the prosecution, prosecutorial misconduct, insufficiency of the government's evidence, jury misconduct, and judicial errors. Jointly, they drafted two chapters, which (to oversimplify) argued that in light of the outcome of the first bombings trial, the third trial had exposed Kimberlin to double jeopardy. Each edited the writings of the other. The table of contents included a twenty-three-page index of the cases cited in the body of the brief. When Morano fretted that his credibility would suffer if the written appeal cited cases that were not precisely germane, Kimberlin replied, "My liberty is at stake." Morano was prone to rhetorical conceits and excesses of his own. He was particularly proud that in framing the duplicity argument, he managed to draw an analogy to—and to quote in a footnote—a lengthy passage from Ionesco's *The Bald Soprano*.

Nile Stanton, identifying himself as chairperson of the Lawyers' Ad Hoc Committee for Brett Kimberlin, attempted to file an amicus curiae (friend of the court) brief with the Seventh Circuit. Stanton's organization, whose membership appeared to consist mainly of himself, was formed in reaction to "deliberate and malicious actions of governmental abuse of power as was demonstrated at the trial level." When Kennard Foster and Jack Thar intervened to block his brief, Stanton was reduced to preaching to the choir, in the form of a congratulatory letter to Gubbins (whose marginality he was somehow unaware of). "Clearly you have seen the tactical positions the Government and defense took to frame some fine-tuned issues, and you've exposed the Government for the Nazi-like actions they took. The brief should be a book that every lover of liberty reads." Kevin McShane, too, wrote to Gubbins: "One of the major impressions that still pervades my memories of Brett's trials is that deep in my heart, *I know that the truth did not win out. I do not know what the truth is* in this case. I do know what it isn't; that is, that Brett Kimberlin is not guilty of the Speedway Bombings." The brief also found a sympathetic audience within the convict population of MCC and among Morano's colleagues in the appellate bar. The novelty and diversity of the issues explored in the appeal made for such irresistible reading that Kimberlin and Morano were able to sell about a dozen copies.

These tributes, though gratifying to Kimberlin, did not solve his fundamental problem, which was that a panel of actual appellate judges—the only audience that mattered—would not read such a long-winded brief. After it was rejected, Kimberlin endured a period of uncertainty, during which the court assigned a partner in a large Chicago firm to serve as his new lawyer. When the Seventh Circuit staff finally agreed to allow the faithful Morano to remain on the case, they also stipulated a compromise on the petition's length: 150 pages. Four months later, Morano refiled the brief, now winnowed to 147 pages—the result partly of deletions but mainly of a smaller typeface, tighter spacing, and narrower margins. Six months after that, on 2 December 1984, oral arguments were held.

Kimberlin did what he could to exploit his media connections. "I called every press person I knew and pumped them up," he said. "Hypnosis was a sexy issue. This was the first time it was being heard in the Seventh Circuit." He had the home phone number of Kreskin, the mentalist and frequent late-night talk show guest, whom he tried to persuade to conduct a hypnosis-debunking performance on the steps of the courthouse. The courtroom proper was filled with on-lookers. A San Francisco trial lawyer named Ephraim Margolin, a hypnosis specialist, split with Morano the forty minutes allotted to the appellants. Though Kimberlin was not allowed to appear in person, he recorded the event in his diary as if he had been an eyewitness: ". . . all the press were there. Margolin was electric and magnificent. Don did good. The government left dejected. All major networks came and interviewed me on camera. ABC and CBS local ran it on the nightly news but NBC shelved it. [*Chicago*] *Law Bulletin* did nice article. All parties thought it went in my favor."

On average, three months was the interval between an oral argument and the court's decision in the Seventh Circuit. Three months came and went . . . then six months . . . a year . . . eighteen months . . . and still the court was not heard from. Kimberlin naturally assumed a conspiracy to delay justice. In the meantime, he had a new ambition: to be released on bail, pending the outcome of the appeal. If only his smuggling conviction was taken into consideration, he had become eligible for mandatory release in the fall of 1981. However, the prohibitively steep bail imposed after his indictment for the bombings—$450,000—remained in effect. Every few months, he would petition Justice John Paul Stevens, of the

Supreme Court, who had jurisdiction over such matters in the Seventh Circuit, to lower the bail. On each occasion, the prosecutors in Indiana registered their formal opposition, and Justice Stevens responded with a blunt denial.

ALMOST as frequently as Kimberlin filed bail-reduction motions, the Bureau of Prisons contrived pretexts for shipping him from MCC back to Oxford, Wisconsin. Kimberlin resisted these efforts for the same reason that he preferred designation to Chicago in the first place—a desire to be closer to his family and his lawyers. Morano was likewise eager to keep him in the neighborhood, and he repeatedly intervened to thwart the BOP. One morning, he showed up at MCC for an appointment and was met by a convict who told him that Kimberlin was being processed for a transfer that would have him aboard an Oxford-bound bus within the hour. Only a frantic dash through several federal courtrooms—in one of which he was threatened with contempt—enabled Morano to obtain an emergency stay of transfer.

The BOP's desire to move him, Kimberlin said, amounted to bureaucratic retribution for his litigiousness. His case manager, Patrick Leddy, who had the most direct day-to-day influence over his prison routines, "just thought it was his job to give me grief because of the serious crimes I'd been convicted of." Also, Kimberlin said, Leddy had it in for him "because I was such a legal beagle." This made it inevitable that Kimberlin would sue Leddy. From Kimberlin's probation officer in Indiana, Leddy learned of the judgment in the DeLong suit. In turn, Leddy notified the probation officer that Kimberlin had been sending Debra Irey $125 a month from his prison commissary account. This information was conveyed to Sandra DeLong's attorney, who obtained a writ of attachment that froze the commissary account. Suddenly, Kimberlin lacked the means to buy toothpaste, shampoo, dietary staples (fruit juice, tuna fish), postage stamps. Even coins for the photocopier or the coffee vending machine were beyond his grasp. He countered by securing a court order that released the attachment, and then he filed suit against, among others, Leddy, the probation officer, and Sandra DeLong's attorney, alleging violations of the Privacy Act and infringement of his rights under the First, Fifth, and Sixth amendments.

By the time this lawsuit worked its way through the courts, the issues were moot. Kimberlin had made it a habit not to use his commissary account in any way that would attract notice, the BOP had finally shipped him to Oxford, and his romance with Irey had foundered. She wanted to get married, Kimberlin said, something he had no intention of doing while still in prison. The longer they were forced to wait for the Seventh Circuit to rule on his appeal, the more acute the tension between them grew. She was unapologetically homesick. Her mother had been so upset when she moved to Chicago that for three months she refused to speak with her. In Chicago, Irey was essentially friendless, all alone except for the time she spent with Kimberlin or at her unrewarding office job. Though one of Brett's legal clients at MCC, a soldier in a Chicago crime family, offered to get Irey work through the Teamsters Union, she ended up returning to Indianapolis instead. For a while, she commuted to Chicago for monthly visits, though she had long been feeling "like I was imprisoned and I hadn't done anything wrong."

KIMBERLIN'S resentment at being transferred to Oxford—he arrived there in September 1985—mingled with apprehensiveness. Only a few weeks before the move, word reached MCC through the grapevine that a guard at Oxford had been decapitated, allegedly by a group of prisoners who called themselves the Aryan Brotherhood. "So I'm thinking: Here I'm going back to Oxford, and they're cutting guards' heads off." He kept his own head immersed in lawbooks, more assiduously than ever. With little to do but wait for the appellate court's decision in his own case, he had more than enough time to work for other convicts. At MCC, he had streamlined his law practice by training what were, in effect, paralegals—convicts to whom he delegated research, typing, and photocopying chores. At Oxford, his methods became even more businesslike. His work assignment required him to put in a couple of hours each morning in the kitchen, filling salt and pepper shakers and napkin dispensers. The rest of the day he spent on the phone, in the exercise room (he had begun to lift weights systematically), or, mainly, in the library.

According to BOP regulations, any cash in excess of $20 was contraband. Though designed to discourage gambling, theft, extortion, and the like, the rule's chief consequence was the artful evasions it inspired. Another equally naïve regulation prohibited convicts from running businesses. At MCC, Kimberlin said, he "got hooked into the whole mob scene" through a convict named Mickey Antonelli. "Personally, I didn't approve of these mob guys shooting people and putting them in barrels in the lake," he said. "But these guys needed lawyers and I needed the money." If anything, the prison rules incited his avarice. The money was there to be made, and this situation offered the piquant intrigue of surreptitiously earning and concealing it. The trick was to route the money through a trustworthy third party on the outside. For several years, this conduit was an Indianapolis woman named Shelly Conner, who as a young teenager had written to Kimberlin at the Marion County Jail and who later sold T-shirts and gathered signatures for the group calling itself the Brett Kimberlin Freedom Committee. She received and deposited checks for his legal work, paid bills, arranged three-way phone calls, conveyed messages to his clients' outside attorneys. Most of the time, she wasn't holding down a separate, steady job. Kimberlin paid part of her rent and all of her phone bill. They spoke daily. She had the air of a lost soul—with men, she was especially shy—and Kimberlin believed that, on balance, he was doing more for her than vice-versa. "I gave her something to do that was interesting," he said. "She cared a great deal for me. Her parents had died; she really didn't have anybody else. I was an important part of her life."

At Oxford, he depended on a different outside facilitator, a freshly sprung ex-con named James Turner, whom Kimberlin met early in his stay at MCC and had anointed his Sancho Panza. Like Kimberlin, Turner was physically small. Temperamentally, however, they bore no resemblance. Turner wore thick eyeglasses, had thinning black hair, and smoked unfiltered Camels, and he was suggestible, garrulous, and high-strung to a nearly farcical degree. "To be very honest with you, I'm a nervous wreck," he once told me. "But you know what? I was born a nervous wreck, so what the hell." There was no indication that he possessed a real aptitude for crime—certainly not for any variety that relied upon cunning and cogitation. He was twelve years older than Kimberlin and had spent his entire working life with the Chicago Transit Authority, until he got briefly diverted into bank-robbing, a detour he could've avoided had he not been a compulsive gambler. In early 1982, he was invited to Las Vegas by an acquaintance who knew that Turner owed a disturbing amount to a Chicago loan shark. A third partner, who happened to be on the FBI's "Ten Most Wanted" list, persuaded Turner to enter a branch of the First Interstate Bank with a note announcing that he was a political terrorist. Turner wore a small microphone on his jacket lapel, through which he could seemingly communicate with comrades outside the bank building. A grenade (neutered, though the bank teller had no way of knowing) dangled from his belt. A dummy switch (in reality, the control button from an Atari video game) was ostensibly wired to detonate the grenade. Though the overall effect must have been breathtakingly unconvincing—Turner made Virgil Starkwell, the Woody Allen character in *Take the Money and Run,* look like Cary Grant in *Charade*—the teller handed over $80,000. Unfortunately for Turner, an off-duty policeman equipped with a two-way radio was in the bank. Three minutes after leaving the premises, Jimmy was in custody. Assigned ten years, he spent forty months in stir and had been paroled a few months, back working for the Chicago Transit Authority, when Kimberlin moved to Oxford.

Kimberlin gave Turner his formal power of attorney and then ordered letterheads printed in the name of James Turner, Attorney-in-Fact. This prevarication circumvented the BOP's authority to open all convict mail except legal correspondence. Whether Kimberlin's clients understood that Turner was not a member of the bar was irrelevant; they knew that Kimberlin was doing the bulk of the work on their cases and that outside lawyers were usually needed to rubber-stamp and file papers formally with the courts. What mattered most to Kimberlin was that Turner was unshakably loyal.

Having Turner at liberty was a lucky break, and so was the fact that Mickey Antonelli, Kimberlin's rainmaker in Chicago, got transferred to Oxford ahead of him. According to Kimberlin, Antonelli told his gangster acquaintances: "Don't settle. Wait until Brett gets here." The result was that "once I set foot inside that place at Oxford, there wasn't one fucking day that I didn't have megawork." Another Oxford convict, Sam Petty, a client who was doing hard time for weapons and drugs, told me, "All the hotshot Mafia guys used to cluster around Brett like ants on a piece of cake." His sales pitch went, "I'm the best guy in the federal system to do your brief. I have a long-standing reputation for winning. Plus I can get almost any lawyer I want to on the phone in a dozen major cities." He wouldn't take a case "unless I could make five hundred dollars a week on it."

His Mafia clients, he said, "always paid well, but they were real ass-holes. The funds always came from these front companies. Jimmy [Turner] would be met by bagmen."

During his peak productivity, he said, he earned between $25,000 and $30,000 a year, "hundreds of thousands of dollars" over the course of his imprisonment. Invisible and therefore tax-free, this income also boasted the crucial advantage of leaving the DeLong family clueless. Toward the end of his sentence, in Memphis, he shared a cell with an electrician who possessed tools to remove the special screws on the prison's electrical outlet covers. At any given time, Kimberlin stashed hundreds of dollars inside walls. As prodigiously as he made money, he spent it—by his reckoning, "at least" half a million dollars. His phone bills often ran over $500 a month. He spent a hundred fifty a week at the commissary for food and stamps. He paid his own legal fees, court filing fees, fees for legal transcripts. When he began taking correspondence courses toward a college degree, there were tuition bills to pay. Debbie Irey and Shelly Conner were not the only women to whom he routinely sent money. Others came along because, according to Sam Petty, "He was a soft touch for a whine over the phone from a woman." Less poetically, James Turner observed, "Frankly, Brett was pussy-whipped." Doing legal work meant feeding "thousands of dollars" to photocopying machines. If there was an angle to be worked on either the income or the overhead side, he naturally took advantage. After someone at Oxford showed him how to short-circuit one of the coin-operated photocopiers, he "beat them out of tens of thousands of copies."

FOR A while, Kimberlin had a sideline selling dirty pictures. At MCC, he had begun to accumulate pornographic magazines, courtesy of a former prisoner and client who got the stuff from a retail vendor in Chicago. Kimberlin described it as "very good quality, full-color— anal, oral, you know, three-way, everything like that." Its shelf life, however, was not infinite. "I didn't know what to do with all of them," he said. "You know, you can only jack off to a magazine once or twice. I mean, you get bored with it. I took them with me when I went to Oxford. I had eighty-seven of these damn things. It was a whole box full. So I got up there and some black guy saw me reading some and he said, 'Hey, you want to sell any of those?' And then this white guy said, 'Do you want to sell any of those?' And I thought:

Well, I'd rather sell them to the white guy than the black guy. So I told the white guy, 'Look, can you sell very many?' And he said, 'Sure, I can sell as many as you got. You give them to me for one-third of the cover price. I'll sell them for one-half of the cover price.' So he was the porno king on the compound. And he made his spending money. And my friend kept sending me the porno from Chicago. I probably made about four or five grand on the damn stuff. Brett Kimberlin, porn dealer. Can you believe it?"

A hitch developed when Kimberlin's supplier—whose own sidelines featured embezzling, burglary, and bank fraud—abruptly landed back in prison. To replenish his inventory, Kimberlin decided to buy through mail-order houses, using Turner as a go-between—an arrangement that proved satisfactory until a distributor aroused Kimberlin's litigious impulses. In January 1987, in federal court in Madison, Wisconsin, Kimberlin sued Crest Paragon Productions, alleging false advertising, breach of contract, mail fraud, conspiracy, and violations of the Racketeer Influenced and Corrupt Organizations Act (RICO). According to the complaint, instead of the thirty magazines and sixteen books Kimberlin expected when he responded to a back-of-the-book advertisement placed by Crest Paragon, he was sent "fifteen pamphlets and three paperback books of low quality." He described this material to me as "real old four-by-six black-and-white pictures that looked like they were from the 1960s and came from England." The tepid paperbacks had titles like *Making a Score* and *Coed Cohabitation*. When Kimberlin wrote a letter demanding the material he had originally ordered, the defendant had the temerity to offer instead "sexual aids," including, Kimberlin noted, "a life-size inflatable doll, dildos, and a vibrating plastic vagina."

Though Kimberlin felt conflicted because "I could have made a fortune on that stuff inside prison if it wasn't contraband," mainly he felt compelled to sue. He asked for compensatory and punitive damages totaling $150,000. After "a fucking Reagan appointee" dismissed the suit on procedural grounds, Brett appealed to the Seventh Circuit but was told he'd have to pay an additional filing fee. "I decided at that point I'd spent enough on this," he said. "So I just blew it off. I never would've sued these guys if they'd been fair to me. They're not supposed to take my money and then not send me the magazines. People fuck with me and try to cheat me, I get pissed off. I don't fuck with people who do the right thing."

24

CAROLYN KIMBERLIN trusted her dreams. At her bedside she kept a dream journal, and every morning, first thing, she recorded fresh dispatches from her unconscious. "Dreams are in the service of wholeness and health," she told me when I asked about this preoccupation. "Every dream is a positive thing. Even the worst nightmare is telling you to pay attention. There's no such thing as a bad dream. If it's in the service of wholeness and health, how can it be bad?" This faith in the intrinsic value and utility of dreams was a dogma that Carolyn had not acquired all on her own. She belonged to two dream-discussion groups; one met weekly, the other monthly. Whenever possible, she attended the annual convention of the National Association for the Study of Dreams, and she subscribed to their monthly newsletter. While Brett was in prison, she often encountered him in her night reveries.

"Sometimes I would see him maybe come to the window in my dreams," she said. "I would visit him or he would visit me. He had that beautiful smile. I would see him where I was. I don't remember talking, but in dreams you don't talk. Most communication in dreams is telepathic. Sometimes he would be at home, out in the yard, at the window. All the time he was in prison, people would ask me whether I would get depressed, and I would say no, he was so uplifting."

One November day in 1986, she had a wide-awake experience that felt singular, an episode that seemed to possess the dislocated, free-floating texture of a dream. On her way from Indianapolis to Oxford to visit Brett, she stopped over in Chicago to pick up Don Morano. A few days earlier, the outcome of Kimberlin's appeal had been announced by the Seventh Circuit. The three-judge panel—Thomas Fairchild, Walter Cummings, and Richard Cudahy—had taken twenty-three months to render a decision. The judges accepted the appellant's claim that he should have been charged with no more than a single count of possession of Department of Defense insignia, rather than four separate counts. Vacating these three convictions, however, did not help reduce Kimberlin's fifty-year sentence. From his perspective, the balance of the court's ruling had not been worth waiting for: a unanimous agreement to affirm the bombings-related convictions and to deny the petition for a new trial.

"I went to Chicago and I wanted to let these people know that Brett was innocent," Carolyn later recalled. "We had waited two years for a decision. So anyway, I just drove up there and I wanted them to know he was innocent and that was that. I knew the building that these folks were in [the Dirksen Federal Building]. It was huge. Stories tall.

"I walk this whole block, past all these windows, all these entrances. I get to this far door and I walk in and get on an elevator, push a button, go up to whatever floor it was. I walk down a hall—walk walk walk walk—and it was a miracle that I went to the right door. And I turn and I walk right into the chief judge's chamber and he's sitting there at his desk. I introduce myself and tell him why I'm there. And suddenly some bailiff or guard comes in. And he's all uptight, but the judge motions"—she waved her hand—" 'It's all right.' I found out later that there are all kinds of security checkpoints in that building, but somehow I had walked into the right door, the right floor, went down the hall and into the right office with nothing to stop me. It was like a fantasy. It was just like you're not using your left brain to figure this out. You're moving, you're in the flow, you just go and there it is. Everything just kind of opened up. You're walking and doors open up and it's like you're just guided. And the judge and I had a nice conversation and I got to plead with him to do what's right. But he didn't do it."

THE LENGTH of the published opinion—over eighty pages—suggested that Fairchild, Cummings, and Cudahy had carefully read the briefs and deliberated the issues. The judges devoted far more space to analyzing the questions raised by the hypnosis and the search of the Chevy Impala than to any of the appellant's several other arguments. Kimberlin and Morano had emphasized the significance of a 1981 New Jersey case called State v. Hurd, which spelled out requirements for conducting hypnosis in criminal investigations. In 1985, the

Council on Scientific Affairs of the American Medical Association adopted as "essential" standards the criteria that were originally applied in *State* v. *Hurd*. Though the Seventh Circuit judges recognized the divergence from these standards in Kimberlin's case, they noted that the Hurd trial decision had preceded Kimberlin's trial by only five weeks. And though they conceded "the danger that persons who have been under hypnosis may be led to testify beyond their genuine memory," they concluded: "We remain unpersuaded that a sweeping rule of inadmissibility is appropriate."

The main opinion was written by Judge Fairchild, the senior member of the panel. In a separate opinion, Judge Cudahy concurred with the majority but expressed concern about the potential unreliability of the posthypnotic testimony. It was "almost impossible," he wrote, "to know with any assurance what role this testimony played in the thinking of the jury." He cited other concerns: that the jury had seen potentially unfairly incriminating mug shots of Kimberlin taken in connection with the military-insignia arrest; that the jury had been exposed to an unholy litany of unrelated deeds and allegations, what Nile Stanton had characterized as the "bad man" tactic. "Many of these matters, taken individually, may not be in themselves of crucial significance," he summarized. "But the cumulative impression on the jury raises real questions of prejudice. Although these and a number of other problems are very troubling, I think the majority has addressed them conscientiously and in a fashion that sustains the result."

Or as one of Kimberlin's former drug-dealing associates—and, by virtue of an eight-year federal prison term for cocaine dealing, an enlightened student of the criminal justice system—interpreted the appellate ruling: "Why did the Seventh Circuit deny Brett a new trial? Because he didn't deserve one. There were probably a dozen constitutional reasons why he should have gotten one. But they just looked at the case and said, 'Hey, he doesn't deserve one.' "

TO PERSUADE the Seventh Circuit otherwise, Kimberlin tried a different approach. Within a month after receiving the Seventh Circuit's opinion, he filed a petition asking for an *en banc* rehearing of his appeal. In effect, he wanted all nine active appellate judges within the Seventh Circuit to recapitulate the labors of the three-judge panel and overrule their decision. He told me that he filed this petition *pro se*—

acting as his own attorney—because "Don [Morano] was so pissed off and burned out on the Seventh Circuit, he just didn't have the energy to do it." In the petition's prefatory statement, however, Kimberlin included a footnote that offered a different explanation: "Brett Kimberlin asks this Court to give him a chance to make his case for rehearing and for suggestion of rehearing *en banc*. Therefore, he alone is making this personal appeal to the Court. What he asks from each judge who reads this is to do so with an open and impartial mind, and while doing so, to ask whether the trial in this case was fair. In asking that question, forget that Brett Kimberlin is the defendant, and imagine that your son or daughter was on trial in this case. After that, Brett Kimberlin hopes and believes that each judge will have the courage to honestly say that the trial was not fair, and therefore, to correct the injustice which has occurred."

One could argue that in urging the judges to imagine their own children in his circumstances, he was appealing not to their sense of fairness or humanity but to their impulses toward corrupt self-interest. Likewise, to beseech the court to "forget that Brett Kimberlin is the defendant" was to concede implicitly that his own mother's appraisal ("that beautiful smile . . . so uplifting . . . he was innocent") was a tough sell. In any event, the Seventh Circuit judges evidently lacked the inclination or the agility to perform such mental gymnastics. Their reply was prompt, pithy, and, once again, unanimous: "Denied."

THE NEXT procedural step, an appeal to the Supreme Court of the United States, was inevitable. An appellant who requests a review before the Supreme Court files what is known as a writ of *certiorari*. At the time—it was now January 1987—the Court was receiving about 4,100 so-called "cert" petitions each year, of which it granted only 175. (Since then, the batting average has dropped even further; in 1994, for example, 94 out of 8,100, and in 1995, 90 out of 7,565.) The likelihood that his filing as a prisoner would be granted, Kimberlin knew, was practically nil. He also knew that a bigger gun than Morano wouldn't hurt, so he wrote to Alan Dershowitz, who was as well known as any criminal trial or appellate lawyer in the country.

On the chance that Dershowitz might decline to take the case—in fact, he never responded—Brett simultaneously sent Carolyn to seek an audience with a colleague of Dershowitz's at Harvard Law School, the constitutional scholar Laurence Tribe. Cynthia Kimberlin was living in Boston, and Carolyn had gone there for a visit. Since she was in the neighborhood, Brett suggested, she should drop in on Tribe. This turned into a variation of her surreal adventure in Chicago. She went to a building called Griswold Hall, where she was told by a receptionist that Tribe wouldn't be in that day. Undaunted, she decided to stick around, until, eventually, she wandered about and "somehow I found out which room was his office and I just went in there. I walked in and there he was. He was supposed to be home, ill. He's telling me he's not even supposed to be there. He told me he was so booked up, he had so many cases. He wasn't hostile. He was taken aback because he wasn't supposed to be there. It was like he sneaked into his office without letting anybody know."

"Tribe just blew my mom off," Kimberlin told me. "He was a total fucking asshole."

GRISWOLD HALL, as it happened, was named after Erwin N. Griswold, a faculty member at the law school from 1934 to 1967 and for over two decades its dean. His years at Harvard were bracketed by tours of duty within the solicitor general's office, which represents the U.S. government in its pleadings before the Supreme Court. From 1929 to 1934 he had been a staff attorney, and when he returned, in 1967, he *was* solicitor general. Though Griswold was, as he liked to say, "a traditional Republican," Lyndon Johnson had appointed him; and after serving during more than four years of Richard Nixon's presidency, he left in 1973 because "President Nixon announced my resignation without consulting me." By then, he had argued 127 cases before the Supreme Court, a figure matched by only two other attorneys in this century. Afterward, he became a partner in the Washington office of Jones, Day, Reavis & Pogue. Moreover, he was listed in the District of Columbia phone directory, which proved convenient when Kimberlin asked his mother to track him down.

"Does he spell his first name with an *I* or an *E?*" Carolyn asked when she thought she'd found the right number. While Brett waited on the line in Oxford, she phoned Griswold and then patched her son into a three-way connection.

"Is this the office of the Erwin Griswold who was the dean of Harvard Law School?" Kimberlin asked the woman who answered.

"Yes, it is."

"Could I please speak to Mr. Griswold?"

"*Dean* Griswold."

"Could I please speak to Dean Griswold?"

When his call was accepted, Kimberlin identified himself, explained that his appeal had just been denied in the Seventh Circuit, and straightforwardly asked Griswold to take the case, pro bono, to the Supreme Court.

"Brett just picked up the phone and called me," Griswold said later. "I get a good many calls from prisoners, and usually I say, 'No, I can't do anything to help you,' and then I try to suggest other sources of help, such as law school clinic people. When he called, I hemmed and hawed. I hate like the devil to tell these poor fellows, 'No, I can't do it.' In this particular case, he was persistent, and he mentioned hypnosis of witnesses, and that struck me as a very dubious practice. Federal regulations prohibit doing it unless it has been authorized in advance by Washington. In this instance, the U.S. attorney turned the hypnosis over to the state police, and then the state police gave the testimony to the U.S. attorney's office. And I thought that was an outrage."

By overnight mail, Kimberlin sent a copy of the appellate brief and other relevant materials, and within two days Griswold had agreed to take the case. Within two weeks, he and two associates completed a draft of the cert petition. In a magisterial gesture, Griswold personally hand-delivered the petition to the clerk of the Supreme Court. He also wrote to the office of the solicitor general, then headed by Charles Fried, asking Fried and his associates to join the request for *certiorari* or to confess error on the part of the Court of Appeals. Instead, the solicitor general filed a brief in opposition.

While the cert petition was still pending, the Court of Appeals in the Eighth Circuit, reviewing a civil suit, decided against the admissibility of posthypnotic testimony. This bolstered one of Griswold's basic arguments: that various circuit courts had issued contradictory rulings on hypnosis, and thus a single standard was required. Regardless of the particulars of Kimberlin's case, the cert petition faced a fortuitous and formidable obstacle. During that same Court term, the justices had already agreed to hear a hypnosis-related appeal, *Rock* v. *Arkansas,* whose fundamental issue was diametrically opposed to Kimberlin's. Vicki Lorene Rock had been convicted of manslaughter in the shooting death of her husband, and her own attorney had her hypnotized to prove her innocence. Also, Rock's original trial took place in a state court, whereas Kimberlin was convicted in federal. Griswold's brief deliberately raised the matter of *Rock* v. *Arkansas* to define these distinctions: "the present case provides this Court with an excellent opportunity to give more comprehensive consideration to the admissibility of hypnotically enhanced testimony in federal courts, and thus to clarify an important question on which other courts, state and federal, have disagreed." The Supreme Court justices—or, perhaps, the young clerks whose task it was to wade through the river of cert petitions—chose to pass up this excellent opportunity. On the final day of the Court's term, Kimberlin's petition was denied.

When I went to see Griswold in the late summer of 1992, he described that event as "a crushing disappointment. Except for the fact that I've had half a dozen other denials in the past ten years, I would say it was a huge disappointment." At the time, Griswold was eighty-eight and still showed up for work six days a week. Five years had passed since his representation of Kimberlin, but they had maintained contact.

"I'm very much interested in the guy," Griswold said. "And as far as the law is concerned, I think he got a bum deal, partly through bad luck on the hypnotic evidence—the Rock case coincidence—and the fact that the opinion in the Seventh Circuit was written by Judge Thomas E. Fairchild, a judge highly regarded by the Supreme Court, an evenhanded, balanced judge, the type of judge about whom a Supreme Court justice might say, 'I don't think I could do better than Judge Fairchild.' "

When I asked Griswold his opinion of Kimberlin's *pro se* skills, he said, "He has nothing else to do. He has plenty of time. He's very bright. He has no background and training. He writes very well. He follows the court decisions, and he will call me from time to time on the phone about some decision that I've never heard of. Both Brett and I keep watching for any cases involving posthypnotic testimony, and we haven't seen any cases since his was decided." He paused, then said, "I guess you could say that despite the denial of cert, the Kimberlin case made an impact, because we haven't seen any other instances of that by the government."

I asked Griswold whether he thought Kimberlin was the Speedway Bomber.

"I haven't any idea whether he did the bombings," he said. "I haven't had a chance to read the entire trial transcript. But I am thoroughly convinced that he did not receive a fair trial. It was never my role to evaluate whether he was guilty or not. It was my role to determine whether events that happened at his trial were in conformity with our legal system, and I was thoroughly convinced that they were not."

AS A LEGAL matter, the bombings conviction was, barring a presidential pardon, for once and for all, irreversible. From Kimberlin, naturally, there would be no resignation or surrender, though a shift in tactics was necessary. If vindication ever came, it would have to be in the court of public opinion, and in that venue Erwin Griswold proved an eminent ally. To have been associated with an unimpeachable man who could've papered several rooms with honorary diplomas and other tokens of his professional accomplishments was a fact to be leveraged to maximum effect. This offered the sort of alchemy that Kimberlin had long since mastered: transmuting defeat into a kind of glory.

The law did allow Kimberlin one last opportunity to ameliorate his circumstances—a motion for sentence reduction, which could be initiated no later than one hundred twenty days after the final disposition of his case. When Kimberlin filed, exactly four months after the denial of cert, the Honorable S. Hugh Dillin, the federal district judge in Indianapolis who had jurisdiction, simultaneously received a letter from Griswold. After explaining how he came to represent Kimberlin, Griswold wrote: "My only contacts—which have been substantial—have been by telephone and by mail. I have met his sister and his mother, who have called on me in my office, and both appeared to be very fine persons, devoted to Brett's interest." Griswold went on to express his doubts about the fairness of the bombings trial: "I have heard enough to make me feel that it is not unlikely that there was a wrong identification. . . . I find myself much concerned about the evidence. . . . If he was not responsible, or if he did not receive a truly fair trial, he has suffered grievously." Finally, Griswold praised Kimberlin as "thoughtful and intelligent" and expressed optimism about his resourcefulness: "If his sentence should be reduced, I think from my contacts with him that he would be well-prepared to enter the outside world. I have found him to be responsible, well-adjusted, and realistic."

In the formal proceeding before Judge Dillin, this yielded no benefit—motion denied. In the years to come, however, Griswold's goodwill provided the underpinning of Kimberlin's credibility. When I reexamine the footings and foundation of the brick wall I built in 1992, I recognize that they rested largely upon Griswold's asseverations. In our conversations then, for example, he said, "I can only tell you that in my relations with him, which were intense five years ago and have continued in minor ways ever since, I have always found him to be reliable, and he has never made a statement to me which turned out to be untrue or misleading." Like Griswold, I had not yet scrutinized the full transcript of Kimberlin's trial, and I had no basis for asking whether his estimation of his former client might be wishful sentiment. Nor did I think to ask what sensations he experienced when he picked up the telephone and heard Kimberlin's voice; not until Brett had been released on parole did Griswold actually shake his hand and look him in the eye. In the meantime, was Kimberlin, for Griswold, entirely real? Or was he not a disarmingly dogged, sufficiently polite, atypically articulate convict who, far better than his neighbors, knew his way around the Constitution and the law library and who had an interesting case, to boot—in other words, as I originally viewed him, a seductive abstraction?

25

APART from Kimberlin's strident insistence that he had been railroaded, his obsession with gaining a new trial derived from the fact that the Bureau of Prisons had him in its clutches for a very long time. From the moment of his sentencing, he knew that, by statute, he would serve at least ten years before becoming eligible for parole. Given that he had been arrested in Texas in February 1979, the earliest he might meet with a panel of examiners from the U.S. Parole Commission was the late summer of 1988. The nature of the crimes he'd been convicted of, combined with his prior criminal history—which parole bureaucrats refer to as "offense and offender characteristics"—posed serious obstacles to his freedom. The Parole Commission's file also contained reports submitted by William Steckler, the judge, and Kennard Foster, the Assistant U.S. Attorney, shortly after Kimberlin's sentencing in late 1981, which plainly intended to simplify and expedite the examiners' task. Judge Steckler: "Defendant seen as a dangerous, sophisticated, and unremorseful offender, necessitating a lengthy prison term for the seriousness of his offenses and for the protection of society." Foster's prescription was succinct and implacable: "This individual should serve within a penal institution his imposed sentence to maximum expiration."

On the positive side of the ledger, Kimberlin had avoided any major violations of BOP regulations. Once, at MCC Chicago, he was caught with a few more dollars in dimes than the rules allowed. That, however, was not the sort of infraction that could have been held against him in a parole deliberation. On paper, he'd been an aggressive self-improver. Depending upon the specific institution a convict is assigned to, opportunities exist within the federal penal system to participate in educational, vocational, and counseling activities— "superior program achievements"—which can potentially enhance one's parole prospects. An official history of good conduct is a prerequisite; such credits will not compensate for a blemished prison record, and a parole examiner or commissioner can also withhold the credits. Or, as a veteran parole attorney explained to me, "Everything the Parole Commission does is based upon your being a good boy to begin with. And you can have all the superior programming there is, but if the hearing examiner feels like saying 'Fuck it, you lose,' then you lose."

MCC Chicago, because it was mainly a way station for convicts en route to long-term assignments elsewhere, didn't offer much in the way of superior programming. Upon Kimberlin's second commitment to Oxford, however, he began signing up for whatever was available. During the next few years—at Oxford and, later, in El Reno, Oklahoma, and Memphis—he assembled an impressive sheaf of superior program certificates: Criminal Personality; Positive Mental Attitude; Introduction to Transactional Analysis; Human Growth; Principles of Motivation and Success; Personality and Stress Control; Goal Setting; Rational Behavior Therapy; Communications I and Communications II; Hatha Yoga Relaxation; Human Resource Development; Drug Awareness, Drug Abuse, and Drug Control; Self-Image; Health Over Forty ("I wasn't yet forty at the time, but I took it anyway").

Also at Oxford, where the University of Wisconsin extension service had an office within the prison walls, Kimberlin began enrolling in college-level courses. He would spend the next six years achieving a Bachelor of Science degree in human services, with a specialization in community legal services, issued by Thomas Edison State College of New Jersey. Along the way, he also picked up an Associate of Science degree from the State University of New York and a paralegal degree from the Blackstone School of Law, in Dallas. His final college transcript showed a cumulative grade point average of 3.96.

JUST AS Kimberlin's superior program achievements offered no guarantee that his parole would be smiled upon, neither did they inoculate him in his interactions with BOP employees. At Oxford, though he lived in what was known as an "honor dorm"—single rooms without bars or locked interior doors, in a clean, quiet, and unviolent ambience—he said the manager of the unit granted the privilege grudgingly. Mainly, it seemed, Fred Westfall resented Brett's legalistic legerdemain. "I would represent inmates before the Institutional Disciplinary Committee," Kimberlin said. "And I would beat almost every case on technicalities. All these BOP idiots would write these incident reports and they would get the date wrong or the time wrong and I would go in and beat these cases, so [Westfall] hated me." This replicated Kimberlin's experience at MCC Chicago, where the fractious dealings with his case manager, Patrick Leddy, had blossomed into a lawsuit.

"Westfall was worse than Leddy," he said. "He was a fucking Nazi. He called me in one day and said, 'Brett, I've been working for the BOP for decades. I'm really pissed off that they started this due-process business.' This guy was such a pig. He had a gut like he was nine months pregnant. Westfall was having a problem with me because I was such a great student in college and I completed every superior programming class they had. He had to sign all these certificates of completion. Not only was I taking these courses; I was telling other people to do this. He tried to bust me several times for getting compensation for doing legal work."

Westfall evidently surmised that Kimberlin was earning money as a jailhouse lawyer, but he lacked proof. When Westfall finally found a convict willing to testify formally against him, the specific accusation was contrived. The details were convoluted and seemingly contradictory: The accuser had a reputation as a snitch, Kimberlin said, and he therefore resisted doing legal work for him; still, though the man "didn't really have any money to pay me," Brett *did* work with him on a sentence-reduction motion. The particulars were of less moment than their main consequence. While the BOP allegations were pending, in September 1987, Kimberlin spent a week in the hole—solitary administrative detention. His isolation ended only when he was unexpectedly put on a plane and transferred from Oxford to El Reno.

Kimberlin said that after he arrived at the Oklahoma facility the BOP investigation exonerated him of wrongdoing. The transfer from Oxford, however, was allowed to stand. If the BOP felt like exercising its prerogative to move prisoners about in an arbitrary fashion, Kimberlin reasoned, he would exercise his counterprerogative to litigate. His administrative complaint about the detention and transfer was dismissed, as was his appeal. He then filed a lawsuit that charged violations of his First, Fifth, and Sixth amendment rights. The defendants were the accusing convict, the prison warden, an investigative lieutenant, and Westfall. Before the lawsuit got very far, Brett told me, he dropped it in exchange for the government's promise to halt a separate investigation by the Internal Revenue Service.

KIMBERLIN took somewhat longer to abandon another lawsuit in which Westfall featured as a bit player. In March 1987, Kimberlin had come across an article in *U.S. News & World Report* about Boys Town, Nebraska, the refuge for troubled adolescents that inspired the 1938 film starring Mickey Rooney and Spencer Tracy. The gist of the story was that Boys Town had evolved and was learning to cope with social pathologies that Father Edward Flanagan, the institution's founder, had not confronted. Also, it was now coeducational. Almost eighty teenage girls resided at Boys Town, and a photograph of one of them, a seventeen-year-old cheerleader named Tiffany Perkins, accompanied the piece. Kimberlin wrote her a letter, and she soon wrote back. He wrote again and received another reply. "Something struck a chord," he later said. "I don't know what the hell I thought, exactly. I guess I just thought I might be able to help her out."

The Reverend Val J. Peter, the executive director of Boys Town, clearly thought that a pen-pal relationship with a federal convict would not prove a great advantage to Tiffany. "I guess they were reading people's mail there—it was like the BOP," Kimberlin said. He began calling Tiffany on the phone. Once, he sent her flowers. Perhaps that was the gesture that made him, as he put it, "the bête noir of Boys Town." After Reverend Peter intercepted a letter and forwarded a copy to Oxford, Westfall called Kimberlin in and chastised him. "It wasn't like I'd written anything sexually perverse or anything," Brett told me. "It was just kind of embarrassing having this guy read a letter I'd written. He said, 'Why are you writing to this young girl? You're a grown man and you're writing to a young girl in a setting where she's trying to get help. Don't you have anything better to do?' He was just trying to lay a guilt trip on me. He told me not to write to her anymore. But that was against BOP regulations. I knew I could write to anybody as long as they weren't in prison. He told me to stop writing, and of course I ignored him."

Using James Turner as an intermediary, he wrote to Tiffany again, and again Reverend Peter intervened with Westfall. So, Kimberlin recalled, "I said, 'Fuck it, I'm suing.' " The Reverend Peter was the sole defendant; because Westfall resided in Wisconsin, including him as a codefendant would've been "a logistical headache" for Brett. In his complaint, he invoked the First, Fifth and Fourteenth amendments, and he persuaded Tiffany Perkins to become a coplaintiff. "She told me I could sue in her behalf, and because she was a minor she was described as suing through me as her 'next of friend.' " The lawsuit prevailed through a series of dismissals, refilings, and appeals, but it finally became moot when Tiffany turned eighteen, left Boys Town, and moved back with her mother in Florida. By then, Kimberlin explained, he had tired of drafting appeals and paying court fees. Exactly where in Florida Tiffany settled wasn't clear, and he contemplated asking a private investigator to track her down. "I didn't know what those assholes told her about me," he said. "They were intercepting the mail. I just wanted to tell her that everything was OK and that I hadn't abandoned her." But he let it go, which was easy enough since, as always, new diversions presented themselves.

WHEN, immediately after his conviction, Kimberlin spent a few months in isolation at Terre Haute, he busied himself with a rigorous exercise regimen, a common prison pastime. Progressing rapidly, he reached the point where each day he did "thousands of sit-ups and push-ups." At MCC Chicago he lifted weights, though not systematically. After he was assigned to Oxford for the second time, he took up distance running, usually doing his laps at six in the morning with a con who was getting in shape for an escape attempt. ("He got transferred to Florida, and he had a gate pass there to cut the grass. One day, he went out the gate, started running, and kept going.") In El Reno, he resumed weight lifting. The institution had one workout area indoors and another outside. While exerting himself on the outdoor pile one afternoon, he was approached by a member of the prison's power-lifting team. Kimberlin, who weighed 110 pounds, was lying on his back and steadily upping the ante until he was bench-pressing twice his weight. In team competitions, power lifters are matched according to weight class, like boxers or wrestlers; each participant does a bench press, a squat, and a dead lift, the total load becoming his score. Previously, the Federal Correctional Institution El Reno team had lacked an able competitor in the 114-pound category.

Now they had an erstwhile ninety-eight-pound weakling who in time would collect a score of trophies along with a national ranking—thus adding to his curriculum vitae one more idiosyncratic adornment.

IN OTHER respects, Kimberlin adapted his usual habits to his new address. Once more, his reputation as a lawyer preceded him. "I walked in and everybody said, 'Jesus, we've got to hire you' "—meaning that not only convicts but also the prison authorities had lined up. He was immediately given a job in the prison's law library, which afforded him unlimited access to a photocopier. He continued to practice law, though less aggressively than before. "In a way, I was relieved to go to El Reno because I was so overwhelmed with work at Oxford," he said. "I just wanted a break for a while. I felt burned out. I refused to take any new cases at El Reno for six months, and I probably took only a dozen new cases while I was there. I made less money at El Reno than anywhere else because I was working in the library and I had to do a lot of things for free that normally I would have charged for."

One of his first greeters at El Reno was James Lewis, whom he'd known at both MCC Chicago and Oxford. At Oxford, they were coplaintiffs in a lawsuit challenging the Parole Commission's guidelines. Kimberlin had also referred Lewis to Morano, who pursued his appeal in the Seventh Circuit—not necessarily an enviable task. Lewis was identified, after all, with an act of terrorism several magnitudes more notorious than the Speedway bombings: the 1982 Tylenol-tampering case, in which unsuspecting consumers ingested cyanide-laced analgesic tablets and seven of them died. In the aftermath of the poisonings, Lewis had written a letter to Johnson & Johnson, the makers of Tylenol, demanding a million dollars in the name of his wife's former boss, against whom he bore a grudge. (For good measure, he sent a threatening letter, in the same boss's name, to Ronald Reagan.) Though Lewis wasn't convicted of the actual tampering—those crimes were never solved—he won twenty years for attempted extortion.

At El Reno, Lewis worked in the cafeteria, and that job posed a threat to his safety because, according to Kimberlin, other inmates failed to distinguish between the poisonings and the extortion attempt. "These other convicts were saying, 'Fuck that. We're not having that fucker working in the kitchen,' " Kimberlin said. "They were saying, 'He put cyanide in Tylenol. We'll kill the motherfucker.' " When Kimberlin complained to the authorities on his behalf, they took no action until Lewis, at Brett's instigation, feigned a health emergency by collapsing dramatically one day in the cafeteria—a moving piece of theater given his history of genuine heart trouble. Lewis then was made a library clerk in the education department. He and Kimberlin had the same supervisor, and the education and law libraries adjoined each other. This posting suited Lewis much better, since he greatly enjoyed Kimberlin's company. With a degree from the University of Missouri, Lewis was a proud and determined autodidact, who'd read widely in the classics and taught himself French and Spanish. Among convicts, he once told me, Kimberlin was "the only person I would defer to intellectually."

Kimberlin would have preferred to reside in an honor dorm—the arrangement he had at Oxford—but new arrivals were consigned to a waiting list. Meanwhile, he was placed in a housing unit called Colorado One, where he befriended a French Canadian doing a long stretch for, among other crimes, murder. Kimberlin said he and his cellmate, nicknamed Frenchie, "got along great." For one thing, they shared an entrepreneurial instinct. Frenchie worked in the kitchen, from which he regularly stole food to put on the black market. What he didn't sell he shared with Kimberlin: "We'd eat like kings." A talented woodworker, he carved a set of miniature furniture that Kimberlin gave to his mother for Christmas. Still, nothing about Frenchie suggested that he was a serious candidate for rehabilitation. One day, Kimberlin said, he rushed into the cell "covered with blood"—evidence that he'd been carving something other than dollhouse rocking chairs.

"He's got it on his hands, his shirt, his pants," Kimberlin continued. "And he hands me this shank. He says he's got to run into the shower. I wrap the shank inside his T-shirt, and he takes a razor blade and starts shredding his pants to flush them down the toilet. I take the shank and bury it in the bottom of a plastic garbage can liner, and that was it. The guy who got stabbed didn't die. He had a punctured lung and was in the hospital for about a month. He never knew what hit him. It was dark, and Frenchie hit him from behind. I think he got paid twenty bucks to stab him. You could get a guy stabbed for a carton of cigarettes."

Kimberlin came to regard that vignette as emblematic of El Reno, a sprawling brick mass that during the Depression had risen from the red soil of the arid western Oklahoma plains. His first day there, as he and another convict stood gazing at the shadowy interior of the main compound, he felt a swell of tension. Hovering à la Hitchcock in the huge elms and bald cypresses and river birches were vast squadrons of grackles. Even for a connoisseur of prison life, this setting had a forbidding austereness that seemed tailor made for the darkest of apprehensions.

But El Reno was also destined to become his Rubicon: the place in time and space at which he would be drawn toward a future that might sever him from his putative past. Because it was here that at last Kimberlin firmly grasped his opportunity to become a quintessential late-twentieth-century American icon—the criminal as victim and celebrity—while simultaneously transcending the infamy of the Scyphers murder and the Speedway bombings. And Brett Kimberlin, so far as I could see, never encountered even a momentary opportunity that escaped his aptitude for exploitation.

26

I N THE simple, familiar paradigm of perspective, parallel lines appear to come together in the distance, when, in reality, they never do. Train tracks recede from view and a convergence, or vanishing point, materializes. This is an illusion, a trick played on the eye, and not especially impressive, since the rational mind hasn't been fooled. Memory, or history, can render a similar effect but lead, in fact, to an ambiguous interpretation. Coterminous lives or events, plotted on parallel time lines and projected into the past, backward, might be said to have intersected. Certain artifacts or documentary evidence might indicate that no convergence has taken place, though in the absence of such data—in a factual vacuum—the lines extending back in time blur and warp. Lacking eyewitnesses, photographs, or business records, Kimberlin could never conclusively demonstrate that he knew Dan Quayle as he said he did. But he understood a precept taught by, among others, Senator Joseph McCarthy: The more damning the accusation, the more helpless, eventually, the denial. For Quayle, the virtually insurmountable burden was to prove a negative—to show that his path and Kimberlin's had never intersected.

On fifteen or more occasions in the early seventies, Kimberlin claimed, he sold marijuana to Quayle. This tale first received a public airing in 1988. Then and later, Kimberlin produced witnesses who, while unable to corroborate these alleged encounters, nevertheless were willing to state that his story itself had a history. In 1976, when Quayle first ran for a seat in the House of Representatives, Kimberlin said, he came across a newspaper photograph, pointed it out to his sister, and told her that years earlier the candidate had been a nickel-bag marijuana customer. (Cynthia Kimberlin later confirmed this "vague memory.") Brett had last seen "Danny" in 1973, he would later recall, and hadn't thought of him since. After all, he'd been otherwise engaged. As of 1976, he had long since stopped peddling nickel bags and was routinely trafficking in multiton shipments from Colombia and Mexico.

When Quayle won reelection to the House in 1978, Kimberlin was still a high-volume smuggler—a fact that (*a*) was suspected by law enforcement authorities and (*b*) was one of their more benign conjectures, following the Scyphers murder and the Speedway bombings that summer. One afternoon two weeks after the bombings ceased, Kimberlin parked a 1970 Chevy Impala teeming with incriminating evidence near a printing shop on the west side of Indianapolis, went inside, and promptly got himself arrested. That same day, Kimberlin tried desperately to bargain for his freedom with FBI and U.S. Army investigators. As a government document—which Kimberlin years later would brandish like an indictment—noted: "[Kimberlin tried to] talk the agents out of formally charging him with any violations in exchange for information which he had concerning . . . drugs . . . and a Congressman of the United States."

That document was a routine presentencing report requested by the court in the fall of 1980, after Kimberlin was convicted of the insignia and seal possession offenses. The passage in question was, in a sense, secondhand, extracted as it was from an FBI report filed at the time of his arrest. That the presentencing report bore the imprimatur of the FBI endowed it with a credibility that the declarations of fellow prison inmates or a Kimberlin family member could never approximate. James Lewis, the Tylenol extortionist, was one of the convicts to whom Kimberlin recited his story—in 1984, at MCC Chicago, Lewis has recalled—and James Turner, the failed bank robber and Kimberlin loyalist, was another. At Oxford, in 1985, Kimberlin befriended and did legal work for Sam Petty, a former associate of the radical black activist H. Rap Brown. "Long before I knew who Dan Quayle was, I heard about this prominent politician who used to be a student and how he had got introduced to him, how he was leery of him, but after a while he would sell him little ounces of marijuana," I was told by Petty. At the time of our conversation, late in 1993, Petty was doing twenty-two years for weapons possession and possession of cocaine with intent to distribute. Mickey Antonelli, who gave Kimberlin his rudimentary lessons in jailhouse lawyering soon after they met at MCC Chicago in 1982, had a similar recollection. "We were talking about some of the politicians that were crooked," said Antonelli, whose record included convictions for bank fraud, bombings, possession of a gun with a silencer, and attempted murder. "When he told me about Quayle, it was that he was selling marijuana to a senator, while he was in law school or college or something. Know what I mean? It was Quayle that he mentioned, but I didn't recognize the name."

Whether or not Kimberlin was telling the truth about Quayle, whatever history his story accumulated between the election campaigns of 1976 and 1988 was tainted by the unsavory pasts of these witnesses. And Cynthia Kimberlin was also, by definition, easily impeachable. Only the author of the FBI arrest report had any true credibility. This document, though it didn't specify Quayle by name and could, in theory, have referred to any of the 434 other members of the House of Representatives, in time became the most valuable nugget of hard data at Kimberlin's disposal. This was *his* circumstantial evidence—though a different sort, he would argue, from the circumstantial evidence the jury relied upon in convicting him of the bombings.

A copy of the FBI arrest report was given to Michael Pritzker and Richard Kammen, Kimberlin's original attorneys. This artifact likely came to rest in some dead-file storage facility, and Kimberlin has never possessed a copy. On 3 November 1980, he attended his sentencing hearing. As Kimberlin reposed the following day in the Marion County Jail, having been freshly handed a twelve-year term for the military-insignia and presidential-seal convictions, Quayle won election for a tour of duty half as long—six years in the United States Senate. Kimberlin's memory of having seen the *presentencing* report when it was filed with the court led, ultimately, to a Freedom of Information Act request that brought a copy into his hands. By then, however, the calendar said late November 1988, and Quayle was the vice president–elect.

EXERCISING his habit of keeping his head on the outside, Kimberlin often spoke on the phone with Lori Levinson. Since adolescence, she had been Cynthia Kimberlin's closest friend, and as adults they both lived in Salt Lake City. During the summer of 1979, while Kimberlin was jailed in Corpus Christi—his drug case there unresolved and the bombing indictments pending in Indiana—Lori and Cynthia made their visit to various points in Texas and also to Bermuda, trying to scrounge drug money owed to either Brett or his brother Scott, to help finance his legal defense.

George Bush's announcement that he had selected Dan Quayle as his running mate occurred on 16 August 1988. According to Levinson, "six or eight weeks before the election"—mid-September, approximately—she had what she considered a revelatory conversation with Kimberlin, during which he talked about the hypocrisy of placing a marijuana user in charge of federal drug enforcement policy. Kimberlin had a somewhat different recollection: "I'm fairly certain that at the time Quayle was nominated she was aware of the situation"—meaning that Levinson, long privy to intimate details of Kimberlin family lore, already knew of his dealings with Quayle. "I think the first conversation wasn't about how I had to do something. It was just that Bush had done this and he was such a hypocrite. I don't remember how she did it, if she told me about it beforehand." Brett was referring to actions that ensued from this telephone conversation. His point was that after urging him "to do something" to make public his allegations, Levinson found him reticent, and as a result, "she did it" herself.

Levinson: "Brett and I were having a conversation and he mentioned it [selling marijuana to Quayle] to me and I just couldn't believe it. I was living here [in Utah], and even though I was from Indiana, I didn't know who Dan Quayle was. During a conversation about politics, Brett said, 'Yeah, I sold that asshole pot a long time ago'—when he was in college or something; I can't remember which. And I said, 'Well, he's got a lot of nerve because he's supposed to be in charge of the war on drugs.' I thought that was hypocritical, and it irritated me a lot. I said, 'You should tell somebody.' I didn't want the guy to win. I'm a Democrat. Brett said no, no, no—he didn't want to tell anybody—and I was, like, 'You *have* to tell people. They have a right to know this information.' And I said, 'Do you mind if I make a few phone calls?' I can't remember whether I asked him that then or in a conversation a few days later. And then I convinced him to let me call somebody. He was concerned about his parole thing, but he finally said I could do it."

A MONTH before the Republican National Convention, Kimberlin had become eligible for parole consideration for the first time since entering prison. Members of the U.S. Parole Commission are presidentially appointed. Logic—superficial logic, at any rate—says that whereas in 1978, when the FBI took Kimberlin into custody at the printing shop, it served his interest to talk about Quayle, by 1988 it had become contrary to his interest to raise the subject. Hence "his parole thing."

On 28 July 1988, at FCI El Reno, Kimberlin appeared before a two-member panel of parole examiners. His most optimistic prospect was that he would be paroled in February 1989. In this calculation, he assumed that the Parole Commission would designate him a Category 7 offender, on a scale in which Category 8 is reserved for felons convicted of the most serious crimes. Another element the Parole Commission took into account was called a salient factor score (SFS), which was a measure, on a scale of zero to ten, of the risk of parole violation, ten representing the lowest risk, zero the highest. Kimberlin here scored a seven. The Parole Commission's guidelines mandated that a Category 7 offender with an SFS of seven had to serve from 64 to 96 months. Exceptions were sentences of thirty years or more, which required a minimum incarceration of 120 months. Kimberlin had already done 114 months and would reach 120 in February 1989. To his surprise, the parole examiners declared him a Category 8 offender, using the death of Carl DeLong as their justification. They then informed Kimberlin of their recommendation: 168 months total, which postponed his release date until February 1993—four years in all. Before this local recommendation could be effected, however, it would have to be ratified by a regional commissioner, in Dallas. Though Kimberlin was angry, he had reason to remain marginally optimistic. "I figured I might have to do another six months fighting them in court," he said later, "but I knew I didn't have to stay in until 1993."

Early in September, though, Kimberlin received more discouraging news. The regional commissioner had decided to defer to the nine-member federal Parole Commission, under a provision that allows for "original jurisdiction." Kimberlin recognized this as an ominous development, one reserved for cases requiring special handling. It was the cloud of the parole deliberations in general and, more specifically, the original jurisdiction referral, he said, that made him reticent when he pondered the possibility of speaking publicly about Quayle.

LORI LEVINSON called "somebody at the Democratic National Committee" but "wasn't getting through," so she called a friend who was a reporter for the *Salt Lake City Tribune*. This reporter "thought it was a great story, but he wasn't interested in becoming the one to break it." Levinson was "aggressively pushing it; I was more fired up than Brett was or he would've been doing the calling himself."

Kimberlin in fact was making some calls of his own, seeking advice on how to proceed. He consulted his father, his appellate attorneys Donald Morano and Erwin Griswold, and some journalists he'd met while incarcerated at MCC Chicago. One of these was Douglas Frantz, who by 1988 was working for the *Los Angeles Times,* and another was Kevin Klose, of the *Washington Post.* Frantz, by peculiar coincidence, had attended DePauw, Quayle's undergraduate alma mater, and had played on the varsity golf team, as had Quayle. A sign of Kimberlin's stress and uncertainty was that he also solicited the wisdom of Buddy Pylitt, who prosecuted him for the Speedway bombings and had since left the government and entered private practice. Calling Pylitt, Kimberlin later acknowledged, was a "stupid move," but he at least knew better than to heed Pylitt's suggestion that he get in touch with the DEA or the Justice Department or the Indiana State Police.

Later, in a conversation with Levinson, Kimberlin brought up the name of Nina Totenberg, the National Public Radio correspondent who in 1987 had broken the marijuana-related story that undid Douglas Ginsburg's nomination to the Supreme Court. So Levinson next dialed Totenberg—and bingo. By now, Kimberlin could recite a well-crafted narrative, and Levinson had taken careful notes, which she duly read to Totenberg, who was sufficiently interested that she agreed to accept a collect call from Kimberlin.

This is Kimberlin's condensed recollection of their earliest conversations: "I said, 'I'll talk, and if you can corroborate this, then go with the story.' She asked me, 'Whom would I talk to to corroborate?' I said, 'Talk to the people who were in the National Guard with him, because I was selling to him when he was in the Guard. Talk to people who were in law school with him, and people right after he got out of law school, as well as old girlfriends of his. Stay away from De-Pauw, because that was before my time—you'd be wasting your time.' She asked whether I would sign an affidavit and said she would send a lawyer to see me. And I said, 'As long as you can keep this to yourself and confront Danny with it, I'll cooperate.' So a lawyer sent by Totenberg came to see me. I gave the lawyer two affidavits. One I wrote by hand and the other was a typed copy. I never thought smoking pot should disqualify someone from holding office, but I realized that it was something the American people should know, given the Reagan-Bush rhetoric about how drug dealers should be skinned alive, shot, and hanged from the nearest tree. I just felt that it was something people should factor in when they were deciding how to vote. So after Nina had these affidavits, she sent a copy to the Bush-Quayle campaign."

Mark Goodin, the deputy press secretary of the Bush-Quayle campaign, later testified that receiving these affidavits from Totenberg had moved him to alert James Baker, the chairman of the campaign. Previously, Totenberg had recounted Kimberlin's charges to Goodin without identifying their source. Totenberg's second conversation with Goodin took place, he said, "within striking distance" of the election—less than three weeks before—and was "something we needed to take very seriously and deal with seriously because of its potential for adverse publicity." Now, given the affidavits, Goodin felt compelled "to move the thing through the chain of command."

"I went to Baker's office," he testified. "And I said, 'There's an issue that has come up that I think requires your attention.' He said, 'I'm in a big hurry. Is it something important?' And I said, 'It's something you need to take a look at. I have a sworn affidavit from a gentleman who claims he sold drugs to Dan Quayle.' He said, 'When was this?' I said, 'Apparently in law school or undergraduate school. I can't remember which.' He said, 'What does the affidavit say?' I gave a capsulized version of it. I think I may have placed it on the desk and he may have looked at it spuriously [sic] and shoved it back and said, 'What do we know about this guy?' I said, 'Nothing.' He said, 'Let's find out.' "

THAT same day, Goodin told the Bush-Quayle campaign manager, Lee Atwater, and Quayle's campaign manager, Stuart Spencer, about the affidavits. The next morning, the matter was discussed during a senior staff meeting presided over by Baker. A check of the Lexis-

Nexis computer databases turned up the comforting information that Kimberlin had been convicted of multiple offenses, among them perjury. In a showdown, the word of a United States senator and a candidate for the nation's second-highest office would be measured against the word of a proven liar and criminal.

Two days after sharing Kimberlin's affidavits with Baker, Goodin became concerned about Totenberg's potential broadcast; Baker agreed that Quayle should be notified. A campaign aide named David Prosperi met with Quayle, who, according to Goodin, insisted "flatly, unequivocally, and without reservation" that he'd never used drugs or purchased any from Kimberlin. Goodin then spoke directly with Quayle, who "left no airspace in his denial."

There was an eight-year age difference between Quayle and Kimberlin, though this gap was narrowed somewhat by Brett's precocity. And while the two men had their comfortable middle-class central Indiana upbringings in common, Quayle's response was intended to suggest they might as well have inhabited separate universes, if not centuries. His biographical time line and Kimberlin's were neither parallel nor convergent; his path and that of the prison convict had never, ever intersected. Bob Woodward and David Broder, in their 1992 *Washington Post* articles about Quayle, referred to his "oddly distant relationship with the great controversies and experiences of his generation." They quoted his friend and senatorial successor, Dan Coats: "I see Dan as someone that really wasn't significantly influenced by those times. . . . [If Bush was] selecting somebody to represent that generation, I don't think Dan is representational." And as vice president, feeling dogged by Kimberlin, Quayle amplified his denial. Journalists who called his press office to ask whether he'd ever indulged in illicit drugs were given this information: The vice president has himself never used drugs. He has never been at a party where drugs were being used. Nor does he have friends who have ever used drugs.

In some quarters, this elaboration smacked of protesting too much. Yet Quayle apparently felt he had no option. It is not known whether he was also mindful that within days of his nomination, a hard copy of a Drug Enforcement Administration file bearing his name had been retrieved from a computer and delivered to the DEA's director—and then to the White House. An equally opaque question is whether, within the highest councils of the Bush-Quayle campaign, the DEA file was ever discussed, especially with reference to the potential damage that could flow from its disclosure. Coincidentally—or, in a sense, not at all—whatever lurked within the DEA database had nothing whatsoever to do with the story Kimberlin was now poised to share with the widest possible audience.

27

THE 1988 Republican National Convention attracted almost twelve thousand members of the media, virtually all of whom, presumably, arrived with clearly defined tasks and expectations. One visitor to New Orleans—Cody Shearer, a thirty-eight-year-old Washington-based independent journalist—had an ostensible agenda that was vague by design. For eight years, Shearer had written—either solo or in collaboration with other young journalists—a political column called "Here and Now," which was distributed by the North America Syndicate to fifty or sixty newspapers about the country. A peripatetic reporter if not a painstaking literary stylist, he was content to dash off inside-the-Beltway–flavored stuff for an invisible, outside-the-Beltway readership. Though the column appeared three times a week, among his friends in Washington journalistic and political circles even his closest pals rarely saw it—a fact that evidently bothered him not a bit. The column was more a vehicle than a destination. Shearer thrived on hoarding and trading information that tended to have a short shelf life. He had contacts throughout the permanent government, as well as plenty on Capitol Hill and in various law enforcement agencies, and he excelled at keeping secrets. A lightly subscribed syndicated column was no cash cow, so how Shearer supported himself was a bit of a mystery. ("Family money" seemed one plausible answer.) Acquaintances knew better than to ask what he was working on at any given time; his response was invariably evasive or elliptical, and this provoked curiosity about how he *really* spent his nine-to-fives. He had a verbal manner that could abruptly shift from wry geniality to bullying aggression; he was a good cop/bad cop team all by himself. Invariably, his sign-off at the end of a phone conversation was "Gotcha." A columnist for the *Boston Globe* once wrote of Shearer: "I've known him a long time and like him, but that wouldn't stop me from looking out the window if he told me the sun was shining." Not the least of his accomplishments was the cultivation of his persona—a *Front Page* throwback, a Washington wiseguy who'd seen and heard everything but was always ready for more.

From the site along the Mississippi River where Bush and Quayle made their first joint public appearance as running mates, Shearer hustled to the apartment he'd rented in the French Quarter. He started making phone calls and within an hour or so had located two of Quayle's former professors from DePauw University and grilled them about his intellectual abilities. After speaking with someone in the university library, he had in hand a fax transmission of Quayle's class of 1969 peers. He interviewed a member of the no-longer-extant draft board in Quayle's hometown of Huntington, learning that during the spring and early summer of 1969 he'd been classified 1-A. Though other 1-A's were conscripted, this man recalled, Quayle was not.

At breakfast the next morning, Shearer encountered Jeff Greenfield, who was covering the convention for ABC News. As the day progressed, Shearer confirmed with a DePauw classmate of Quayle's the draft board story. That evening, during an ABC broadcast, Greenfield acknowledged Shearer on the air, citing his enterprising legwork on what had become the story du jour: that Quayle had apparently received preferential treatment before enlisting in the Indiana National Guard. The shadow cast by this revelation, of course, became the prologue to a more general and enduring set of doubts about Quayle's worthiness, if circumstances demanded, to serve as president.

A journalist who had worked for Shearer on "Here and Now," but in 1988 was employed elsewhere, witnessed him developing this Quayle story, only to see his scoop eclipsed by the horde of reporters who pounced upon and began to scrutinize Quayle's past. "He got the dog to bark once," the journalist recalled—his point being that the experience left Shearer with an inordinate desire to hear the dog bark at least one more time.

Back in Washington in early September, Shearer learned from a source within the DEA that, as he put it, Quayle "had a problem with drugs." This information came from a career DEA employee, someone Shearer had known for almost twenty years, spoke with often, and regarded as highly credible, but the source could offer no details. Using the DePauw yearbook as a reference text, Shearer began tracking down Class of 1969 grads and asking, in essence, Was Quayle a doper? He made fifty or sixty such calls, he said, and "was getting nowhere."

THOUGH a time came when cynics insinuated that the Quayle vice presidency was a perverse masterstroke by George Bush—a blood indemnity, a guarantee that no one would dare an attempt on his life—of course it's far more likely that he believed he was doing the country a favor. Likewise, from the moment of the nomination, a mobilization of counterforces was animated by an equally sincere belief that any peaceful action tending to prevent Quayle from assuming a position in the line of succession was a legitimate exercise of patriotic duty.

Steve Fawley thought he knew something, and it suddenly inflated in importance. A DePauw alumnus, Fawley had graduated three years ahead of Quayle. If their paths had crossed there, Fawley was unaware of it. But no matter. It was Fawley's impression that, years later, his life and Quayle's had indeed overlapped. During the late seventies and early eighties, while living in east-central Illinois, Fawley became marginally involved with a cocaine ring that marketed a variety of the drug they called "crink." Most of the other dealers lived in Bloomington, Indiana, or nearby rural Brown County. At their laboratory headquarters, cocaine base was refined in a way that gave the final product a faint blue or pink wash. "It was so pure you couldn't cut it," Fawley remembered. The coke retailed for two hundred dollars a gram, and from conversations Fawley had overheard—at least one of them in the processing lab—he concluded that Quayle had been a customer.

In July 1982, after the ring was infiltrated by an informer, seventeen people either copped pleas or went to trial. Most drew prison terms, ranging from six months to ten years. Two of the indictees had dealt extensively with Kimberlin years earlier; during one trial, for instance, newspaper articles noted that an electronic money counter that was seized as evidence had originally belonged to Kimberlin. But this was merely a sign of how small the pond they were all swimming in actually was. Kimberlin did no business with the cocaine ring, nor did what Fawley believed to be the truth about Quayle and drugs have anything at all to do with Kimberlin. Indeed, the name Brett Kimberlin meant nothing to Fawley.

After being sentenced to three years' probation and paying a modest fine, Fawley arranged to have his probation supervised in northern Vermont, where he resettled. He was still residing there in the summer of 1988, teaching at a school for adolescents with special needs. Vermont suited Fawley's sensibilities. He looked like an aging hippie—biblike graying beard, paunch, general Jerry Garcia profile—and he lived like one too. Most people didn't call him Steve or Fawley, because he also had the cheery nickname Coyote—not an allusion to the animal but a play on "Quixote." Not surprisingly, he had the politics to match. He almost always voted Democratic, and now he wanted to tell a story that, by his standard, possessed salutary partisan potential.

"I thought taking a swipe at the ignorant privileged would certainly not harm my self-image," he later said. "It wouldn't bother me to look into the mirror in the morning. It was not an agonized, thoughtful decision. It felt more like what goes around comes around—I was the what-comes-around part—given my sense of Quayle's politics and what they meant to the world."

On two occasions, according to Fawley's recollection, reference had been made to small amounts of the ring's cocaine being conveyed to Quayle. In both instances, the same individual—a friend of several of those who were later prosecuted—was present. The first such discussion took place when the processing lab was installed in the town of Martinsville; Quayle was then a congressman. The second conversation occurred after Quayle had become a senator, and the locale was the Brown County property of John Calhoun, another of Quayle's DePauw contemporaries. "It was common knowledge that some of the coke coming through our domain was ending up in Dan Quayle's possession," Fawley said. "It wasn't big news to us. It was just happening." During the 1988 Republican National Convention, Fawley was visiting Calhoun, who in the meantime had spent four years in prison and had been on parole for two years. Together, Fawley said, they watched scenes from the convention on television. "I said to Calhoun, 'Let's do him,' " Fawley remembered. "And Calhoun was intrigued, but only intellectually."

Fawley decided to proceed on his own. He didn't feel comfortable using his real name or his nickname, so he invented another moniker. For this undertaking he would identify himself as the Owl, because "an owl's a wise bird and he knows a lot." The Quayle nomination was only a few days old when Fawley confided in a friend, Cindy Cole, who was the executive director of the school where he taught. Cole's reaction was identical to the response Kimberlin evoked when he told Lori Levinson that he had sold marijuana to Quayle. "You have to tell somebody," she urged Fawley. "This just isn't right." Cole suggested that he give the story to a big newspaper, and they thought of the *Washington Post* and its Watergate investigation. On August 26, Fawley made a cold call to the *Post*. He got through to the national desk and spoke first to a clerk and then to a reporter—brief conversations that generated no evident interest and left Fawley with a sense of frustration.

About a week later, Fawley recorded an entry in his journal: "I think I'll give up on Quayle thing. Nobody's willing to go down"— by which he meant that neither Calhoun nor the corroborating friend would help him advance the allegation. However, partly because of Cole's encouragement, he did not fold his tents. One day, Cole was having a conversation with Ben Cohen, one of the eponymous founders of the Ben & Jerry's ice-cream empire. (Though Cohen and Cole later married, at the time the two were only friendly acquaintances.) A few years before, in his capacity as a Vermont icon, Cohen had given a graduation speech at the school where Fawley and Cole worked. Now Cole was lobbying him to support a vocational training program that required federal assistance—funds the Reagan administration was cutting off. Four more years of a Republican White House wasn't her idea of a radiant future. "Steve got discouraged because the *Washington Post* thought he was some sort of yahoo," she recalled later. "The election was gearing up and Quayle was saying all these stupid things about drugs. I thought Quayle was being really hypocritical. And then I told Steve's story to Ben. And Ben said, 'Well, I know somebody he should talk to.'"

EARLIER that summer, Ben Cohen had taken a stroll on a California beach with Chuck Blitz. Though neither long-standing nor intimate friends, they had much in common. Both were imaginative, energetic, enterprising, thirty- or forty-something guys who had become politicized during the sixties and who, by the eighties, had become wealthy. Their definition of fun included saving the planet. From where Blitz spent most of his time—a spacious house in Santa Barbara that he shared with his wife and young children, up a steep slope overlooking the ocean—the planet appeared to be both endlessly marvelous and exquisitely fragile. Blitz's admirers described him as "very bright and creative" and "a real out-of-the-box thinker" and "impassioned about his causes." To his detractors, he was "a rich guy who feels guilty that he doesn't have to work for a living" and "a confused, well-meaning manipulator." If you asked Blitz how he'd accumulated his money, he would make vague noises about real-estate investments. To causes deemed worthy he contributed ample sums of time and dollars. Though he didn't insist upon anonymity, he did believe that the most successful tactic in these endeavors was to maintain a low profile. He was a proficient networker. When I invited one of his activist cohorts to define exactly who Blitz was and what he did, he replied, "Chuck Blitz is a guy who spends a lot of time on the phone."

One object of Cohen's visit to Santa Barbara was to enlist Blitz's support for "One Percent for Peace," an organized effort to pass a law in Congress that would set aside a small portion of the Pentagon budget for international peace-through-understanding activities. While walking on the beach, Cohen talked about "redirecting money out of the military into meeting basic human needs" and "building bonds of peace between nations instead of walls of fear." Blitz offered a shortcut prescription: the most effective way to bring about a shift in military priorities, he told Cohen, would be to elect a Democratic president in 1988.

Sometimes you took the high road, Blitz knew, and sometimes the most expedient path. And—an unspoken corollary—occasionally the latter option involved maneuvers the opposition would no doubt criticize as dirty tricks. (A further corollary: the opposition should know, since they invented dirty tricks.) In 1988, for instance, Blitz was interested in airing in the press, with as much substantiation as possible, any information about George Bush's rumored extramarital affairs. On the one hand, this was unseemly business; on the other, it could be justified as the realpolitik price of saving the planet. Blitz was therefore delighted when, one day in late September, he played the messages on his telephone answering machine and heard the exuberant voice of Ben Cohen saying, "Hey, Blitz-o. Good news! I found the guy who sold drugs to Dan Quayle."

Blitz set to work. He listened to Fawley's story and arranged for Ira Rosen, a producer at "60 Minutes," to hear it as well. Rosen, in turn, brokered a conversation between Fawley and the "60 Minutes" correspondent Mike Wallace. After hearing Fawley's buildup, Wallace impatiently asked the only question that mattered from his perspective: Had he been an eyewitness to a drug transaction involving the vice-presidential nominee? When Fawley allowed that he hadn't, Wallace lost interest. If not "60 Minutes," Blitz calculated, then who? He discussed the matter with a political soul mate, John Richard, who was one of Ralph Nader's closest associates. Both Richard and Nader, it turned out, had been friendly with Cody Shearer for more than a decade, and Richard had once rented a room in Shearer's house in Washington. No one doubted anyone else's political sympathies. Which was how Shearer became the next recipient of a phone call from the tipster who introduced himself as The Owl.

28

Weeks slipped by without Cody Shearer turning up any witnesses or evidence to nail down what his DEA source had originally told him. He'd talked to "hundreds of people," mainly in Indiana—college and law school acquaintances of Quayle—and come up with nothing more than "secondhand stories." Fawley's phone call seemed like the stroke of good fortune that could put him back in the game. Election Day was now a month away. Delivering a single-handed scoop mattered less than developing a story that would hold together, and Shearer felt he needed the resources of a large news-gathering enterprise. He called a friend, Michael Duffy, who years earlier had worked for him on his column and had since become a *Time* correspondent. Duffy was sufficiently interested to discuss the outlines of the story with his boss, Strobe Talbott, the Washington bureau chief of *Time*.

This was a proposal that Shearer could perhaps have taken up directly with Talbott, considering that for seventeen years they had been brothers-in-law. At Yale, Talbott was a classmate and close friend of Cody's older brother, Derek, and then he married their sister, Brooke, who was Cody's twin. Another very close friend of Talbott's was the charismatic young governor of Arkansas, Bill Clinton. The two had shared quarters while attending Oxford University as Rhodes Scholars in the late sixties. By the fall of 1988, Talbott had established himself as one of his generation's leading writers on Soviet affairs, arms control, and diplomacy. Clinton, for the moment, was in a temporary downward spiral, the consequence of having blown a golden opportunity at the Democratic National Convention. Presenting the nominating speech for Michael Dukakis, the governor held forth with a bladder-testing piece of oratory, overstaying his welcome so egregiously that the crowd cheered when he said, "And in conclusion."

As a practical matter, it made sense for Shearer to approach Duffy rather than Talbott. When it came to journalism, Shearer's style seemed to unnerve Talbott, and a sort of Chinese wall existed within the family. On one side was a self-made mandarin destined to become the deputy secretary of state, and on the other was a raffish gumshoe type who worked out of an office that resembled a newsprint recycling facility and who found it invigorating when the phone rang at midnight and a pal in Langley, Virginia, or a caller identifying himself as the Owl or the Hyena or Mr. Magoo offered some deep background on a story involving the Department of Commerce, the baby in the manger, and the Trilateral Commission.

That the election was imminent weighed in Shearer's favor. Talbott agreed to meet with Fawley, who traveled from Vermont to Washington for a weekend sit-down with several *Time* staff members—a blind date that began inauspiciously. Shearer and Fawley had difficulty finding each other at the airport and arrived over an hour late for a group interview with Talbott, Duffy, and two other reporters. One of the participants recalled the encounter as "a three- or four-hour debriefing during which the Owl drank most of a bottle of something." Fawley articulated what he considered a well-informed hypothesis, and the *Time* people countered with "What did you see?" and "What do you know?" It occurred to Shearer that "they thought this guy had flown in from Jupiter." Fawley's admission that he had already approached the *Washington Post* and "60 Minutes"—shopping his story around town, as it were—didn't boost his credibility or cause *Time* to itch with excitement. Elaine Shannon, who'd covered the DEA and drug-related stories for the magazine, did some follow-up reporting that altered no one's initial impressions. Shearer and Fawley moved on.

The more Fawley talked, the more likely it became that other reporters would soon get wind of the story. Despite the misfire at *Time*, Shearer believed that Fawley's tale was basically truthful, and he wasn't about to loosen his proprietary grip. By phone, he began conversing with various members of the erstwhile Indiana cocaine ring, some of whom he traced with help from an Indianapolis private detective whose bill was eventually paid by Chuck Blitz. The pursuit of John Calhoun proved especially slippery. He was one of the ring's leaders, and Fawley had placed him in the room when drug deliveries to Quayle were allegedly discussed. With Shearer and Blitz, Calhoun was not exactly elusive, but reticent. So determined was Blitz to get Calhoun to talk that he enlisted the aid of an old friend, Baba Ram Dass (né Richard Alpert), the psychologist who, along with Timothy Leary, his fellow faculty member at Harvard, in the early sixties pioneered the notion that the broad proliferation of psychedelic drugs such as psilocybin and LSD offered the most felicitous hope for remaking American society. After learning that Calhoun was an admirer of Ram Dass and a student of his writings, which included the counterculture bible *Be Here Now,* Blitz persuaded Ram Dass to appeal to him to 'fess up. Later, Calhoun reported to friends, "For me, getting a call from Ram Dass was like, if you're a Catholic, getting a call from Mother Teresa." But to no avail. Ram Dass later said that Calhoun "was very loving and friendly, but basically he stonewalled me. I thought he knew something." According to Calhoun, "Ram Dass refused to believe me. He kept it up. It was like talking to a cop. I told him, 'I would swear on my hand-bound copy of *Be Here Now* that I really didn't sell cocaine to Dan Quayle.' At that point, he finally realized that even if I was lying, I was not going to change my story for their benefit."

Shearer felt that Calhoun's coyness derived from his parole status—and was proof of incriminating knowledge. A friend of Calhoun's later explained that "his problem was that he loved the attention and he hated the attention." Fawley described to Shearer an apparent pattern of favorable handling that Calhoun received while in prison—a transfer from a medium-security facility in Minnesota to a minimum-security coed camp in Kentucky, where Calhoun's wife was also incarcerated, as well as a pair of five-day furloughs after she was released. According to Fawley, this coddling took place after someone in Quayle's Senate office intervened with the Bureau of Prisons. The implication, of course, was that Quayle was doing a favor for an old friend. Blitz, meanwhile, worked on Fawley's other source: the never-arrested, never-indicted friend of several ring members, who allegedly knew of Quayle's cocaine use. This person was an architect then living in southern California. Blitz invited him up to Santa Barbara—enticing him, the architect later complained, by disingenuously suggesting, quid pro quo, a possible architectural commission.

After *Time* dropped out, Shearer approached NBC News. He called Tom Brokaw, with whom he was on friendly terms, and raised the prospect that if properly primed—by, say, a call from a network anchorman—Calhoun would come clean. Brokaw demurred, referring Shearer to Brian Ross, a reporter who specialized in investigative stories, and Ira Silverman, a producer. They began their own legwork, and Ross was able to confirm through one of his own sources that Quayle did indeed have a DEA file. When Ross's source attempted to view the file's contents, which required penetrating the Narcotics and Dangerous Drugs Information System database (NADDIS), he was rebuked by a superior in the Washington office of the DEA. "He almost didn't survive," Ross recalled. "He was challenged: 'Why the hell are you accessing this file?' It was all very tantalizing."

IN RETROSPECT, Shearer's motives—competitive instinct, partisan proclivity, or a fluid combination of the two—seem difficult to parse. He was on no one's payroll and therefore felt free, while loosely collaborating with NBC, to seek other alliances. From a friend who worked at National Public Radio, he learned that Nina Totenberg was working on a Quayle-and-drugs story. For the first time, Shearer heard the name Brett Kimberlin. Less than two weeks remained until the election. Shearer knew no specifics—only that, in effect, his stock had split.

When Kimberlin first spoke with Totenberg, she promised not to discuss his allegations with anyone else until Quayle had been confronted with his affidavit. By now, the Bush-Quayle campaign had seen the affidavit and, through whatever channels, the story was spreading. After Michael Isikoff, a *Washington Post* reporter who was pursuing Brett, had a phone conversation with Carolyn Kimberlin that left her feeling agitated, Brett complained to Totenberg about leaks within NPR. Several days earlier, however, Brett himself had told Kevin Klose, a deputy national editor of the *Post,* that he was thinking of going public with his story, and Klose assigned Isikoff to follow up. Isikoff began to hear about Kimberlin as "part of the mix of political gossip at the time—somebody in the Bush campaign told somebody at the *Post* that they were getting these inquiries. . . . It was going to be the killer story that people talk about during a campaign." (Ultimately, Isikoff spoke with Kimberlin a few times by phone and also interviewed Erwin Griswold, after which he concluded a memo to his editors with "there wasn't enough there to publish a story.")

The disparate participants in these events, whose energies all briefly coalesced with the subject of illicit drugs and electoral politics, cannot agree on a who-knew-what-when chronology. Relations between the reporters involved, as well as their dealings with their sources, were marked by a blithe promiscuousness. Kimberlin, notwithstanding the demand for confidentiality that he imposed upon Totenberg, proved to be almost indiscriminately accessible. Tail-chasing gave way to tail-swallowing, which is to say that unintentional comedy gave way to grotesquerie. As Shearer shifted his focus to Kimberlin—thanks to what was indeed a leak within NPR— Totenberg was picking up the trail of the Owl. Chuck Blitz, by his own account, was "talking to political people and journalists across the board." When, inevitably, Totenberg found her way to Blitz, he asked whether she'd been dealing with Kimberlin and she said no. Blitz knew that she was dissembling but nevertheless pointed her in the direction of Calhoun and the architect. Shearer later claimed that he had no idea Blitz was freelancing in this manner—and, yet, Blitz told me that he "had no capacity or desire to do anything independent of Cody." When Shearer got in touch with Totenberg and suggested that they might be able to help each other, she denied that she was working on a story involving Quayle and drugs. When Totenberg spoke with the architect, he insisted that the Owl's story was fantasy, not memory. "I told her that there was nothing to the rumors she'd heard," the architect told me. "If I had some information that would have derailed Quayle, I would've freely given it. But I wasn't going to make up a story about it."

As a ROUTINE matter, federal prison inmates are subject to monitoring of their phone calls. The official reason for this policy is the preservation of institutional security. In principle, only calls made from phones specially reserved for conversations between prisoners and their attorneys are immune to such eavesdropping. Many of Kimberlin's phone conversations that took place after he gave his affidavit to NPR were preserved on tape by local officials at El Reno. The ambivalence Kimberlin expressed when he first spoke with Totenberg never wholly disappeared, as the tapes demonstrate, but it was superseded by his eagerness to be a player in presidential politics. He spoke of his sense of obligation "to the American people to let them make an informed decision." He expressed a fear that if his allegations about Quayle's drug history were not made public until after a Republican election victory, "then they may have another paralyzed presidency, which would be terrible for the country."

Kimberlin's agenda, whether good or bad for the nation, immediately benefited the phone company. As the campaign entered its final week, his contacts with the outside world were more numerous and diverse than ever. Instinctively, he played reporters off one another, alternately flattering them and letting them know that he was receiving entreaties from their competitors. When both NBC and CBS expressed interest, Kimberlin assured a CBS producer, "I told you I wanted to talk to you before anybody else. I mean, Tom Brokaw is OK, but I like Dan Rather much better." Two days earlier, he had told Nina Totenberg that he wanted her to break the story because NPR had been his "lifeline" in prison. Kimberlin's technique was not foolproof. "It's my impression that Brett was looking for somebody to peddle this story," said Douglas Frantz, then of the *Los Angeles Times,* explaining why he didn't take the bait. "He had James Lewis [the Tylenol extortionist] call me to vouch for his credibility."

Two or three times a day, Kimberlin made collect calls to Totenberg, and after his initial contact with Shearer, on November 1, he spoke with him just as frequently. Kimberlin seemed impressed with the reporting Shearer had done on the cocaine ring. From Shearer he learned that Quayle had a DEA file, and they laughed about Quayle's official disclaimer about drugs, drug parties, and druggie friends. There was still a missing piece, however, as Shearer explained: "We need other bodies, we need other people."

Shearer asked for the name of an eyewitness who had attended the fraternity party where, Kimberlin said, he met and first smoked dope with Quayle. Though Kimberlin would later name Larry Harvey, who for better or worse was dead, he now said only that he was trying to get through to someone who might remember details of the party. He had in mind Larry's sister, his old girlfriend Susan, whom he hadn't spoken with in years. He told Shearer that NPR would broadcast the story if he passed a polygraph, though he was reluctant. "Personally, I'd rather undergo hypnosis than a polygraph," Kimberlin said. "It depends on the operator . . . and it also depends on how you feel. And, you know, if I'm trying to withhold the name of a person at this frat party, it might show deception. . . .

So there's all kinds of problems with those, and plus they're not a hundred percent reliable." A credible corroborating witness, presumably, would have obviated a polygraph.

THURSDAY, November 3—Election Day minus five—Brian Ross made a formal request for NBC News to conduct an on-camera interview with Kimberlin. He spoke with Rodger Benefiel, the El Reno warden's executive assistant, who was also in charge of media relations, and was offered an interview date a week later. Unless access to Kimberlin was granted before the election, Ross replied, NBC News would air a report that the Bureau of Prisons had obstructed the interview to protect Quayle's candidacy. Now the prison staff consulted with superiors in Washington, including J. Michael Quinlan, the director of the BOP, a deputy attorney general, a deputy associate attorney general, and the chief of staff of Richard Thornburgh, the Attorney General. Mark Goodin, the Bush-Quayle campaign's deputy press secretary, later testified that he, too, was regularly in touch with the Justice Department: "Over a fairly substantial period of time, it is fair to characterize my contact with the Department of Justice as fairly close contact."

In the end, the BOP decided to expedite the interview—it would take place the next day—but only after weighing the possibility of placing Kimberlin in isolation, or "administrative detention," for allegedly having violated prison procedures in arranging his contacts with the media. (An associate warden at El Reno later testified that Kimberlin had committed no such violation.) A subsequent memorandum from Quinlan to Frank Keating, an associate attorney general, cited "Kimberlin's fundamental lack of credibility" as the basis for his calculation that, ultimately, NBC would choose not to broadcast the interview. What quite likely had been a bluff by NBC thus had provoked a counterbluff by the chief executive of the Bureau of Prisons.

Late the next morning, the interview was videotaped in Benefiel's office. The session lasted forty-five minutes, during which Kimberlin recited his well-oiled spiel—the frat party, the ensuing phone call from "D.Q.," the meetings in the Burger Chef and motel parking lots. During a conversation with Totenberg, Kimberlin had said, "Tom Brokaw is coming out to see me tomorrow." Actually, the NBC emissaries were a reporter named Kevin Dunn and a crew from Atlanta. By El Reno, Oklahoma, standards, however, the event had sufficient celebrity heft and news value to arouse the interest of Ray Dyer, the editor of the *El Reno Daily Tribune*. The previous day, he had learned of the NBC meeting from a prison employee and himself had spoken with Kimberlin on the phone. When the NBC team arrived at the prison, a *Daily Tribune* photographer was waiting for them. Within ten minutes, Kimberlin phoned Dyer and told him the interview "went real well." Dyer replied that he had a shot of the NBC crew, and "we're going to put it to the wire—the Associated Press."

The *Daily Tribune* (circulation 5,000) was published every weekday afternoon at two o'clock. That day's headline and subhead read: QUAYLE PROBE COMES TO FCI, INMATE SAYS THAT HE SUPPLIED SENATOR DOPE. The story, under Dyer's byline, ran about five hundred words and included a synopsis of Kimberlin's allegations as well as his criminal convictions. "A Quayle campaign worker in Washington, D.C., this morning called Kimberlin 'a little Charlie Manson,' and said that he did not want his name used in any story about Kimberlin because he is afraid for his family," Dyer wrote. A prison official, who also requested anonymity, told Dyer that the press "is calling here like crazy." The warden, Tom Martin, was quoted as saying that only NBC had filled out the forms required for an interview with a prisoner. The campaign worker denied that Quayle knew his accuser and also contended that the candidate had never made statements about legalizing marijuana. Dyer, however, had spoken with a librarian at the *Fort Wayne News-Sentinel* and confirmed that in March 1977, the newspaper had quoted Quayle, during his first term in Congress, calling for a "serious" look at decriminalization.

TWO P.M. Oklahoma time was noon in Santa Barbara. There, Chuck Blitz, on his Pacific promontory, received a facsimile copy of the *El Reno Daily Tribune*'s front-page story. In Blitz's recollection, the fax reached him before noon—a physical impossibility. Perhaps Blitz's advance knowledge, courtesy of Shearer, that the *Daily Trib* piece was coming, or perhaps the general intensity of the occasion, left him with a memory at once vivid and imprecise. By the end of the day, the phone company was even richer. Armed with a list of newspapers and radio and television stations, also courtesy of Shearer, Blitz began making calls all over the country. Along the way, an assistant provided him with additional numbers. "I can work the phones when I need to, and I've been known to make a hundred calls in a day," Blitz said. "That day I made two hundred fifty calls." Affecting a southwestern twang, Blitz would get an editor or a news director on the line and explain that he'd just read an interesting item in the *El Reno Daily Tribune*. He would recite choice excerpts—emphasizing Kimberlin's claim of having "sold marijuana to Quayle fifteen to twenty times between 1971 and 1973"—rather than the "little Charlie Manson" characterization. Then he provided Ray Dyer's phone number.

Before publishing the story and transmitting it on the wire, Dyer had forewarned the Associated Press bureau chief in Oklahoma City that a scoop was en route. The bureau chief, after consulting with the AP's national assistant managing editor in New York, decided not to forward Kimberlin's unsubstantiated allegations further along the wire. Still, the effect of Shearer and Blitz's joint enterprise was to circumvent the news wire. In 1988, the *El Reno Daily Tribune* did not own a fax machine. To respond to requests for copies of the article, Dyer went to the nearby office of an insurance company. He dispatched "twenty-five or maybe fifty" fax copies, which in turn triggered a barrage of calls to the prison from journalists demanding interviews with Kimberlin. Around three-thirty, while working in the library, Kimberlin was summoned to the office of the warden's executive assistant, who, according to Kimberlin, "was all agitated." Their conversation lasted only a few minutes. The logistical demands of arranging dozens of individual interviews threatened to overwhelm the prison administration, so Benefiel proposed an expedient solution: a press conference at seven o'clock that evening, in the main visiting room. Kimberlin would have his say, the reporters would ask their questions, and Benefiel's task, as a media liaison, would be simplified and fulfilled. Kimberlin instantly agreed, and signed an authorization form.

FROM Benefiel's office, Kimberlin went to a telephone and dialed Totenberg, but she was on deadline and couldn't take the call. He then phoned Shearer, to tell him about the press conference. Earlier that day, Kimberlin had spoken with a private investigator in Indianapolis, a woman named Barbara Bumbalough. After the Supreme

Court declined to hear his appeal of the bombings convictions, Brett had retained Bumbalough because he wanted her to find hypnosis witnesses and persuade them that their identifications of him had been mistaken—a prelude to a motion to have his convictions vacated. Kimberlin's immediate circumstances had precipitated a pair of more urgent requests. He asked Bumbalough to get in touch with Susan Harvey, hoping she would confirm that a decade and a half earlier he'd done marijuana business with a customer named Danny. He also had Bumbalough rummaging through old files that Nile Stanton had placed in storage, specifically for a copy of the FBI arrest report from 1978, with its reference to "information which [Kimberlin] had concerning . . . drugs . . . and a Congressman of the United States." For the moment, Bumbalough had no encouraging news. The arrest report hadn't turned up, and she informed Kimberlin that her conversation with Susan Harvey wasn't "very friendly. . . . Right off the bat, she said you were somebody that she knew a long time ago and she wanted nothing to do with you whatsoever."

In his call to Shearer, Kimberlin omitted this closing detail. Without identifying Susan by name, he allowed that Bumbalough's interview "didn't go very well." Hearing this, Shearer questioned the investigator's competence and proposed that he would've been more successful. "Does this woman [Susan Harvey] know about Danny?" he asked, and Kimberlin answered, "Yeah. She could be very helpful if she remembered certain things. But that's the problem—she won't even talk." At that hour, Shearer was mainly preoccupied with the NBC interview, and he was awaiting the outcome of discussions in New York, where editors at "NBC Nightly News" were deliberating. Though he didn't say so to Kimberlin, he felt reassured knowing that if NBC broadcast its story, it would beat the press conference by an hour, more or less.

Kimberlin had only a few minutes left before he was due to report to his unit for a prisoner count—a daily 4:00 p.m. routine. He reviewed with Shearer the four basic issues he would discuss at the press conference: his dealings with Quayle; the existence of the DEA file on Quayle; the 1982 investigation of drug use on Capitol Hill and the likelihood that Quayle had been a target of that inquiry; John Calhoun's transfers within the federal prison system, information that originated with Fawley. (A prison employee in El Reno had given

Kimberlin a printout of Calhoun's transfers and furloughs, but there was no tangible evidence of Quayle's influence or motives.)

Kimberlin asked Shearer, "What else do you want me to say? Come on, Cody."

Shearer reiterated the four topics.

"All right," Kimberlin said.

"I mean, everybody's trying to find out all these answers," Shearer replied.

"I'll put it all out tonight. Bye."

Following this phone conversation and the prisoner count, Kimberlin went to the gym, where, for an hour and a half, he honored his daily body-building regimen. He then hurried back to his residential unit to clean up and get to the conference room well before seven o'clock. James Lewis accompanied him from point to point. The accumulating stress was almost tangible, and Kimberlin seemed rushed and distracted. Midway between the gym and the unit, Lewis placed a hand on Kimberlin's shoulder, stopping him in his tracks.

"Take it easy," the man known as the Tylenol extortionist told the man known as the Speedway Bomber. "Slow down. Savor this. This is history."

29

EVEN Kimberlin, who disdained the idea that fate ever tripped a lever or squeezed a trigger, who believed that you made your own luck, couldn't deny that a dynamic life featured turning points at which luck enhanced or impaired one's designs. Indeed, he had now been delivered to such a turning point. In the absence of a higher form of intervention—which, in this case, masqueraded as a lower form of inanity—he could not have achieved single-handedly what came next: his apotheosis. A sinuous pattern of dominoes, many of them set in place by people who were certainly not Kimberlin's deliberate allies, began to topple at optimal angles at opportune moments.

The press conference never took place. The fifteen or so newspaper, radio, and television reporters who showed up were presented with a memorandum from the warden's executive assistant: "Unforeseen developments have come up since arrangements for the interview were set up this afternoon. There will be no interview tonight. We will take any requests for a personal interview tonight and arrange the interview at a later time." Determining what happened between the scheduling and the cancellation, as well as what happened to Kimberlin during the subsequent hours and days, as well as why and how these events occurred, provided the grist for litigation that dragged on for several years.

In the course of the litigation, certain undisputed facts emerged. Mark Goodin of the Bush-Quayle campaign, having learned of the press conference from a reporter, called the Justice Department's office of public affairs, was told that the Bureau of Prisons had arranged the event, and responded, "I just never cease to be amazed." Since first hearing, weeks earlier, an account of Kimberlin's allegations from Nina Totenberg, Goodin said, he "was monitoring it [the Kimberlin matter] on a daily basis." Now it seemed that he "was about to be overtaken by events."

During a conversation with Loye Miller, the director of public affairs at the Justice Department, Goodin expressed shock and dismay: "This Kimberlin fellow apparently is going to have a press conference. I'm amazed."

"Well, amazed or not, he's going to have one," Miller said. "It's within his rights to have one, according to the rules and regulations."

"I am bowled over," Goodin replied.

According to Miller, Goodin "noted the obvious: that the closer to the Tuesday election the story were to break, the more attention it was likely to get, and the better the chance that it could have at least some adverse effect." According to Goodin, Miller said, "I will be happy to keep you apprised of developments." Miller called his public affairs counterpart at the BOP, as well as the executive assistant to Attorney General Richard Thornburgh. In turn, Goodin briefed his colleagues, among them James Baker, chairman of the campaign; Lee Atwater, the campaign manager; and Stuart Spencer, who was managing Quayle's campaign. Quayle himself was told of Kimberlin's looming press conference. At least one other official from the campaign—someone other than Goodin—also got in touch with the BOP to discuss the situation.*

Michael Quinlan, director of the BOP, personally issued the cancellation order. Kimberlin, frustrated that he was not going to meet the press after all, did the usual: he made phone calls—to his mother, Totenberg, and Shearer. By the time he spoke with Totenberg, she'd already heard the news from Loye Miller. Totenberg did not entirely share Kimberlin's frustration; an aborted press conference meant that a story she had tried to develop for weeks would not be disseminated by other reporters.

"Welcome to the Polish government," Shearer began, when Kimberlin reached him shortly before 9:00 p.m. After they discussed how all this had come about, Shearer continued, "Let me tell you something. What we may be seeing here is a total news blackout. Absolute total news blackout."

"How can that happen?" Kimberlin asked.

---

* That such a call took place was disclosed in a memorandum prepared by Michael Quinlan and sent to Frank Keating, an associate attorney general. Kimberlin and his attorneys speculated about who the caller might have been—the list of suspects included James Baker or someone acting on his direct orders—but the identity of the caller has never been revealed.

"What do you mean, how can that happen?" Shearer replied. "It's easy. Welcome to America."

Timing was everything. The next deadline for Shearer's syndicated column was three days away, so he was unable to file a story that would have any effect upon the outcome of the election. He urged Kimberlin to approach various media outlets directly, and he rattled off the phone numbers of television and radio stations in Oklahoma, as well as numbers for the *New York Times* and the *Boston Globe*. Kimberlin told Shearer that he had already heard that the cancellation order had come "from the top," but he did not literally know that Quinlan was involved. Oddly, when the director's name came up, Kimberlin referred to him as "a decent guy, from what I understand." Perhaps, he suggested, if Shearer could get in touch with Quinlan, he might act in his behalf. Who knew? The right words from Quinlan might discourage his minions from "put[ting] me on a bus and ship[ping] me to Timbuktu."

"Yeah, that's the other thing," Shearer said. "They may try to move you out."

"But I think this would make it look worse than if I talked to them [the press]," Kimberlin said.

"Of course it does."

This exchange was both prescient and shadowed by ignorance. If Kimberlin had known that it was Quinlan who stifled the press conference, he would have offered a wholly different appraisal of the director's character. Nor did Kimberlin or Shearer have any inkling that rather than being shipped out of El Reno, the convict was about to be buried deep inside. To his first edict, Quinlan soon added another: Kimberlin was to be placed in "administrative detention"—removed from the general population and locked away in a four-by-six cell commonly known as "the hole." This event was and is unique in American penal history. At the time, almost 45,000 inmates populated the federal prison system. Never before had the director of the Bureau of Prisons personally ordered that an inmate be put in the hole.

KIMBERLIN's travelogue of his particular journey:

"There were guards all over the unit, watching every move I made. The whole atmosphere was charged. Everybody could feel it—

not just me. It was, 'Oh shit, something big's going to happen.' Very spooky. It was around eleven o'clock that night. I'd just gone into my cell. I remember I was looking in my locker for something—a toothbrush, maybe. All of a sudden, my door swings open and there were all these goons coming at me—half a dozen prison guards screaming at me. They grabbed me and took me outside my cell and threw me against the wall, spread-eagled me, kicked my legs out. I said, 'What's going on,' and they said, 'You *know* what's going on!' One of the cops said, 'Kimberlin, you're fucking with the wrong people.' At one point, I turned around, and they screamed at me to look at the wall. They said, 'Put your hands behind your back.' They handcuffed me behind my back, and I said, 'Where am I going?' They said the hole. I asked what for. They said, 'You *know* what for!' The next thing I know, they're hauling me down the stairs without a coat. It was cold out that night. The hole is way across the compound, a quarter mile. Instead of just letting me walk, they wheelbarrowed me—lifted the handcuffs up in the back so it pulled on my shoulder sockets, so I had to walk bent over. I had to walk like that the whole way. They were telling me to shut up. When I got to the hole, they strip-searched me. I was shaking like a leaf. Both in fear and cold."

Kimberlin's detention did not amount to solitary confinement. Another convict shared the hole with him, a man in his seventies with a serious coronary complaint. The hole was large enough for a bunk bed and a toilet-sink unit—"but not large enough to practice my golf swing."

In the event that anything untoward might happen to him, Kimberlin had taken the precaution of giving James Lewis and other convicts the phone numbers of Shearer, Totenberg, and his mother. Within the next few hours, all three received calls relaying the news of his detention.

THE OFFICIAL explanations for the cancellation of the press conference and Kimberlin's subsequent detention had about them a gang-that-couldn't-shoot-straight character that made them almost endearing. In a letter to Senator Joseph R. Biden, Jr., written six weeks after the events, Quinlan stated that "the Bureau's policy . . . does not authorize inmate press conferences." This versus Loye Miller's accurately informing Mark Goodin—the very day the conference was to have taken place—of Kimberlin's "rights to have one, according to the rules and regulations." If inmate press conferences weren't allowed, why were reporters given a statement that attributed the cancellation to "unforeseen developments"? How could such language apply to a matter of policy? Why were Quinlan's colleagues—among them the regional director in Dallas, with twenty years of service, and the El Reno warden, who'd served the BOP for thirty years—unaware that any such policy existed?

Describing the detention order, Quinlan wrote to Biden: "During the evening hours of November 4, based on a report from the media that Mr. Kimberlin had expressed concerns for his personal safety, he was placed in administrative detention pending an investigation relative to his possible need for protection." A memorandum prepared by Loye Miller and addressed "To Whom it May Concern" referred to "a telephone call from a very disturbed Ms. Totenberg," which took place at "perhaps 11 p.m." During this conversation, Miller wrote, Totenberg recounted two telephone calls that she had received—one from Kimberlin, who "complained bitterly about the cancellation of his press conference," and the other from an inmate who reported that Kimberlin had been sent to the hole.

In the Quinlan-Miller version of this episode, Totenberg was cited as the source of information ("based on a report from the media") that Kimberlin feared retaliation from other inmates. Quinlan and Miller adhered to this story line in the face of strong evidence to the contrary: one, that the late-night conversation between Totenberg and Miller took place *after* Kimberlin had already gone to the hole; two, that Kimberlin swore in an affidavit that "while I was in the detention unit I was informed that I had purportedly expressed fears that other inmates would harm me. . . . I neither perceived, nor had I expressed, such fears"; three, that the prison's own wiretaps yielded no record of Kimberlin expressing these fears to Totenberg; four, that as Totenberg swore in an affidavit, "it became clear to me that the Department [of Justice] was using me as the excuse for isolation—that I was supposed to be the person who quoted Kimberlin as saying his life was in danger. I immediately told Loye Miller that was untrue and that I had never said any such thing."

Discrepancies accumulated that would have had Kafka crying plagiarism. If Kimberlin was placed in detention for his own protection on the basis of information from a third party, why wasn't the standard procedure followed—an interview to confirm that he indeed feared for his safety? Why was he manhandled and verbally abused by the guards who escorted him to the hole? Why did the papers ordering his detention contain the notation: "NO! MORE CALLS FOR THIS INMATE / per Lt. Garvue"? How was it that Lieutenant Garvue, in charge of the unit that housed segregated inmates, later could neither recall giving such an order nor explain the basis for it? And how was it that, eventually, Miller himself denied ever having spoken directly with Quinlan about Kimberlin? Ultimately, the Justice Department's own inquiry into these events concluded: "Just when and how that information [that Kimberlin feared for his safety] reached Director Quinlan, who was then in Chicago, remains obscure."

THE NEXT day, Saturday, November 5, was a busy one for Totenberg, Miller, and James Jones, the director of public affairs for the BOP. In her affidavit, Totenberg referred to a "series of conversations" with Miller and Jones. During one of these conversations with Miller, which Totenberg characterized as "fairly acrimonious," she realized that the pretext for placing Kimberlin in detention was a statement she had never uttered. The journalistic contours and import of the Kimberlin story were shifting.

From Totenberg's sworn declaration: "I demanded that Kimberlin be permitted to call me so that I could make sure he was all right. I don't know how many conversations I had that day with Loye Miller and with the Bureau of Prisons spokesman, but they both seemed quite hysterical. . . . I reiterated my position that the Department [of Justice] was making a story of a non-story by trying to shut this man up when under normal circumstances his uncorroborated statement could not be used. Mr. Miller, extremely agitated, made various accusatory remarks about my professionalism, which of course only made me rather suspicious."

Another interested party with whom Miller spent significant time on the phone that day was Mark Goodin. From Miller's memorandum: "Also Saturday, Goodin called from the Quayle campaign to ask what was happening with Kimberlin. He said that Totenberg had told them that the Justice Department's alleged persecution of Kimberlin was likely to cause National Public Radio to air a story, which would of course highlight Kimberlin's claim that Quayle had purchased drugs. He said they were poised to have Quayle vigorously deny the allegations if they did become public. He said that for the entire previous weekend, Nina had kept the Quayle camp on tenterhooks while she debated whether to air the story following her telephone interviews with Kimberlin."

The warden on duty that weekend assigned Lieutenant James Monk, whose title was special investigative supervisor, to review the tapes of Kimberlin's phone calls for evidence that he feared for his safety. This task was completed by early Saturday evening—Monk having turned up nothing—and after less than twenty-four hours in the hole, Kimberlin was allowed to rejoin the general population. From that moment—and continuing for the next several weeks, Kimberlin believed—he was kept under special surveillance. "They had a lieutenant assigned to watch me," he said. "They were following me all the time; it was like the KGB. And they were trying to pretend they weren't watching me. It was almost comical." This scrutiny wasn't successfully intimidating; if anything, he considered it a sign that he was a force to be reckoned with. Moreover, it was his impression that Totenberg's threat to air the story of his detention had prompted his release—proof that his allies outside the prison could and would protect him from further abuse. "I felt like things had been equalized," he said later.

Kimberlin resumed his telephone routines, staying in touch with Shearer and Totenberg and also speaking with reporters who, after the conference was canceled, had filed interview requests. He granted one to WBAI, a listener-supported radio station in New York City. From Shearer, he learned of a plan to gather a group of reporters Monday morning at the Mayflower Hotel in Washington, where they could converse with Kimberlin by means of a speakerphone. This hastily arranged event was devised by Chuck Blitz and John Richard, the Ralph Nader associate who a month earlier had brought together Shearer and the Owl. Blitz was renting the meeting space at the Mayflower and covering other costs, but he didn't intend to leave California to be there in person. By Blitz's own account, Nader himself vehemently urged him to show up. "It's like Iwo Jima," he claimed Nader told him. "It's pivotal. It's the end of the war. You've got to go. You've got to be there."

Blitz was making similar entreaties to other minor players. Carolyn Kimberlin was by then living in a Maryland suburb of Washington, and Cynthia happened to be visiting. The constantly ringing phone and the uncertainty over what Brett had got himself into greatly unnerved Carolyn, and out of deference to her mother Cynthia declined to appear at the Mayflower. Nor was Blitz able to induce Lori Levinson, who'd guided Totenberg to Kimberlin in the first place, to make an eleventh-hour journey to Washington from Salt Lake City.

"Chuck Blitz called, and he's saying, 'Whatever you want. Whatever you need,' " Levinson recalled. "He wanted me to go to Washington. But I couldn't go, because I'd just had a miscarriage. Chuck had told me that I was a heroine because I had convinced Brett to talk to Nina. He was a real salesman, telling me how proud I should be, that I was saving the country. A real flowery guy. And I thought: Whoa—the guy [Quayle] just smoked pot. I'm not trying to save the country." (The Kimberlin wiretaps recorded a conversation with Levinson, who complained that Blitz had been willing to pay for a coach, but not a first-class, airplane ticket.)

Lieutenant Monk, meanwhile, having digested the telephone tapes made before Kimberlin's detention, was given a new assignment by the weekend warden: to monitor Kimberlin's calls contemporaneously, rather than reviewing them later. By Sunday evening, the warden had left town because of a family emergency. His replacement, an associate warden, stopped by the telephone monitoring facility, listened to a conversation in which Kimberlin urged a reporter to attend the Mayflower conference, and learned from Lieutenant Monk what was being hatched. By the next morning, the principal warden, Tom Martin, was back on duty at El Reno and reporters were calling the Bureau of Prisons and the Justice Department in Washington about the press conference, which was scheduled to begin at ten o'clock.

Mark Goodin, who otherwise would've spent Monday in his office, made plans to travel that day with Quayle, in case the candidate needed a handler to face Kimberlin's charges. As things turned out, Quayle didn't need any help. At nine forty-five, Kimberlin was again taken from his cell, handcuffed, strip-searched, and escorted to the hole. A prison log contained the notation: "No Phone Calls." Loye Miller later told the *New York Times* that, as in the first instance, the decision to place Kimberlin in detention had been made by Quinlan. And in his memorandum, Miller noted: "It was certainly my understanding at the time that it was this attempt to hold an unauthorized press conference which directly caused him to be segregated once again." That same day, seven cassettes containing recordings of Kimberlin's phone conversations were sent directly to Quinlan. When Quinlan's chief of staff was asked under oath to characterize this action, he acknowledged that it was "uncommon."

Later, seeking to justify the second detention, Quinlan explained that Kimberlin had violated a prison regulation prohibiting third-party phone calls—that is, a call that one party forwards to another. The phone call in question was one that Kimberlin had made the previous Friday, to Boston, when he tried to reach John Sasso and Susan Estrich, the vice chairman and manager of the Dukakis campaign. After his collect call was refused, Kimberlin had a friend in Indianapolis arrange the forwarded call. (Neither Sasso nor Estrich was available, so Kimberlin spent a few minutes chatting with a secretary: "I'm the marijuana dealer that sold pot to Dan Quayle when he was in law school, and I've been hounded by the press for the last week and—" "Where do you live now?" "I'm in prison and—" "You're in prison?")

Not until Monday morning did it become necessary to punish Kimberlin for this offense; he had previously been placed in the hole "for his personal safety." Now the pretext changed. Even if the pretext had a legitimate basis, the BOP's regulations required that Kimberlin be allowed a hearing before the punishment could be imposed. Why hadn't official concerns about the call to Dukakis headquarters been raised following Lieutenant Monk's review of the tapes, two days earlier? Why was Kimberlin once again placed in detention when no BOP regulations prescribed such punishment for this infraction? Because it was a harvesting season in El Reno and Washington, such niceties of due process got overlooked. This time Kimberlin stayed in the hole for a week.

UNABLE to come up with compelling corroborative evidence, Totenberg and National Public Radio never did broadcast a story. "I had conflicting feelings about that," Totenberg said later. "I drafted a memo that was a model of what the story would be. The news director and I discussed it, and we decided no, we're not going to go with it. And I agreed." NBC begged off as well, reporting neither Kimberlin's original allegations nor the news of his detentions. And so, in the days before the election, the public exposure that Kimberlin's story received was limited to the *El Reno Daily Tribune* article, WBAI, and a local radio show and a television news broadcast in Los Angeles that noted the cancellation of the first press conference—very nearly the "total news blackout" that Cody Shearer had posited.

ON ELECTION Night, Kimberlin said, a prison guard came to the hole and said, "Kimberlin, you're in big trouble now."

Kimberlin said, "Why?"

The guard said, "Bush won."

KIMBERLIN'S second detention ended on November 14, with an administrative hearing during which he was found guilty of having made a third-party call, was warned not to repeat the offense, and lost two days "good-time" credit. A month later, after he appealed, the good-time credit was restored.

Good-time credit was a commodity that Kimberlin badly needed. The day that he was released from the hole, the Parole Commission issued its decision. The parole examiners whom he'd met with in El Reno that July had suggested that he serve a total of 168 months, which translated into a release date of February 1993. Though this was a much longer incarceration than Kimberlin believed the guidelines allowed, it was far less than what Victor Reyes, the regional commissioner to whom the report was forwarded, felt he deserved. The appropriate guideline range, as Kimberlin perceived it, was 64 to 92 months. Overruling the examiners, Reyes sent the full Parole Commission in Washington a recommendation that Kimberlin serve 240 months, which would've kept him in prison until 1999. Despite their vote to reduce Reyes's recommendation by twelve months, the verdict that greeted Kimberlin as he emerged from the hole was much worse than he had anticipated. The government intended to lock him up until February 1998.

30

I N WAYS both direct and not, Cody Shearer continued to follow
the story. The day after Bush and Quayle were elected, he published in his syndicated column a summary of what Kimberlin
would've said if he'd been able to have a press conference. He disclosed the existence of Quayle's DEA file and placed it in the context
of the 1982 Capitol Hill drug investigation, then described a memorable encounter with Quayle at a political rally near Baltimore the
previous weekend. While shaking the candidate's hand, Shearer asked
whether he was aware of the DEA's interest in him. Quayle jerked
away, Shearer wrote, and replied, "That's the most absurd question
I've been asked in this campaign." More than fifty newspapers subscribed to Shearer's column through the North America Syndicate—
not enough, apparently, to stir a measurable response. "I remember a
couple of newspaper editors calling," he said. "But there was no great
flurry of activity. By then, the voters had spoken, it was no big deal,
life was going on."

Shearer turned to a friend, a young journalist named Aaron Freiwald, who covered the Justice Department for *Legal Times,* a weekly
publication affiliated with *The American Lawyer.* The lead story of the
19 December 1988 issue bore Freiwald's byline and the headline ISO-
LATION FOR INMATE WITH QUAYLE CLAIMS; WITH ELECTION NEARING,
OFFICIALS PLACED PRISONER IN SOLITARY, BARRED PRESS. Freiwald had
spoken with many of the principals, including Quinlan, Miller, and
Goodin. He confirmed that Goodin had been in regular contact with
the Justice Department and that he had "briefed Campaign Chairman
James Baker III on Kimberlin's status five times during the final days
of the campaign." Referring to the second detention, Miller said:
"The Bureau of Prisons caught on that he was going to hold another
press conference, so they put him back in." Though Quinlan told
Freiwald, "We have nothing to hide. Inmates just don't have press

conferences," the reporter arrived at a different understanding: "Kimberlin's handling by federal prison officials, and the intense interest in his activities among top GOP campaign aides, suggests that a supposedly apolitical system was being guided by political consideration." Exploring Kimberlin's background, Freiwald interviewed Buddy Pylitt, who identified himself as "a lifelong Democrat [and] a law-school classmate and acquaintance of Quayle" and said, "I don't know how anyone can give credibility to anything [Kimberlin's] saying." From Erwin Griswold, he elicited a countervailing judgment: "I've never had any reason to question his comments to me. I've been very much impressed with him." Freiwald also spoke with David Dorworth, the Parole Commission analyst who had reviewed Kimberlin's case and who explained that his parole date was pushed back because his crimes had resulted in the death of Carl DeLong. Freiwald wrote: "As far as the timing of the Parole Commission's decision, issued the day Kimberlin was released from solitary confinement, Dorworth says: 'On the surface that looks bad. But the fact that the hammer came down on him after this [Bureau of Prisons] stuff came up is just coincidence.' "

TOTENBERG, of course, saw Freiwald's story. On the eve of the 1992 election, I asked whether reading it after the 1988 election had given her second thoughts or persuaded her to pursue the facts once again.

"Since I was involved, I thought it was inappropriate," she said.

Then, perhaps, should someone else at National Public Radio have explored the matter?

Totenberg said, "We didn't think it was enough of a story—it was in a legal publication—to merit a follow-up."

Later still, I asked her to elaborate, and she said, "When they put Kimberlin in solitary, I tried to get people at the [Bush-Quayle] campaign—I was talking to Mark Goodin—to talk to someone at the Justice Department and find what these guys at the Bureau of Prisons were doing. But Goodin refused. He said, 'If we call Justice on this, we're dead meat.'

"At some point, you have to say either the story's not there or you've been manipulated. As far as I'm able to recall, nobody could ever say that they'd done something really awful to Kimberlin. Nor could I determine that, say, Jim Baker had given the order to put him in solitary. Now, *that* would have risen to the level of a real story. I didn't have anything reliable in the way of sources. My recollection is that *Legal Times* had some circumstantial evidence that higher-ups in the campaign had been involved in this episode of putting him in solitary. I think I remember making a call or two to determine whether there was more to this *Legal Times* story. I remember being interested by it but not floored. And I really shouldn't have been interested any more, because I was personally involved. Anyway, I couldn't verify anything."

In LATE November 1988, from the Freedom of Information Act, Kimberlin finally obtained a copy of the 1980 presentencing report that alluded to his offer to the FBI to trade information about drugs and a congressman. When Shearer told NBC News producer Ira Silverman that the document had turned up, he asked whether, had it become available a few weeks earlier, the network would have broadcast its taped interview with Kimberlin. Silverman replied, "I'd like to think that if we'd had a copy of that before the election, it would've made the difference."

THE SELF-JUSTIFYING explanations that Quinlan proffered to Freiwald—"We have nothing to hide. Inmates just don't have press conferences"—were elaborated in a memorandum that the BOP director sent to Frank Keating, his superior at the Justice Department, and in a letter to Joseph Biden, the chairman of the Senate Judiciary Committee. In his opening paragraph to Keating, Quinlan noted that the Kimberlin matter had "received additional media attention in the last several days." Biden's interest had been kindled by a letter from Kimberlin, who asked for an investigation of his detentions, and the senator promptly wrote to Quinlan, requesting an official BOP review of its handling of the prisoner. Ultimately, what seemed most resonant and curious about Quinlan's official correspondence with Keating and Biden—even more than the hollowness of his labors to superimpose "policy" after the fact—was the peculiarity of his timing. Both the memorandum and the letter were dated December 22, 1988—the same day that Kimberlin, as he later swore in an affidavit, was, for the third time in seven weeks, "seized . . . and forcibly marched to the detention unit . . . strip-searched at the unit, then locked into a cell, without being afforded a pre-detention hearing." The alleged offense that precipitated this third detention was, again, a third-party telephone violation.

The day before Kimberlin's return to the hole, he spoke with a reporter for a television show produced by *USA Today,* and split-screen shots of him and Quinlan appeared on the air. He'd also been a guest on a call-in radio program in Los Angeles, whose producers had solicited comments from Quinlan. The BOP's director of public affairs, James Jones, arranged with a subordinate, Richard Phillips, to get copies of Kimberlin's phone conversations from this period. (Phillips later testified that he didn't know why the request was made, but added that "there was a great deal of media interest" in Kimberlin. He also said that this was the first and only time he'd been asked to obtain records of a convict's phone conversations.)

To carry out this order, Phillips spoke directly with Lieutenant Gale Williams at El Reno. For at least two days after the publication of the Freiwald article, Williams monitored and recorded Kimberlin's calls, and he played some of the tapes over the phone for Phillips, who was also taping copies of the calls at his end. Supplementing this endeavor, Williams sent Phillips by overnight mail cassette recordings of Kimberlin's December 20 and 21 conversations. The recordings that Phillips made picked up the byplay between himself and Williams, including an exchange in which Phillips noted that he wanted to get the "attorney call . . . into the director [Quinlan]."

Kimberlin's third detention lasted one day. According to his affidavit, he was "released on December 23, 1988, by an official from the El Reno FCI who implied that while he might catch some flak for releasing me, he would do so anyway since there was no justification for my detention and he didn't want to see me in the hole over Christmas." The "attorney call" that Phillips wanted to get "into the director" was a conversation between Kimberlin and Steve Salky, a parole lawyer in Washington. Salky wasn't in his office when Kimberlin tried to reach him, and without his knowledge, a receptionist forwarded the call to Salky at a third location. If the good soldiers in El Reno hadn't been monitoring Kimberlin's phone conversations with his attorney, they would've had no pretext for the third detention.

In their avidity, the prison personnel skipped the due-process requirement of a predetention hearing. And of course, to gather their specious evidence they focused their eavesdropping on what by rights was a privileged conversation between attorney and client—a flagrant flouting of the BOP's own regulations. An administrative hearing held the next month resulted in Kimberlin's vindication—he was exonerated of any third-party phone violation—and the particulars of the third detention also provided him with a potentially valuable long-term asset, an unlawful-wiretapping claim against the U.S. government.

NOT LONG after Freiwald's article appeared in *Legal Times,* Kimberlin received a letter from Paul Alan Levy, a staff attorney with the Public Citizen Litigation Group, which was founded by Ralph Nader. Levy had read the article and was eager to assist with any redress Kimberlin might seek from the BOP, and Kimberlin naturally seized the offer. Also as a result of Freiwald's article, Kimberlin was approached by a lawyer familiar with the case of George Hansen, a former Idaho congressman who, while incarcerated at a federal prison camp in Virginia in 1986 and 1987, regularly held press conferences attended by newspaper, television, and radio reporters—events, Hansen swore in an affidavit, that "the Federal Bureau of Prisons [had suggested] to accommodate press interest in me."

In February 1989, the Public Citizen Litigation Group filed a Freedom of Information Act petition for tapes of Kimberlin's phone calls, memoranda pertaining to his detentions, and other prison records. Though the government tried to resist this request, by summer Public Citizen had received some documents, as well as cassette copies of some of the calls. Because the Nader organization's resources were limited, Levy and his colleagues sought to persuade one of the large law firms in the District of Columbia to represent Kimberlin on a pro bono basis. They approached the 370-member Arnold & Porter. Irvin Nathan, head of the firm's pro bono committee, agreed to explore the case and assigned it to two young associates, Howard Rosenblatt and Robert Threlkeld.

In December 1989, after satisfying themselves that Kimberlin indeed had a case, Rosenblatt and Threlkeld filed an administrative claim with the BOP, under the Federal Tort Claims Act, alleging unlawful imprisonment, assault and battery, and property loss (Kimberlin said that weight-lifting equipment, a radio, and personal papers had been removed from his cell during his first detention), and asked for $25,000, the maximum damages allowable. The lawyers were guided by a strategic assumption that they stood a better chance of victory in an administrative proceeding than in a constitutional claim against the government. Moreover, as Freiwald speculated in one of his continuing articles in *Legal Times,* an administrative proceeding afforded a more likely forum for a settlement that would grant Kimberlin an earlier release on parole.

By statute, the BOP had six months to respond; almost to the day six months later, the claim was denied. The letter from the Dallas regional counsel of the BOP did, however, contain something that Kimberlin's attorneys were delighted to have in writing—confirmation that Quinlan had personally canceled the first press conference, and that the second detention occurred because Kimberlin had intended to talk with reporters over the telephone. According to the BOP regional counsel, Kimberlin had six months "in which to bring suit against the United States . . . should you wish to do so."

Two weeks later, on 2 July 1990, Kimberlin filed a suit in the United States District Court for the District of Columbia. Named as defendants were Quinlan, Miller, and the United States of America. Invoking the First Amendment, Kimberlin's suit alleged that Quinlan and Miller, "while under color of federal law, intentionally and wantonly violated plaintiff's right of freedom of speech." Additionally invoking the Fifth, the suit charged that Quinlan and Miller "intentionally and wantonly violated plaintiff's right to due process."

Appealing the denial of Kimberlin's administrative claim against the BOP, the suit also sought damages "for tortious false imprisonment, assault, and battery." Then, under the Omnibus Crime Control and Safe Streets Act of 1968, the suit proposed that the wiretapping of Kimberlin's phone calls was intended to facilitate and further the "defendants' scheme to silence, isolate, and retaliate against Kimberlin as a result of his statements concerning the vice-presidential candidate." Finally, the suit alleged that the wiretapping was done "for the improper purpose of supplying information to Bush-Quayle campaign officials regarding Kimberlin's statements and the level of media interest in such statements."

· · ·

BEFORE the Supreme Court decided a 1971 case known as *Bivens* v. *Six Unknown Named Agents of the Federal Bureau of Narcotics,* individual citizens had no standing in court to sue federal officials for violating their constitutional rights. In the Bivens case, the Court ruled that citizens could indeed sue federal officials for compensatory and punitive damages when their rights were breached. The Court decision did not, however, revoke the protection federal officials enjoy under a concept known as "qualified immunity," the roots of which are centuries old. The right to sue does not in itself cancel immunity. The attempt to reconcile two competing interests—the right to sue federal officials, and the desire to protect these same officials so they can go about their business of running the country—is a matter that the courts are still wrestling with. When Kimberlin filed suit, nearly two decades had passed since *Bivens* became law, and more than twelve thousand claims had been filed. Of those, only thirty were decided for the plaintiff at the district court level, and twenty-six of those were later reversed on appeal. Only four *Bivens* claims resulted in paid judgments.

The Kimberlin suit was assigned to Judge Harold H. Greene, a senior and much respected jurist. He was the judge who delivered the famous ruling that led to the breakup of AT&T. He also presided over the trial of John Poindexter in the Iran-contra affair. To strip Quinlan and Miller of their qualified immunity—the fundamental prerequisite for a lawsuit for damages to proceed to trial—Kimberlin's attorneys had, first, to persuade Judge Greene, that Kimberlin's constitutional rights were "clearly established" at the time of his detention; and, second, to demonstrate that his allegations of wrongdoing were supported by concrete facts and evidence. Within three months, the government filed a motion to dismiss. Meanwhile, defeating the government's persistent opposition to discovery, Rosenblatt and Threlkeld had begun the process of obtaining government documents and taking depositions. Among the motions they filed was a request to depose Quinlan and Miller. The government opposed this motion, and Judge Greene ruled in its favor.

In early August 1991, Greene delivered his opinion, and for once it wasn't what the government and the individual defendants wanted to hear. Though he dismissed Kimberlin's Fifth Amendment claim and decided he had no jurisdiction over the assault-and-battery claim, he ruled in Kimberlin's favor on false imprisonment, illegal wiretapping, and the First Amendment violation. He used the terms "concrete," "tangible," and "facts and evidence corroborative" in reference to the plaintiff's claims. Overall, the judge's decision constituted a huge victory for Kimberlin. Stripping Quinlan and Miller of their immunity, it opened the door for their depositions to be taken; also, in the opinion of the federal district court, the case could now proceed to trial. Kimberlin's full day in court would be delayed, however, because within a month of Judge Greene's decision the government filed notice that it would appeal to the United States Court of Appeals for the District of Columbia Circuit. And this next step would turn out to be only a way station, an extended leg of an excursion that would consume years before arriving, at last, in the councils of the United States Supreme Court.

31

N O ONE familiar with Kimberlin could have expected him to respond passively to his detentions or his dealings with the Parole Commission. He dispatched his letter to Senator Biden soon after returning from his second trip to the hole, then wasted no time in expanding the battle to other fronts. That *Kimberlin* v. *Quinlan et al.* found its way to the Supreme Court, however, was a tribute only to the constitutional issues it addressed and the tactical artistry of his lead attorney, Howard Rosenblatt. What promised to be the chef d'oeuvre of Kimberlin's long career as a litigant was, it turned out, the only complaint ever filed in his name for which he was not the chief strategist. Which was just as well, because he had his hands full being a victim.

The lawsuit's provenance—an unsolicited offer from a public-interest law firm—helped legitimize Kimberlin's casting of himself as a casualty of systematic persecution. After the bombing trials, petitions circulated by the Brett Kimberlin Freedom Committee, with Carolyn and Cynthia Kimberlin as key operatives, had said: "Three years ago Brett Kimberlin was targeted for destruction 'at all costs' by the Indianapolis U.S. Attorney's Office." While awaiting sentencing, he had written to the U.S. attorney: "I promise you that I will not end my fight for liberty and justice until I am vindicated. I promise you protracted litigation on all fronts. I promise you appeals on all levels. I promise you that someday I will win and I will be liberated. . . . I promise you that I will fight for my Constitution, drafted by my Founding Fathers." Now, having been placed in isolation three times, apparently because he had tried to exercise his First Amendment rights, he fully entered the big time. Now he could sport the badge of political prisoner.

Still and all, drawing attention to this cause demanded even more dedication than he had exhibited while promoting himself, a decade earlier, as a victim of vindictive prosecution. Once Bush and Quayle entered office, the mainstream media had virtually no use for him. Sympathetic journalists like Cody Shearer, Norman Solomon, and Aaron Freiwald found other stories to follow, as well as agendas that extended beyond the duty to accept Kimberlin's collect calls. The incrementalism of the redress process—the twenty-month lapse, for instance, between the first detention and the formal filing of the lawsuit—was another liability, with much-diminished news value. Kimberlin settled for a shotgun approach, calling "everybody in the media and politics that I'd been involved with at one time or another." His sense of martyrdom was rejuvenated. If he knocked on enough doors, something had to give.

WITH names and addresses that Kimberlin claimed Shearer had provided, he wrote letters to prominent people of wealth and left-of-center sympathies—Robert Redford, Norman Lear, Pamela Harriman—asking for financial help or other favors. He wrote to a Hollywood movie producer, pitching an autobiographical drama that would depict both himself and Quayle embroiled in "the political skullduggery that occurred"; listening to the tapes of his wiretapped conversations, he assured the producer, was like "reading a thriller novel." To big hitters with conservative pedigrees such as Edwin Meese and Elliot Richardson he wrote letters identifying himself as the son of "a Republican lawyer from Indiana." When he wrote to rock stars including Jackson Browne, Steve Winwood, Neil Young, Don Henley, and Frank Zappa, he added personal blandishments: "I really like your new song," "I saw you on 'Saturday Night Live,' " "I love your new album." What better time to revive the Brett Kimberlin Freedom Committee, and wouldn't a benefit concert be an ideal way to kick it off?

In Chicago, his factotum James Turner followed up by telephone, explaining that Kimberlin himself would soon be calling from prison. "I had all these addresses and phone numbers," Kimberlin said. "Like Madonna. I wrote to Madonna first and got a letter back saying to call. Jimmy was calling Madonna's publicist. I called Don Henley at home, and he said, 'How the fuck did you get this? This is an unpublished number.' I wrote to David Crosby several times. John Denver I wrote to several times, and he never wrote back. Neil Young I wrote to several times, but I never got an answer. Zappa's people were really cool, they were nice. I called Stephen Stills at home many times. I got to know his son pretty well."

IN FEBRUARY 1989, the BOP transferred Kimberlin from El Reno to Memphis. As always, he resented the move—capricious authorities sticking you wherever they pleased—but, again as always, he quickly adapted. In Oklahoma, he'd begun accumulating credits toward a college degree, in no small part because he knew that it would enhance his parole prospects. At Memphis he was able to continue these studies, and he also began working toward a paralegal degree. Though he'd worked in the law library at El Reno, his "legal practice" had slackened. Here it would accelerate once more. The first new case he took, he said, involved a convict who'd drawn more than twenty years for a drug offense, a sentence Kimberlin got reduced by half. The grateful convict "knew all the drug people, knew all the mob people, he was very well respected, and he started bringing me a lot of cases, which he filtered so I wasn't getting any rats." Kimberlin agreed to represent a Ukrainian émigré named David Sushansky, who was also doing drug time, and who became his closest friend in the joint. And when Kimberlin wasn't occupied on behalf of other prisoners, he collaborated with two pro bono attorneys on an appeal of the Parole Commission's decision in his own case.

A FEW months after arriving at Memphis, Kimberlin wrote a letter to Norman Gorin, a producer for "60 Minutes." The two had met years earlier when, as Gorin described it, he was trying to develop a story about "someone who was put away who was a model citizen but was convicted with posthypnotic testimony." Because the Speedway bombing case "wasn't clean," Gorin decided not to use it, and eventually he gave up on the idea altogether. But in the spring of 1989 Brett had a different tale to tell. Remembering that Kimberlin was articulate, Gorin flew to Memphis, where they spent the better part of an afternoon together. Kimberlin recounted his alleged experiences with Quayle and showed Gorin the copy of the 1980 presentencing report. "My reaction was that this was all very interesting," Gorin told me. "But not very sexy as far as '60 Minutes' was concerned."

Kimberlin told Gorin that Cody Shearer had explored the general subject of Quayle and drugs, and Gorin subsequently arranged for CBS to put Shearer on the payroll as a researcher. They met with Don Hewitt, the show's executive producer, after which, Gorin recalled, "Don was willing to roll the dice for a while, spend some time and money." Shearer introduced Gorin to the DEA source from whom he'd first learned that the agency had a file on Quayle. Gorin independently confirmed the truth of this, though he wasn't able to get a printout of the file. Another source showed them the diagram of the 1982 Capitol Hill drug investigation that identified "Don Quayle" among dozens of potential targets. Gorin then arranged, and CBS paid for, an alumni reunion of the Indiana cocaine ring—John Calhoun and associates—whose members Shearer had become familiar with through Steve "The Owl" Fawley. Through the Freedom of Information Act, Gorin got copies of correspondence between the BOP and Quayle's Senate office regarding Calhoun's prison transfers and furloughs. Calhoun himself, however, convinced Gorin that Quayle had no direct role in facilitating his movements through the prison system. The Indiana gang, Gorin concluded, was a red herring courtesy of Fawley, since no one would corroborate his story that some of their product had gone up Quayle's nose.

That fall, Gorin and Shearer did turn up a couple of titillating leads. The data-entry work for the DEA's computer database—the Narcotics and Dangerous Drugs Information System, or NADDIS—was farmed out to private contractors. Gorin and Shearer met with several aggrieved employees of one such contractor, Ebon Associates. Many of the data-entry personnel, it seemed, engaged in what they referred to as "window-shopping." For fun, they'd scope out certain celebrities or public figures to see if they had been named in DEA investigations. The day after Quayle was chosen as Bush's running mate, some of these browsers discovered the existence of his file. The computer's security system made it possible to identify the snoops, some of whose reprimands included two- or three-week unpaid suspensions. Gorin and Shearer wined and dined them, hoping in vain that one had printed out Quayle's file. Then, in the spring of 1990, after almost a year of trying, they at last obtained hard copy from two separate sources, about 250 pages of NADDIS printout. The contents were summaries of investigative interviews, uncorroborated raw reports from agents in the field. Buried within this mass of data were three paragraphs that referred to Quayle.

WHAT did the passages about Quayle say, and what did they mean? In the summer of 1982, in Indianapolis, a drug dealer named Charles Parker was arrested and charged with selling methaqualone (Quaaludes). Hoping to ingratiate himself with law enforcement, he described a cocaine transaction that he claimed had occurred a few months earlier at the Indianapolis Press Club between Quayle and a dealer named Terry Carson. According to Parker, while he waited at the bar at the club, Carson passed cocaine to Quayle in the men's room. Parker also said Carson claimed to have sold Quaaludes to Quayle. When Carson was later subpoenaed and questioned, he admitted telling Parker about this transaction but insisted that he'd made it up in order to impress a buddy. One paragraph of the NADDIS printout was a distillation of Parker's version, and two others gave Carson's rebuttal. Hoping the former was in fact truthful, Gorin and Shearer pursued him.

Along the way, they came across this tantalizing information: In the wake of Parker's statement, an assistant U.S. attorney in Indianapolis placed a call to the Criminal Division of the Justice Department in Washington and spoke with a lawyer, David Hopkins, who was a liaison with the DEA. Hopkins made a notation in his diary: "Received call from AUSA in Indianapolis seeking advice re simple possession case on Senator Quayle. Advised [Justice Department] position was to commit resources on simple possession when person is in a position of trust. He stated reverse undercover [sting] contemplated—sale by state defendant to senator, and DEA had permission to do so. I recommended he or his boss clear details with [Hopkins's superior] before it happened. Called [Hopkins's superior] and advised him."

The AUSA in Indianapolis was—small world—Kennard Foster, who led the prosecution of Kimberlin for the bombings. In a conversation a decade later, Foster told me that no sort of "sting" on Quayle was ever contemplated. Rather, he said, he merely was following routine procedures by sharing the fact that a serious allegation had been made against an elected official.

In the summer of 1990, Hopkins, by then retired to private practice, showed Gorin and Shearer his diary. Six weeks after the first entry, he made a follow-up notation to the effect that the case seemed not to be going anywhere because of a "hang-up between state prosecutor . . . and informant/defendant"—that is, Parker—over what sort of plea bargain Parker could cut in return for setting up Quayle. Missing from Hopkins's diary was any explanation of how a state prosecutor could seize control of a case that was of interest to federal prosecutors. Not long after making the second entry, Hopkins left the Justice Department. There is no evidence that the investigation of Quayle went any further. One possible reason was that in December 1982, Parker was again arrested for selling drugs, which made him unavailable to participate in a sting or any other worthwhile law enforcement endeavor. Gorin and Shearer, however, were inclined toward a more arcane explanation: the case died because the entire Capitol Hill investigation was dismantled in the summer of 1983. A possibility they apparently discounted was that the Quayle inquiry came to naught because Parker's allegations were groundless.

IN INDIANAPOLIS, during the winter of 1991, Gorin and Shearer met with Parker, who recently had been released from a state prison. Shearer wore a hidden recording device and got Parker to hold forth on what he'd told the Indiana authorities about Quayle more than eight years earlier. Back in New York, Gorin informed Hewitt that he had a tape of Parker admitting a relationship with Quayle. Finally, Parker agreed to sit for the "60 Minutes" cameras. As the interview approached, the air of anticipation was palpable. "When I first told Don Hewitt about seeing the flow chart, he was enormously pleased," Gorin recalled. "And when we had Parker on the audiotape, he was even more excited. If this paid off, it would be a significant political story—potentially one of the big stories in the history of '60 Minutes.' We all thought: My God, if this is true, the second-highest elected official in the country might be forced to resign."

On a Friday in April 1991, with Morley Safer asking the questions, "60 Minutes" filmed an interview with Parker in a hotel suite in New York, and according to Gorin, "He was wonderful." The next day, Parker was given a polygraph test.

Gorin: "When the idea of a polygraph came up, there was initial reluctance by some of my bosses at '60 Minutes.' But the more I thought of it, the more I thought it would be prudent to get the best corroboration possible. And so we hired a guy who was a former FBI agent who specialized in polygraphs. On Saturday, the polygraph expert came in. Parker failed the polygraph. He gave all these reasons. He was apologetic. He said something with Quayle had happened and he was a witness to it. He said he had padded his involvement, and so on. But he insisted there was really something to it. We sent him back to Indianapolis. Then we spoke and he said he wanted to do it again. He wanted to talk some more. So we gave him another polygraph, four weeks later in Indianapolis, and he failed again. It was in a motel off the Indianapolis beltway. The last I saw of Charles Parker, he was wandering down a road near an interstate-highway off-ramp in Indianapolis."

Before the polygraph, CBS had hoped to confront Quayle with the Parker interview.

Shearer said, "It would have been a fucking nightmare."

Gorin said, "I think I saved CBS's ass."

CITING what he regarded as multiple flaws in the U.S. Parole Commission's handling of his case, Kimberlin appealed. He challenged his designation as a Category 8 offender; he was not legally responsible for the death of Carl DeLong, he said, and therefore belonged in Category 7. He objected to the case's having been earmarked for "original jurisdiction"—review by the full nine-member national panel. He felt he'd been given insufficient credit for his superior-program achievements (the college credits and self-improvement certifications). In February 1989, the Parole Commission—the same panel whose ruling he was challenging—rejected his appeal. One of the commission's arguments was that his responsibility for several dangerous explosions merited his allocation to Category 8.

Kimberlin took the appeal to the next level—the U.S. District Court for the Western District of Tennessee—and there he won a big round. Judge Jerome Turner found that the Parole Commission had violated its own rules; there was no provision for upgrading multiple Category 7 offenses into 8s. The court ordered that Kimberlin be given another hearing, and on 1 March 1990, the case was submitted to a new panel, which affirmed his good standing in Category 7 but nonetheless suggested that he serve 180 months—a year longer than the original panel had recommended at El Reno in the summer of

1988; five years less than Victor Reyes, the regional commissioner, had recommended before forwarding the case to the full national commission; and four years less than the national commission demanded. On 27 April 1990, the Parole Commission accepted this new, month-old recommendation, and Kimberlin was given a parole date of 13 February 1994. Again he appealed, and he was similarly denied. In April 1991, he requested that the hearing be reopened because he'd completed an associate of arts degree. Neither did this petition fly. Any new information Kimberlin wished to submit—superior-programming achievements, Publishers' Clearing House giveaways, what have you—would have to wait until January 1992, when he was next eligible for a formal review.

OTHER than articles in alternative newspapers in San Francisco, Memphis, and Milwaukee, Kimberlin's parole struggles didn't arouse anyone in the media. To his way of thinking, the whole deal was QED—he was being held prisoner not for the bombings but for daring to speak out about Quayle—even if the details were dense and intricate. The lawsuit against Quinlan, Miller, and the government was an easier matter for journalists to grasp, and in August 1991, when Judge Greene ruled that the case could go to trial, this development was briefly picked up in the press.

After reading a magazine account of Judge Greene's decision, Garry Trudeau created a week-long series of "Doonesbury" cartoon strips in which Quayle, depicted as a feather, was paid a late-night visit by an anthropomorphized marijuana joint. According to Trudeau, the series prompted "virtually no reaction." One person who did react was Shearer. First, he said, he called Quayle's office for comment and was told by a staff member, "We're glad this crap is coming out in August, when nobody is paying attention." Then, at the suggestion of a mutual friend, he called Trudeau to correct what he interpreted as a factual error: one of the strips seemed to imply that Kimberlin had been released from prison. Shearer volunteered to share some of the information he'd been gathering, and Trudeau—who once wrote, "With me, it's *never* personal. At the risk of sounding like Sonny Corleone, it's my job"—embraced the offer.

In November, Trudeau was back at it with a three-week-long series about Quayle and drugs, in which Shearer appeared in the role of

Rick Redfern, investigative reporter. The strips focused mainly on Quayle's DEA file and included a subplot with a keypunch operator who described the phenomenon of window-shopping à la NADDIS. Other strips depicted Redfern having phone conversations with Kimberlin and alluded to his detention, his knowledge of Quayle's DEA file, and the status of his parole case.

The seven hundred or so newspapers that subscribed to "Doonesbury" received the first series of strips from the Universal Press Syndicate a week before their publication. Immediately, strongly negative reactions came from many quarters. The *Boston Globe* reported that "Quayle, asked specifically if there is a DEA file on him, replied, 'Not to my knowledge' "—this despite his run-in with Shearer the weekend before the 1988 election, when he was informed point-blank of the file. (It also seems unlikely that Quayle would have been ignorant of the fact that, only a week earlier, Jeff Nesbit, the director of communications for the Vice President, had been deposed in connection with Kimberlin's lawsuit and had been asked by Howard Rosenblatt, "Are you aware or were you ever told about the existence of any government files containing allegations of drug use by Dan Quayle?")

No; what Quayle told the *Globe* was: "Who cares what a comic strip may or may not say about me or anyone else? I have no idea what the 'Doonesbury' strip is but you ought to treat it as a comic." Of Kimberlin, Quayle said, "He's a convicted felon. Geez. I mean he's in jail." The *Los Angeles Times* quoted David Beckwith, the Vice President's press secretary, as saying, "Both Garry Trudeau and Universal Press Syndicate know for a moral certainty that the allegations were proven to be false. Yet they are proceeding anyway. I think that is outrageous."

Also quoted in the *Los Angeles Times* and several other newspapers was Don Hewitt, who delivered what sounded like a spurned lover's account of his experiences with Charles Parker. Hewitt said, "This guy not only flunked the lie detector test, but he broke down and cried in front of Morley Safer and said that he had made it up because he wanted to get out of jail." In fact, at no point did Parker break down and cry. Nor did Parker have reason to lie to get out of jail, because he was already free. In a *Newsday* story that went out over the national wires, Hewitt said, "Cody Shearer has been trying to get this story placed somewhere. He finally talked Garry Trudeau into doing it." In fact, Norman Gorin had approached Shearer—on behalf of CBS and, of course, Hewitt. And Trudeau needed no coaxing when he embraced Shearer as a collaborator.

More than thirty papers refused to publish the strips. Trudeau was also attacked in a number of editorials and op-ed columns; in a speech on the Senate floor by Senator Harry Reid of Nevada, who accused him of McCarthyism; and implicitly, according to David Beckwith, by the Quayle family dog, a black Labrador named Breezy, who threw up while watching a morning news broadcast about the controversy. As the backlash gathered force, it became clear to Trudeau that Hewitt was going to great lengths to discredit him and Shearer alike. For the first time in his career, Trudeau began to keep a log of his phone calls. After one conversation with Morley Safer, he noted that Safer had told him that Hewitt was "probably out of control" because CBS hadn't been able to get the story.

This perception was shared by Gorin, who later commented on Hewitt's reaction to the strips: "It was bullshit—all this public sanctimony about how [Hewitt's] standards were so high. Hewitt told the press, 'We knew the guy was a liar.' . . . When the polygraph came down, Hewitt was absolutely crushed. Because Parker blew the polygraph, Don Hewitt couldn't dine out on the fact that we had the story that brought down an administration—because we didn't have the goods. It got him into a deeper and deeper funk. He must have had fantasies of sitting down with Ben Bradlee at the table of the high priests of journalism. . . . In Hewitt's mind, the whole thing was bullshit because '60 Minutes' hadn't been able to prove it. Don's problem is that if something comes out of his mouth, then it's true."

Gorin, who had worked for "60 Minutes" since 1971, left the show in 1991 and retired.

THE "DOONESBURY" episode seemed to unhinge the federal drug enforcement bureaucracy, forcing it into high damage-control mode. Four days before the first installment was published, the DEA acknowledged that Quayle had a file. In interviews, two former heads of the DEA said that accusations of illegal drug use by Quayle had been made by two convicts, Parker and Kimberlin. In an accompanying statement, the DEA noted that Parker's 1982 "allegations were pursued to their source and were determined to be untrue." Kimberlin's accusation, though uncorroborated, could not be "proved" false.

A week later, in Indianapolis, an even more remarkable mini-drama unfolded. Jack Thar, the assistant U.S. attorney who shared with Kennard Foster the prosecution of the Speedway bombings, invited a reporter from the *Indianapolis Star* to his office and disclosed the records of the 1982 investigation of Quayle, including the text of the DEA file. Though this action exposed Thar to reprimand or even prosecution—to reveal the contents of criminal-investigative files is a violation of federal law—he let it be known that he was acting with the approval of Deborah Daniels, the U.S. attorney. This revelation made Thar's gesture seem even more paradoxical. Deborah Daniels, a Republican appointee, was the sister of Mitchell Daniels, who had been the White House political director under Ronald Reagan and, during the 1988 presidential campaign, a close adviser to Quayle. Thar, however, was a lifelong Democrat, and acquaintances in Indianapolis, among them journalists, later said that he'd been known to make highly unflattering remarks about the Vice President.

Still, whatever aversion Thar felt toward Quayle could in no way compete with his profound, implacable contempt for Kimberlin. Kevin McShane, who worked with Nile Stanton on Kimberlin's defense in the bombings case, said, "It's always been my feeling that Jack wanted to get Brett convicted and go on to the next case, and his problem is that Brett won't go away." Kimberlin was more succinct: "Jack Thar hates me more than he hates anyone on earth."

As if to underscore this sentiment, two months after revealing the DEA file to the *Indianapolis Star*, Thar intervened to oppose Kimberlin's parole. When a federal prisoner enters the prison system, any prosecutor involved in his conviction is allowed to file with both the Bureau of Prisons and the Parole Commission something called a Form 792. This document allows a prosecutor, at his own initiative, to comment on how those agencies should respond to the offender. The two other prosecutors in the Speedway bombings—Foster and Buddy Pylitt—each filed a Form 792 within a year of Kimberlin's sentencing. In the summer of 1988, at the time of Kimberlin's first application for parole, Thar did nothing. In January 1992, however, when Kimberlin's case was back before the Parole Commission for an interim hearing, Thar finally spoke up.

Kimberlin's parole attorney was Alan Chaset, who before entering private practice had worked for three years on the Parole Commission and, before that, for fourteen years training federal judges on its operations. "At the time of the original conviction, sentencing, original parole hearing, Thar personally did nothing," Chaset observed. "It's not terribly unusual for a prosecutor to communicate with the Parole Commission around the time of a parole hearing if one takes place within several months of conviction. But to do it eleven years later, after two hearings—really, you can count on the fingers of one hand the number of times that has happened."

Parallel to Kimberlin's parole application, he had pending with the United States pardon attorney a request for a presidential pardon or sentence commutation. (He had filed a similar request in 1989, which George Bush formally denied not long after entering office.) In the spring of 1992, Thar wrote to the pardon attorney. He also called and strongly disparaged Kimberlin to at least one attorney who he knew had written a letter in support of the pardon petition. To Howard Rosenblatt, Brett's pro bono lawyer, it seemed that Thar's actions were an extension of the political interference that formed the basis of Kimberlin's lawsuit, and he filed a motion with Judge Greene to obtain a copy of Thar's letter to the Parole Commission. The government opposed this motion, and Judge Greene deferred any ruling. Aaron Freiwald explored the coincidence of Thar's release of the Quayle DEA data and his opposition to Kimberlin's parole in *Legal Times*. "They don't have a damn thing to do with each other," Thar told Freiwald. "It just happens I had the bad roll of the dice to be involved with both." David Beckwith told Freiwald, "People can see conspiracies in the God-damnedest things."

A journalist I know in Indianapolis told me that Thar told him, "The day Brett Kimberlin gets out of prison is the day I carry a gun."

When the Parole Commission finished its review, the prospective date of Kimberlin's release remained unchanged—13 February 1994. A letter submitted by Kimberlin's unit manager in Memphis, elaborating upon his "excellent institutional adjustment" and "extremely valuable" contributions to the weight-lifting and inmate-wellness programs, had cut no ice. The hearing examiners who met with Kimberlin wrote that though he had been "essentially a model inmate who has accomplished much since being incarcerated . . . the aggregate of subject's criminal behaviors precludes an earlier release." The national commission accepted the panel's findings. When Kimberlin appealed, he argued formally for the first time that the Parole Commission was being vindictive because of his allegations regarding

Quayle. When the commissioners dismissed this appeal, their vote was unanimous. "Your claim that the Commission's decision in your case is based on vindictive political considerations is without merit," they informed Kimberlin. "The Commission's decision was based on the aggravating circumstances relating to your offensive behavior."

32

I N TERMS of mass appeal, having Garry Trudeau in one's corner offered even better value than Erwin Griswold's imprimatur. The "Doonesbury" cause célèbre achieved serendipitously, and far more effectively, what Kimberlin had been trying to accomplish for the better part of three years. He was news again. The buzz galvanized momentum he could ride through the 1992 election—still a year off, though the contest for the Democratic nomination was well under way. In October 1991, a month before Trudeau's strips began to appear, Bill Clinton formally announced his candidacy, and this set the stage for a steep rise in Kimberlin's political currency.

Cody Shearer's entire family became preoccupied with Clinton's candidacy. Eventually, his older brother, Derek, would take a leave from Occidental College to become an economic adviser, and their sister, Brooke, would travel regularly with her close friend Hillary Rodham Clinton during the campaign. (The tangible rewards would be, respectively, appointments as ambassador to Finland and director of the White House Fellows Program. Though Brooke's husband, Strobe Talbott, officially remained at *Time* as a columnist and chief diplomatic correspondent, he was destined to become the deputy secretary of state.) For Kimberlin, the prospect of a Clinton nomination and victory in the general election loomed like so many more dominoes, all of them magically toppling. He foresaw not only a friendlier audience for his pardon and parole petitions but real levers that, when pulled, would trigger liberation and glorious vindication. Who could have anticipated such a realignment of the political firmament when, in 1988, Cody began nosing around in Quayle's putative past? At last, the dog might bark for the second time—and bite.

As the "Doonesbury" hoopla percolated, the *New York Times* took note with an editorial headlined WAS THIS PRISONER SILENCED? A few months later, in May 1992, the *Times* followed up with a lengthy story by Stephen Labaton, a former law school classmate to whom Howard Rosenblatt had given access to depositions he'd taken from various officials of the 1988 Bush-Quayle campaign, the Justice Department, and the Bureau of Prisons. Griswold, for his part, offered this assessment of Kimberlin's parole case: "It looks like there has been a strong internal reaction against him. Where he was making progress toward an early release date, that suddenly has dried up and apparently from suggestions in high places." The story filled a half page inside the Sunday *Times,* including a large photograph of a clean-cut Kimberlin looking soulful and sober, with the headline EVIDENCE LINKS '88 BUSH CAMPAIGN TO EFFORT TO SILENCE AN ACCUSER OF QUAYLE. A few weeks later, in a *Times* op-ed column, Anthony Lewis quoted Kimberlin on his relationship with the sainted Griswold—"He writes to me. He never forgets my birthday. He's been like a grandfather to me"—and concluded: "[W]hether Vice President Quayle bought marijuana is a question of no importance. But it matters a lot if officials manipulated the Federal prison system at the behest of a political campaign. That question should be explored in the way best designed to get the facts promptly: a Congressional hearing."

And by that point, a congressional investigation—if not a specific congressional hearing—had already begun. Labaton's article got the attention of Senator Carl Levin of Michigan, then chairman of the Senate Subcommittee on Oversight of Government Management. In late June, Levin sent to Michael Quinlan and Loye Miller lengthy and detailed letters that spelled out questions raised by his subcommittee's scrutiny of the BOP's handling of Kimberlin. Neither Quinlan nor Miller responded, and the reply that Levin did receive—an assistant attorney general's recapitulation of Quinlan's many previous self-contradictions—deepened his suspicion that important facts were being concealed. A second letter from the senator, in mid-August, itemized remaining unanswered questions but also failed to yield satisfactory explanations. Levin, a liberal Democrat, had placed himself in a tricky position. He wanted to avoid any suggestion that his subcommittee was doing Kimberlin's bidding or that he, personally, was politically motivated.

Kimberlin, meanwhile, hoped literally to cash in on these developments. Armed with fresh press clippings from the *Times* and other sources, he sent grant requests to potential benefactors—primarily foundations and generous Democratic donors. "My reason for contacting you is because of your reputation as a staunch supporter of justice . . ." Chuck Blitz provided networking assistance in this endeavor, which paid off. A Washington organization called the Drug Policy Foundation funneled to Kimberlin a total of $5,000 from two progressive philanthropies, the Tides Foundation and the Ottinger Foundation. An environmental-activist friend of Blitz's, Jeremy Sherman, gave Kimberlin another $5,000. Peter Lewis, a Cleveland insurance executive who during the two years leading up to the 1992 election contributed more than $250,000 to the national Democratic Party and individual candidates, helped Kimberlin with a gift of $500 and, later, a loan of $10,000. In *USA Today,* Kimberlin read an article about a New York businessman, Daniel Lehner, who had a habit of bailing nonviolent offenders out of jail at Christmastime. James Turner called Lehner, Kimberlin pursued him for weeks, and Lehner finally forked over $2,000.

To read, in *Newsweek,* that "the Kimberlin case could be a factor in the '92 race" was nothing if not a heady experience. There had been moments in 1988 when he was given to grave utterances about the implications "for the country" of his revelations about Quayle. Four years later, he fancied himself a full-fledged player. As the campaign intensified, Kimberlin interpreted the stagnation of Bush-Quayle as evidence of his own handiwork. He discerned a direct correlation between his political persecution and the poor poll ratings and desperate Republican flailings. "The government made a major blunder in not settling this lawsuit four years ago," he told me. "It's the abuse of power that generates the publicity. If they had treated me fairly and paroled me years ago when I should've been paroled, I would have been a blip in the political-history books. But it's like Watergate. They created the monster. That's what they've done. They've had every opportunity to settle this case. We told them in the tort claim that we were going to file a civil suit if they didn't give us what we wanted. They should have said, 'OK, we'll give him what he wants. Let's nip it in the bud.' And now it's a snowball. This is like an albatross around these guys' necks—Quinlan, Quayle, the campaign."

THAT preelection summer, when I wandered into Kimberlin's orbit, I did so without recognizing how intricately he had constructed the ziggurat-like belief in his victimhood. Nor did I grasp that I was about to be incorporated within it—that I had unwittingly joined the flock that Kimberlin would later refer to as "my strongest supporters." He saw no reason not to have it both ways: ipso, any journalist who wrote about him needed only to look at the facts to be appalled at the injustice of his circumstances; facto, even the most disinterested observer, having absorbed the evidence, would subordinate the pretense of impartiality to the righteousness of advocacy. I ignored the paradox, assuring myself that I was building a separate structure—*my* brick wall.

My article appeared in *The New Yorker* when Election Day was slightly more than a month away. In the course of my reporting, I had several conversations with staff members of Senator Levin's subcommittee, as well as a conversation with Levin himself, during which—crossing the line from impartiality to advocacy—I urged him to hold public hearings. Levin, to his credit, resisted this misguided advice. Instead, he waited a decent interval—four days after the *New Yorker* piece was published—and unobtrusively released a report that ran to eighteen single-spaced pages. The document dispassionately laid out the known facts leading up to the press-conference cancellation, explored the three detentions, contrasted Kimberlin's and the official version of each of these episodes, and posed more than a dozen pointed questions, the answers to which would remain elusive as long as Quinlan and Miller remained unavailable for depositions. "Based on the information reviewed and having been denied by the Justice Department two requested interviews, I can only conclude that the Bureau of Prisons did, in fact, take action against Brett Kimberlin for political purposes," Levin wrote.

Simultaneously, Levin sent a letter to Richard J. Hankinson, the inspector general of the Justice Department, calling on him "to investigate this matter as soon as possible." Such an investigation, Levin knew, would require Quinlan and Miller to respond to his questions. In a speech Levin entered into the Congressional Record but didn't deliver orally, he explained why he wasn't holding hearings: "Were these ordinary times, I would convene a subcommittee hearing and call these individuals and others to testify. . . . However, these are not ordinary times—we are in the final month of a Presidential election—and holding a hearing would probably lead to charges of politics. That would deflect the public's attention and the attention of the agencies involved from the important substance of the issues involved." In a front-page story that appeared in the next day's *Times*, Stephen Labaton wrote that "in a departure from past practice," Levin had not called a news conference to herald the report and had declined interview requests. He also noted that Levin's findings reflected a consensus of the subcommittee's Democrats and Republicans and that there was no dissenting report, "as there often is in response to conclusions with political implications."

DESPITE the fact that Kimberlin was still locked up, he was unmistakably on a roll. Each day brought new invitations to give television and radio interviews, and he could afford to be selective. In the wake of the Levin report, Kimberlin and I appeared on the "Today" show. Two days later, having filed a successful Freedom of Information suit to obtain copies of certain tapes made from the El Reno wiretaps, CNN broadcast round the clock a story about the monitoring of Kimberlin's privileged phone conversations with his attorneys. That story was picked up by the Associated Press and reported widely.

Even more unwelcome, from the perspective of the Bush-Quayle reelection campaign, was the timing of oral arguments in *Kimberlin v. Quinlan, Miller et al.*, which took place in the District of Columbia Court of Appeals on October 16—less than three weeks before Election Day. Extra seating had to be set up in the courtroom to accommodate the crowd, which included Griswold, Trudeau, and a sizable media contingent. The spectacle seemed to confirm Kimberlin's assertion that the Bush administration would've been wise to settle the case in its embryonic phase. The day of the oral arguments, I published an op-ed piece in the *Times* that urged James A. Baker III, in his dual capacity as White House chief of staff and chief executive of the Bush-Quayle reelection campaign, to come clean. Who, I asked, was the unidentified Bush-Quayle official who called the BOP in 1988 to ask about Kimberlin's media contacts? When did Baker first examine Quayle's DEA file? How did Bush react when he learned about the file? Who said what to whom, and when?

The basic issue confronted by the three-member panel of appellate judges had nothing to do with Quayle or, for that matter, with the details of Kimberlin's detentions. Rather, the question was how much evidence of wrongdoing a plaintiff needed to present in order to override the qualified immunity enjoyed by federal officials. The Supreme

Court decision in the 1971 Bivens case didn't set a clear standard by which citizens claiming violation could bring actions beyond the initial complaint to the discovery stage. Rosenblatt's remarkable achievement had been to persuade Judge Harold Greene, who heard the case at the district court level, that plaintiff Kimberlin satisfied the standard—even though, according to the precedents in the D.C. Circuit, he plainly had not. Most other circuit courts recognized a more lenient standard, but the prevailing rule within that circuit didn't consider circumstantial evidence sufficient; the plaintiff had to show "direct evidence." Rosenblatt already had presented an abundance of circumstantial evidence. The fundamental flaw of a direct-evidence rule in this case, he argued, was that it unreasonably required nothing less than a confession from the defendants that they had knowingly violated Kimberlin's clearly established rights.

En route to the Court of Appeals, Kimberlin had expanded his pro bono legal support group. A collaborative amicus brief was filed by the American Civil Liberties Union, the Reporters Committee for Freedom of the Press, and the Washington firm of Covington & Burling; another notable D.C. firm, Wilmer, Cutler & Pickering, was handling Kimberlin's parole appeal. There was no telling how long the Court of Appeals would take to render a decision. Until then, he benefited from other forms of advocacy. In response to Senator Levin's call for an investigation by the inspector general—an investigation the Justice Department announced would indeed take place—letters expressing concern about Kimberlin's treatment were sent to the attorney general, William Barr, by representatives of Amnesty International, Human Rights Watch, and the Harvard Law School Human Rights Program. Though none of these organizations explicitly labeled Kimberlin a "political prisoner," he would later state that he had been certified as such. He could then go on to cite Griswold, as I quoted him in *The New Yorker,* or Garry Wills, who, despite taking me to task in his syndicated column for excessive credulity, opined that "it should be disturbing to any American, regardless of party, to think that our government machinery can work, under a cover of lies, evasions, and intimidation, to make a political prisoner here."

THE ADVANTAGE of that designation, Kimberlin believed, was that "there weren't too many in the United States, and I thought it would help me to stand out." He wrote a letter to the president of the MacArthur Foundation, requesting a grant "to spread the word about my status. . . . I do believe that I will be officially declared a 'political prisoner' by several international human rights groups." A "large grant in the $20,000 range," he explained, would "help me continue this important fight for civil, human, and constitutional rights."

The other consequence of bona fide certification, he assumed, was that it would help him get out. In a letter to Victor Reyes, the south central regional commissioner of the U.S. Parole Commission, he requested a reopening of his case "in light of favorable information," including the fact that "several human-rights groups are poised to declare me a political prisoner." His parole date was still fifteen months away on the day that Bill Clinton and Al Gore defeated George Bush and Dan Quayle. "If Clinton gets elected, I'm out, I know I'll get a pardon," he had told me months earlier, in one of our first conversations. I hadn't questioned that statement, nor did I dwell upon its implications or exigencies. Rather, I supposed Kimberlin imagined the new President completing his inaugural parade up Pennsylvania Avenue and, as he entered the White House, pausing to sign an executive pardon. Such a scenario seemed to me no stranger than, say, the notion that I'd been sucked whole and cast adrift inside Kimberlin's narcissistic universe, a black-and-white realm of dreams and schemes and factoids, a galaxy far beyond the gravity-bound realities of politics and logic and justice.

33

ERCIFULLY, my invitation to the Clinton-Gore inauguration—a delusional notion traceable to job-related stress—managed not to turn up in the mail. Nor did Kimberlin face the option of trading his prison khakis for a rented tuxedo. But unlike me, Kimberlin felt the President-elect should be given a chance to correct this oversight, and he asked me to intervene. Which is how—the thought still makes me wince—I ended up placing a call in early January to Joan Baggett, director of political affairs for the inauguration, seeking her help in obtaining a furlough that would allow Brett to attend the festivities. His motives, he instructed me to explain, were unselfish; someone from the inspector general's staff was due to interview him the day after the inauguration, and he was willing to spare this civil servant an inconvenient trip down to Memphis. As it was, I conveyed Kimberlin's message to an assistant and never got a call back.

In the following months, Kimberlin did his best to ignore the multiple ironies inherent in Clinton's assumption of power. The basic paradox was that if, in principle, the Parole Commission should have been immune to partisan influence, then the mere presence of a Democrat in the White House couldn't legitimately raise Kimberlin's expectations. But this wicket was much stickier. If the Clinton administration didn't commute his sentence or otherwise facilitate his early release, might that imply that he was not, in fact, a political prisoner? Or, even if Clinton did think of him as such, how politically savvy would it be to supersede the authority of the career employees of the Justice Department who, contra Kimberlin's Bivens action in the courts, saw themselves as defending the long-term interests of the federal government? Perhaps, after all, he would've stood a better chance of getting out sooner if the election had gone the other way. The early missteps of the Clinton presidency, especially the aborted nominations of Zoe Baird and Kimba Wood as attorney general, didn't help. Kimberlin's grievances weren't prominent on any official's list of priorities.

Thus Kimberlin was reduced to what he knew best—attacking from multiple, marginal angles. For instance, while Clinton's third attorney general nominee, Janet Reno, prepared for confirmation hearings, Kimberlin wrote to every member of the Senate Judiciary Committee, urging them all "to ask tough questions . . . about the Justice Department's handling of my situation" and explaining, "As you surely know, I am the Bush/Quayle political prisoner." At least one senator, Paul Simon of Illinois, received from Brett's lawyer Rosenblatt a written draft of a prepared question. During the hearings, Dennis DeConcini, of Arizona, asked Reno whether she would review the Kimberlin case, among others, as a way of rehabilitating the credibility of the Justice Department, and she replied that she would explore the cases "as vigorously as possible . . . [to] make an informed judgment."

"My theory was to keep the pressure on all sides and hope that something would break," Kimberlin told me. One thing that did break—though not in a way that benefited Kimberlin directly—was Michael Quinlan's tenure as director of the Bureau of Prisons. Quinlan's formal resignation came a month after the election, though he'd been on a vaguely defined leave of absence for some time. An AP story published several weeks before he officially quit was headlined DIRECTOR OF FEDERAL PRISONS HAS GONE MISSING IN ACTION, and its lead was: "Has anyone seen the director of the federal Bureau of Prisons?" Ostensibly, Quinlan resigned for medical reasons—his valedictory letter cited "continuing, although not life-threatening, health problems"—but his leave-taking was obviously involuntary, and the Kimberlin affair its defining factor.

IN JUNE, Rosenblatt and Shearer met with Webster Hubbell, Hillary Clinton's former partner in the Rose Law Firm and, at the time, the associate attorney general, with authority over the civil side of the Justice Department. Hubbell, Rosenblatt understood, "was extraordinarily powerful . . . the man to see." It was Rosenblatt's impression that Hubbell had agreed to the sit-down as a favor to Shearer but wasn't versed in the specifics of the case. The meeting didn't last long, and Hubbell said little. Though Kimberlin's lawsuit sought unspecified monetary damages, his immediate goal was freedom. For his part, Rosenblatt was content to pursue the lawsuit, which he felt addressed an important constitutional issue, but Kimberlin wanted him to pursue Hubbell. Implicit in Rosenblatt's presentation was that his client was seeking extrajudicial relief, and he knew better than to expect an immediate, salutary settlement. Hubbell, meanwhile, had the advantage of knowing that if he listened and took no subsequent action, the unresolved issues would still be addressed by the inspector general and the courts. Which is indeed what ultimately happened. (Whereas what ultimately happened to Hubbell was that he left Washington and government service in 1994 and a year later took up residence in a federal correctional institution, having pleaded guilty to mail fraud and tax evasion after bilking his former law partners and clients out of almost $400,000.)

KIMBERLIN continued to seek new avenues of influence. With an introduction from Blitz, he found his way to Alan Greer, a Miami attorney who was active in Democratic politics and whose wife, Patricia Seitz, had practiced law with Janet Reno. More than once, Kimberlin described Greer to me as "a big fan of mine." He wanted Greer, either directly or through his wife, to urge Reno to call Dean Griswold "and ask his advice on what to do." (Griswold had been a law school professor of Reno's and had already explained to Kimberlin that it would be improper to approach the attorney general on his behalf.) During an American Bar Association convention, Greer did speak to Reno, who, he later said, "took a few short notes, said she couldn't promise anything, and said she'd look into it." Greer added that "there must have been ten zillion people [at the convention] standing in line, asking her to look at this and that." Kimberlin also tried to persuade Anthony Lewis, of the *New York Times,* to intercede with Reno at the same ABA meeting. He wrote to John G. Healey, the executive director of Amnesty International, asking him to write to Reno "and urge her to release me." Nothing came of this request. Aryeh Neier, of Human Rights Watch, who had written to Reno's predecessor, William Barr, agreed to follow up with a letter to Reno. Several months went by before the attorney general responded, and her reply invoked the inspector general's report and the pending status of Kimberlin's litigation.

Each passing day brought Kimberlin closer to his parole date, a fact that had the incongruous effect of both diminishing his incentive to settle and exacerbating his restlessness. In a letter to Griswold, he wrote: "The A.G.'s office has been swamped with people supporting me. . . . I also know that several senators asked. . . . We are also anxiously awaiting the D.C. Court of Appeals decision. . . . If patience is a virtue, I am a saint by now." When his sister and her friend Lori Levinson were planning a trip to Washington, he reported to me that he had exhorted them "to go see Hubbell, Reno, or the President or all three." A few weeks later, he had James Turner send a fax to Clinton's scheduler, asking for a meeting between his mother and the President. Carolyn herself called Hubbell's office, trying to arrange an appointment. Kimberlin asked Trudeau to try to put pressure on Hubbell to settle, rather than having to endure another round of "Doonesbury" strips—a suggestion Trudeau had no intention of acting upon. The day of the Branch Davidian holocaust, in Waco, Texas, Kimberlin called me to provide running commentary on what he was following on CNN. He condemned the federal agents as "a bunch of dumb sonsofbitches," adding, "And what'll happen now is Janet Reno will be so busy answering questions about this she won't pay any attention to my case for a month." When Vincent Foster, the deputy White House counsel, committed suicide in midsummer, Kimberlin characterized him as "that asshole who killed himself"—the implication being that Foster not only lacked spine but also had interfered with Hubbell's capacity to focus on his case.

Kimberlin struck a more sympathetic, even empathetic tone when he wrote to Hubbell a few weeks later. The letter said, in part: "I want to extend my sincere condolences to you for the death of your friend and colleague, Vince Foster. I know how difficult it must be to reconcile all of your feelings about that tragic loss. The biggest question you must want answered is, Why did it happen? I kept asking that question for years after my younger brother, Scott, was killed by a hitchhiker. My suffering will last a lifetime and yours will too. I have, however, come to terms with it simply by telling myself that I had the pleasure of his companionship and love for the 24 years he was alive. I hope that you too can realize that Vince blessed your life for many years and the fond memories you have of those years will, in the long run, diminish the profound sadness you feel now. I realize that your plate has been full since your confirmation and you have to deal with the pressing matters of the day. I am writing, however, to ask for your kind intercession in seeing that I am released from prison. . . ."

That same day, Kimberlin also wrote to Reno, Senators Simon and Levin, and Kathleen Hawk, Quinlan's successor as director of the BOP. He had a new goal: release as of 13 August 1993, under a regulation that allowed a qualified prisoner to serve as many as six months at the end of a sentence in "community custody." In Kimberlin's case, this would have meant residence in either a halfway house or his mother's home, with restrictions that amounted to an attenuated form of house arrest. In his letter to Hawk, Kimberlin explained that during her recent visit to the Memphis federal correctional institution, his attempt to arrange an audience had been thwarted by the prison staff. He told me what he had in mind. "I was going to ask her about my house arrest," he said. "They always bring these big shots to my unit because it's the best one here. I asked my case manager if I could talk to her, and he said yes. But my unit manager found out and said to me, 'Brett, I don't want you to get within fifty feet of that woman.' I said, 'I just want to whisper something in her ear.' I'd say, 'Hey, Kathy, you owe me.' And when she said, 'Owe you for what?' I'd say, 'I got you your job.' "

As PART of standard BOP procedure in anticipation of parole, Kimberlin underwent a psychological evaluation in May 1993. A BOP psychologist, Dr. Steven Thomas, found him "friendly, cordial, alert . . . [with] no evidence of hallucinations, delusions, or illusions . . . in the 'superior' range of intelligence." He also noted a tendency toward "name dropping (e.g., 'I write and call Tony Lewis, a famous columnist for the *New York Times,* and talk regularly with Garry Trudeau of "Doonesbury." '). Most statements made were attempts at embellishing personal accomplishments and telling the evaluator what a great fellow he is. . . . [Kimberlin] attempted to speed up the process with statements such as, 'I really need to get this completed as soon as possible. I expect to get released shortly' or, 'When will you get this done and over to the unit? I need to get things rolling.' " Summarizing, the psychologist wrote: "Mr. Kimberlin maintained a facade of being very cooperative and friendly. However, testing clearly reveals that he was evasive and defensive in attempting to present himself in a very positive fashion. . . . He denies responsibility/guilt for the current convictions and steadfastly indicates that he is only guilty of 'selling some pot when I was younger.' . . . In conclusion, Mr. Kimberlin is a high profile, highly publicized individual with no history of mental health related problems. He continues to maintain that he is a 'political prisoner' and innocent of any wrongdoing. He will likely continue to maintain this view of himself and be defensive and evasive in relations with authority figures. When confronted with other areas that contradict this 'image' he will likely use his considerable skills to persuade significant others that they are wrong about him."

A FEW weeks after the meeting in Hubbell's office, when Kimberlin had yet to grasp that the Clinton administration wasn't going to help him out, he told me, in a spasm of frustration, that he thought Rosenblatt and Shearer were underplaying their cards. "I just get the feeling that they're not pushing the Hubbell thing hard enough," he complained. "I want Howard to go back to Hubbell. . . . I feel like let's rock 'n' roll. And it seems to me like Cody could be a lot more aggressive. He can call Hubbell and say, 'What're you gonna do?' He can write him. He can fax him. He can follow up. Jimmy's called Hubbell's office two or three times this week. Jimmy's the only one who stays on things."

The devoted James Turner, the bumbling bank robber who had befriended Kimberlin at MCC Chicago, Brett told me, had been "talking to the fucking White House like crazy. He knows everybody there—Stephanopoulos, McLarty. . . . Jimmy is telling them, 'I want an appointment with the President!' " In the late summer of 1993, in Chicago, I spent an evening with Turner and gained a deeper insight into how Kimberlin marshaled his self-promotional crusades. "What I do for Brett I do from my heart," Turner said. Nothing I saw or heard indicated otherwise. He was living alone in a studio apartment on the north side, a three-block walk from the Chicago Transit Authority maintenance garage, where he earned seventeen dollars an hour. He worked odd hours and somehow squeezed in his prodigious labors for Kimberlin, the most telling evidence of which was a thick bundle of long-distance phone bills. Kimberlin was reimbursing him for the calls, which averaged five hundred dollars a month.

Clearly, Turner, who in person seemed all nerves and naked insecurity, possessed on the phone a fearless alter ego, filled with an unabashed willingness to hector and implore. During the fall of 1992, when Turner's daily rounds included calls to people in the upper echelons of the Bush-Quayle reelection campaign, he would identify himself as "a loyal Republican and friend of the Kimberlin family." His message was that "Bush needs to do something for Brett Kimberlin immediately or the media will have a field day. If you think the Anita Hill story was big, wait until this Kimberlin business hits the news." When he tried to get in touch with Jimmy Carter, he was preying on the former President's humanitarian instincts. When he called the Ross Perot campaign, he began, "I'm sure you receive lots of kook calls. Rest assured, I am not one of those callers." Then he offered to help the Perot forces "make use of this scandal." In notes that he made to prepare for a conversation with a Parole Commission attorney, he wrote: "I'm a good family friend for years. I'm calling you on my own, without anyone knowing. I need a few moments of your time. Join in motion for bail and confess error in the appeal. Let's clean this up and deal with it now. . . ." There were days when Turner would run through a list of calls—to the BOP, the pardon attorney, the Parole Commission, the White House—and, when he was finished, call the same parties all over again. At one point, he was sending so many faxes to Hubbell that even Kimberlin advised him to stop because the effort had become counterproductive.

As Turner and I pored over the phone bills and other artifacts of his exertions, I said, "You're either a saint or the most loyal of friends."

"Or a schmuck," he replied. "If I had any political clout, he would definitely be out."

Turner showed me his bound copy of the brief Kimberlin and Donald Morano had submitted to the Seventh Circuit in appeal of the Speedway bombings verdict. It was inscribed, "To my friend Jimmy. With many thanks, Brett, May 1, 1984." The cement in the bond of their friendship was Turner's belief that Kimberlin had saved his life in prison. When Turner was being prosecuted for bank robbery, he had given the government information that led to the conviction of an accomplice who was chummy with mobsters. Kimberlin, in the course of his jailhouse lawyering, wrote appellate briefs for several convicts with mob connections and learned that another prisoner at MCC Chicago, intending to reciprocate, had "put a hit on Jimmy." According to Brett, "I spoke with someone I knew in the government," and "they neutralized the threat."

There was one occasion, Turner told me, when he declined his friend's call. This was in the late autumn of 1990, during the weeks preceding America's entry into the Persian Gulf War, when Kimberlin cooked up a maneuver that, in its dubiousness, surpassed his previous efforts to liberate himself. The Iraqi invasion of Kuwait and the likelihood of a broader conflict had placed in jeopardy thousands of foreign civilians then living in Iraq, mainly in Baghdad. These people constituted the so-called "human shield," the sitting ducks that Saddam Hussein was threatening to station at military bombing targets, thereby lessening the potential for a massive aerial assault by the United States and its allies. It was Kimberlin's elaborate conceit that, as "a political enemy of the Bush administration," he was someone Saddam could trust.

Kimberlin twice wrote letters to Mohammed Al-Mashat, the Iraqi ambassador to the United States, the first of which his mother hand-delivered to the embassy in Washington. In the letters, he volunteered his services as a go-between. Not all the fine points were spelled out, but the bottom line was that the Americans would be released and, for his efforts, Kimberlin would score a rewarding public-relations coup. "Here's the logic," he later explained to me. "My personal motivation was obviously to bring attention to my own case, but at the same time to do it with this high-profile humanitarian mission. Jesse Jackson or Muhammad Ali could go over there and get a hostage out, and here I had been portrayed in the media as a political prisoner for a couple of years. So the plan was for Hussein to release these hostages—the human shield—to my mother." Carolyn, who apparently felt equal to this task, told me that when she went to the Iraqi embassy "to see the head honcho," she took with her "a whole package of materials about Brett."

When Turner received instructions to call the embassy and urge the Iraqis to act upon the proposal, he balked. Turner consulted another respected friend. "My friend told me, 'Jimmy, you've been in trouble before, but until you get involved with that you don't know what trouble is,' " Turner recalled. "That was the only time I refused to do something for Brett. Since his IQ is 150-plus and he's brilliant, I take his word for just about everything. If he had pushed it, I probably would've called. Do you think I would have gotten in trouble?"

. . .

DESPITE Kimberlin's colossal efforts, not to mention the efforts of those who responded to his solicitations for help, his parole date never advanced. Through a BOP administrative process, he did succeed in obtaining ninety days of community custody—time he was allowed to serve in a halfway house in the District of Columbia—instead of the pro forma thirty days. His overall parole case, a habeas corpus proceeding, was argued in June 1993 in the U.S. Court of Appeals for the Sixth Circuit. The decision came down four months later, and it upheld a lower court's finding that political vindictiveness had not been a factor in the Parole Commission's 1990 decision that he would have to serve the full 180 months. During the oral argument, Renee Todd, of Wilmer, Cutler & Pickering, emphasized that Kimberlin's sentence represented an increase of 108 months over the guidelines for a Category 7 offense. Though Todd raised the matter of political vindictiveness in her written brief, she didn't refer to this in open court. As the Court of Appeals opinion noted, somewhat curiously, "In the absence of proof or an allegation of actual vindictiveness, no lawful basis exists to set aside the Commission's sentence." Because the judges' decision was unanimous, and especially since Kimberlin's transfer to the halfway house was only a few weeks away, the notion of a further appeal was moot.

In a broader context, the parole ruling could be seen as a relatively minor setback. In July, the first of two installments of the report by Inspector General Hankinson was completed, and the verdict, though mixed, tended to exonerate Quinlan and Miller. The report concluded that "overall . . . Brett Kimberlin was treated differently and held to a stricter standard of conduct than other convicts" and that this treatment derived from his allegations about Quayle. However, "the available evidence suggests . . . that this disparate treatment was not due to any conspiracy to silence Mr. Kimberlin for partisan political reasons." Rather, the special handling was attributed to a departure from "traditional BOP methods of resolving problems associated with inmate conduct and with press contacts." Elaborating upon this thesis, the inspector general found that after the first detention, "most of the decisions . . . were made solely by FCI El Reno personnel without Central Office direction." In other words, any abuse Kimberlin suffered came at the hands of freelance rogues. Quinlan claimed he had neither requested recordings of Kimberlin's privileged phone conversations nor listened to tapes that were delivered to him. The investigators found inconsistencies in Quinlan's explanation that Kimberlin's first detention came about because he had expressed fears for his safety. Nevertheless, they accepted at face value Quinlan's declaration that he had "never spoken to anyone in the White House or anyone associated with the Bush/Quayle campaign, or anyone at the Republican National Committee, or anyone that—who is ever [*sic*]—political in nature." James Baker, in a written response to questions from the inspector general, stated that he "did not suggest to anyone in the Government that [Kimberlin] be detained." Kimberlin's complaints about the substandard physical conditions in the hole were also discounted: "Administrative Detention, as Mr. Kimberlin experienced it, was not the equivalent of 'solitary confinement,' nor were the conditions of confinement oppressive or so significantly different from those of his usual housing cell as to amount to harsh treatment."

Initially, the report attracted little notice, and its contents became widely known only in mid-September, after the Associated Press obtained a copy under the Freedom of Information Act. Senator Levin called the report "a major disappointment" and expressed skepticism about its conclusions, a sentiment echoed in some newspaper editorials. The *New York Times* chose a canine metaphor, describing Hankinson and his staff as "Justice Department bloodhounds" who turned out to be a "kennel of toothless bureaucrats." Kimberlin naturally had a more caustic reaction: "a fucking whitewash." As a practical matter, Rosenblatt, who told me that the report was "seriously flawed," recognized that it reduced even further the possibility of winning a worthwhile settlement of the lawsuit.

DURING the final weeks of Kimberlin's incarceration, other adverse judgments accumulated. On consecutive days in October, the decision came down in the parole case argued by Renee Todd, and the inspector general delivered the second installment of his report. The latter document, a detailed investigation into Kimberlin's allegations of politically vindictive treatment by the Parole Commission, had the effect of corroborating the former. All the living members of the Parole Commission were interviewed, and all said that their votes on Kimberlin's initial application for parole—when he was classified in Category 8 and given a total of 228 months—were cast well before they heard his allegations about Quayle. Of course, even after being reclassified in Category 7, Kimberlin was still required to serve nine years above the sentencing guidelines. This, according to the inspector general's statistical analysis of departures from sentencing guidelines, "was not unique." Nor did the investigators embrace Kimberlin's contention that the Parole Commission had failed to give him sufficient credit for his superior programming. In short, "Our review did not disclose evidence that any of the actions taken in regard to Mr. Kimberlin's parole were politically motivated."

The other unpropitious development was the Court of Appeals' decision in *Kimberlin* v. *Quinlan et al.,* which was announced almost exactly a year after oral arguments had been heard in the D.C. Circuit. By a 2–1 vote, the panel reversed Judge Greene's 1991 finding that Kimberlin had presented concrete facts and evidence of a violation of his clearly established rights. The majority opinion, written by Karen Le Craft Henderson, a Bush appointee, rejected Kimberlin's claim that the actions taken by the BOP had flowed from an unconstitutional motive—a desire to curb his First Amendment rights. That Kimberlin had been allowed to meet with the crew from NBC News before the detentions, and that he had been permitted telephone and media contacts during detention, Henderson determined, made any unconstitutional motive "particularly unlikely." Nor had Kimberlin satisfied the so-called heightened pleading standard that ruled in the D.C. Circuit—the requirement that a plaintiff in a Bivens action, in an initial complaint, show direct rather than circumstantial evidence of wrongdoing by a federal official. "In sum," Henderson wrote, "Kimberlin relies only on inference and weak circumstantial evidence, notably the timing of events, to support his claim of unconstitutional detention by Quinlan and Miller."

A Reagan appointee, Judge Stephen Williams, joined Henderson in the majority, albeit with obvious ambivalence. His concurring opinion focused on the distinction between direct and circumstantial evidence, agreeing on the direct-evidence precedent. At the same time, Williams was willing to second-guess both himself and that requirement: "This is not to say that circuit law is correct." Because Williams was clearly uncomfortable with the local standard, he proposed a re-examination "en banc"—that is, a review by all ten appellate judges in the D.C. Circuit.

Judge Harry Edwards, who had been appointed by Jimmy Carter, wrote a strident dissent that exceeded in length the combined opinions of Henderson and Williams. At least three justices then on the Supreme Court had found, in other cases, that the direct-evidence rule was a "nonsensical" mistake that had "no foundation in reason or in case law"—and, as Williams suggested, "ought to be reconsidered by the [appellate] court en banc." To continue to uphold such a standard, he added, would have the effect of "eliminat[ing] all civil rights actions involving unconstitutional motive." He concluded: "I simply cannot imagine that the judiciary of the United States will shut the doors of the courthouse and refuse to allow Kimberlin's suit to proceed for the specious reason that his complaint is based on circumstantial evidence."

Kimberlin reacted to this reversal with remarkable equanimity. If he lost in the Court of Appeals, it was a foregone conclusion that Rosenblatt would carry the case to the next level: first, an en banc review within the D.C. Circuit, and then, if necessary, an appeal to the Supreme Court. Kimberlin found this prospect hugely tantalizing. "If the Supreme Court grants cert, this could become our biggest glory," he told me. "This could be the biggest deal of all. We could make very important law." And that was where things stood when, a month later, Kimberlin walked out the front door of the Memphis federal correctional institution, stepped into a taxi that transported him to the downtown terminal, and there boarded a Greyhound bus, heading for Washington and whatever he decided to make happen next.

34

I've created this, my release, and I'm going to be living in that creation," Kimberlin had told me as he counted down his last days as a prisoner. Coming from someone else, such a remark would have struck me as pop-psych cant, flavor-of-the-week existentialism, but I knew that Brett had in mind a concrete plan, a short- and long-term agenda, all nuts and bolts. The Parole Commission, too, had ideas about how he should and shouldn't be spending his time. The conditions of his release included a full financial disclosure, the surrender of his pilot's licenses, drug counseling and periodic drug testing, and a one-year travel restriction that limited him to a fifty-mile radius of the Washington metropolis. Of these strictures, only the last seemed onerous; he was in a hurry to get rich again, and he wanted to roam freely wherever his entrepreneurial instinct led him.

One cloud that darkened his fiscal future throughout his incarceration had, for the time being, become less menacing. This was the $1.6 million judgment awarded to Sandra DeLong ten years earlier for her pain and suffering and for the wrongful death of her husband, Carl. Kimberlin had appealed the verdict and judgment to the Indiana Court of Appeals, citing various grounds, foremost that he could not be legally responsible for an injured victim's suicide that occurred four and a half years after the original injury. The appeal also challenged the foundation of the DeLongs' complaint, an interpretation of a state law that made the fact of a criminal conviction admissible in a civil tort proceeding. The law in question was passed four years after the Speedway bombings, and Kimberlin maintained that it shouldn't have been applied retroactively. Because of procedural delays, which Kimberlin blamed largely on the trial judge, Michael Dugan, the Court of Appeals did not render a decision until March 1993. The court found that Kimberlin was not responsible for Carl's suicide, but it let stand Sandra's award for compensatory and punitive damages. While this improved Kimberlin's balance sheet by re-moving a $1.25 million contingent liability, he was by no means home free. He still owed Sandra $360,000.

Hoping to restore the wrongful-death award, Sandra's attorney filed a petition to transfer the case to the Indiana Supreme Court—a procedure similar to a writ of certiorari. This motion was denied. Kimberlin also filed a petition to transfer, seeking a reversal of the $360,000 judgment. The Supreme Court justices agreed to entertain this appeal, and as he left prison their opinion was pending. In 1983, at the time of the original verdict, Kimberlin sought protection by having himself legally declared a pauper. His status had since changed—he had received the first of several installments of his share of the advance royalties from this book—but he still had no intention of paying. No matter what the Indiana Supreme Court decided, Kimberlin felt confident that he would prevail with the help of a trump card that he claimed to have held close to his vest for ten years. It was Kimberlin's contention that the DeLong litigation had been tainted from the beginning and that the source was Judge Dugan, who was corrupt.

In 1988, a federal grand jury in the southern district of Indiana indicted Dugan on forty counts of extortion, bribery, and related charges that arose from his supervision of an insurance company case. At a trial the following spring, the jury returned a guilty verdict on twenty-five counts, and Dugan drew a sentence of eighteen years. No other judge in Indiana history had received so harsh a punishment for misconduct. Several months earlier, and at Kimberlin's request, Nile Stanton gave a handwritten affidavit that set forth his "best rec-ollection" of a solicitation by the judge—an offer to deliver a pro-Kimberlin verdict in the DeLong suit. At the time of the alleged bribe, Stanton had no direct role in Kimberlin's defense, which was being handled by one of his associates, David Hennessy. During a chance encounter at a bar in downtown Indianapolis, Stanton swore in his affidavit, Dugan "after general chit-chat . . . said something like—and nearly in these exact words—'Your man would do okay if he had the bread.' I confirmed that he meant Brett Kimberlin. He said, 'Of course,' and I stated that I had nothing to do with Brett's civil cases, to which he responded, 'Like hell.' Nevertheless, Judge Dugan ex-plicitly said that 'he could do okay for ten.' I'm sure those were his exact words. My best judgment at the time, and to this very day, is that he meant that he would rule in Brett's favor in the civil case for $10,000. . . . At the time, it was very evident to me that, albeit quite drunk, the judge . . . was soliciting a bribe."

Stanton went on to recount a follow-up conversation, by telephone, in which he and Dugan spoke in code—using the phrase "ten days" to mean ten thousand dollars—a conversation in which "the meaning was *very* clear to me." Stanton stated that he discussed the matter with Kimberlin and advised him not to pay. "Brett told me to tell the judge to 'get fucked,' but I did not relay the message. I paid no bribe and there was never a further discussion about it."

THOUGH the subsequent proof of Dugan's malfeasance lent credence to the affidavit, Stanton's own credibility had suffered in the intervening years. The period the affidavit referred to—two years after the bombings trial—was chaotic for him. He'd gone through an untidy divorce, his second. He was making plenty of money but spending more than he could afford. His attention to administrative details, always spotty at best, became even more lax. He moved at a frenetic pace that was fueled by more than natural adrenaline. People familiar with Stanton told me they suspected he'd been abusing cocaine during the Speedway bombings trial. Before I got around to asking him directly, he volunteered that he used cocaine frequently in the early eighties.

Stanton drew a romantic distinction between "criminals" and "outlaws," and he thought of many of his own clients as belonging to the second category—endearingly anarchic and basically harmless. For his part, he cultivated a persona that combined raffishness with moral righteousness. "I just have always believed that while you aren't supposed to throw stones, you should be willing to overturn tables. I was raised to believe if you have a light, let it shine," he once told a newspaper interviewer, gracing with lofty First Amendment sentiment his aptitude for bombast. In early 1983, he appeared in a video produced by the publishers of an Indianapolis alternative magazine. On camera, he fondled his .38-caliber Smith & Wesson and in a sardonic manner spoke about the sorts of dangerous people who shouldn't carry guns, including police officers. A few months later, as he left a health club where he'd been playing handball, he was arrested by the Indiana State Police and charged with one count of marijuana possession and one count of dealing cocaine.

A photograph in the next morning's *Indianapolis Star* showed Stanton wearing tennis clothes and handcuffs. The drug charges were supported by questionable testimony from a cocktail waitress moonlighting as a police informant. The cocaine Stanton was alleged to have "dealt" to her weighed in at 38/1000th of a gram, and after laboratory analysis none of the evidence remained. The drug charges were dropped before the case came to trial, and Stanton eventually filed a $24 million lawsuit, naming as defendants the Indiana State Police, the Marion County Sheriff's Department, individual law officers, and a Marion County deputy prosecutor. No civil litigation, however, could undo the harm that Stanton's arrest had inflicted upon his law practice. In February 1984 he filed for bankruptcy, and from there his downward slide gathered momentum.

Several clients filed allegations of professional misconduct with the Indiana Supreme Court Disciplinary Commission. A recurring complaint was that Stanton had taken retainers for work he then failed to perform. In May 1986, he issued a press release and announced a news conference to rebut these accusations. The release discussed in detail various mitigating factors. Some clients, Stanton said, had recanted their grievances. Others were simply criminals—as opposed to outlaws—whose testimony could not be trusted. By then, however, it was too late: he had been disbarred by the Indiana Supreme Court.

The disbarment, as Stanton interpreted it, was an act of willful vindictiveness by the established order. Along the way, he had compounded his problems by picking a fight with the Internal Revenue Service. Kimberlin, among Stanton's defenders, explained this dispute by saying, "Nile was opposed to a government policy that funded a war machine." That Stanton had been raised a Quaker did not, however, exempt him from paying federal income taxes. In Marion County, he was jailed briefly for contempt of court after falling in arrears on his child-support payments. Exactly a year after his disbarment, he pleaded guilty to a misdemeanor charge of driving while intoxicated. (He had been arrested while urinating beside his automobile, its engine running.) Indiana had ceased being a congenial place for him to live. A month later, with his tax dispute unresolved, he surreptitiously left the country. He went first to Canada, then to Scandinavia, and finally to a southern European port, where he lives today.

FOR KIMBERLIN, the queer and inauspicious turns in Stanton's life proved inconvenient. Stanton was the only friendly witness who could support his charges against Judge Dugan. He was also the most forthright exponent of the dogma that the investigation and prosecution of the Speedway bombings amounted to a grotesque miscarriage of justice. In another affidavit, Stanton swore that during the bombings trial, which occurred while Quayle was campaigning for the U.S. Senate, Kimberlin had mentioned that he, Quayle, had years before been a marijuana customer. Stanton, a law school classmate of Quayle's, went on to state, "When Brett Kimberlin told me this, I did not doubt for a moment that it was true." The revelation reminded Stanton of an occasion when he encountered Quayle emerging from a room thick with marijuana smoke.

In 1992, I was tempted to report in *The New Yorker* the contents of this affidavit, along with Stanton's anecdotal recollection, but I could corroborate none of the charges, nor was it clear what the anecdote exactly proved. At Stanton's suggestion, I tracked down a classmate who he claimed had been in the room and presumably had witnessed Quayle smoking pot. When I called this person, an attorney then living in southern Indiana, the conversation had barely begun when he said, "Tell Nile I'm glad he was disbarred. And tell him I'm not interested in talking to anyone who's been talking to him." At which point he hung up. No array of mitigating factors could erase the stubborn reality that Stanton, as Kimberlin's champion or in general, had become easily impeachable. Even if he was telling the truth about Dugan, about Quayle, or in general, his affidavits were practically worthless. Grudgingly, Kimberlin admitted as much. The net effect, he told me, was that if the Indiana Supreme Court ruled against him and the DeLong judgment continued to bedevil him, he would probably turn to the no-longer-honorable Judge Dugan—his fellow convicted felon—and ask him to give a sworn statement acknowledging that he'd invited a bribe.

AS KIMBERLIN exited prison, he seemed to be in love. His inamorata was Juliya Chupikova, a young Soviet émigrée with whom he had sustained a relationship for more than three years. It was meant to be, he told me, as if their attachment had been cosmically ordained—an eventuality as inevitable as the extraordinary coincidence that had brought them together in the first place.

In 1987, a Washington-based correspondent for the Soviet news agency TASS had written an article about Kimberlin which focused on the use of posthypnotic testimony in the bombings prosecution. Even in the era of glasnost, the TASS dispatch had a bit of a Cold War spin, a flavor of look-what-they-do-to-accused-criminals-in-America! Kimberlin added the correspondent, Nikolay Turkatenko, to his roster of media contacts and made an effort to stay in touch. Shortly before Gorbachev visited Washington for a summit meeting with Reagan—in December 1987, months after the Supreme Court had declined to hear the appeal Griswold submitted on his behalf—Carolyn delivered to Turkatenko at the TASS offices in Washington a packet of materials about Brett. Her goal was for Turkatenko to pass them along to the Soviet ambassador, who would in turn give them to Gorbachev, who during his conversations with Reagan would raise the matter of Brett's unjust prosecution and imprisonment. "It was a human rights issue," Carolyn explained later. In anticipation of a 1990 meeting between Gorbachev and Bush, Kimberlin addressed a letter to Turkatenko to bring him up to date. He enclosed copies of Aaron Freiwald's *Legal Times* stories and other clippings about the 1988 election and the denial of his parole. "I am writing this letter to again ask for your kind intercession in my case. I realize that my situation is somewhat of a 'hot potato.' However, the topic of a political prisoner is never an easy subject to deal with, no matter what country is involved."

Again, Carolyn paid a visit to the TASS bureau, but Turkatenko was no longer stationed in Washington. Nevertheless, according to Brett, subsequent articles about him appeared in the Soviet press. Though he never actually saw them, he told me that Juliya Chupikova, who was then a teenager living in Ukraine, read at least one. And this was the extraordinary coincidence: Chupikova was the niece, by marriage, of David Sushansky, who was Kimberlin's closest friend at the Memphis federal correctional institution.

In my earliest conversations with Kimberlin, he described the diversity of his interest in things Russian. First, there was Juliya, who "loves me to death." Then there was the fact that he had studied Russian for four semesters while working toward his college degree.

Sushansky gave him extracurricular oral instruction, Kimberlin told me, and to refine his reading and writing skills he translated stories by Pushkin, Tolstoy, and Chekhov. The articles about him in the Soviet press, he added, had made him well known among Russian human rights activists, and in turn he'd helped families seeking political asylum in the United States. When I went to visit Carolyn in the summer of 1992, I learned that an émigré family—a man, a woman, and a teenage boy—was renting the bottom floor of her house. That same summer, Brett and Sushansky had volunteered to assist Task Force Russia, a newly established U.S. Department of Defense agency whose role was to investigate rumors of missing American servicemen, from the Second World War through Vietnam, who reportedly had turned up in Soviet prisons. Sushansky had a proposal, and he used Kimberlin as his middleman to present it to the Task Force Russia brass: If the U.S. Army would arrange his release from prison, Brett and his Russian pal would guide them to Ukrainians who could provide information about missing Americans.

About once a month, Sushansky spoke by phone with his family in Ukraine. During one of these conversations, Kimberlin said, Chupikova mentioned to her uncle that she had read a newspaper article about a heroic American political prisoner, and Sushansky told her that the prisoner was his close friend. Kimberlin and Chupikova began corresponding, exchanging letters every couple of weeks and speaking by phone once a month.

When the relationship began, Chupikova was a blond, blue-eyed eighteen-year-old with a round, cherubic face. Kimberlin kept dozens of her photographs in his cell and obviously felt protective, referring to her as "my baby." Another description was "very aristocratic." She craved the life of the mind, he said, and in prison of course he felt the same lack: "I don't have any intellectual stimulation in here until I get on the phone."

In May 1990, with a plane ticket paid for by Kimberlin, Chupikova flew from Kiev to New York and then traveled to Philadelphia, where she stayed with Sushansky's wife, her aunt. She enrolled in an intensive English-study program and, in time, improved her visitor's visa to a student's. One of her plans was to study voice—she was a "high soprano with perfect pitch," Kimberlin told me. He soon was footing the bill for her private lessons with a teacher who "told her she had the clearest and most beautiful voice she'd ever heard, I think."

SEVERAL attorneys who had worked with Kimberlin, either on his own cases or in the course of his jailhouse practice, suggested he would have no trouble finding work as a paralegal after his release. This possibility failed to excite him. "Administrative law, immigration law, criminal law—I know that stuff cold," he said. "But if I go to work for some law firm, I can't make the kind of money I want to make and have the kind of fun I want to have." Banging his head against the wall so that some convict could wind up doing nine years instead of ten—he'd had enough of that. He thought he could do "a lot better" in the music business, which also offered the attraction of collaborating with Chupikova.

To demonstrate to his probation officer the brightness of his economic prospects, he prepared a typewritten itinerary and self-employment agenda that referred to Chupikova as a "singer, model, artist" and listed as one of their prospective undertakings a "recording and video project—Juliya Chupikova as singer and recording artist and Brett Kimberlin as song writer and manager." During his final stretch in Memphis, he wrote song lyrics at the rate of almost ten a month. Some had political themes, others were brazenly sexual, many were romantic ballads. At times, he sounded as if Chupikova had become his muse. "I'm working on one right now, called 'Waiting to Meet,'" he told me one day. "It's a love song, kind of about me and Juliya." Clearly, he'd given much thought to what life with her would be like. She had visited him only once while he was in prison, and their physical relationship had not yet begun. She was still a virgin, he said; this complicated the challenge of developing intimacy with someone who was in many ways a stranger. "I tell her things that I want to do sexually and she says, 'Oh, I can't imagine that,'" he told me. "I've got to take it slow, so I don't blow her mind."

Otherwise, he was not inclined to forbearance or patience. He was eager indeed to find a composer who would write music to accompany his lyrics. "I might just go to some people in the music world who I respect and ask them to cowrite with me," he told me. "You know, like Sting or Paul McCartney. I don't have any trouble calling people up. You know me, I always go straight to the top."

As usual, Kimberlin's hyperbole was more than idle talk. He had been home only a few weeks when he had business cards printed up, naming his enterprise Brettsongs. He made it a point each week to read *Billboard,* the music-trade publication, and he studied such books as *Breaking into the Music Business, The Complete Handbook of Songwriting, Successful Artist Management,* and *Moguls and Madmen.* He linked up with a songwriter who lived nearby and who in turn introduced him to competent studio musicians. Before long, he'd produced a demo tape, something he could send to prospective artist-management and recording companies. He had not yet been inside the recording studio when he put together a promotional brochure—a glossy gold folder that included a bound volume of lyrics titled "Songs of Passion," photographs of himself and Juliya in various poses (together on a love seat; Juliya standing in front of a Christmas tree; Brett in his weight-lifting room, shirtless, with his blue jeans strategically unzipped), as well as a capsule biography heralding the arrival of a pair of new pop icons:

Success depends largely on timing. The time is right for Brett and Juliya. Together, they form a rare combination of musical, cultural and theatrical talent.

Brett is American; he grew up on rock and roll in a musical family. At odds with the right-wing Administration during the 1980's, he was jailed as a political prisoner. While there, he experienced first-hand the suffering of the underclass and the cynicism of governments. He became a champion for those less fortunate and rose above the evil around him.

It was while in prison that Brett wrote 29 "Songs of Passion." These songs will resonate in the hearts of people throughout the world because of their insight, honesty and directness. Moreover, many of them will, through controversy, raise the consciousness of people everywhere. Brett's combination of social consciousness and anger, as represented in these songs, brings comparisons to Lennon and Sting. He has a strong, melodic voice and a keen sense of music. In addition to being in shape and handsome, he is a savvy businessman who operates without fear of success. Indeed, he is firmly in control of his life; he has no bad habits, has been a vegetarian for decades, and practices yoga, meditation and exercise daily. . . .

Juliya is Ukrainian; she was raised under the specter of Communism and saw the lost hope and despair of an entire nation. She coped by immersing herself in art and music at the best schools. After being noticed for the clarity and brilliance of her high soprano voice, she studied Italian opera at a special college and was chosen the most beautiful and talented diva.

Disillusioned with the lack of opportunities in the former Soviet Union, Juliya decided to come to America. Through serendipity, Brett began writing and calling her. To overcome the language barrier, he studied Russian, and shortly after Juliya turned nineteen, he brought her to America. Over the next three years, she diligently studied English and took private singing (opera) lessons. Although trained in the classics, Juliya has a keen ear for popular music and trends. Moreover, she is exceptionally beautiful, shapely and sexy. As with Brett, she has no bad habits and is motivated, driven and intelligent.

Brett and Juliya have an agenda; they want nothing less than to be a phenomenon and to change the world for the better with their music and personalities. They want to bring the world closer together and give hope to those who have little or none. They want to have fun, stir things up and make lots of money for themselves and everyone who works with them. They hope to usher in the 21st Century with incredible passion and joy.

35

DURING the summer of 1993, when Kimberlin was still locked up in Memphis and still angling to get out sooner than the Parole Commission intended, I made a couple of extended trips to Indiana. A year earlier, I'd spent three days in Indianapolis, photocopying clippings in the library at the Indianapolis Star/News Building and talking to journalists and lawyers. On my return visits, I did more of the same, and I added detours to Quayle's hometown of Huntington and to Bloomington and its rural environs. Kimberlin suggested I speak with people he said were friends of his or other family members—"friend" often meaning someone involved in the drug trade—and I also tracked down people connected to the cocaine ring Steve Fawley claimed had supplied Quayle.

Given what I'd already published in *The New Yorker*, I had no friendly sources in law enforcement. So it struck me as odd when certain people Kimberlin referred me to spoke of him quite disparagingly; if I closed my eyes, I could imagine I was listening to cops or government attorneys. When that novelty wore off, a deeper feeling replaced it—the sensation that, as forewarned, I'd entered a black hole, a dense and perhaps impenetrable expanse of doubt.

I WAS looking for people who fell into two categories: those who knew Kimberlin and would talk about his early years, and those who might know something about Quayle's early years. One of the first people I met with was Woody McDermott, who, conveniently, had done business both with Kimberlin and with Fawley's cocaine ring. He'd also spent over five years in a federal prison, after the coke ring was busted. It was McDermott who told me Kimberlin envisioned himself as "a robber baron" and who recalled that, in the early seventies, when the other Indiana hippie dope-dealers were talking about peace and love and universally expanded consciousness, Kimberlin was fixated on money and power and "figuring out the angles." McDermott asked for a copy of my *New Yorker* piece, which he returned the next day decorated with marginalia. What I'd written, he declared, was "revisionist history." Though this wasn't at all what I'd wanted to hear, I was nonetheless grateful. In retrospect, I regard it as a watershed—the moment I knew I'd have to engage in rigorous self-revisionism, and the point at which my narrative acquired an unanticipated plot.

The implication, of course, was that I'd been taken for a ride. When I examined how this happened, I found that my respect for Kimberlin's particular gift was, if anything, enhanced. He'd done a skillful number on me. In return, I owed him my best efforts. Long before I developed serious reservations about Kimberlin's credibility, I was mindful of Janet Malcolm's famously devastating thesis in *The Journalist and the Murderer,* the notion that journalism is a confidence game in which the reporter holds a stacked deck—"preying on people's vanity, ignorance, or loneliness, gaining their trust and betraying them without remorse." Kimberlin and I concurred that I would write a book over which he would have no control or veto and that he would be compensated for his cooperation. When I suggested that he consult a lawyer to review our arrangement before the project began, he chose not to. Later, I interpreted this as a bluff, a nothing-to-hide gesture intended to boost my confidence in him.

"Like the credulous widow who wakes up one day to find the charming young man and all her savings gone," Malcolm wrote, "so the consenting subject of a piece of nonfiction writing learns—when the article or book appears—his hard lesson." What we were involved in, I concluded, was an extension of Malcolm's mordant dialectic. In our *folie à deux,* there would be no credulous widow, only two ostensibly charming young men. The relevant question in my mind, however, was not a simplistic "Who's conning whom?" but instead: "Given the stakes dictated by Kimberlin's proven and apparent deeds, why shouldn't I play his game?" On balance, I felt there was no choice, even if truth necessitated a kind of counterdeception. Any frontal challenge to Kimberlin, I knew, would provoke only defensive hostility. I assumed *he* assumed he could always stay several steps ahead of me. To disrupt that illusion, I feared, would cause my work to implode. The trick, above all, was to keep him talking. He had set the original terms, and I was leveling the playing field.

ONCE I compared Kimberlin's renderings of certain incidents with the recollections of other witnesses, the recurring theme of "jumping the connection" almost always emerged. When a dope dealer jumped a connection, he eliminated a middleman, hoping to cut his costs without increasing his risk. Now, both literally and figuratively, it seemed that Kimberlin had this same habit. Figurative instances were narratives in which he claimed center stage, though in reality he'd participated at a distant remove or not at all. Or, when it suited his purposes, he might do just the opposite, ascribing to others acts he in fact had performed himself.

Brett once told me an elaborate tale that combined the literal and the figurative. On two occasions, he said, he went to New Jersey to buy hashish and got ripped off. The first misadventure, in 1970, cost him $1,800 yet had a semihappy ending. The go-between who lured him to New Jersey later introduced him to Leo Casas, his famous Mexican connection. Before long, Kimberlin jumped the connection and started dealing directly. Then, within a year, he jumped *that* connection and did business with Casas's supplier, Papa Reyes, who became his primary source on the Tex-Mex border. In 1973, Kimberlin said, he went back to New Jersey for a $40,000 transaction in which his customers Randy and Ricky Stovall were also involved. Somehow the deal went south, and the enraged Stovalls ended up kidnapping a confederate of the thieves, who covered the loss with funds his girlfriend retrieved from a safe-deposit box. Brett thus described the instant of the rip-off: "We were in one car and the people we were supposed to be buying from were in another car. The middleman was in our car. And so I don't remember exactly what happened, but we got close to the place where we were supposed to get the hash from. And he said, 'You got the money?' I said, 'Yes, I got the money.' I showed him the briefcase with $40,000. He said, 'OK, give me the briefcase.' And to make a long story short, they steal the money from me. . . . After that I never went to New Jersey again."

As it happened, Woody McDermott recognized this particular story and identified its basic flaw: Kimberlin wasn't there. The telltale lacuna—"And so I don't remember exactly what happened"—was a mass of details McDermott remembered exactly because he *was* there, along with Kimberlin's close associate Justin Farrell. The hash deal took place because Kimberlin's bread-and-butter Mexican pot had become too mundane to compete with the Colombian redbud that lately had hit the market. After McDermott told Kimberlin he needed to diversify, Brett came up with a hashish source in New Jersey. When McDermott asked how well he knew these people, he replied, "I know them well enough to send Justin." So McDermott and Farrell went to New Jersey to make the buy. "I had five thousand dollars of my own money in this," McDermott said. "Which was *all* the money I had."

There was indeed a rip-off—$40,000 at gunpoint—and in its aftermath there was indeed a kidnapping. "I was running the whole shakedown on the middleman," McDermott said. The Stovall brothers made a cameo appearance to provide some muscle, and then McDermott and Farrell held the middleman hostage for three days. "We tied him up," McDermott said. "We started out in East Orange. Then we made a series of stops. We took him to a motel. Then we took him to upstate New York. All through it, Justin was talking on the phone to Brett in Indianapolis. When Brett tells the story, he says it's the girlfriend who goes to the safe-deposit box. Wrong. It's the *guy* that goes in, not the girlfriend; we've got her in the diner across the street from the bank. We're holding the girlfriend. I tell [the middleman], 'One false move and you'll never see us again, and you'll never see your girlfriend, either.' I go inside the bank with him. I'm there, supposedly filling out an application for a safe-deposit box—I'm wearing a coat and tie, I've got short hair—because I'm keeping an eye on him. We get the money and let him go. Brett never left Indianapolis."

Julie Johnson, Farrell's girlfriend, confirmed McDermott's chronicle and pinpointed what was defective about Brett's recapitulation of another violent rip-off—the Halloween 1971 middle-of-the-night encounter with gun-toting thugs from Dayton, a payback for jumping a Mexican connection. In Kimberlin's version, the intruders pounded on the door of the house in Zionsville, shouting, "Open up! Open up! DEA!" and then captured him as he prepared to jump from a balcony, tied him up, and made off with $32,000. Again, according to Johnson, Kimberlin wasn't actually present. The bad guys had come looking for him—"Where's Brett? We're gonna kill him"—but it was Farrell they tied up, terrorized, and robbed. Johnson's account was supported by Tim Young, a dealer who started doing business with Kimberlin when they were both sixteen. "I was told about the robbery the next day, and I believe the figure was $24,000, not $32,000," Young recalled. "From what I was told by both of them, Justin was there but Brett wasn't. Brett was sleeping at his parents' house that night. And I remember that when these guys came in they said, 'Open up! Open up! *FBI!*' They couldn't have said 'DEA!' because the DEA didn't even exist; it was still the Bureau of Narcotics and Dangerous Drugs. If Brett had been there, he would've told me so."

There were similar stories whose only corroborating witnesses were dead or otherwise unavailable—Kimberlin's tale, for instance, of being robbed by a junkie in Bloomington when he was sixteen years old. The specifics of that one never struck me as especially plausible—a hundred-pound kid wresting a .38-caliber gun from a junkie—but it was virtually impossible to prove it a fabrication. What mattered about such vignettes was their portrayal of a fearless, at times even heroic, protagonist. The tale-teller was a short fellow who needed to be looked up to, who consistently sought relationships with females much younger than himself, who could boast to an eighteen-year-old woman he'd just met on a bus that he was "one of the strongest men in the world."

WHEN his high school girlfriend Susan Harvey, then in her early twenties, lay comatose in the hospital after a terrible car accident, he saved her life—so he said. Her doctor had told the family to "pray for her to die, that she probably wouldn't come out of it." Kimberlin, the sole believer in her recovery, "stayed by her side for literally three months." He had mystical experiences in her hospital room, where he spent a lot of time in "meditation and affirmation." To discourage scarring, he salved her wounds with vitamin E. "The fucking nurses would go crazy. They thought I was nuts." After visiting hours, he would sneak into her room and hide under the bed. One day when they were alone, Susan was writhing in pain, and he "felt her presence, her soul, kind of leaving her body, kind of rising up from her body and getting ready to go out the window." This perception was overwhelming. She was dying because "nobody believed in her anymore"—nobody except Brett. He told her, "Susan, I want you to know I love you very, very much, and I don't want you to die." And promptly her soul "snapped right back into her body."

Kimberlin advised me to speak with Susan's mother, who he assured me was quite fond of him. "He was a nice teenager, I think,"

Darlene Harvey told me. "But my children said I didn't know him very well." Brett's ministrations, she asserted, had not been beneficial. "We hired private-duty nurses so Susan wouldn't fall out of the bed, but they were worth nothing. I went in one evening after work and found this one nurse had gone to eat and left her alone. So that was that, no more private nurses. I guess after that Brett and his mother would slip in the back door to visit her. He poured oil on her stomach, which was all cut open from surgery. It was vitamin E or something like that. The surgeon was so outraged—he read the riot act to me. Brett didn't nurse her back. He might have thought he did. 'Nursing her back' is a figment of his imagination. The surgeon said if that oil had gotten into her stomach cavity it would have killed her. Brett thinks one thing, but the doctor thinks another, and I'm sure the doctor knows more about this particular situation." Susan Harvey refused to be interviewed, allowing only that she wanted "nothing to do with Brett Kimberlin."

THE LIFE Kimberlin couldn't save belonged to his brother. However, he said, he'd done the next best thing by solving Scott's murder. As noted earlier, he told me that while in the Marion County Jail, he'd called acquaintances in Dayton, learned the name of the motel where Scott had been staying, persuaded a clerk to give him a list of phone numbers dialed from the room, and referred the police to an unfamiliar number, which then guided them to the killer. "It was my quick detective work that solved this crime."

QED or not. All this—as with Brett's reference to the "hitchhiker" in his condolence letter concerning Vince Foster—was in fact considerably more complex. The truth fell into my lap during a painfully awkward conversation with Brett and his mother. From the outset, the very idea of this book offended Carolyn. So what if it put money in Brett's pocket? Nothing I could write would do her any good. She made her feelings plain to Brett and Cynthia, and I was hardly surprised. Brett's claim of innocence rested on the theory that Scott was somehow involved in the bombings, and even if my reporting absolved him, someone she nurtured and loved would still stand accused of these heinous crimes. "I don't want to be the mother of the Speedway Bomber," she once complained to Brett, outside my presence, and he replied, "Mom, you already are." Her sensitivity to inflection was acute. Frequently, she responded contentiously to my queries, as if my imprecise choice of a word or phrase had crudely perverted reality; or else she glared at me with a look at once hurt and amused, apparently marveling that I had never been taught manners. My right to ask questions at all seemed the most outrageous offense. Thus an uncomfortable silence often yawned between us, a void pregnant with her resentment at this gross injustice. No matter what I published, she would be seen as having failed at motherhood.

One afternoon, the three of us, seated in Brett's living quarters, downstairs in Carolyn's home, talked about Scott. She cried as she described identifying her child's corpse, and the crying continued as she recalled testifying during the trial of his killer. She told of driving to Dayton with her former husband and his second wife, of meeting on a Saturday with a homicide detective who said he couldn't really get started until Monday. That weekend, she said, they began their own investigation. They canvassed motels along the interstate south of Dayton, and at the third stop she found Scott's name in the guest register. She persuaded the clerk to provide the list of outgoing phone calls, which she then gave to the detective. One of the numbers led directly to a material witness, and the killer, George Shingleton, was arrested within a week.

Another jumped connection. I avoided eye contact with Brett as Carolyn spoke. And I never chose to raise the subject with him again.

KIMBERLIN'S first major infraction, the felony perjury conviction that plagued him like an infestation of fleas—that made him eligible for the explosives possession charge, made it possible to dismiss him as a chronic liar when he popped out of the woodwork to talk about Quayle—was itself a setup, he explained, a consequence of perjury by David Pacific and John Buckley. Its precursor had been the cocaine offense that resulted in his conviction for juvenile delinquency. This was the only time in his life he'd sold cocaine, he insisted—just bad luck and legal harassment. Then Pacific and Buckley came along and shamelessly claimed he sold them LSD when in fact they "had a laboratory making LSD."

But the evidence I turned up suggested otherwise. Sometimes Brett himself placed the proof in my hands. In files pulled from Carolyn's attic, I found the transcript of a July 1972 federal court hearing to determine whether he should be prosecuted as a juvenile or an adult on the cocaine charge. This included testimony from Gerald Alpern, the aforementioned psychologist who appeared as a defense witness:

> Q. What drugs did he tell you he had dealt in?
> A. Well, he told me that he had both furnished mari-juana and on a few occasions cocaine to friends. . . .
> Q. So this sale in question is not the only time he has told you that he has sold cocaine?
> A. If I understand your question correctly, did he tell me he had sold cocaine more than once. . . . Yes, he did.

And there was this colloquy when the prosecutor asked *Kimberlin* whether he'd sold cocaine on occasions other than the single trans-action for which he was charged:

> Kimberlin: I have been associated with people that sold it, yes.
> Prosecutor: Have you sold it yourself?
> Kimberlin: Yes.

In 1992, when Kimberlin told me he trafficked only in marijuana and hashish—besides cocaine just that once—he stated emphatically that he had never sold LSD. "I don't remember ever selling any hal-lucinogens. I mean, it's possible, like, five hits of this or that. But it's not in my memory base." He also said, "I've never even seen am-phetamines." Yet the same court transcript contained his testimony that he had dealt in small quantities of LSD and methamphetamine. He had bought amphetamines and given them to his girlfriend, he said, because she was trying to lose weight.

Kimberlin exploited the fact that Pacific and Buckley were ar-rested on drug charges in October 1971, when, according to a report in the *Indianapolis News,* more than $20,000 worth of laboratory equipment was confiscated. But in a 1994 meeting, Pacific told me the "laboratory equipment" was actually vegetable-canning para-phernalia plus a few flasks and petri dishes. What the state police originally identified as "48 quarts of psilocybin, an ingredient used in hallucinatory drugs," was the by-product of his and Buckley's failed experiment to synthesize psilocybin. They had never, he maintained, tried to manufacture LSD. Why go to the trouble when the finished product was so accessible at the cost of about seven cents a hit?

"So you and Buckley weren't making acid?"

"Oh, no. Good heavens, no," said Pacific—a quaint-sounding denial that encouraged me to check with the prosecutor. Scott Miller, a former assistant U.S. attorney who'd headed a Bureau of Narcotics "strike-force grand jury," stated that Pacific and Buckley weren't manufacturers of LSD but mere jobbers. Though Miller suspected that Kimberlin was one of their suppliers, he opted to pursue a perjury indictment rather than a drug indictment. The government's general impression of Kimberlin was corroborated by Tim Young, who told me Brett was his source in several "multithousand-hit deals."

"I probably sold fifty to seventy-five thousand hits of acid in my life, over a year and a half period," Young said. "Purple microdot and orange sunshine are two that I remember. How much from Brett? All of it. I don't remember ever buying acid from anybody but Brett. He sold it to me about ten thousand hits at a time. If he said he never sold acid, he's a lying motherfucker. Guarantee."

Kimberlin's grand jury testimony made it evident that the government didn't really need Pacific and Buckley to hang him. At one point, as Miller probed inconsistencies between his testimony and previous sworn statements, he said, "Now you're trying to get me for perjury."

In 1992, Kimberlin assured me that Pacific and Buckley had confessed in 1988 to Cody Shearer and Barbara Bumbalough, his private investigator. Shearer, however, told me he'd never questioned them about LSD or perjury; he was interested merely in whether they knew of any dealings between Kimberlin and Quayle, and their reply was negative. Bumbalough, as well, recalled inquiring only about Quayle. "Perjury? No. I never discussed anything with them along those lines. None of that rings a bell with me as to why I was talking with them."

Sifting through this little heap of mendacity, I asked myself whether Kimberlin lied for sport or whether an assortment of small lies coalesced into a gang of tar babies that then encircled him. When I first heard about Pacific and Buckley, they amounted to an interesting brick in my wall; their role in Kimberlin's life never rose to a sinister level. Ultimately, they signified his willingness to stay wedded to a falsehood despite black-and-white evidence to the contrary. My metaphor metamorphosed. The Pacific-Buckley factoid—the news report of their arrest, along with Kimberlin's claim of their perjury to frame him for same—was no longer a constructive brick but one of many blind turns in a labyrinth of misinformation.

KIMBERLIN'S denial that he was the Speedway Bomber left open the question of who might have been. Absent a confession from the "real" bomber, any "definitive" answer could imply guilty knowledge, so Kimberlin spun polymorphous scenarios. During the third trial, Nile Stanton's promise to unmask the malefactor backfired when Scott Bixler's alibi for the last four bombings also absolved Scott Kimberlin. Nevertheless, as Brett argued his innocence in the appellate courts and the press, he maintained that the two Scotts must have been involved, because they lent him the Chevy Impala. In time, he added a hypothetical accomplice, Joe Majko.

Majko was one of the stray suburban urchins Carolyn took under her wing, which rescue failed to launch him on the straight and narrow. He dropped out of school at sixteen and by the time he earned his high school equivalency diploma, aged twenty, was residing at the Indiana State Reformatory, in Pendleton. The most sympathetic appraisal of Majko I heard came from a defense attorney: "Joe's the kind of fellow who, if you get him hanging around guys who go to church camp, he'll go to church camp. But if you get him in a bar with guys who say, 'Let's go buy some drugs,' and maybe one of them turns out to be a government informer, he'll do that."

Buying drugs wasn't actually Majko's preferred method. For years, his chief occupation was burglarizing pharmacies, often by breaking through walls or ceilings.* Drugstore Cowboy notwithstanding, Majko's vicissitudes never seemed to interfere with his loyalty to the Kimberlins. He dutifully menaced Kelly Merritt, the main government witness in Brett's cocaine case. After Brett had a falling-out with Woody McDermott—over a jumped connection, predictably—McDermott chased him through the neighborhood near the Good Earth, pummeled him in broad daylight, and warned he'd be back. For three days and nights, Majko, Scott Kimberlin, and a

---

* Majko once made headlines by perforating a ceiling inadvertently. While awaiting a court hearing in the Indianapolis City-County Building, he escaped from a holding cell by removing an overhead panel. As he tried to crawl toward freedom, a sudden plunge deposited him on a philodendron in the office of the aptly named Judge John Downer.

couple of cohorts unobtrusively stationed themselves in the Good Earth parking lot, firearms at the ready. By his account, McDermott luckily got wind of the ambush before blood was shed. Another time, after Scott and Brett had a serious disagreement with some dealers in Zanesville, Ohio, Majko and Bixler disguised themselves as police officers and, as Majko put it, "got our shit back, the pot and the money."

Along with the affidavits Stanton gave in 1989 about Judge Dugan's bribe solicitation and his smoky encounter with Quayle during law school, he produced a third sworn statement, which in effect fingered Majko for the bombings. Before Brett's third trial, prompted by an indication from Greg Kimberlin "that Joe Majko wanted to talk to me about Brett's case," Stanton sent a law clerk to interview him in prison. The clerk reported "that Majko knew 'everything' about the bombings," including the " 'rock-hard fact' that Brett Kimberlin was not the bomber." These statements struck Stanton as "hyperbole," but he subpoenaed Majko, who gave testimony implicating Bixler and Scott Kimberlin—testimony the jury, of course, found unconvincing.

Years passed before Stanton's suspicions focused on Majko directly. In 1984, while representing him in a drug possession case, Stanton began to speculate that Majko, who was six inches taller than Brett, more closely fit the physical descriptions offered by the hypnosis witnesses. More time—including Stanton's disbarment—elapsed before he went to Pendleton and confronted Majko. Though Majko disclaimed responsibility for the DeLong bombing and one other, he neither confirmed nor denied a role in the remaining six. On a follow-up visit, Stanton failed to get him to sign a statement affirming his partial culpability. According to Stanton's affidavit, Majko wouldn't formally admit anything as long as the appeal of his conviction was pending before the Indiana Supreme Court. Assuming that Stanton, though impeachable, gave a truthful affidavit, did that mean Majko had told him the truth?

In September 1993, I went to see Majko at the Westville Correctional Center, in northern Indiana, where he was doing five years for possession of a controlled substance.* He told me the following story:

---

* Majko had received an additional thirty-year term under Indiana's "habitual criminal offender" statute—a variation of the three-strikes-and-you're-out principle—but eventually won this more lenient sentence.

In July 1978, having been released from jail in Wisconsin, he returned to Indianapolis, where one afternoon he got a call from Scott Kimberlin, telling him to come to Bloomington and to bring along a heavy-duty black rubber raft. He arrived at an A-frame Scott had rented in the woods, just missing Bixler, who'd departed a few minutes earlier. "Scott says, 'Come on, we're gonna go try something.' We go out to this lake. It might have been Monroe Reservoir. He's got this gym bag. We take the raft and go out there and he sets the bag on this other raft. . . . When we're paddling out to the middle of the lake, I'm asking him what was in the bag and he wouldn't tell me. He said, 'You'll see.' And then when we got back on shore he told me it was a bomb. He said, 'It'll go off in a few minutes.' And it did. . . . He just wanted to see if it would work. And it worked."

At a later date, he continued, Scott Kimberlin sent him to the Graham Electronics store in the Glendale Shopping Center to buy timers. "I think I picked up four timers," he said. "And I picked up a packet of nuts and bolts, I think, and I gave them to him, and that's the last I ever seen of them." Finally, Majko told me, "Scott was wanting me to set the bombs off," but he refused.

I related Majko's story to Brett, who was naturally delighted. Several weeks later, I repeated it in Carolyn's company. This was during the same conversation in which I discovered that she, rather than Brett, was the source of the "quick detective work" that helped solve Scott's murder. Carolyn's reaction was anything but delighted. Nothing I said had altered the pedigree of the Speedway Bomber. Upon reflection, I realized Majko's story didn't make my life any easier, either, since it didn't jibe with my evolving portrait of Brett.

By his own admission, Majko had a habit of making things up as he went along. His testimony at the third trial included perjury—the account of overhearing a conversation between the two Scotts in Colorado, during which Bixler allegedly said, "I didn't mean to mess up that man's leg." Why give that testimony? I asked. "Because I didn't like the way Thar was fucking with me." The trial transcript showed, however, that Majko had made this statement during direct examination by Stanton. And the government's cross-examination was conducted by Kennard Foster, not Jack Thar.

Majko's story contained other holes. First, that the alleged test-bombing on the lake occurred before his birthday, July 27. The murder of Julia Scyphers took place on July 29. Before that date, no one in the Kimberlin family had any beef with the Speedway police, or vice versa. Second, in fact three timers were sold on 2 September from the Graham Electronics outlet at the Glendale Shopping Center. This was the only multiple purchase of Mark Time timers from that store during the relevant period. (Brett acknowledged visiting the shopping center late that afternoon, shortly before closing, but denied going into Graham Electronics.) Even if Majko bought four timers and accoutrements at Glendale, he couldn't possibly have given them to Scott Kimberlin, because earlier that day, the two Scotts had flown from Bloomington to Louisville. Third, and finally, Majko told me Scott Kimberlin had shown him a bomb. When I asked what it looked like, his depiction in no way matched the model constructed by the ATF. The timer, for instance, he described as "tan and egg-shaped, like a little kitchen timer." A Mark Time job, I pointed out, was blue and white and rectangular. He replied, "It's been so long ago, and I was eating Quaaludes."

When I juxtaposed my Majko interview with Stanton's affidavit, I knew that parsing the truth was a practical impossibility. Where did that leave me? Bixler, an alumnus of the federal witness protection program, had again successfully disappeared; even if I'd been able to depose him, he no doubt would've contradicted Majko without illuminating Brett's role. Brett, of course, accepted Majko's narrative at face value, citing it as further proof of his innocence. "With the evidence I had before, two and two equaled Joe Majko," he told me. "Now I have no reason to doubt that maybe somebody else was involved. I've always thought Scott Bixler was involved, but I didn't know how much. Joe could have bought some of the timers, Bixler could have bought some of the timers, maybe Bixler and Scott [Kimberlin] made the bombs or tested the bombs. And then maybe somebody else planted them. Or maybe Scott and Scott planted the first four and split town—talk about a perfect alibi—and let somebody else plant the rest."

To accept Brett's interpretation, one had to (a) find Majko generally credible and (b) embrace the import of his courtroom testimony that Scott, not Brett, controlled the Tovex. Such a proposition became untenable once I grasped that when it came to who did what with the Tovex, Brett had told me an intricate, maddening lie.

STANTON'S primary goal in putting Majko on the stand was to elicit testimony that in the autumn of 1978, after the bombings, he'd helped Scott move his belongings from the A-frame to a commercial storage facility and that among the items was a cardboard carton labeled EXPLOSIVES. This dovetailed with the testimony that Greg and Kevin, hindered by the hearsay doctrine, had been prevented from giving during Brett's trial for illegal possession of explosives. If the court had permitted, they would have sworn that Scott, not Brett, assumed control of the Tovex after blasting was done in Jackson County in 1975.

Suppose Scott possessed a carton of Tovex around the time of the bombings. Did that prove he controlled the Tovex during the preceding three years, or that he built or planted the bombs? An intuitive leap was required; once I made it, I was confident I'd deciphered the message embedded between the lines of Brett's convoluted explanation of what happened to the Tovex.

According to Brett, his architect, Stephen Miller, took the seventy leftover sticks of Tovex from the Jackson County construction site and stored them at his home for a few months before calling to say he didn't want that stuff around. So Brett sent Scott to pick it up. Miller held on to four sticks for personal use—potential root cellar excavations—and gave Scott the rest. When the ATF traced the Tovex to Miller in 1978, the agency threatened to charge him with improper storage of four sticks. To avoid prosecution, he signed a statement and gave grand jury testimony that failed to mention either having originally retained seventy sticks or the retrieval by Scott. Since Miller's "primary concern was his own ass," Kimberlin and his attorneys accommodated him. Though Brett never explicitly discussed with Miller his testimony ahead of time, one of his attorneys—"probably Nile"—reached an agreement that allowed Miller to shape his story to avoid a possible charge of having illegally stored the bulk of the Tovex.

All quite interesting—at points, not unpersuasive—except that every other participant contradicted it.

When I asked the ATF's Patrick Donovan whether he or his partner, Ben Niehaus, threatened Miller, he said, "Definitely not. Miller may have asked me if he'd done something wrong. My response would have been that he might have technically had a misdemeanor violation for the way they [the four sticks] were stored. But we weren't interested in that. There wasn't any need to put any pressure on Miller anyway, because he was cooperating."

When I asked Miller whether he ever possessed more than four sticks, whether Scott came to his home to pick up the bulk, and whether he could recall his encounter with the ATF, he said, "If I took not four but fifty or seventy sticks, I would remember that. Oh, yeah. I went out of my way to hide the four—I was very aware of my two kids and the four sticks—so I would remember having an entire carton. . . . The long and short of this thing is Brett's saying Scott came and got the explosives. Had that been true, then when I was informed that Brett was suspected of the Speedway bombings, my mind would've initially gone to Scott. And the thought that Scott was involved never crossed my mind. . . . I don't recall ever being threatened by ATF people about my involvement in how I stored the Tovex. I wasn't worried about that."

When I asked Kevin McShane, Stanton's cocounsel, whether he had agreed to disregard Miller's wrongdoing, he said, "I don't think he told me anything different than what his testimony was. I don't have any recollection of him saying anything different. If he'd told anybody associated with the defense that things were other than his testimony, I can assure you we would have beat him over the head with it. We would have impeached him with that. He was a government witness. We wouldn't have cared if Steve Miller and Brett were best buddies. We would have asked about it."

I asked Stanton this same question—did he agree not to reveal that Miller had stored the entire load of Tovex? "That would be suborning perjury. I wouldn't protect him over my client, that's for damn sure. I wouldn't have backed off of Steve Miller if it was something critical to my client. I don't recall Miller telling me at any time that he was afraid of the ATF. He certainly didn't say, 'I want to present one thing but another thing is true' because he was afraid of the ATF. I wouldn't have gone along with that shit."

In this context, another bit of dissimulation by Brett seemed, if not exactly benign, relatively incidental. At the third trial, he testified that Scott had taken possession of the Tovex to supervise further blasting in Jackson County, specifically tree-stump removal. This was perjury, he admitted to me. There was no more blasting at the Jackson County property. For three years, the Tovex lay fallow . . . until the Speedway bombings.

DESPITE Majko's problematic credibility, I concluded that he knew something. He was confessing not to being the culprit but to being a would-be tool of a hybrid Speedway Bomber, a cog in a multiform conspiracy. I would never be able to say for certain how all the parts fit together, but it had become impossible to believe Brett knew nothing. Even Stanton, though he steadfastly rejected the government's one-man-band theory of bomb-builder and planter, finally conceded the likelihood that Brett was somehow involved. A few days after I first spoke with him about Stephen Miller's testimony, Stanton called back to say he was greatly disturbed by the implications of Brett's lying. "It just bothers the fuck out of me," he said. "I've racked my memory about whether Miller and I even had a conversation. Even if we did, why would I agree to suppress information like that at the expense of my client? The answer is I wouldn't have. It's incomprehensible that I wouldn't pound Steve Miller on the witness stand if he had told me what Brett told you he said. That's just impossible."

Stanton was correct that the disparate pieces never fit together precisely as the prosecution contended, and it was those flaws that empowered Brett Kimberlin to obscure the truth. He did his cleverest work in the interstices, and I spent months wandering through his disclaimers and prevarications before deciding, finally, that this was a case of homework, along with truth, being eaten by the dog, pissed on by the cat, and buried in the backyard. In Kimberlin's case, the scenario was: I didn't do the bombings; my brother Scott did, or else his friend Scott, or maybe my brother's friend Joe. Besides, it wasn't really bombings that put me in prison, but a right-wing political conspiracy. The government is corrupt, and I've always been a prisoner of war. If the eyewitness, Lynn Coleman, lied, then everybody else is a perjurer. If hypnosis witnesses were impeachable, the entire case is a dishonest confection.

When Kimberlin delivered a similarly sanctimonious oration at his sentencing hearing, he apparently believed in his innocence. At the end of the day, I decidedly did not.

HAVING come this far, I couldn't resist contacting Leonard Harrelson, the polygraph examiner retained by Kimberlin's attorneys before the first trial. Without providing details, Rick Kammen told me that when he and Michael Pritzker surveyed the results, "We didn't want to breathe a word about Harrelson to anybody." The fact of the polygraph became public knowledge only because Kimberlin boasted to the *Indianapolis News* that he'd passed with flying colors—an assertion he repeated to me. "I flunked one question about whether I'd ever possessed explosives, and Pritzker asked me why that would be so," Kimberlin said. "I told him it was because I'd handled explosives in 1975. I told him to have Harrelson ask the question more specifically to 1978. And then I passed."

Proponents and detractors of polygraphy agree that its accuracy depends greatly on the skills and biases of the examiner. For that reason above all, despite its effectiveness as an investigative tool, courts bar polygraph results as evidence. Kimberlin treated polygraphy with the same double standard he applied to hypnosis. When hypnosis witnesses identified him as the purchaser of bomb components, the unreliability of hypnosis was to blame; when they described a suspect whose physical dimensions didn't match his, hypnosis worked. Likewise, he told me, "I don't believe polygraphs, because I've seen them beat many times. I've seen them wrong." Yet he trumpeted the successful outcome of his session with Harrelson. And in 1988, he toyed with the prospect of a polygraph to substantiate his allegations about Quayle.

When I approached Harrelson, I had a couple of goals. In a way that felt almost prurient, I wanted to verify that his findings coincided with my conclusion about Kimberlin's culpability. Thanks to the unsubtle hints I'd received from Pritzker and Kammen, I already knew the answer, but I had no idea whether Harrelson would speak freely. If so, he might also confirm—and this fact could not be impugned the way the polygraph results might—that Kimberlin had told me yet another brazen lie.

Harrelson lived in Chicago, where, in his early seventies, he remained professionally active. He had administered over fifty thousand polygraphs, he said; his credits included the My Lai massacre, the Boston Strangler case, and the JFK assassination. To maintain storage capacity, he routinely destroyed records from old cases and therefore had long ago discarded the Kimberlin file. Nevertheless, he remembered the case clearly.

"I went into it with a completely open mind," he said. "His attorney [Pritzker] told me what he was interested in knowing. I encountered Kimberlin and found him to be an extremely obnoxious, cocky little guy. We talked, I formulated the questions, and I ran two or three different tests. His tests indicated that he failed every relevant question. He bragged to me about flying drugs and outrunning government planes and dumping drugs when they were chasing him. And that was the truth.

"He made a lot of admissions about a lot of things. I don't know if you're aware of the fact he admitted the drug things. He flunked the test every way in the world with regard to why I was testing him. I asked him questions about obtaining material for making the bombs and about the actual placing of the bombs. He made admissions in general but denied that he placed the bombs.

"I think Kimberlin's the type of person that if you talked to him face-to-face you wouldn't even need a polygraph. But he was a good subject for the polygraph because he reacted much better when he lied than some people do. There are certain types of individuals that do not react to a large extent, and he did; he reacted to a very large extent. I was using a three-channel instrument measuring pulse rate and blood pressure and changes within those, breathing patterns, and sweat-gland activities.

"The attorney didn't want a written report, because when their clients flunk they don't want it in their files. I gave him the graphs [polygrams] because he wanted them in case somebody tried to get smart and subpoenaed them. It's not common to give up the polygrams."

When Harrelson referred to the polygrams, I recalled hearing that during the first trial Pritzker, out of some macabre impulse, had framed a portion of one and hung it on the wall of his office. Two responses that indicated a striking degree of deception were: "Do you love your father?" and "Do you know anything about the eight bombings?" Kimberlin answered affirmative to the former, negative to the latter. Kammen, who also saved a copy of this same polygram, recalled, "It was as if Brett's heart skipped several beats. His heart just stopped at that moment." I asked Pritzker if Kammen's characterization was accurate, and he replied, "I don't think his heart stopped. Exploded is more like it."

WORKING WITH Donald Morano on his appeal to the Seventh Circuit, Kimberlin applied himself to the transcript of the third trial with Talmudic rigor, and his notes included a detailed index of the testimony. After the appeal was filed, the transcript, which totaled more than seven thousand pages, came to rest in a federal storage facility in Chicago. For a long while, I immersed myself in the details of the case by referring to newspaper accounts, appellate briefs, and the Seventh Circuit's published decision, though not to the transcript itself. When I at last accepted the inevitable—that I needed to consult the verbatim testimony of certain witnesses—Kimberlin's thorough index enabled me to isolate the pages I needed.

I adverted to the transcript after a clumsier-than-usual attempt by Kimberlin to mislead me. One of my secondary sources was a lengthy February 1983 *Chicago Reader* article by Deanna Silberman, entitled "Is This Man the Mad Bomber of Speedway, Indiana?" Her answer leaned sufficiently in the direction of reasonable doubt for Kimberlin to circulate photocopies among journalists. I was especially struck by Silberman's description of a melodrama during the spring of 1978, two months before the death of Julia Scyphers, when Kimberlin was prevented from seeing Jessica Barton. After Sandi Barton instructed Brett to stay away from her younger daughter, "he became very upset and said it wasn't worth going on anymore." When I asked whether he'd actually threatened suicide, Kimberlin told me Silberman had the facts wrong; Sandi had given no such testimony. "It never happened," he said. Later, I came across an *Indianapolis News* clipping that described Sandi's court appearance: "Mrs. Barton said after she ordered Kimberlin to stay away from the child, Kimberlin threatened suicide because 'life was not worth living' without [Jessica]." The same article reported that in June 1978, Sandi "forbade Kimberlin to speak to [Jessica] after he hit the child on at least two occasions and took the daughter's puppy when [Jessica] refused to talk to him."

Calling the Bartons for clarification wasn't an option, because Sandi, after a single brief phone conversation, had refused to talk with me further, and Yvonne and Jessica, whom I approached through an intermediary, were completely inaccessible. To avoid a fractious encounter with Kimberlin, I alluded to the *News* clipping in a manner of innocuous befuddlement, and he modified his denial only slightly. "I don't believe any of that testimony," he said. "I don't think [Sandi] said it. Number one, I didn't take the dog until July, and it was because Jessica was supposed to do something and she didn't, and I thought it was a good punishment. I don't remember what it was. It was just for a couple of days. . . . [Sandi] never forbade me to

talk to Jessica, ever. The point is that anything about me being depressed about not seeing Jessica was after her grandmother was killed
and she was kept away from me. Nothing like this happened before
her grandmother was killed. This stuff about how I hit her—I didn't
even hit her; it was just a smack on the face, a year and a half earlier,
because she lied to me. This was, like, in early 1977. I just smacked
her and said, 'Don't lie to me.' "

The notion of Kimberlin admonishing anybody not to lie both
amused and galvanized me; I had no choice but to retrieve from storage the transcript of Sandi's testimony. On pages 4532 and 4561, I located the colloquy that confirmed what the *Chicago Reader* and the
Indianapolis News had reported. Confronting the naked evidence of
this particular deception left me feeling momentarily deflated, if not
downright insulted. Did Kimberlin think I was stupid? Getting an appointment at the federal archive proved a mild inconvenience, transcript copies cost fifty cents a page, and I had to hire someone in
Chicago to go to the archive and pick up the pages—but I'd had
tougher days at the office. Did he think I was lazy? How could I maintain my presumption of his innocence, or my refusal to acknowledge
his guilt, if he insisted on lobbing fat juicy ones in the vicinity of my
overhand smash? What next—a confession? Hardly likely, I reassured myself. This had been a glaring lapse by Brett, but as long as I
remained in character—a talented amateur, never quite able to see
into the heart of the game—we could keep the rally going.

WILLIAM Bowman, an associate of Kimberlin's and the only person
ever publicly identified as a serious suspect in the murder of Julia
Scyphers, passed two polygraph examinations. Nine days after Bowman made his first court appearance, Fred Scyphers, the only eyewitness, dropped dead. With that, the investigation reached what seemed
a permanent impasse.

To recap my findings up to this point: The day of the murder, a
Saturday, Kimberlin made a trip to Martinsville, half an hour southwest of Indianapolis, to the home of Rodney Fint. While driving back
to the city, he said, he got an urgent message from his sister on his
beeper. He found a roadside pay phone, and Cynthia, who had heard
the news from Yvonne Barton, told him Mrs. Scyphers was dead.
"This was early afternoon, one o'clock. I think she was killed at

twelve-thirty p.m." He asked Cynthia if Mrs. Scyphers died in a car accident, but she didn't know. Yvonne, meanwhile, wanted Brett to help track down Sandi and Jessica in Texas.

Fint was known to be involved with Kimberlin in the pot trade. What was really going on that day in Martinsville? I asked.

"I went down there in the morning. It had to do with some business, probably to pick up some money. I don't remember what it was. Some routine thing."

In a subsequent conversation, he told me he remembered the purpose of the trip after all. He had gotten a new shipment of T-shirts at the Good Earth, and Rodney's daughter, Lisa, and a friend of hers each wanted one, so he drove to Martinsville to deliver them. He didn't mind going out of his way, because he was having a romance, if you could call it that, with Lisa's friend, who was then fifteen years old. "So I'd taken those T-shirts down there that morning. It had nothing to do with business."

During a 1982 deposition, Jack Crosby, who at the time of the murder was living in Austin and married to Sandi's sister, Louise, gave the following testimony:

"The thing that I recall most is the day that we had gotten the word that Louise's mother had been murdered [so] we tried to make contact with Sandi because she was not in Indianapolis. She'd told us that she was coming to Texas and was—I can't remember whether it was doing a favor for Brett or some such thing, but that she was going to stop by Austin on her way back. So, we knew she wasn't in Indianapolis, and then we got the word that Mrs. Scyphers had been murdered. We had no way of contacting her and I had called Brett to find out whether he knew where she was and if he could get in contact, how could we get in contact. It was a strange conversation. . . . The affect of the conversation didn't match up with the emotions of the circumstances. I felt that he was being very coy and cute at a moment when an individual had been murdered. And I remember saying to him, 'Mrs. Scyphers has been killed and we need to get ahold of Sandi.' He said, 'Oh, she was in a car accident?' I said, 'No, Brett, she was shot and we need to get ahold of Sandi. Could you help us?' And there were hems and haws and he said, 'Oh, she was in a car accident?' And I said, 'No, Brett, she was shot. How can we get ahold of Sandi?' And, I remember, a third time he asked, 'Oh, she was in a car accident?' And by that time I was getting relatively aggravated and I probably said something to the effect, 'No, damn it, she was not in a car accident. She was shot. Will you help us or won't you?' And he made some kind of comment, 'Well, I'll see what I can do. Maybe I can take care of it.' "

Julia Scyphers wasn't shot until three o'clock. Allowing time for her to be taken to the hospital and officially pronounced dead, it would've been at least four o'clock, probably later, before Kimberlin would've been paged by his sister. As it happened, other people were in a position to fill in some of the hours that were missing from his narrative. Though none of these witnesses wished to be identified, there emerged an account of the day's events—indelibly engraved in memory—that was sharply at odds with Kimberlin's version. Kimberlin, according to this contrary narrative, wasn't dropping off a couple of T-shirts in Martinsville; he was consummating a multiton marijuana deal. And he wasn't heading away from Martinsville by midday, because the dope transaction didn't get started until late afternoon. At five o'clock, the early edition of the local television news was broadcast from Indianapolis.

"We were in the middle of a weighing operation," one participant told me. "And Brett said he wanted to go watch the news. What was strange was that he wanted to break routine in the middle of a deal involving thousands of pounds of marijuana and go watch the news. We had the scales and the load in the garage, and to see the TV we had to enter the house and climb a flight of stairs. The Scyphers murder was the lead story, and Brett reacted with surprise. He said, 'My God, that's Sandi's mom!' He made a phone call immediately. . . . He didn't deny anything that day, because he wasn't accused of anything."

Granting latitude for a highly evolved type of deviousness, this account of how Kimberlin first heard about the murder could be reconciled with Crosby's. But neither version, of course, could accommodate Kimberlin's chronicle of the day's events.

IN KIMBERLIN'S first petition to the Parole Commission, filed during the summer of 1988, he included two references to the Scyphers murder. His main purpose was to rebut what he said was erroneous information contained in a presentencing memorandum prepared by the government in 1981. With Morano's name appearing on the parole brief as the attorney of record, Kimberlin wrote: "The police finally concluded that the murderer was a local drug addict who died of an overdose shortly after the murder."

While in the aftermath of William Bowman's polygraph exams it was, in fact, briefly speculated that the drug addict cited by Kimberlin might have been a suspect, no one close to the murder investigation ever regarded that as a creditable theory. Several law enforcement people to this day believe that Bowman pulled the trigger and then somehow beat the polygraph. Others, while hastening to point out their lack of fondness for Kimberlin, doubt Bowman's involvement. However, all parties agree—and this includes Speedway police detectives who worked the case, as well as the present Speedway police chief, who was on the force at the time of the crime—that the murder of Julia Scyphers remains unsolved and is therefore, officially, an open investigation.

Soldier of Fortune, a magazine enjoyed by gun nuts and right-wing militia sympathizers, featured in May 1996 an article critical of the ATF. Discussing the careers of a husband-wife pair of dissident ATF agents, the article mentioned the Speedway bombings and Kimberlin's "murder conviction." When Kimberlin became aware of this, he was outraged, he told me, to the point of contemplating a libel suit. He had a valid complaint. Never, *ever*—as Brett himself liked to say—had he been charged with, much less convicted of, murder.

36

I'M GONNA say, 'Hi, Danny, remember me? From law school?' Cody told me to call him 'Mr. Vice President,' but fuck that, I've always known him as Danny. I'm not gonna change now."

Midmorning in May of 1994, I'd just arrived in Washington on the Delta shuttle, and Kimberlin, behind the wheel of his Mercedes 300, was transporting us the short distance to a shopping mall in Arlington, Virginia. There, at a Brentano's bookstore, the author of the political memoir *Standing Firm,* launched on a thirty-city publicity tour, was scheduled to appear at one o'clock to inscribe copies for the faithful. This rendezvous was my idea—a chance to see Kimberlin and Quayle face-to-face. Would I witness a reunion between long-standing acquaintances or simply a first and ludicrous meeting?

THE PREVIOUS summer, serendipitously, Quayle and I had our own initial encounter. Fortuity placed us on the same 7:00 a.m. flight from New York to Indianapolis. Running late, I caught a glimpse of the tanned and fit-looking former veep just as boarding began. Humbly, minus an entourage or any other imperial trappings, he had a garment bag slung over his shoulder; less humbly, he was riding in first class. Recent news reports had noted that, as part of a literary endeavor, he intended to turn the tables on certain journalists who had covered his vice-presidency. What a break! Without having to run a gauntlet of advisers warning Quayle not to squander his time on the noxious likes of me, I could corner him and volunteer to be interviewed. And if he agreed, once he was done asking questions I had a few in mind for him. ("So, this business of having no friends who ever used drugs—are you troubled by the implication that you have virtually no friends, period?")

En route to the coach cabin, I paused at Quayle's seat, interrupting his banter with the flight crew.

How was the writing coming along? I asked.

Coming along real well, he said affably.

"I understand you're interested in speaking with journalists who wrote about you during your vice-presidency." I reached for my wallet and removed a business card. "And I've written about you. At length and unfavorably."

He looked at the card, still smiling, no bells ringing.

"Brett Kimberlin."

"Oh," Quayle muttered, his chirpy pleasantness evaporating.

An uncomfortable five seconds, then five more. "Anyway, I'd be eager to get together with you," I said. "If I don't hear back from you soon, should I follow up by contacting your publisher?"

"No," Quayle said, with admirable equanimity. "I have your card. You'll be hearing from someone."

Marilyn Quayle was waiting at the arrival gate in Indianapolis, and as the traffic flowed toward the baggage claim, I contemplated introducing myself to her as well, but discretion prevailed. A lot of good it did me; neither Quayle nor anyone in his office ever did call. I let a couple of weeks pass before I got in touch with his editor, who explained that the journalists the author felt like sitting down with ran along the lines of Bob Woodward, David Broder, Len Downie, Dan Rather, and Brit Hume. It didn't "behoove" Quayle to meet with me, the editor said. After consulting a dictionary, I agreed; I was beneath behoovability. The first printing of 200,000 copies sold out, and *Standing Firm* ascended the best-seller lists without benefit of either my piercing insights or my public evisceration.

KIMBERLIN and I were two and a half hours ahead of schedule when we pulled into the parking garage adjacent to the mall. "I wish I'd brought my goddamn camera," he said. "Can you imagine having a picture of me and Quayle?"

I'd been balancing a laptop computer on my knees, and now I was fishing inside my briefcase for a notebook and pen. "I feel," I said, "like we're on our way to an assassination."

"I know," Kimberlin said, laughing. On the seat lay a copy of *Standing Firm,* which he'd bought the previous day. "My mom was outraged. She said, 'I can't believe you paid for his book.' " Brett showed up on page 71 (the 1988 election) and page 262 (the 1992 election). "Look at this. Notice how he never says in here that I was arrested for smuggling? Only perjury and bombings. He says I maimed two people. Two people weren't *maimed*. And he says '60 Minutes' investigated me for two years. They didn't investigate me for two years. They decided right off the bat not to do me."

Brentano's was sandwiched between a Gap Kids and a Nordstrom's, which operated an espresso bar and had created an ersatz sidewalk bistro. A trio of Pinkertons and a store manager were stationed outside the bookstore. We sat at a café table and tried to blend in with the early-bird Quayleophiles. Being seen with a copy of *Standing Firm*, however, seemed to make Kimberlin self-conscious; after reviewing the passages that mentioned him, he turned the book facedown.

"Are you nervous?" I asked.

"Not at all," he said, shaking his head. "I'm as cool as a cucumber. This is fun." He wore black trousers, black wingtips, a white dress shirt, tinted aviators, and a white-blue-and-turquoise nylon windbreaker. His light-brown hair was neatly trimmed. "The last time I saw Danny, my hair was about shoulder length. But when I first met him, it was down to my butt."

Why, I asked, did he plan to begin the conversation with a reference to law school, given that he and Quayle hadn't attended law school together?

"When I say, 'Remember me? Indiana Law School, 1972,' I want to see how he reacts, and ad lib it from there. I might say, 'You have me in your book, and there are some errors.' And he'll say, 'Well, who are you?' And I'll say something like, 'Brett Kimberlin, the guy you say is doing fifty years in jail. But I'm not. I'm out. I'm right here.' "

At noon, a line began to form. Twenty or so people were allowed to wait inside the store. Kimberlin and I took our places in the mall corridor, at the head of a queue that grew steadily until eventually we were joined by about three hundred other pilgrims. I'd bought three copies—one for myself and two to give to ironic friends. At twelve-thirty, a Brentano's representative delivered unwelcome news: the author would sign no more than two books per customer, and there would be no time for personalized inscriptions. This doomed a pathetic fantasy I'd been nurturing; confident that Quayle wouldn't remember my face, I'd planned to say, "Mr. Vice President, I'm sort of an aspiring author myself, and I would love it if you could inscribe my book 'To Mark, Good luck with your writing.' " But now, no dice. Sotto voce, I told Kimberlin we'd clearly entered a zero-tolerance sector. "Any funny stuff," I said, "and our asses are going to get yanked right out of here." A skinny, bespectacled man with a video camera stood five yards away and captured us on tape. "Look out," I whispered. "That's the Zapruder film." And so, presumably, the grassy knoll was over yonder, past the escalator.

PRECISELY at one o'clock, heralded by cheers and applause, Quayle took a leisurely, majestic stroll through the mall. Perfectly groomed, per usual, he wore a dark suit, a white shirt, a black-and-white print necktie, and a bright smile.

"I'm excited," Kimberlin said. "This is fun. It's been a long time. I like this. I'm going to ruin his day. You watch. I'm absolutely going to ruin his day. As long as I don't get lynched by the right wing."

A smooth assembly line mobilized. We were instructed to open our books to the title page, and each copy was handed to a lackey who passed it to Quayle, who had mastered the ability to scrawl an illegible signature while sustaining heynicetameecha-goodtoseeya palaver at the rate of about four happy campers a minute. Suddenly it was my turn: an instant of eye contact, not quite a smile, clearly no trace of recognition, then—*zip, slash, autograph*—the books were back in my hand. I edged a few feet away as Quayle greeted his next admirer.

"Hi, Dan," Kimberlin said.

Quayle looked up and, without changing his expression, signed his name. In what seemed a perfunctory monotone, I heard him say "How ya been?" This was supposed to be the moment of truth— Kimberlin confronting Quayle with "Hi, Danny, remember me?" But it never happened.

"Here," Kimberlin was saying.

What? Why wasn't Kimberlin following the script? Why wasn't he revealing himself? Instead, he was smiling faintly and saying, "I'm glad you're running for President in 1996, I'll be seeing you then." And Quayle was nodding, appreciative of the friendly tidings. The encounter lasted less than half a minute, another autograph-seeker advanced, and Quayle kept the chatter going.

Kimberlin sidled over to me. "He recognized me!" he said, his voice pitched with excitement. "He knew me. Did you see that? He recognized me a hundred percent."

I was stunned and, momentarily, dumbstruck.

"Did you hear what he said? He said, 'Where have you been?' I couldn't believe that. He asked me where I've been. He *knows* where I've been."

"What are you talking about, Brett? He didn't say 'Where have you been.' He asked you *how* you've been."

"Mark, he fucking said, 'Where have you been?' He asked me how I've been and then he said, '*Where* have you been?' He clearly, *clearly,* knew me. He kind of caught me off guard by saying 'How've you been?' real casually. It reminded me of an old dope deal, where they say, 'Hey, how've you been?' under their breath—like, at a concert of something, when they're passing something and they don't want to make it seem like they're doing what they're doing."

"*Brett,*" I said, suddenly aware of the pulse in my temples. "He said 'How are you?' or 'How've you been?' or whatever he said because that's just small talk. It doesn't mean anything. He's just chatting people up as they come through. What makes you think he recognized you?"

"There's no doubt in my mind. He totally fucking knew who I was. Why would he say 'Where've you been?' if he didn't know who I was?"

I CAME to this conclusion:

The Quayle story was Kimberlin's most successful creation, the invention that propelled him further than any other. Someone he knew, but not Kimberlin himself, had either sold or claimed to have sold pot to Quayle—and he appropriated this for himself. A likely source was Larry Harvey, who Kimberlin said had witnessed their first meeting. By the time Quayle first ran for Congress, in 1976, Harvey and Kimberlin were no longer in touch; without fear of contradiction, Brett could safely boast to his sister that he'd done business with Quayle. By September 1978, when he told the FBI that he knew something about a congressman and drugs, Harvey had been dead almost a year—a shotgun wound to the head, self-inflicted, according to the coroner in Columbus, Indiana.

Kimberlin chronically interjected himself into other people's stories by jumping narrative connections. He said his relationship with Quayle began in 1971, while passing a joint around an Indiana University fraternity house. Woody McDermott, who was later introduced to Kimberlin by Harvey, lived in the Sigma Chi house in Bloomington in 1966 but moved to a private apartment a year later, along with a fraternity brother named J. D. Watson. And Watson, McDermott said, was Harvey's only other close connection to fraternity life.

"In a frat house, you don't get past the foyer if they don't know you. And Larry Harvey was never a member of any fraternity. I was very tight with Harvey at that time. I don't believe Harvey ever met Brett at any fraternity house. Larry Harvey did not associate with straight people. He would not be in a fraternity house. No way. And Harvey was a liar. Maybe *he* knew somebody else who smoked dope with Quayle."

Why, I asked McDermott, would Kimberlin bother to mention in 1976 that Quayle had been a customer? "It was a parlor game in the trade: 'Guess where my pot ended up?'—with this Indiana Pacers forward or that cop or some politician. So all of a sudden it's 'your' pot. *You're* selling it to these guys, even though you're doing it through four people and three words-of-mouth. It's 'Ha ha ha! I know about this guy's private life and he doesn't know I know it. So I own him.' "

Above all, basic business principles suggested Kimberlin had tampered with the truth. By his own account, more than a year before he met Quayle he began receiving regular shipments of Mexican weed from Leo Casas—two or three hundred pounds, twice a week. In late 1971, after he jumped the Casas connection, Papa Reyes was supplying him with a ton a week. Also, in the fall of 1971, he bought into the Good Earth. With all that on his plate, why go out of his way every few weeks to meet Quayle at the Burger Chef to sell an ounce or two?

Tim Young, who dealt large quantities of LSD and marijuana supplied by Kimberlin, told me that "by late 1970 or early '71, Brett was in the kilo or the multikilo business." By 1971, Young had dropped out of school and was living with a woman several years older. "I can remember having a hundred pounds in her house, and Brett was my only source," Young said. "Nineteen seventy-one, it's guaranteed that he's not selling any small amounts, not even single pounds. No doubt in my mind. He kept his personnel down pretty much to a minimum. If he had a ten-pound-a-week customer, he'd give him to me—that was in 1971. By the spring of 1972, I'm probably doing fifty a week and he's probably doing five times that. When I heard that Brett said he'd met Quayle at a Burger Chef, I didn't believe it, because in my experience, when you dealt with Brett you did business on his turf. You went to his parents' house and he crawled out his bedroom window, which was over the garage."

In 1972, Kimberlin said, his associate Justin Farrell quit the marijuana trade and moved to New York to pursue a rock 'n' roll career, taking with him $250,000. According to Kimberlin, his generosity and ingenuity enabled Farrell to prosper. Fine. But again, why would someone making so much money that the trickle-down was putting a quarter-million bucks in a partner's pocket go out of his way to sell nickel bags to a remote chance acquaintance?

Did my hypothesis validate Quayle's claim to lifetime membership in the Just Say No Club? Hardly. When Bush selected his running mate in 1988, more than a few of Quayle's acquaintances in Indiana scratched their heads at the strangeness of it all. And when Kimberlin popped up, he stirred conjecture and gossip aplenty. Kimberlin had what seemed a plausible story, yet in effect he redeemed Quayle simply by virtue of who he was. I spoke with reputable Indiana lawyers who told of receiving calls from clients claiming firsthand experience with Quayle and drugs. Even if Quayle was guilty of hypocrisy, however, what benefit was there in being linked with his accuser? "Had the source of Quayle's problem been someone other than Brett, these people might have come forward," one lawyer told me. "But nobody felt like getting into bed with Brett Kimberlin."

I spent four years asking questions about Kimberlin, and along the way I never met a soul who could offer genuine corroboration of the fable that brought him to my attention in the first place.

INSTINCT told me to flee the bookstore; if I hung around Kimberlin much longer, I feared, my cover would be blown. (The pounding inside my brain—was this how a cerebral hemorrhage announced itself?) Still, I was transfixed, as if I'd come in contact with high voltage. Opposite where Quayle sat, about ten feet away, was a cordon sanitaire for members of the press. I stationed myself there, behind a reporter who was holding a white legal pad. As he raised the pad to add some notes, I saw that he had scribbled *Where have you been?*

"The question 'Where have you been?' " I asked. "Is Quayle saying that to a lot of people?"

"Yes, he is," said the reporter, who identified himself as Graham Fraser, Washington bureau chief of the *Toronto Globe & Mail*.

I motioned to Kimberlin. "Brett, this reporter is writing down what Quayle says as he gives autographs. He tells me Quayle has said 'Where have you been?' to a lot of people."

"I heard him say it to at least one person," Fraser said.

"Was it me?" Kimberlin asked.

Fraser regarded him for a moment and replied, "Yes, it was you."

Kimberlin smiled triumphantly. "Quayle asked me where I've been because I'm an old friend of his. I'm in the book. I used to be his marijuana dealer." He showed Fraser his listing in the index, then opened his wallet and revealed his driver's license. Fraser seemed satisfied that Brett Kimberlin was Brett Kimberlin, whatever that might mean.

"He keeps looking at me," Kimberlin said, nodding in the direction of Quayle. From what I could tell, Quayle was signing books and, without breaking stride, maintaining his bonhomie. Occasionally, his gaze would take in the foreground, of which we were a part, but he seemed focused on the immediate task. "See that?" Kimberlin nudged me. "Quayle knows exactly who I am. I've got him nervous now."

I went to the cashier and sold back my third, unautographed copy. When I returned to the press area, Kimberlin was talking to the bespectacled man with the videocam, who, it turned out, worked for a fundamentalist Christian cable television outfit. Their conversation ended abruptly after Kimberlin introduced himself as an "old friend of Dan Quayle's" and explained what that meant.

Jiggling change in his pocket, Kimberlin asked, "Want me to continue making him nervous?" I studied Quayle for traces of nervousness, detected none, and told Kimberlin I'd had enough. As we wandered into the mall, he kept it up. "He recognized me a hundred percent. It was just like the old days. His exact demeanor, like—it was like, 'We have a secret.' "

I said, "I thought you were going to say, 'Hi, Danny. Remember me?' What happened?"

"I don't know. It just seemed formal. I planned to say 'Danny.' I don't know. I guess it was because of the atmosphere of the place."

"Don't you think it would have had a more striking effect if you'd called him Danny?"

"I don't know. Just with the timing and everything combined, I just didn't do it."

We rode an escalator down one flight and scouted for a place to eat lunch. There were more than two dozen choices, each one serving faster food than the next. I found a vendor that specialized in turkey (sandwiches, burgers, salads), and Kimberlin settled for Chinese, at Panda Express. As we ate, Kimberlin perused the photographs in Quayle's book, one of which showed him as a young father, with tousled hair and long sideburns. "That's how I remember him," he said. "Exactly. He was much more casual. Much more normal. He wasn't all combed and groomed the way he is now. He let the wind blow through his hair."

My sandwich, I realized, was inedible—a mealy pale-pink slice of tomato, lettuce that looked as if it'd spent a few days in the mail, and strangely bonded turkey material.

"He said, 'How have you been?' And then it was like he corrected himself. It became 'Where have you been?' He wouldn't have said that to somebody he didn't know. No way. It wouldn't make any sense to say it to somebody he didn't know. He hates my guts, but I don't think he wanted to make a scene. After every signing he would look at me. It was almost like paranoia."

Kimberlin paused, surveyed the mall crowd, and said, "Can you believe these people?" Six months earlier, as he prepared to leave prison, he had told me, "I feel like I'm kind of the conscience of the country right now. I have this eagle's-eye view of the situation. Everybody else seems to have these very restricted, myopic views of what's going on." Now he soared above the throng—a mythical self-creation, the moxie and talent behind a vanity production, as well as his own starstruck audience. A fortune cookie had come with his lunch. Kimberlin opened it, smiled with satisfaction, and passed me the message: *Your ability to juggle many tasks will take you far.*

37

KIMBERLIN'S love affair with Juliya Chupikova was not, after all, meant to be. Even though the capsule biography he wrote to promote "Songs of Passion" described her as "exceptionally beautiful, shapely and sexy" and a creature of "no bad habits," they'd been together only a few months when he decided the whole thing was a mistake. She had continued to live in Philadelphia, commuting to Washington in a brand-new Nissan Maxima for long weekends. After they split up, Kimberlin repossessed the car as well as several of his power-lifting trophies.

When their relationship was still cordial, I engaged Chupikova in a brief but illuminating conversation one day—her twenty-second birthday, as it happened—at Carolyn's house. I wanted to know whether she had saved copies of any articles about Brett that appeared in the Soviet press. What articles? I repeated the touching drama Brett had related—of how, while still living in Ukraine, she read a newspaper story about an American political prisoner, and how she mentioned this while speaking by telephone with David Sushansky, her uncle and Brett's fellow convict, and how this extraordinary coincidence sparked their romance and . . . She obviously hadn't a clue what I was talking about. "I never read anything political," she said. "Brett saw pictures of me that my uncle had in prison." For almost a year, she explained, Kimberlin pestered Sushansky for her address. When their correspondence finally began, she had just turned eighteen. He wrote in English, and she had someone translate into Russian. They didn't speak on the phone until she arrived in America and began to learn the language.

There seemed no point in asking Chupikova about a letter drafted for her signature and sent in April 1992 to the U.S. pardon attorney. The letter referred to "a number of favorable articles that were written about [Brett] by TASS and *Pravda,*" and described how "Brett was regularly talked about like a folk hero among those in the reform movement in my country." As we spoke, I also realized that Kimberlin's archives—a trove, he said, that included his diaries, copies of virtually every letter he'd written from or received in prison, every newspaper and magazine clipping—would contain no translations of stories by Pushkin, Tolstoy, or Chekhov. How were Brett's transliterative skills? "He speaks Russian to say 'Hello,' 'How are you?' He reads it some. But he doesn't write it."

Juliya's disappearance from the radar screen forced Brett to do a certain amount of editing; he purged her from the "Songs of Passion" press kit. Now he was a solo act, single-handedly poised to usher in the twenty-first century with incredible passion and joy. This turn of events, however, did not alter his friendship with Sushansky, to whom, in Memphis, he had been close for more than four years. In the summer of 1992, when they volunteered to find missing American servicemen in the former Soviet Union, each hoped to curry favor—Sushansky with the Immigration and Naturalization Service, which was planning to deport him at the end of his prison term, and Kimberlin with either the Parole Commission or the pardon attorney. During Brett's early conversations with the Task Force Russia desk at the Defense Department, however, he didn't mention any quid pro quo. Rather, he explained that Sushansky, prompted solely by humanitarian concern, was uniquely qualified to pursue the truth about Americans swallowed by the gulag. A Task Force Russia representative, Colonel Arthur Parr of the U.S. Army, accompanied by a lieutenant colonel, went to Memphis to meet with Sushansky, and discovered to his consternation that Brett was part of the package.

"We heard from Kimberlin very soon after Task Force Russia was set up," Colonel Parr told me. "He claimed that Sushansky had all kinds of information to give us, none of which he would disclose over the phone. Sushansky was apparently saying, 'Get me out of jail and we can solve everything in two weeks. All the outstanding POW/MIA cases.' This is what they purported. It was highly unlikely we were going to have two convicts released to the responsibility of the United States Army. But we decided to talk to them because our job was to elicit information and see whether it made sense. We wanted to ask Sushansky what he knew, but Kimberlin wanted to grandstand and orchestrate their presentation. Sushansky said, 'I know everybody'—Brezhnev's son-in-law, or whomever—'I've got connections everywhere. Get me out of jail and we'll go to New York and Ukraine and conduct the interviews.' We said, 'But what do you know?' He was offering very little specific information, which was contrary to what Kimberlin had built up when he first called us. There was never any full-faith disclosure on what they could provide, and the few names that we were given never led anywhere. Again and again, we had to request even the smallest bits of information—Sushansky's mother's phone number in Ukraine, for instance—and always we were met with 'They won't trust you without us'–type remarks. Actually, our experience in the former Soviet Union was quite the opposite. We'd ask questions and the people we approached would look at us suspiciously, but then, once we explained what we were doing, they would open up."

After the Task Force Russia ploy fell through, Kimberlin offered a cynical postmortem: Colonel Parr had seen him on television talking about Quayle; Parr hated "the draft dodger" Bill Clinton; Sushansky had valuable information the U.S. government wanted to cover up rather than risk making the reform regime in Russia look bad. When I repeated these charges to Colonel Parr, he dismissed them as absurd.

Following Kimberlin's release, he continued to labor on his friend's behalf. Sushansky had been sentenced to eight years for possession with intent to distribute heroin, and he indeed faced deportation once he had done his time. But there was a hitch: Sushansky was a Jew who had been stripped of his citizenship when he left the Soviet Union in 1979. Meanwhile, the Soviet Union had dissolved and the newly established Republic of Ukraine wouldn't permit his return. In June 1993, he was transferred from Memphis to an Immigration and Naturalization Service (INS) facility in Louisiana, where he languished along with about fifty other detainees in similar straits.

This man-without-a-country hook provided material Kimberlin could work with, and during the late winter of 1994, articles about Sushansky's dilemma turned up in the *Chicago Tribune* and *Legal Times*. Both stories gave more than equal time to Kimberlin's new role as a public citizen. The latter, a lengthy front-page feature headlined BRETT KIMBERLIN, WASHINGTON LOBBYIST, portrayed the indefatigable polymath—self-proclaimed human rights activist, inveterate litigant, budding professional musician—and focused on his ability to cultivate the powerful. He had approached Howard Rosenblatt, hoping that Arnold & Porter might file a suit challenging the INS policy. Though the firm declined to add Sushansky to its pro bono roster, Kimberlin helped persuade two other lawyers, one in Washington and the other in New York, to take the case.

BOTH articles updated Kimberlin's lawsuit against Michael Quinlan, Loye Miller, and the BOP. At that point, Kimberlin was awaiting the decision of the D.C. Circuit Court of Appeals on his request for an *en banc* review. In early spring, with one judge recusing himself, the court voted 5–4 to rehear the case—but Kimberlin needed six ayes to succeed. Only superficially, however, had he lost the round. As usual, there was a complex subtext. Judges on both sides submitted opinions reflecting a desire to pass the ball to the Supreme Court. This echoed the vote six months earlier, when Judge Stephen Williams, though concurring with the three-member panel's majority finding that Kimberlin had not fulfilled the D.C. Circuit's heightened pleading standard—the requirement that in order to overcome a federal official's qualified immunity, a plaintiff must provide direct evidence of wrongdoing—had questioned the wisdom of this precedent. Other circuit courts had rendered contrary rulings; clarification was necessary. Meanwhile, a parallel debate had been brewing for months within the Justice Department. This took the form of a disagreement between the civil division and the office of the solicitor general. Attorneys within the former regarded Quinlan and Miller as their clients. The staff of the latter, however, concluded that a defense of the direct-evidence standard would undermine that office's credibility with the Supreme Court. No doubt lawyers in each camp believed their positions reasonable—a worthy balancing of a basic constitutional right on the one hand and, on the other, the freedom of government officials to do their jobs without fear of meretricious lawsuits. In the end, the solicitor general prevailed, and the Justice Department formally withdrew its representation of Quinlan and Miller. Now the defendants were obliged to retain private counsel, with the consolation that taxpayers would foot their bill.

Rosenblatt, of course, immediately drafted a writ of certiorari, and in January 1995 it was granted. "You're talking to a Supreme Court litigant here," Kimberlin announced when he called with the news. Rarely had he sounded more buoyant. The oral argument—the uplifting spectacle that Kimberlin had hopefully anticipated as "our greatest glory . . . the biggest deal of all"—was placed on the docket for the final day of the Court's term.

FOR KIMBERLIN, poetic justice would truly have been served if he had entered the Supreme Court chamber in the sublime company of Erwin Griswold. Alas, two months before the cert petition was granted, Griswold died, at the age of eighty-eight. This was one of a string of personal setbacks that Kimberlin endured as 1994 drew to a close. In October, the funeral of his paternal grandmother, Louise Bicknell, had necessitated his first trip back to Indianapolis since Judge Steckler, in 1981, ordered him to leave town for fifty years. Within two weeks of burying his mother, Greg Kimberlin was diagnosed with lymphoma, and despite immediate radical chemotherapy, his condition rapidly deteriorated. On Christmas Day, Brett returned to Indianapolis, to his father's bedside. During this vigil, he said, they had a conversation from which he derived great comfort. "I asked him if he'd been satisfied with his life—if he had any regrets, whether he'd have gone about things differently. I told him I was sorry if I'd done anything to hurt him, and he said, 'No, it's OK, it's all part of growing up.' "

Three days later, Greg died, in the presence of his wife, Peggy, Brett, and Cynthia. "It was very peaceful, quiet," Brett reported when we spoke that afternoon. "He seemed very resolved. It seemed like he knew we were there. Even last night, as we were leaving, he was unable to talk and he was breathing real hard, but I said, 'Dad, if you can hear me, blink your eyes.' And his eyes were closed, but you could see him try. I felt like when we got there this morning, he became much more peaceful. We told him it was OK to go—go in peace. We all cried, and that was it. Today, I've been dealing with the arrangements. He didn't want a funeral. He wasn't religious at all. He disliked churches immensely. He didn't believe in Jesus Christ. He didn't believe in the Trinity. He wanted to be cremated and he wanted a party."

A friend of Brett's stepmother had advised him not to stick around for the memorial service, but he rejected this counsel and was glad he did. "We had a nice celebration. About two hundred people came. This jazz combo played for about an hour, and then there were speakers—old friends of Dad's. They talked about all the things he liked to do, about how he was always a good lawyer and a good friend. I'd made the decision to be the person who met all the guests. I stood there when people signed the guest book and shook hands with every single one of them, stood there with my chin up and my chest out and a smile on my face. It was a very high-class crowd—lawyers, judges, accountants, doctors. There was no negativity toward me at all. Everyone was so warm and supportive. People said to me, 'Oh, I'm sorry your dad died.' And I said, 'Don't feel sorry. Dad lived a great life. He doesn't want you to feel sorry. We don't want any tears here.' That was the atmosphere—jovial and happy. Everybody went out of there smiling and feeling good. I was the master politician. I made everybody who came through there feel good. Like the secretaries who worked with him. I said, 'Dad always talked about how great the secretaries at the company were.' Someone told me, 'Brett, you should be running for public office.' "

THE MORNING of the Supreme Court oral argument, I rode downtown with Brett, Carolyn, and Monika Kosior, a twenty-year-old Pole who had replaced Juliya Chupikova as his romantic interest. Brett wore a black suit, a white shirt, and a gray print necktie, and was driving a brand-new 1995 Mercedes 300E, courtesy of Greg's life-insurance proceeds. Along the way, we passed the halfway house where he'd lived for three months after his release from Memphis. The date was 26 April 1995, a week after the bombing of the Alfred P. Murrah federal building in Oklahoma City. The prime suspect, Timothy McVeigh, had been apprehended, but Kimberlin was skeptical. "I was reading the paper this morning, and they said they'd found traces of ammonium nitrate in this guy's car and I just yawned. It was like when they said they found monomethylamine nitrate in my car. I have a very jaundiced view of how they're going about this."

We made a quick stop at Howrey & Simon, to which Rosenblatt had brought Kimberlin's case after leaving Arnold & Porter a year and a half earlier. Four blocks from the White House, the firm occupied nine floors of a sleek eleven-story building that had acquired instant celebrity when it was used in several scenes of *The Pelican Brief* movie. In the lobby, Brett and Monika posed while Carolyn snapped pictures.

This photo opportunity meshed with Brett's cinematic sense of the occasion. The nation's capital was at the peak of its springtime radiance, and the name "Kimberlin" was about to be uttered in the highest court of the land, attended by an audience of reporters from all over the country, among them several of us who had helped advance his legend. Nina Totenberg was there, and Anthony Lewis had come from Boston. And this time the plaintiff was approaching the Supreme Court not as the Speedway Bomber but as a First Amendment champion.

The rules of the court allowed each party thirty minutes. Quinlan and Miller were represented by Michael Martinez, of the Washington firm Holland & Knight. Remarkably, Rosenblatt was joined by a deputy solicitor general, William Bender, to whom he had yielded ten minutes of his time to argue against the D.C. Circuit's heightened pleading standard. However, on another crucial issue—the so-called appealability question—Bender and Rosenblatt parted company. According to the reasoning proffered by Rosenblatt, the matter should've been settled when Judge Harold Greene ruled, at the district court level, that Kimberlin had in his initial pleading provided "concrete" and "tangible" evidence that his "clearly established" rights had been violated. In other words, at that point the case ought to have proceeded to discovery and trial, with the defendants denied the opportunity to appeal. The Justice Department officially disagreed.

Though the attorneys' presentations and questions from the bench included occasional references to Kimberlin and Quayle, the colloquy took place on a rarefied plane galaxies removed from what had or hadn't occurred almost twenty-five years earlier in the Burger Chef parking lot back home in Indianapolis at the intersection of Kessler Boulevard and Michigan Road. Justices Sandra Day O'Connor and Ruth Bader Ginsburg were the most active interrogators. Both asked Rosenblatt whether the defendants had been entitled to an appeal of their summary-judgment motion, and he naturally responded in the negative. When Rosenblatt pressed further and argued against the heightened pleading standard, Justice Stephen Breyer brought him up short, pointing out that, as far as the Supreme Court was concerned, the issues were mutually exclusive. If the matter shouldn't have been appealable, Breyer was saying, then the Court had no jurisdiction regarding the heightened pleading standard.

When the hour was up, Kimberlin was not done imbibing the great glory of it all. Outside, at the foot of the western steps of the Supreme Court building, Rosenblatt and Martinez paused to answer questions from reporters, and Kimberlin basked in the noonday sun and whatever media attention came his way. To a reporter from the *Indianapolis Star,* he said, "I'm a very dogged person. If I make a decision to do something, I follow it through. When we initiated this suit, we knew we would take it all the way." Two middle-aged couples—men in dark business suits, apparently accompanied by their wives—descended the steps. Kimberlin approached, his right hand extended, and addressed one of the men. "Hi, what's your name?"

"Michael Quinlan."

"I'm Brett Kimberlin."

Quinlan was at a complete loss for words. "Well-l-l," was all he could utter, though what he actually seemed to be saying was that he suddenly felt unwell. He leaned away from Kimberlin, disengaging the handshake, and abruptly walked away. This happened so quickly that neither Carolyn nor Cynthia nor Monika, all of whom were brandishing cameras, managed to get a snapshot. Again, I woefully realized, as with the Kimberlin-Quayle tête-à-tête at Brentano's, here was a glorious momentary meeting that would never be captured on film.

KIMBERLIN still had unfinished business with the Supreme Court. In June 1993, the Indiana Court of Appeals reversed the $1.25 million wrongful death finding against him in the DeLong case; then, a year later, the Indiana Supreme Court restored it. He requested a rehearing, the motion was denied after several months, and an appeal to the U.S. Supreme Court became his only recourse. Three weeks after the oral argument in *Kimberlin* v. *Quinlan et al.,* he filed a writ of certiorari. Because Donald Morano had rejected his paltry offer of $2,000 to handle this phase of the case, Kimberlin ended up representing himself (*pro se*), officially claiming pauper status. His cert petition recapitulated the briefs in the lower courts and dwelled at length upon the alleged bribe solicitation by Judge Dugan. As a practical matter, the mere fact of *pro se* representation greatly reduced the likelihood that cert would be granted. Kimberlin, however, was confident he would soon make an encore appearance. I asked whether he wasn't concerned that the Court, having just heard his suit against Quinlan and Miller, would be disinclined to grant a hearing in a separate case. Not at all, he said. "It makes it certain they'll read my brief. And if they read it, I think they'll be pretty appalled at what happened to me."

But if cert was denied—what was his worst-case scenario?

"For the DeLongs to get the money from me, they have to have a writ of attachment," he said. "I can go to Indiana and say they can't have the money because this bastard solicited a bribe. Even if it got past that, they would have to bring that writ to Maryland and ask a judge here to enforce it. And the judge here would have another hearing. And I would explain why this judgment should be voided, and I would stand a better chance in Maryland because of all the taint in Indiana—what with Dugan winding up in prison. And even if I lost here, I could appeal here. I could have this in litigation for twenty years. I'm not paying for something I didn't do. I'm not giving a penny."

In October 1995, as the Supreme Court opened its new term, Kimberlin's cert petition was indeed denied. By then, however, he had received advice from an Indiana attorney that convinced him he had nothing to fear. "That judgment against me is worthless," he told me. "I found out Indiana has a statute of limitations on any judgment ten years or older. If they don't renew it within that period, it's as if it never happened. And they've never bothered to renew it. So none of this matters anymore. I'm home free."

MOREOVER, in the meantime the Supreme Court had rendered its opinion in the suit against Quinlan and Miller: in Kimberlin's favor, unanimously. But the decision was steeped in irony. After years of wrangling about direct versus circumstantial evidence, after reams of briefs about the heightened pleading standard, the justices left those conflicts unresolved, basing their decision solely on the issue of appealability. The week before the oral argument in *Kimberlin v. Quinlan et al.,* the Court had heard *Johnson v. Jones,* a case in which an allegation of police brutality formed the basis for a charge of misconduct by a government official. In that case, which originated in state court, the defendant cited qualified immunity in an unsuccessful motion for summary judgment, and the issue then traveled all the way through the appellate process. Rosenblatt was thoroughly familiar with *Johnson* v. *Jones,* and when, during his own oral argument, Justices O'Connor and Ginsburg alluded to the question of appealability, he knew that a decision had been reached, though not announced, in that case. The die had been cast. His reply—no, the defendants' summary-judgment motion should not have been appealable—happened to be one that the Court was already comfortable with.

Months of procedural tactics and diversions ensued, but the great hurdles had finally been cleared, and the case was ready to return to the district court of Judge Harold Greene, where it had originated, some five years earlier, in July 1990. Judge Greene conferred with the opposing attorneys, announced a cutoff date for discovery, and arranged his calendar so that the case was likely to go to trial in the fall of 1996. If Kimberlin won, he would be entitled to unspecified damages. If he lost, it seemed virtually certain that he would appeal and appeal and appeal. He would milk every last drop. With sufficient pro bono legal resources, he could keep going until, by comparison, Charles Dickens's *Jarndyce* v. *Jarndyce* would seem an ephemeral spat.

WHEN I undertook my reporting about Kimberlin for *The New Yorker,* I spent several hours one day with Cody Shearer in Washington. In the late afternoon, we went to a photocopying shop to duplicate some documents, among them the DEA's printout, from its NADDIS database, of the three passages that referred to Quayle. There was other material that I was grateful to have, and I asked Shearer what, essentially, was in this for him. He replied, "Let's just say that if this wasn't an election year you'd be paying for this stuff." That conversation was a fresh memory when I decided to write a book. I would need to ask Shearer questions in the future, and I knew I couldn't develop the sorts of connections he boasted in Washington. He assured me that there were as-yet-undisclosed portions of the DEA file, and that if anyone could lay his hands on this material it was he. In those days, the likelihood that Quayle would run for President in 1996 seemed quite high. How might his campaign be affected if my book exposed unrevealed portions of the DEA file?

Eventually, Kimberlin and I signed an agreement with Shearer stipulating that he would perform "research services" for which we would compensate him from our shares of the advance royalties. Though I expected Shearer to be congenial and cooperative, neither he nor I suffered any illusions that our relationship was other than a business transaction. Nor did I expect him to function as a research assistant in any day-to-day sense. Basically, I wanted him to do one thing: come up with the rest of the DEA file.

At a certain point, late in the summer of 1993, before Kimberlin had been paroled, I shared with Shearer the basic revelation of my reporting—that Kimberlin was far less noble and credible than originally assumed. I soon regretted this disclosure, which permanently complicated my dealings with Shearer. From that moment on, he frequently distanced himself from events in which he clearly had played a substantial role. He often claimed not to remember whatever I was asking about, though we both knew he had a prodigiously retentive memory. Many of my questions were rather innocuous, which made all the more vexing the ad hominem reactions they could incite. Neither Shearer's histrionics nor his historical revisions, however, could push me into disliking him. Though I found his best-defense-is-a-good-offense harangues grating, I managed not to take them personally.

Mainly, I sympathized with Shearer. A friend of Bill Clinton's who'd done what he could in 1992 and didn't want to be associated with anything that might embarrass the President in 1996, he'd placed himself in a tough spot. After one of Shearer's tirades, I had a conversation with a journalist who knew him well, and he recounted an exchange with Hillary Clinton. Shearer was in the room at the time, and the First Lady, in an aside, asked the journalist, "Do you believe the things Cody says?" And the journalist replied, "Cody says a lot of things that on the surface seem crazy or improbable, but a lot of them turn out to be true."

When it came to Kimberlin, I concluded, Shearer had surely been seduced by a combination of his own competitive instinct and Washington gamesmanship—but mostly, and above all, by Kimberlin's manipulations. A lot of us, in varying degrees and lengths of time, had similarly been taken in. And how much, really, had Shearer benefited? Aside from his piece of the advance paid for this book—a trifling amount, he often complained, barely sufficient to offset the headaches and hefty phone bills Kimberlin had burdened him with—it's hard to say that he got much out of it. What the enterprise definitely did not yield was any more incriminating documents from Quayle's DEA file.

In January 1994, Kimberlin did something that struck me as typical, simple, and ingenious. He filed a Freedom of Information Act request for Quayle's DEA file. The request was rejected. Of course he persisted, arguing that *he* was working on a book and that a precedent for releasing the file to the press had been established in November 1991, when the assistant U.S. attorney Jack Thar disclosed a portion to the *Indianapolis Star.* After a year of unsuccessful entreaties to the DEA, Kimberlin filed suit in the District of Columbia. In April 1995, Judge Stanley Sporkin ruled in his favor, but DEA lawyers dragged their feet for eight months more before coming up with the goods. The actual file totaled nine pages, and though many portions were redacted, the substance clearly did not extend beyond the single alleged 1982 episode at the Indianapolis Press Club—the charges made by the discredited Charles Parker and the disclaimers made by the braggadocio-prone Terry Carson.

Because Kimberlin had gone about this quietly, none of the proceedings in Judge Sporkin's court were ever reported by the media. The day that the file finally arrived in the mail, mid-December 1995, he faxed me a copy. By then I'd long since opted for the exasperation of having Shearer ignore my phone messages rather than provoking his bullying evasions whenever we did speak. For months he'd teased me by failing to give up one of his sources, whom he described as a former law enforcement officer in suburban Virginia, whose participation in the 1982–83 Capitol Hill investigation could shed new light on Quayle's obscure role. The obstacle, Shearer always maintained, was a quid pro quo. "My guy," as he called him, wanted a job in the Clinton administration. If Shearer could arrange that, the source would talk with me. But the job kept not materializing. Then the terms changed; "my guy" wanted to do private investigative work, and Shearer was supposed to introduce him to some high-powered lawyers who would engage his services.

Perhaps what Shearer kept feeding me wasn't deliberate bullshit; still, it was the functional equivalent. In any event, when Kimberlin faxed me the DEA file, I knew exactly what to do with it. I called and asked whether he would mind running an errand: Would he please make another copy of the file, attach a typewritten unsigned note that said *Cody: Merry Christmas,* place it in a plain envelope with no return address, and mail it to Shearer from a Virginia suburb? Kimberlin was happy to oblige. Three days later, Shearer called, sounding festive. "My guy came through with the file," he announced. "I just got it in the mail." I said this was great news, and asked him to fax me a copy.

Shearer and I occasionally spoke on the phone after that, and once he even arranged a useless ten-minute conversation with "my guy." None of our subsequent dealings, however, brought me a fraction of the pleasure of that particular December surprise.

38

WHEN Howard Rosenblatt drafted the complaint in *Kimberlin* v. *Quinlan et al.*, he sought unspecified damages rather than, say, ten million dollars or some other juicy sum, because, he later explained, "we were unwilling to inject a flamboyant drama into the claim." Nevertheless, the thought often occurred to his client that such flamboyance would only be fair. By statute, Kimberlin's wiretapping claim could bring $100 a day, up to a maximum of $1,000, with a provision for supplemental punitive damages. The tort claim—his alleged physical manhandling by prison guards—was, as a practical matter, superseded by the Bivens action, which at least hypothetically was far more lucrative. If Rosenblatt could persuade a jury that Kimberlin had been deprived of his First Amendment rights, illegally confined and harassed during three episodes of false arrest, and treated vindictively by the Parole Commission, punitive damages were a real possibility, though any award would have to take into account the reality of the defendants' ability to pay.

Even as Kimberlin spoke optimistically of the lawsuit's possible rewards, he was prudently cultivating fallback sources of income. His share of the royalties from this book was one such contingency. However, in the scope of his long-term fiscal plans, my labors would render a modest emolument. "I want to have five million dollars before I move out of my mom's house," he had told me as we rode the bus out of Memphis in November 1993. "I figure that will take me a year or two at the most."

Either Kimberlin genuinely believed he would cash in as a pop minstrel or he was bluffing at the top of his form. In the spring of 1994, minus the vocal accompaniment of the recently deaccessioned Juliya Chupikova, he spent a couple of days in a recording studio with a composer-arranger and session musicians, laying down tracks for three of his songs. When I asked him to describe his style, he said, "Pop rock, soft rock, a little country—crossover—because that's how you get the big money." To make certain I didn't miss the point, he added, "I'm doing this for the money. I'm doing it for fun and creativity too, but it's mainly for the money. It's like vengeance. I can go out there and say things and reach a huge audience, and it's kind of a revenge on all the people who hate me. Can you imagine if I have a number-one hit and I'm all over the radio—every time Jack Thar turns on the radio, there's Brett Kimberlin? Success is the best revenge. These people who wish me ill, who lied about me, made up these stories, turned me into this monster, will just turn green with envy. Every quote from Thar over the years has been 'God! How can you believe this guy?' All this publicity I've gotten will now be working for me. My lyrics are very potent, and they'll touch a lot of people. I see myself as being in the Phil Collins mold more than, say, in the Michael Jackson mold. I can't be fake that way. I have to be real."

Subsequently, I received regular bulletins about Kimberlin's artistic struggle, an endeavor that required periodic redefinition. Trying to entice artist managers and entertainment lawyers and record companies, he dispatched packages that included, along with a bio and lyrics and a demo tape, color photographs with poses ranging from sweetly smiling sincerity to bare-chested beefcake—juxtapositions as jarring as Julio-Iglesias-meets-Merle-Haggard. During the summer of 1994, he announced that he had become a client of "the best entertainment lawyer in the business," who also represented Madonna. Then, a few months later, he reported having "got rid of" the lawyer: "Yeah, he's in the middle of some Madonna negotiations and he keeps putting me off." If Kimberlin doubted himself, he didn't let it show. Without missing a beat, he would regale me with the praise flowing from other quarters—say, from the entertainment lawyer in New York who reportedly declared, "Brett, I don't just like your music, I *really* like it." Or So-and-so, "who's, like, one of the best engineer-producers in the history of music, called me last night and said, 'Brett, I've never told anybody this, but your stuff is great and you're gonna have a major record deal. It's got commercial written all over it. It's got radio play written all over it.' " Or: "Several labels say they want to hear more material. I'd like to go back to the studio and record some more. So I'm writing a couple of songs. One, called 'Fountain of Youth,' is about a guy who searches all over the world for the Fountain of Youth and finds it between a girl's legs." Along the way, Kimberlin pondered the image he wanted to project on MTV. When he bought himself a guitar—previously, he had played only bass—he said he intended to become merely "competent, not great . . . because if there's going to be any kind of videos, I just don't want to look like an idiot."

The vagaries of the path to rock stardom led him at one point to attempt a shortcut through the familiar terrain of politics. Realizing that Bill Clinton had better name recognition than Juliya Chupikova, he found a new muse and came up with a ditty called "Return to Camelot," which he decided would make an ideal Democratic Party theme during the 1994 midterm elections. By August, he'd maneuvered his way into a meeting at the Washington offices of the Democratic National Committee (DNC). In preparation, he wrote a preamble: " 'Return to Camelot' was inspired by the election of President Clinton. The simple yet profound lyrics embody the values and ideals of the Democratic Party—caring, sharing, peace, tolerance and understanding—and embrace positive change for the good of the world. Its melody and emotional harmonies touch a universal chord. In focus groups, people have commented that they 'feel' the song resonating inside their souls." One evening, I found the following message from Kimberlin on my answering machine: "The meeting went extremely well today at the DNC. And it appears they're going for it." The next day, he filled in the details: he had met with a Democratic operative whose title was Chief of Media, along with his assistant; the DNC people "really like the song, they want to use it in feel-good fundraising promotions and local, regional and national elections"; they asked for ten copies of the tape to submit to firms that coordinate Democratic advertising nationally and regionally. "They brought up money and I said I didn't want to talk about money, they had to do that with my lawyer. I said, of course, I wanted to make money, but that I was there to talk to them as a creative artist."

Did the DNC people recognize him?

"I just presented myself as an artist. I'm not down there tooting my horn about this other stuff. I wanted to deal with them straight up. I didn't want them feeling they owed me a favor. I couldn't get a sense of whether they knew who I was."

The synergistic possibilities excited him. After reading a *Playboy* interview with the entertainment tycoon David Geffen—from which he gleaned that "Geffen is a great supporter of Clinton's; he's, like, one of his best friends"—he imagined his dealings with the DNC as "kind of a stepping-stone." Rather than bother with a cumbersome royalty agreement, he was willing to sell "Return to Camelot" to the Democrats outright, because "even if I just make ten grand or so, this opens doors." In other words: today the President's party, tomorrow a major record label. Such great expectations, however, proved premature. Neither the national committee nor any of the several individual senatorial or gubernatorial campaigns he approached came through with an offer for "Return to Camelot." When this gutter-ball result became evident, he complained, "These Democrats! You wonder how they win any damn thing." Sure enough, the midterm elections turned into a Republican triumph.

By the time the 1996 presidential campaign got rolling, though Kimberlin still didn't have a record deal, his artistic evolution was gaining momentum of its own. After a trip back to the recording studio, he emerged with "my debut album." Instead of *Songs of Passion,* the album was now called *Escape from Hell,* and he referred to his accompanists as "my band," which he had named Payback. The songs were "completely different from anything I've done before. This represents a major shift in my style. It's more of an alternative sound now." Some of the numbers—the title cut, for instance, which was about a prison break, complete with a helicopter, a warden shouting through a megaphone, and gunfire—were "almost like Nine Inch Nails." Others featured him singing "with a more Kurt Cobain–like voice."

That no record company had yet signed Kimberlin up, he calculated, could work to his advantage. He set up a web site on the Internet, where he posted the following information about *Escape from Hell:* "The album's dark and edgy songs are in-your-face, anti-conservative, anti-PC, anti-authoritarian . . . so different and controversial that many record labels will not touch it for fear that they will be subjected to criticism from the right-wingers and family-values censors."

DISPLAYING his own brand of conservative wisdom, he continued to hedge his bets by diversifying his business interests. His pal David Sushansky, after almost two years in legal limbo, was finally released by the Immigration and Naturalization Service in May 1995 and deported to Ukraine—which, and not entirely by coincidence, was about to become a frequent destination for Kimberlin himself. Despite the unfriendly denouement of his romance with Juliya Chupikova, Kimberlin had to admit that, in a roundabout way, the relationship paid off. When she settled in Philadelphia and began to study English, one of her classmates was an émigré named Julia Kariman. Along with her husband, Yevgeny Lerner, and her teenage son from a previous marriage, Kariman faced an immigration predicament. Lerner was a Jewish refusenik who, during the seventies, twice had been arrested at a Moscow synagogue and had difficulty finding steady employment. Julia had held a responsible position in the Russian Ministry of Justice, where all went well for her until she married Yevgeny, in 1987. At that point, she later maintained, her security clearance and certain perks were revoked, and she thereafter was assigned minimal, perfunctory tasks. During the late winter of 1991, the family arrived in the United States on tourist visas, and by summer they were ready to seek political asylum. Chupikova discussed their situation with Kimberlin, and before long she was assuring Julia Kariman that her boyfriend, Brett, a political prisoner in Tennessee, could somehow help them out.

Kimberlin tried to get Arnold & Porter involved, but the firm's pro bono committee declined. Instead, he was referred to an immigration specialist, Elliot Lichtman, who agreed to take the case for a fee and also advised the Lerner-Kariman family to move to the Washington area. By the summer of 1992, when I went to visit Carolyn Kimberlin, they had lived for nearly a year in the lower level of her house (the same quarters Brett would later occupy). Yevgeny, a mechanic who'd opened an auto body shop, was at work when I dropped by, so I met only Julia and her son, Alex, a sixteen-year-old high school student eager to master English. Because of a backlog, more than three years passed before the family's immigration status was favorably resolved. While the asylum request was pending, Alex one summer decided he wanted to return temporarily to Ukraine. Kimberlin told me he'd made the necessary visa arrangements—by appealing directly to the regional counsel of the INS, in Baltimore.

My second encounter with Alex took place in the late spring of 1996, in Donetsk, Ukraine. By then, he and Brett, along with Alex's father, had become partners in a variety of ventures, and in the process the Karimans had discovered new reasons to admire Kimberlin's special skills at making necessary arrangements. "Who is Brett Kimberlin?" I asked Alex one day, as we rode in a chauffeured Volga to a business appointment at a steel factory in the port city of Mariupol. This was the same rhetorical question I'd asked myself years earlier as the Greyhound delivered us to Washington. "Who's Brett?" Alex said. "Basically, Brett is someone who takes care of all our problems. He's like a doctor. He cures everything."

THE FIRST time I heard Kimberlin mention Valentin Kariman—Julia's ex-husband and Alex's father—was in November 1994. Valentin had come to the States for a few weeks on business, the nature of which defied concise description. "He's a bigwig in the Ukrainian government," Kimberlin told me. "He's got all these businesses. He's a multimillionaire. Now he wants to buy oil from America. So I've been busy helping him out. I've been talking to Shell, Exxon, Mobil. I tell them I'm representing the Ukrainian government and I want price quotes on engine oil. He doesn't want crude oil, he wants refined engine oil. So that's what I've been doing—talking to shippers about shipping container loads of oil over there. . . . He wants to send me an invitation from the Ukrainian government. I talked to my parole officer about it, and he kind of wigged out. But I think if I had a letter from the Ukrainian government, he might let me go."

The more I heard, the more incredible it sounded. By then, Kimberlin's tendency to count unhatched chicks—another form of jumping the connection—had infected me with a knee-jerk skepticism. Which, in retrospect, seems shortsighted. Given what I understood about the reshuffling of the post-Communist economies of Eastern Europe—a swamp comically underregulated and overregulated at once, a looter's playground where white-collar opportunism and knowing the right people meant everything and moral temporizing was the surest way to kill a deal—I owed Kimberlin the benefit of the doubt. Once again, he had found his natural milieu.

"It looks like I'm going to be sending some oil over there, about twenty metric tons," he told me the next time he called. "I finally got a real good price. If this works out, I can do this on a regular basis and make some buckos. You know, this is exactly like dealing dope. I always looked at pot as a commodity. This is just a different commodity. You're transporting it from one country to the next and trying to get the very best price. And as far as dealing with government officials is concerned, I feel very experienced."

An alarm of sorts sounded a few days later, when Cody Shearer heard from his brother-in-law, Deputy Secretary of State Strobe Talbott, who wanted to know what the hell Kimberlin's involvement was with the Ukrainian government. It seemed that Valery Shmarov, the Ukrainian deputy prime minister and minister of defense, had come to Washington on state business and, after an official meeting with Talbott, requested a private audience. Evidently, it was Shmarov's intention to include Valentin Kariman in this private meeting. Kimberlin, meanwhile, had informed Kariman that he had a parallel pipeline to Talbott via his good friend Cody Shearer. Kariman was no doubt impressed, but Talbott was definitely not pleased; no such meeting would take place. According to Kimberlin, "Cody called me and said, 'Is there any funny business going on? My brother-in-law's as straight as an arrow.' And I told him, 'Cody, Kariman has a reputation as an incorruptible reformer. He's trusted by all these high government officials.' "

What was it, I asked, that Kariman had wanted to discuss with Talbott?

"What if Shmarov and Kariman are involved in some self-dealing? There could be something going on," Kimberlin replied vaguely. "But the way I look at it, who the fuck knows? Cody says Strobe wants to know why I'm involved. He says if I'm lobbying for foreign countries or foreign firms, I have to register. I told him, 'Cody, I'm not a lobbyist. I'm just a go-between.' Nobody can fathom me, especially somebody who's very straight. They don't know how I can do all the things I do. Well, that's just the way I am. But I've never conned anybody, I've never ripped anybody off, I'm very reliable and credible to people I deal with. But somebody hearing that I've been in jail, that I've got a record—they're going to be naturally cautious. That's why I tell Kariman I don't want to be present at any of these meetings. I'm a behind-the-scenes guy. I don't want the limelight."

Thus began a relationship that, from all angles, appeared amicable and rewarding. The Karimans were traders who had positioned themselves to open and supply markets for an expanding array of Ukrainian state-owned and privatized enterprises. Kimberlin's task, in effect, was to run their Western branch office—buying and selling, enlarging the margins, figuring out the cheapest and most expedient means of delivery. One week it was twenty tons of motor oil, the next it was three hundred tons of hydraulic fluid. He found himself soliciting bids for automobile parts and chicken parts. When we spoke, his bulletins sounded even more hyped than the news about his music career. He was "close to wrapping up" a $2 million powdered milk sale . . . a 300,000-ton steel deal . . . a multimillion-dollar financing for an oil-recycling plant. He was being courted by Americans who wanted to build low-cost housing in Ukraine. He was educating himself in the recondite ways of the Export-Import Bank, the U.S. Agency for International Development, the European Bank for Reconstruction and Development, the Overseas Private Investment Corporation.

Kimberlin made his first trip in July 1995, moving from Kiev toward the Azov Sea, spending time along the way in Dnepropetrovsk, Donetsk, and Mariupol, much of it in the company of a trio of American businessmen who were pursuing oil-exploration joint ventures with the government and the Karimans. A month later, back in the States, he was the point man on a $2 million barter transaction that sent 50,000 Goodyear tires to Turkmenistan and natural gas flowing to Ukraine. Though the profit margin was quite slender, the Ukrainian government fronted $1 million, a convenient float that Kimberlin and the Karimans were able to ride for several months while making other investments. For Kimberlin personally, the best part was that the front money wound up briefly in his bank account, long enough for him to flash his statement at his parole officer. Flourishes like that—or the photographs of himself, Valentin Kariman, and Leonid Kuchma, the Ukrainian president, taken during the United Nations fiftieth-anniversary celebration—proved useful when Kimberlin would request permission, every couple of months, to leave the country.

AT A CERTAIN point, I realized, I had to see this new action for myself. And so, one day in June 1996, I wound up seated next to Kimberlin on an Air Ukraine craft—a Greyhound with wings, its incommodiousness alleviated by endless free drinks—bound from New York to Kiev. Because sleep was impossible, Kimberlin had plenty of time to explain the nature of his bold partnership. "Valentin is Mr. Automotive in Ukraine," he said. "Nobody knows more about cars than Valentin." Proof of the esteem in which President Kuchma held him was the title he carried: "advisor to president of Ukraine for economics, with a speciality in automobiles." Pre-perestroika, Valentin lived in Russia and ascended the hierarchy of Lada, the state-owned car manufacturer. When the Soviet Union came apart, he returned to his native Ukraine and founded Lada Makom, the first privately owned dealership in the republic. For years, dozens of customers would line up each morning outside his suite at the Hotel Kiev, in Donetsk. As he branched out, Lada Makom grew to 120 employees. There was an administrative office not far from the city center, a warehouse and car repair complex on the outskirts, an auto parts dealership, a grocery store, a small department store, residential real estate, and a large interest in a domestic air cargo company. Increasingly, Lada Makom did business with the gargantuan Ilyich steel manufacturing plant, in Mariupol. In the reconfigured Ukraine, certain contracts were restricted to domestic companies, such as Lada Makom, while others, because they involved hard currency, were better suited to foreign-owned entities. The partnership between the Karimans and Kimberlin was called Lada Express, a Maryland corporation. Brett's crucial importance, beyond his general resourcefulness and legwork, was that he legitimized Lada Express's foreign ownership.

Kimberlin's life always turned hectic in advance of his travels. This time around, he had the added distraction of closing on the purchase of a five-bedroom house, only a few minutes by car from his mother's. This acquisition left him cash-poor, and to remedy the situation he was working on a dozen deals at once. He showed me a bundle of fresh faxes: the Ilyich plant needed $110 million to upgrade a steel-rolling assembly line, and Kimberlin was chasing financing; a trader in Texas wanted a price on steel pipe to ship to the United Kingdom; Valentin wanted price quotes on used ambulances; an American company in the Midwest had a client who wanted to buy 10,000 tons of reinforcing rods; a broker in New York wanted a price for 10,000 tons of steel to send to Colombia; Ukrneft, the state-owned oil enterprise, needed to rejuvenate more than 3,000 antiquated oil wells, and Kimberlin was talking with a Texas bioengineering outfit about a joint venture. Kimberlin's pet project, at the moment, was a proposal to ship prefabricated "tornado-proof and earthquake-proof" homes from Illinois to Dnepropetrovsk, where they could be erected atop the flat roofs of low-rise apartment buildings.

Dnepropetrovsk was our first stop, a five-hour drive from Kiev, and our plan for the next four days was to adhere to Kimberlin's standard itinerary. The scenery along the highway revealed a Day-Glo lushness—oceans of wheat, barley, corn, oats, and sunflowers, the proverbial breadbasket described lovingly in geography books—as well as rampant industrial pollution.

"Does it look like Indiana?" I asked Brett as our driver dodged the ubiquitous potholes.

"No, it feels a lot better than Indiana, a lot freer," he said. "No police. No parole officers." (Which proved accurate only as far as Dnepropetrovsk, where we were arbitrarily pulled over by a cop and shaken down for a million karbovanets—about five dollars.)

Kimberlin's Russian was better than Juliya Chupikova had indicated—"improving by leaps and bounds," he explained—and it seemed passable when he met with Vadim Kozlov, an architect involved with his prefab housing scheme. Kimberlin introduced me as *avtor moey knigi* ("the author of my book"). In turn, he described Kozlov as "the leading architect in Dnepropetrovsk"—an odd distinction, I thought, in an astonishingly blighted city where a million people lived in dingy concrete and brick buildings and nothing seemed plumb.

We arrived in Donetsk early the next afternoon. For the next two days, before putting me on a plane back to Kiev, Kimberlin and Alex Kariman, a tall, handsome, and remarkably poised twenty-year-old mogul, showed me the sights, such as they were. We made two trips to the Ilyich steel plant, toured the Lada Makom offices and car-repair facility, and logged many idle hours in the suite at the Hotel Kiev, where the furnishings included taupe velvet furniture, a chandelier, a mastiff named Dascha, an Afghan named Akbar, a bodyguard named Sergio, a red telephone linked into a private network of government ministers and VIPs, and a yellow telephone that led directly to President Kuchma. Valentin, a prematurely white-haired but otherwise youthful man in his late forties, joined us for the first trip to the Ilyich plant. After dinner that evening, this seemingly contented if not outwardly joyful workaholic excused himself to go meet a plane bearing the head of Ukresources, the government purchasing agency.

The next morning, Valentin and the Ukresources chief were off to Crimea on unspecified business. That same day began on a satisfactory note for Kimberlin. Before we left for Ilyich, where I was to be shown the site of an oil recycling plant that Lada Express hoped to have up and running by year's end, Alex handed Brett a document to sign. This turned out to be a one-year agreement, by Lada Express, to supply 20,000 tons of coke—the carbonized coal used in blast furnaces—to Illych every month. The coke would come from a factory north of Donetsk, and Alex calculated that the profit to Lada Express would be between four and five dollars a ton, or from $960,000 to $1,200,000 for the contract.

"That's how this works. Sometimes they just tell me, 'The deal's done. Sign the contracts,' " Kimberlin said. "I guess I won't be able to keep on saying I never sold large quantities of coke."

If I understood the numbers—and when I checked with Alex, he said I did—Kimberlin's share of the contract would be worth between three and four hundred thousand dollars. If this was all a con, an elaborate dog-and-pony show for my benefit, then the government of the world's third-largest recipient of American aid was in on it.

Evidently, Alex had learned well a lesson Kimberlin claimed credit for having conveyed. "When we first started out, Alex was bringing me these deals that were for a thousand tires, five hundred tires, a hundred tons of steel, and it was just overwhelming. I said, 'This is crazy. It takes just as much time to do a small deal as a big deal, so why waste our time on small deals?' Actually, it's harder to do a small deal, because you can't get a good price, the profit margin's not there. I said let's just focus on the big deals. So we completely changed our outlook."

When Kimberlin told me this, of course I thought of a corollary: it takes just as much time to sell a nickel bag of marijuana as a hundred pounds, so why waste your time on the nickel bag?

I NEVER got a bill for my two nights at the Hotel Kiev—Valentin, I assume, picked up the tab—but otherwise I would've split it with Kimberlin, since we shared a room. We stayed down the hall from the Karimans' suite, and both nights Brett hung out there for a while after I retired early to commune with my laptop computer. The final morning, I rose before the sun, plugged in, and sat down in an armchair, working while Kimberlin slept. You will not be passing this way again, I told myself. Kimberlin awoke about seven-thirty and, while still in bed, did fifteen minutes of Transcendental Meditation before we exchanged a word. For a long while, I had known what I was about to say.

"You know, Brett," I said, "this is where the book ends. I came here with you because I hoped it would give me a scene I could use, and I think it did. I want you to have the last word. Remember how you told me to pack a bathing suit, because we might get to spend some time at Melekhina, on the Azov Sea? Well, I conjured this fantasy of us lying there on the beach sunning ourselves. And I imagined how great it would be if you would turn to me at a certain point and say, 'Only in America.' But then things got busy and we never made it. I hate to lose that as an ending, though, so I have a favor to ask. You wouldn't mind if I made that scene up, would you? What if I just pretend we went there? What if I write it up as if it really happened and end the book with that line?"

Kimberlin was propped on his elbows, looking utterly satisfied, smiling, then chuckling. "Sure, go ahead," he said. "Do it. Make it all up. Make the whole thing up."

DOONESBURY © 1992 G. B. Trudeau. Reprinted with permission of UNIVERSAL PRESS SYNDICATE. All rights reserved.

Appendix

IN THE SPRING OF 1995, I received a letter from Kimberlin in response to my request that he compile a list of specific ways in which he had been deprived of a fair trial.

"I have trouble believing in conspiracies, per se," he wrote, in a prefatory paragraph. "Rather, as in my case, the people who lied or let a lie go uncorrected had their own agendas. They did not all get together and say, 'Hey, let's conspire to railroad Kimberlin.' Instead, each saw an opportunity to further his or her agenda and each did so, knowing full well that the others would wink at it or look the other way."

What follows are salient passages from the letter—which, its preamble notwithstanding, reveal if nothing else a conspiratorial mind busily at work. More than thirty times in the document, Kimberlin used the words "liar" or "lies" or variations. These were augmented by frequent repetitions of phrases such as "ethically corrupt" and "morally bankrupt." Also included below are my interpolations, derived from interviews with Kimberlin, his attorneys, government agents who participated in the bombing investigation, and government attorneys who were involved in the trials or the appeal.

The suitcase

"The timers were clearly planted in the suitcase. My theory is that Ben Niehaus hatched the idea and probably planted the four timers the evening I was arrested. I believe that he did not inform all the others at the search that he had done it but rather had them present at the moment of discovery to add credibility to his deed. What great theater having the AUSA and the others there, but how odd when they were ostensibly only searching for army patches. The suitcase was in the back seat of the car when I was arrested. The agents who testified about the search all said that the suitcase was unzipped and lying open when they popped the trunk. It wasn't until the third trial . . . that Nile asked the judge to order the Govt to provide all the pictures of the search—which they had previously hidden from us. Those pictures revealed that the suitcase was in fact zipped up and not at all open."

When Kimberlin said Niehaus planted timers "the evening I was arrested," he meant during the overnight hours, while the car was left unsecured in the printing shop parking lot.

Patrick Donovan, of the ATF, appeared as a witness before the grand jury and at all three of Kimberlin's trials. At the third trial, he testified he learned of Kimberlin's arrest 21 September—the morning after it occurred. In a conversation with me, he filled in details of what he said was his "clear recollection" of that day. Around nine-thirty, he was at the Speedway Police Department headquarters, conducting a daily briefing of the bombing investigation team, when a call came from Buddy Pylitt at the U.S. attorney's office. An FBI special agent, Chester Lucas, had come to Pylitt's office to complete the paperwork necessary to charge Kimberlin formally with the Department of Defense officer impersonation and military insignia and presidential seal possession offenses. This was how Pylitt first became aware of Kimberlin's arrest. After hearing this news from Pylitt, Donovan announced it to Niehaus and the other gathered investigators.

That day, two search warrants were issued: one for a search conducted by the FBI in the parking lot, the second for a search conducted by the ATF. The latter began in the parking lot and was completed after the car was towed to the garage of a federal office building, where the swabbings that revealed Tovex residues were taken.

Among documents Kimberlin received in 1983, in response to a Freedom of Information Act (FOIA) request, he came upon an FBI telex that mentioned the presence of an "AUSA"—assistant United States attorney—at the first search. Kimberlin extrapolated: the AUSA was without question Foster or Pylitt; the AUSA was a potential witness; the AUSA should have disqualified himself from prosecuting the case; as a consequence, the entire proceeding was tainted.

An FBI special agent named John Yara testified that the first search began at 3:00 p.m. Niehaus testified the timers had been spotted by Yara "just a few seconds after the trunk was opened." Donovan told me that within minutes he received a phone call from Niehaus. In the affidavit supporting the second search warrant, Donovan stated he arrived at the search site at 4:15. An AUSA arrived at approximately the same time. Whether the AUSA was Foster or Pylitt didn't matter, because Kimberlin's claim was a red herring. The presence of an AUSA, though noted in the FBI telex, had no significance because the AUSA arrived after the first search was well under way. Therefore, no government attorney happened to be in the audience for the startling moment of "great theater" that Kimberlin imagined.

In his letter to me, Kimberlin argued that a deliberate deception had occurred and that it underscored his fundamental assumption: "The AUSA . . . did not correct the lies of the agents when they testified about the suitcase and who was present. Clearly, if they will lie about those things they will lie about the timers."

As I was writing this appendix, Kimberlin told me he was rethinking the timer-planting scenario, entertaining the possibility that it had taken place in broad daylight, immediately after the trunk was opened. Niehaus remained the prime suspect, but Kimberlin wouldn't rule out Yara and Donovan as accomplices. He had been rereading the transcript of an evidentiary hearing—also known as a suppression hearing—that preceded the second trial. "I was so taken by the blatant lies about the search I decided that clearly several agents—at least two—were lying or covering up the lie," he told me. "So why would they have to do it the day before, if everybody's on board? I would say Yara is definitely lying and Niehaus is lying. I think Donovan is cosigning the lie when he says the suitcase is open and the timers are in plain view."

A claim that law officers had concocted the most incriminating piece of evidence was not likely to be well received by Judge Steckler or the jury, Nile Stanton knew.

The only choice left was to attack the legality of the search; thus the suppression hearing. Stanton wanted to convince the court that the suitcase was zipped and sealed when the trunk was opened and that the terms of the FBI's search warrant didn't allow an examination of its contents. The government's position was that the suitcase was unzipped sufficiently to reveal the timers. The suitcase was made of soft, flexible leather and had a two-tabbed zipper that extended along three-quarters of its perimeter. When fully unzipped, it would fold open and lie flat, allowing access to an interior compartment.

With Donovan on the stand being cross-examined by Foster, and with the suitcase available for demonstration purposes, Judge Steckler interrupted and questioned the witness directly:

STECKLER: "You say it was split. Was it open?"

DONOVAN: "It was unzipped, it was opened up."

STECKLER: "It was unzipped?"

DONOVAN: "Unzipped. There is a zipper that goes around the outside of the bag. It was unzipped and it was laying open and at that point I saw the four timers were located in the suitcase."

Nile Stanton questioned Donovan further:

STANTON: "Does it stay open by itself when it's unzipped? Is it unzipped clear down to the sides?"

DONOVAN: "I believe it unzips all the way down to the bottom."

STANTON: "So it's just open like that?"

DONOVAN: "No, it's not open like that."

STANTON: "How was it open? It was still standing upright?"

DONOVAN: "No, it was not, it was laying on one of its sides."

When Niehaus testified, he was asked by Kevin McShane, Stanton's cocounsel, "Who opened the suitcase itself?"

NIEHAUS: "When I first saw the suitcase it was already open, it was unzipped and laying open."

McSHANE: "Would you demonstrate for the Court as best you can. I notice there are quite a few zippers."

NIEHAUS: "It was laying open in a cocked position about like this [indicating] in the bottom of the trunk."

Transcript passages such as this, with their show-and-tell stage directions, left room for conflicting interpretations—what did "laying open in a cocked position" mean?—as did photographs taken during the first search. When I studied the photographs myself in Donovan's office, I saw that at least one side of the suitcase was zipped. The opposite side of the suitcase, however, photographed from another angle, appeared to be unzipped for three-quarters of its length—an opening that could have made the contents partly visible. (Imagine a sandwich that has been slapped together hastily; the slices of bread are not flush, and the sandwich filling is exposed.) There was no photograph that showed the position of the zipper tab on the third side. At the suppression hearing, Niehaus replied affirmatively when Foster asked whether the contents were "in plain view"—a phrase with a specific Fourth Amendment implication.

Kimberlin sent me a pair of photographs that showed the suitcase in slightly different positions. In one, a box of lead balls was partly obscured. In the other, the suitcase had been moved to expose the price tag on the box. The suitcase was at least partly unzipped, but in neither photograph was it "laying opened in a cocked position." Nor did either reflect how the timers could have been in plain view. These photographs, Kimberlin said, proved Niehaus and Donovan had lied. If they were the only photographs, I would have been inclined to agree. But I had seen other shots, from other angles, in Donovan's office. And Judge Steckler, who had seen all the photographic evidence, ended the suppression hearing with a ruling for the government: the first search had been legal, both suitcase and contents admissible as evidence.

Kimberlin told me that the existence of the photographs—"which they had previously hidden from us," according to his letter—was a fact that "just slipped out" when Niehaus testified at the third trial. If the government had not unfairly concealed the photographs—in order, Kimberlin alleged, to cover up the illegality of the search—Steckler would have found for the defense during the pretrial suppression hearing. This assertion, however, was difficult to square with the fact that when the photographs were introduced at another evidentiary hearing during the third trial—Stanton forced the court to revisit the question—the result didn't change. The judge looked at the photographs, concluded the suitcase wasn't fully zipped, and declared the first search legal.

If Judge Steckler wrestled with the disturbing notion that the timers had been planted, he kept that to himself. Donovan, meanwhile, asked me, "If we're going to plant something in the trunk, why not make sure there's no question that the suitcase is open? Wouldn't we unzip it all the way? Wouldn't we make certain that the timers were glaringly visible, so that the legality of the search wouldn't become an issue?" He paused, then added, "Look, Kimberlin complained that the search was illegal. The judge disagreed. And what finally matters is that, zipper or no zipper, the timers were inside his suitcase."

The trunk lock

"The trunk lock was lied about by the ATF. Niehaus testified that it was damaged and the key wouldn't fit. Foster then told the judge that the lock was damaged and they couldn't use the key in it. They hid the lock from us until Nile got Steckler to order them to give it to us and take it to the locksmith. . . . Finally, the locksmith eventually testified that he made a key for the lock and didn't have to alter it."

If, according to Kimberlin's initial surmise, Niehaus acted alone late at night to plant evidence in the trunk, he did so, Brett told me, by picking the lock. ("It's not hard to do. You use this tool that looks like a little pistol and that has these attachments that slide into the lock. You pull the trigger and it kicks this little tool, which pushes up all the tumblers. I've never used one, but I've seen them. You just pull the trigger, and it takes about five seconds—*boing!*")

In his trial testimony, Niehaus explained that Yara, executing the first search warrant, used a crowbar to break into the trunk. During the struggle at the time of his arrest, Kimberlin managed to slide the car keys beneath a photocopying machine inside the printing shop. A few days later, the keys were found and turned over to the government. At the trial, Foster asked Niehaus whether he'd tested these on the trunk lock. Niehaus answered, "Yes, sir, but the trunk lock was—during the opening procedure at the time the search warrants were executed, the trunk lock was damaged."

As a rebuttal witness, Stanton subpoenaed a locksmith named Richard Freund. At the defense's request, the lock cylinder had been retrieved from a government property room and given to Freund, who made a new key for it. If the lock's interior mechanism had been seriously damaged, Freund said, he would not have been able to fabricate the key. Neither of the keys Kimberlin had tossed beneath the photocopier fit the trunk lock, Freund added.

According to Kimberlin, the government knew all along that the tossed-away keys did not fit the lock, and this knowledge launched the government's mendacious suggestion, as expressed by Niehaus, that if the lock hadn't been damaged, one of the keys would have opened it. Maladroitly, the government failed to foresee that the defense would bring in a locksmith to expose this lie.

Donovan told me what Niehaus meant to convey with his testimony was that the lock cylinder had been punched out when the trunk was pried open, and Niehaus reasonably assumed it could not be tested. In light of the locksmith's findings, however, Niehaus's testimony sounded, at best, incomplete, if not disingenuous.

Still and all, Kimberlin's labored complaint about the trunk seemed tangential— a tree standing alone in a broad clearing. Many of his arguments seemed internally dissonant; together they were cacophonous. His logic fit neither an innocent nor a conspiratorial motive. The government believed Kimberlin possessed a trunk key, which, for whatever reason, was not on his person when he was arrested—a bit of legerdemain that he later tried to make the most of. A coat hanger, rather than a crowbar, was used to enter the passenger compartment. Otherwise, at the time of the search there was no meaningful distinction, for evidentiary purposes, between the passenger compartment and the trunk. If a government agent was going to plant timers in the suitcase, why would he bother to move the suitcase to the trunk? Kimberlin's wallet and other belongings were found in the passenger compartment, so what purpose was served by placing the suitcase elsewhere? Or why not place the wallet inside the suitcase? Why not have a trunk key made and add that to the tossed-away key ring? Small screws and nuts used to modify the timers had been bought from Graham Electronics, so why not plant some of that along with the timers? The paper bag containing security officer badges and embossed plastic nameplates, which Kimberlin acknowledged purchasing and which he insisted had been left on the car's backseat, was also found in the trunk. A receipt was found with the badges, but Kimberlin's name wasn't on it. Again, what advantage was gained by planting this evidence in the trunk?

Electronic surveillance

"The ATF and AUSAs repeatedly stated that there was not any electronic surveillance in the case. However, it was later learned after trial that FOIA showed that tracking devices were used (probably on my truck and Sandi's car) and wires were put on certain phones, probably my mom's and Sandi's. If we had been given the reports prior to trial, we may have learned certain exculpatory information."

According to Donovan, the government did indeed obtain a warrant to deploy two electronic tracking devices, but they were never installed. Kimberlin correctly surmised the government's intentions: one of the tracking devices would have been placed on his truck. Also, a government agent confirmed to me that certain phone calls had been "electronically monitored." Because this monitoring did not include any conversations Kimberlin was a party to, however, the government had no obligation to disclose this fact. Nor did the monitoring yield exculpatory information, which Kimberlin also would have been entitled to.

Hypnosis guidelines

"The government repeatedly lied about the existence of hypnosis guidelines. . . . This was a deliberate falsehood by the Govt to gain a tactical advantage."

In retrospect, the gathering of posthypnotic testimony from six witnesses stands out as the most specious feature of the prosecution case. A negative scientific consensus about the usefulness of hypnosis as a criminal investigative tool long ago became standard, and the shoddy manner of the hypnosis was profligate: the shallow training of the hypnotists, who moreover were law enforcement officers rather than independent qualified psychiatrists or psychologists; the presence of other law enforcement officers during the hypnosis sessions; the failure to document preliminary interviews with the hypnosis subjects or to videotape the hypnosis sessions—all this was conspicuously skewed.

Kimberlin's charge that the government "lied about the existence of hypnosis guidelines" raised an ancillary issue, a question of form more than of content. Under FOIA, Kimberlin requested hypnosis-related documents from the Justice Department and from the ATF, which is part of the Treasury Department. A 17 January 1983 letter to Kimberlin from Bob Pritchett, the chief of the ATF's disclosure branch, in Washington, noted that the "only policy statement concerning this matter [was] contained in ATF O 3210.7A. Prior to the publication of this order the Bureau followed guidelines established by the Justice Department."

From the FOIA documents, Kimberlin culled the following: (1) a December 1968 Justice Department memorandum headed "The Use of Hypnosis in Interrogation of Witnesses"; (2) an ATF internal routing memorandum, dated 4 October 1978, which accompanied a draft of the guidelines set forth in ATF O 3210.7A; (3) an ATF telex dated 15 September 1978, sent from the criminal enforcement division in Washington to all special agents in charge of ATF field offices. The telex said: "It comes to our attention that Hypnosis has been used as an investigative aid. It is imperative that all future requests for the use of this technique be approved by this office. . . . Bureau headquarters approval may be given after consultation and review to insure that the Department of Justice guidelines and policies are adhered to. . . ."

The Justice Department guidelines, as defined in December 1968, included an admonition to avoid leading questions, an injunction Kimberlin said was ignored in his case.

Kimberlin also referred me to transcripts of suppression-hearing arguments over the admissibility of the posthypnotic testimony. If it could be shown that the government ignored its own procedures—and the transcripts, Kimberlin said, revealed that the government consciously misled the court on this point—the defense would have been able "to suppress the hypnosis or argue to the jury that it should not rely at all on the hypnotic testimony." Before the first trial, Michael Pritzker questioned Watson Beatty, the resident agent in charge of the Indianapolis field office, who supervised Donovan and Niehaus. "I employed the standards that were required by the Bureau of Alcohol, Tobacco, and Firearms at the time," Beatty said, explaining that this meant he had to receive the approval of his supervisor, the special agent in charge of the Louisville, Kentucky, district office. Asked by Pritzker whether he obeyed "standards promulgated by the Department of Justice or FBI for the performance of hypnosis," Beatty said he had complied, adding that this meant receiving approval from "my immediate supervisor."

During a suppression hearing held before Kimberlin's second trial, Nile Stanton questioned Virgil Vandergriff, the Marion County sheriff's deputy who, along with Brooke Appleby, an Indiana State Police sergeant, conducted the hypnosis sessions. The following exchange took place:

STANTON: "Would you please indicate to us what these guidelines are?"

VANDERGRIFF: "O.K., at the time the hypnosis sessions were conducted in 1978, there were no guidelines by anyone and—"

STANTON: "The hypnotic session. Would you explain what you mean there?"

VANDERGRIFF: "The hypnotic sessions in relationship to this particular case. I believe the only guideline the federal government had at that time was that it was to be cleared in Washington, D.C. That was about the only guideline they had at that time. . . ."

Vandergriff's apparently self-contradictory response was the sort of thing Kimberlin had in mind when he wrote me that "The government repeatedly lied about the existence of hypnosis guidelines. . . . This was a deliberate falsehood by the Govt to gain a tactical advantage." Official clearance for the hypnosis had come from a supervisor in Louisville, not in Washington. Kimberlin regarded this as less an excusable error—Vandergriff, who was not an ATF employee, misapprehending the bureaucratic flow—than a conscious prevarication.

I sent away for a copy of ATF O 3210.7A—a 194-page pamphlet entitled "Investigative Priorities, Procedures and Techniques." The last of the twenty-one chapters was titled "Investigative Employment of Hypnosis."

One of the hypnosis sessions took place 21 October, another on 1 November, 1978, and they were conducted by Appleby. Kimberlin ascribed much significance to the 4 October date of the ATF routing memorandum, which referred to a document called "Chapter T: Hypnosis as an Investigative Technique." Here was proof, he told me, that established guidelines had been violated and that the government compounded its crime by denying the guidelines' existence.

But this was not the case. Plainly, Chapter T was the draft of a gestating policy. When it was published, 14 December 1979, it had become "Chapter U: Investigative Employment of Hypnosis."

The hazard of a sedulous journey through this maze of regulatory history was that it obscured a simple irony: the posthypnotic testimony, when you totted it up, was less than compelling. The physical descriptions offered by the Graham Electronics employees generally pointed toward a suspect taller and heavier than Kimberlin. Two of the employees were unable, in open court, to identify Kimberlin positively as the person they had served. Judge Steckler routinely reminded jurors not to assign greater importance to the posthypnotic testimony than to other evidence. One is left wondering, finally, how heavily the posthypnotic testimony weighed in the context of the full body of evidence.

Yvonne Barton's "hypnosis"

Ben Niehaus, Kimberlin alleged, "withheld information about [Yvonne] being hypnotized."

Here was a curiosity that fell into the subcategory "Department of Weird & Complex Coincidences." In December 1981, Sandi Barton's sister, Louise Crosby, gave a deposition in connection with the personal-injury lawsuit Carl and Sandra DeLong filed against Kimberlin. In her deposition, Crosby described an event that preceded her testimony at the third trial. Niehaus, she said, phoned her at her home in Texas and told of receiving a call from a man who reported having hypnotized Sandi's daughter Yvonne at a dinner party in Indianapolis a few months after the bombings. As that third trial progressed, the man read a newspaper account of Sandi Barton's alibi testimony. The caller told Niehaus that Sandi had to be lying when she said she spent 1 September 1978 with Kimberlin, because Yvonne, under hypnosis, had recalled having dinner that night with her mother in Brown County, Indiana—far south of Indianapolis. Niehaus wanted Yvonne to appear as a witness. Crosby, who was acting as de facto legal custodian for her nieces, told Niehaus she didn't want Yvonne to have to testify.

"I said I was almost sure that she was [at home] in Speedway at the time of the bombings from a letter or something she had written," Crosby testified in her deposition, adding that Niehaus told her "OK, we'll just drop it; we won't pursue it if you are pretty sure."

The conversation stirred Crosby's memory: "I am one of these people that saves things forever, and I started looking back through old stuff I had saved, and I guess because I really felt close to the kids at that time right after Mom's death and when they were living with Dad, she [Yvonne] had written me almost daily for a while when I came back, and I found that letter in a box of old letters that I had in the kitchen cabinet."

And so it was that Yvonne Barton became a prosecution witness after all—testifying she had indeed written a letter to her aunt, dated 1 September 1978, in which she described her mother's driving her home from work the first night of the bombings.

Several months after Louise Crosby's deposition, Yvonne signed an affidavit in the presence of an attorney representing Kimberlin. She described the dinner party and noted a male guest who "said he was an amateur hypnotist." The man tried to hypnotize two other female guests, including his wife, "without apparent effect." When he tried to hypnotize Yvonne, she "decided to play along." Later in the evening, she told the man and the other guests "that she was just playing along."

When Niehaus asked "about this incident his information about it did not agree with this affiant's recollection." In other words, if Niehaus had accepted as true and accurate the amateur hypnotist's account of having successfully hypnotized Yvonne—or the content of any "posthypnotic" statements she might've made to the would-be mesmerist—he was sorely mistaken.

Kimberlin viewed these facts from a polar perspective. Yvonne could not have eaten dinner with her mother on the night in question, because Sandi was with him. Moreover, if the defense had known of Yvonne's hypnosis, "we could have attacked the credibility of the other hypnotic witnesses and attacked Yvonne's testimony as inconsistent." By Kimberlin's reckoning, this was evidence of the government's duplicity. "They used hypnosis when it went against me," he wrote, "but withheld it when it could have helped me."

But a contorted fallacy formed the core of Kimberlin's complaint. In a conversation with me before I'd read Louise Crosby's deposition, he said, "Niehaus called up Louise Crosby and said, 'We've got a problem with Yvonne's testimony because this guy who hypnotized her said she was in Brown County on September first.'" The deposition, however, indicated a quite different sequence: Niehaus heard about the dinner-party hypnotism; Niehaus called Crosby to say he wanted Yvonne to testify that she and Sandi had gone to Brown County the first night of the bombings; Crosby remembered that Yvonne had been in Indianapolis that night and produced a letter of corroboration; and only *then* was Yvonne enlisted as a witness. The hypnosis anecdote and the letter from Yvonne to her aunt were mutually exclusive; sequentially and logically, the latter could negate the former, but not vice versa.

If Yvonne Barton "had just played along"—which meant the Brown County episode hadn't occurred—then, by definition, no posthypnotic statements even existed for the government to share with the defense. Whether Yvonne's "hypnosis" was just an empty parlor trick or something more substantial, the government itself had not conducted the hypnosis, and the prosecution therefore had no obligation to inform the defense that it had transpired. Nor had Niehaus or the government attorneys failed to disclose exculpatory information. An ATF agent went to the Burger King where Yvonne was employed and returned with a copy of a time sheet showing she had worked the night of September 1. In the end, Niehaus, apparently in hopes of impeaching the defense's chief alibi witness, had stumbled across evidence that was both more tangible than the dubious dinner-party hypnosis—a document, as opposed to hearsay—and more inculpatory.

Tovex

According to the government, the swabbings of the Chevy Impala and Kimberlin's Mercedes produced traces of monomethylamine nitrate (MMAN), a primary ingredient of Tovex. According to Kimberlin, "the ATF, its chemists, and the Govt all lied repeatedly about the traces of Tovex. . . . I know for a fact that no Tovex was ever in my Mercedes, and I don't believe that Tovex was ever in the Impala."

The government put on the stand four ATF chemists who had examined bomb debris or sweepings and swabbings from the two cars. What Stanton's cross-examination of these chemists established, Kimberlin told me, was that MMAN occurred so commonly—in "paints, thinners, solvents, urine, fuels, etc."—it was meaningless as a chemical indicator.

Part of Stanton's strategy during cross-examination was indeed to suggest that MMAN occurred both in nature and in commercial products other than Tovex, but the expert witnesses resisted these suggestions so persuasively that their testimony was never seriously weakened. George Peterson, the first chemist called by the government, testified that MMAN is a measurable ingredient in only one family of products, Tovex and Tovan. He went on to say that unnitrated monomethylamine is found in "extremely low concentrations" in nature, concentrations too low for it to combine readily with nitrates. It was "theoretically possible" for MMAN to occur naturally, but if it did, Peterson said, it would be impossible to detect. In products other than Tovex that contain unnitrated monomethylamine, like soap, "we have never been able to find it. It has reacted with other material and it becomes a different chemical compound."

Michael Gerard, the next chemist, said much the same thing: MMAN was found only in Tovex and the Tovan family of explosives; methylamine alone might be a constituent of dye, insecticides, solvents, and paint removers, but it was not detectable in the final products; and MMAN was "not used" in products other than Tovex and Tovan.

When Stanton tried to get Gerard and William Dietz, his successor on the stand, to imagine a chemical environment other than Tovex that might sustain MMAN, they were skeptical. In an acidic soil sample enriched with dog urine, he asked, "Would you be reasonably apt to find monomethylamine nitrate?" Gerard maintained that he would not be, but neither would he rule it out. To Dietz, Stanton put the question this way: "If cleaning fluids or some types of solvents were used to clean out a vehicle, do you know whether or not it is possible for any solvent to combine with any nitrates and to leave monomethylamine nitrate?" Dietz responded it was "chemically possible" but not probable. Leroy Stewart, the final chemist to testify, confirmed what Peterson had said about the quantity of monomethylamine in nature, saying that in explosives, the concentration of monomethylamine—MMAN was not mentioned—is "absolutely higher" than in urine. Later, Stanton revisited the inquiry with Dietz, who seemed most responsive to the suggestion of ubiquitous MMAN. Stanton asked whether it would "surprise" Dietz to find MMAN at a body shop where paints and thinners had been used. Dietz responded, "It would surprise me, yes."

With these questions, Stanton meant to inspire doubt about the MMAN the ATF had found on the Mercedes, which had been tested after it spent time in a body shop near Dayton. With his suggestions that MMAN is fairly common, he hoped generally to neutralize the chemists' findings. The effectiveness of Stanton's cross-examination depended on the jury's confusing monomethylamine, which is fairly common, with monomethylamine nitrate, which is rare. But Stanton didn't get much out of the cross-examinations—in sum, three concessions that an occurrence of MMAN outside Tovex was not utterly impossible. None of the chemists had ever seen it, though; two said it would not be detectable, even if it existed; and one said its existence would surprise him. This was not the conclusive moment for the defense that Kimberlin remembered. To witnesses in the courtroom, it didn't even look like reasonable doubt.

If Kimberlin knew "for a fact" that his Mercedes was free of Tovex—and if he believed the same to be true of the Impala—why didn't he and his lawyers run their own tests to prove it? It was impossible, Kimberlin said. The government had so thoroughly swabbed the bomb scene, the cars, and their contents, that there was no MMAN left to test. The defense was thus deprived of a chance to prove the MMAN had never been there in the first place.

Donovan, however, said that while the cars themselves might not have been testable, the defense could've asked to look at the floor mat or the debris—or, at the very least, could've had the ATF rerun their testing procedures in the presence of their own chemists. Stanton and Kimberlin never chose to do this. Instead, in 1987, after the Seventh Circuit upheld Kimberlin's conviction, he produced an affidavit from a professional chemist and chemical engineer, Carl J. Abraham, who concluded that in the absence of spectra or spectrographs, the government's chemists had insufficiently documented the presence of du Pont products. "The analysis and presence of the du Pont materials would be documented with spectra of the material obtained in relationship to known or standard materials," he testified. "The failure to produce such spectra is a deviation from standard and accepted scientific methods."

After reviewing Abraham's deposition, ATF chemist Dietz was puzzled and suspected Abraham didn't have all the facts. For one, Dietz said, spectrography was not itself a chemical test but a means of interpreting test results: the chemical tests used by the government on the cars and the bomb scene didn't require spectrographic interpretation because they didn't *produce* spectra. "It is for this very good reason why spectra and spectrographs were not available for Dr. Abraham's inspection." He cited two papers from the *Journal of Forensic Sciences* (vol. 2, no. 2 and vol. 28, no. 3)—unfamiliar to Abraham, perhaps, because he had worked not in forensic but in commercial chemistry—that recommended a multiple thin-layer chromography system (TLC) coupled with chemical visualizing sprays as a means of identifying explosives such as the du Pont products. These were the tests the ATF had used; neither required spectrography to interpret. From Abraham's brief testimony, it seemed he hadn't seen all the government's results and had been informed only that there were no spectrograph results to examine. Without knowledge of the other recommended tests for the du Pont explosives, Abraham had erroneously concluded that, without spectrography, there was no proof of Tovex.

To believe that Kimberlin's conviction represented a widespread effort to frame him required the postulation of a sophisticated, ingenious, and illegal network of his enemies—nothing less, it seemed, than a "conspiracy per se." Sometimes the ingenuity with which Kimberlin credited the ATF specifically seemed too generous. For instance, on 20 September 1978, the day of Kimberlin's arrest and the impounding of the Impala, the ATF agents involved in the search did not have the lab results from the bomb scenes. If the government had wanted to lace the Impala, they would've needed to guess exactly which substance—Tovex, that is, and not dynamite or TNT—would link Kimberlin to the bombings. Additionally, the ATF was unlikely to have known that Kimberlin had been using Tovex to excavate his property three years earlier.

Secret room

Even if Sandi Barton had been with Kimberlin the night of September 1, the prosecution tried to show that he still could've planted the first four bombs without her knowledge by leaving his house via *the secret room*.

In 1975, not long after moving into the rented house in Eagle Creek, Kimberlin subdivided a walk-in bedroom closet, creating a hidden interior "dead space" about ten feet square, accessible by a hinged wall panel activated by an electromagnetic switch. Wooden shelves lined the walls of the secret room, and inside, Kimberlin told me, he stored "a bunch of silver, valuable rugs, and stuff that I didn't want people to know about if they robbed the house." The room's other purpose was to provide a refuge in case an intruder entered the house.

While cross-examining Kimberlin, Foster introduced the prosecution theory that the room also served as an escape route. Originally, a retractable ladder had been installed in the ceiling above the secret room, providing access to the attic. Floorboards laid across the attic joists created a path to a window above the garage. An employee of the Indianapolis Department of Parks and Recreation, which owned the house, discovered the secret room after Carolyn Kimberlin vacated the property in 1979. During the rebuttal phase, this employee testified that, in the spot where the ladder had been, he had pulled down the ceiling molding and removed a drywall cap. Earlier, Kimberlin had testified that the drywall ceiling replaced the retractable ladder in 1975. The prosecution wanted the jury to believe the drywall had been installed after September 1978, and it showed the jury photographs of the opening in the ceiling. The display of these photographs, Kimberlin felt, amounted to one more travesty. "This was just more theater by the Govt," he wrote. "If I had wanted to leave, I would have simply gone out the window or the door but the Govt wanted the jury to think that I was some kind of weirdo who had secret egress and exits."

If Kimberlin had omitted the final phrase of this passage, I would've shared his feeling that, in this instance, the prosecution had overstepped its rights. Sneaking into a hidden room and traipsing through your own attic on your way to plant bombs—this was unapologetic, hard-core, bad-man imagery, superabundant proof of Stanton's lament that the government was more interested in locking up a caricature of Kimberlin than in addressing the facts at hand. Yet, though I doubted the government's scenario, I found Kimberlin's logic defective in a different sense. Somehow he had forgotten describing to me in lavish detail the hidden features of his Jackson County compound: the hundred-yard escape tunnel from his basement to the woods; the trapdoor in the upstairs closet leading to the vertical passageway; the gun rack built into the wall of the vertical passageway, opposite a vent. Unless Kimberlin's self-righteous allegation that "the Govt wanted the jury to think that I was some kind of weirdo who had secret egress and exits" was intended ironically, it was laughable.

Perjury

The testimony of several witnesses, Kimberlin said, was a series of orchestrated lies. He was most aggrieved by Ron Confer and Lynn Coleman, who shared a reward of about ten thousand dollars after the trial. "He [Confer] lied pure and simple and the ATF and Govt knew it," Kimberlin wrote. "Confer is a lying opportunist who, along with the others who lied and who condoned the lies, must carry the burden of his lies on his conscience for the remainder of his life."

Testifying before the grand jury, Confer had said one thing: he had never seen Kimberlin possess explosives. Testifying at the second and third trials, he told an utterly different story: he had seen a cardboard carton of explosives in the cargo area of Kimberlin's truck. He offered a plausible, if not necessarily truthful, explanation of how his memory had been refreshed. Jurors in the second trial who'd expressed doubts about Confer's credibility nevertheless voted to convict Kimberlin. How damaging was Confer's testimony at the third trial? Was he lying or telling the truth? A stalemate: Kimberlin's word versus Confer's.

Of Coleman, who gave no grand jury testimony and signed no statements, Kimberlin wrote: "Nothing, not one detail he gave, held up to scrutiny. He was . . . out of work . . . simply trying to get the reward, and the Govt relied on him as its bombshell witness. . . . It is a routine requirement when a person gives conflicting statements or is a crucial witness to give them a polygraph to see if they are telling the truth, but the agents did not do that with either Confer or Coleman. They winked at them and let them lie."

Coleman's trial testimony indicated that he was not "out of work," but rather that he had both full- and part-time jobs. The reward money, which he shared with Confer, came from the Speedway Shopping Center Merchants Association, a group of retail store owners who were alarmed by a persistent decline in business after the bombings. Cross-examining Coleman, Stanton asked, "Do you have any direct interest in the outcome of this case?" and "Is there any benefit to you as a result of testifying in this case?" Both times, the response was "No, sir." Neither Confer nor Coleman had a mercenary motive, Donovan told me, because at the time of their testimony neither was aware that any reward existed. Only two months later, when Kimberlin filed defamation-of-character lawsuits against both witnesses, did Donovan arrange for them to share the reward money to defray their legal expenses.

According to Coleman's testimony, his first contact with the government occurred in February 1981—several months after the first trial ended. By chance, a member of the Marion County Sheriff's Department was moonlighting as a private security guard at a grocery store where Coleman worked. Coleman told the deputy he'd witnessed the planting of the first bomb, the deputy duly repeated this conversation to a deputy United States marshal, and Coleman's name got passed on to the ATF. When Donovan and Niehaus went to interview Coleman, they were surprised to find he believed the prosecution of Kimberlin had ended. Coleman was aware of the hung jury but didn't realize the case would be retried. In Coleman's narrative, his wife, Judith, witnessed virtually everything he did. Lynn Coleman was quite reluctant to testify, and his wife was even more adamantly opposed to either of them getting publicly involved. Kimberlin told me Mrs. Coleman was reticent because "she knew her husband was lying and she refused to sign off on it." But Donovan told me Judith Coleman was spooked by the Scyphers murder; she feared Kimberlin would arrange to have prosecution witnesses killed.

Should Confer and Coleman have been given polygraphs? "We didn't administer a polygraph to a single witness in this case," Donovan said. "It is decidedly not a quote-unquote routine requirement. So why would we administer one to Ron Confer or Lynn Coleman?"

Stanton made a game attempt at rebuttal. He subpoenaed another shy witness, a jewelry store owner, Leonard Wechsler, whose place of business was two doors from the furniture store where Coleman reported having window-shopped just before Kimberlin pulled up in a Mercedes and planted a bomb in a receptacle. The explosion shattered the windows of Wechsler's shop. If the timing had been slightly different, his loss would've been incalculable. Only minutes earlier, Wechsler's wife and three children had been waiting in a station wagon in front of his store. By chance, Mrs. Wechsler drove to the rear of the store so her husband could load some lumber into the car. Another vehicle parked in her spot as soon as she vacated it, and the bomb reduced it to a total wreck.

Before completing his testimony, Wechsler volunteered, "I would like to make one statement: That I am not a friend [of Kimberlin]. I'm here only because of the paper [subpoena] and the federal law that says I must be here. I am not here as part of the defense. I definitely want the bomber caught. That is my only concern. And I am here just because I have to be."

Still, Wechsler contradicted Coleman in two respects. First, though he and his family parked their station wagon very near where Coleman reported having parked, and within the same time frame, Wechsler had no memory of seeing either Coleman's red subcompact or Kimberlin's white Mercedes. Second, Coleman testified that there were "very few" other cars in the parking lot when he saw the Mercedes go by. Wechsler recalled that between 9:15 and 9:30 p.m., the lot was starting to fill with cars, and he said that at one end the traffic was "pretty heavy."

Coleman's testimony seemed problematic on other grounds. His primary observations had taken place through a pair of rearview mirrors at a distance of about a hundred feet. The entire encounter—from the moment the Mercedes pulled alongside his car until it drove away—lasted "probably a minute." Though he positively identified Kimberlin in court, he had no memory of the Mercedes driver's hair color or whether he had a beard or was clean-shaven. (That summer, Kimberlin had grown a rather feathery beard.)

In 1992, I had a phone conversation with Wechsler. He was no more eager to be interviewed than he'd been to testify when subpoenaed by the defense. While he expressed no sympathy for Kimberlin, he said, "I never understood the jury. I knew Coleman was lying. My personal observation is this testimony was fabricated to accommodate the prosecutor's need to rid the street of Brett Kimberlin. I think they [the government] forced this guy off the street. They had some other things on him that they couldn't nail him on, so they did this."

Wechsler was not alone in this belief. After the verdict, Rick Kammen, one of Kimberlin's original attorneys, had a conversation with a fellow trial lawyer, who mused, "Well, I guess the only thing to say is that the government seems to have framed the right guy."

. . .

A FOOTNOTE to this footnote: By odd chance, Leonard Wechsler was the president of the Speedway Shopping Center Merchants Association, which had offered a ten-thousand-dollar reward for information leading to the conviction of the Speedway Bomber. This money was later split by Confer and Coleman. What might a diehard conspiracy theorist make of such an anomalous coincidence?

But in general, and in conclusion, Go Figure.

Acknowledgments

I SET TO WORK on this book thinking I could get the job done within a certain amount of time and, as things turned out, my budget estimate was off by I hate to say how much. Two editors, Sonny Mehta, of Knopf, and Tina Brown, of *The New Yorker*, proved remarkably forbearing, and I'm deeply grateful.

Gary Fisketjon, of Knopf, accompanied me wire to wire, providing superb editing, energy, wit, and friendship. Pat Crow, who edited my initial *New Yorker* story about Brett Kimberlin, scrutinized the final manuscript and galleys and offered valuable suggestions for improvements. My gratitude to these other current or former *New Yorker* colleagues: Bill Buford, Lincoln Caplan, Bruce Diones, Blake Eskin, Daniel Hurewitz, Cressida Leyshon, Bill Vourvoulias, Ren Weschler, and Dorothy Wickenden.

Working with Rob Grover, of Knopf, was like being equipped with several extra vertebrae. Thanks also to Janice Goldklang, Marjorie Horvitz, Katherine Hourigan, Melvin Rosenthal, and Elise Solomon.

For legwork and research assistance, I depended greatly upon Anne Gilbert, Audrey Duff, and, especially, Virginia Heffernan.

Members of the library staff of the *Indianapolis Star/Indianapolis News*, which is headed by Sandra Fitzgerald and Cathy Knapp, were unfailingly gracious and accommodating. Barbara Hoffman and Dawn Hall put up with my long-distance requests at all hours and always tracked down what I was looking for. Early on, Joe Gelarden, of the *Indianapolis Star*, Dan Luzadder, of the *Rocky Mountain News*, and Bill Shaw, then of *People* magazine, shared their insights about Kimberlin and the mythology that has enveloped him.

From Cody Shearer, I learned lessons about journalism that might otherwise have eluded me.

Some of the sources for this book cannot be mentioned by name. Among those who can be mentioned and who extended themselves in ways that I particularly appreciated were: Robert Berg, Alan Chaset, Norman Gorin, Kevin McShane, Donald Morano, Howard Rosenblatt, Norman Solomon, Nile Stanton, and Garry Trudeau.

For wise counsel, thank you Joy Harris, Adria Hillman, and Jeremy Nussbaum.

As ever, my parents, Alex and Marjorie Singer, offered love and support, and my sons, Jeb, Reid, and Timothy, love and ideal companionship. And Caroline Mailhot reminded me, in countless ways—always with the rarest grace—that one day this book would indeed be completed and a new chapter could begin.

A NOTE ON THE TYPE

THE TEXT of this book was set in Sabon, a typeface designed by Jan Tschichold (1902–1974), the well-known German typographer. Based loosely on the original designs by Claude Garamond (c. 1480–1561), Sabon is unique in that it was explicitly designed for hot-metal composition on both the Monotype and Linotype machines as well as for filmsetting. Designed in 1966 in Frankfurt, Sabon was named for the famous Lyons punch cutter Jacques Sabon, who is thought to have brought some of Garamond's matrices to Frankfurt.

Composed by North Market Street Graphics,
Lancaster, Pennsylvania
Printed and bound by R. R. Donnelley & Sons,
Harrisonburg, Virginia
Designed by Virginia Tan